THE ALTERNATIVES TO WAR

The Alternatives to War

From Sanctions to Nonviolence

JAMES PATTISON

OXFORD
UNIVERSITY PRESS

OXFORD
UNIVERSITY PRESS

Great Clarendon Street, Oxford, OX2 6DP,
United Kingdom

Oxford University Press is a department of the University of Oxford.
It furthers the University's objective of excellence in research, scholarship,
and education by publishing worldwide. Oxford is a registered trade mark of
Oxford University Press in the UK and in certain other countries

First Edition published in 2018
Impression: 3

Published in the United States of America by Oxford University Press
198 Madison Avenue, New York, NY 10016, United States of America

British Library Cataloguing in Publication Data
Data available

Library of Congress Control Number: 2017960750

ISBN 978–0–19–875520–3

Printed and bound by
CPI Group (UK) Ltd, Croydon, CR0 4YY

Acknowledgements

This is my third book and it has been the most challenging to write, although also the most rewarding. The book is ambitious: it aims to provide a comprehensive account of the ethics of the alternatives to war. I could not have completed it without much support. In 2014, I was awarded a two-year grant by the Arts and Humanities Research Council (AH/L003783/1). This time was crucial for the project and I thank the AHRC for it. I have also benefited greatly from comments, discussions, and written feedback on draft chapters. I'm indebted in this respect to Kirsten Ainley, Thomas Biersteker, Pojanath Bhatanachareon, Vittorio Bufacchi, Simon Caney, Phil Cunliffe, Patrick Coy, Graeme Davies, Ned Dobos, Liz Ellis, Toni Erskine, Cécile Fabre, Christopher Finlay, Adrian Gallagher, Jess Gifkins, Jonathan Gilmore, Luke Glanville, Harry Gould, Michael Gross, Aidan Hehir, Fred Hjorthen, Randy Janzen, Chris Mills, Valerie Morkevicius, Bob Murray, Yasmine Nahlawi, Brian Orend, Jason Ralph, Ruben Reike, Massimo Renzo, Heather Roff, Don Scheid, Christine Schweitzer, Michael Skerker, Danny Statman, John Thrasher, Jean-Baptiste Jeangène Vilmer, Michael Walzer, Jennifer Welsh, Leif Wenar, Rob Whittaker, and John Williams. I would particularly like to thank Eamon Aloyo, Daniel Brunstetter, and John Lango, who generously read and commented on a whole draft of the book. I would also like to thank Dominic Byatt at OUP, for his enthusiasm and unparalleled efficiency, and the anonymous reviewers for OUP for their very constructive comments and suggestions.

Manchester has been a stimulating and supportive (if wet and grey) environment. I thank several of my colleagues (past and present) for helpful discussions and for comments on draft material, including Richard Child, Stephanie Collins, Steve de Wijze, Stephen Hood, Mark Reiff, Miriam Ronzoni, Christian Schemmel, Liam Shields, Hillel Steiner, Jon Quong, and Maja Zehfuss. We are fortunate at Manchester to have engaged, motivated, and bright students. In 2016–17, I taught two courses based on material from the book. This was very helpful for clarifying my thoughts and I thank the students for their valuable suggestions (including for the title of the book!). Thanks are also due to Bolarinwa Adediran for his research assistance.

One of the privileges of being an academic is the opportunity to speak at various venues across the world. I have been lucky enough to present material from the book at over thirty conferences, workshops, and seminars, including in Atlanta, Baltimore, Birmingham, Brittany, Canterbury, Dublin, Durham, Florence, Frankfurt, The Hague, Leeds, Ljubljana, Manchester, New Orleans,

Oxford, Reykjavik, Sheffield, Sicily, and Warsaw. I am grateful to the participants and audiences for their insightful questions and reflections.

Some of the material from this book has been published in an earlier form elsewhere, although I have updated and developed much of my earlier anaylsis. Parts of sections 3.2 and 3.4 first appeared in 'The Morality of Sanctions', *Social Philosophy and Policy*, 32/1 (2015): 192–215. The first part of chapter 5 draws on 'The Ethics of Diplomatic Criticism: The Responsibility to Protect, Just War Theory, and Presumptive Last Resort', *European Journal of International Relations*, 21/4 (2015): 935–57. Sections 6.1–6.3 draw on material from 'Unarmed Bodyguards to the Rescue? The Ethics of Nonviolent Intervention', in Michael Gross and Tamar Meisels (eds), *Soft War: The Ethics of Unarmed Conflict* (Cambridge: Cambridge University Press, 2017). Chapter 8 (especially section 8.3) draws on some arguments first presented in 'The Ethics of Arming Rebels', *Ethics & International Affairs*, 29/4 (2015): 455–71. I am grateful to the publishers for the permission to use this material.

Finally, I would like to thank my wonderful wife, Claire, for her continuing love and support. I dedicate this book to our daughter, Isabelle.

Contents

1

The Alternatives to War

1.1 INTRODUCING THE MEASURES

Wars and military intervention almost always involve death and destruction. They annihilate civilians in bombing raids, destroy infrastructure, lead to soldiers suffering mental and physical injuries, and tear apart societies. Doing nothing in response to mass atrocities and significant aggression, however, leaves civilians to face abuses of their basic human rights by government forces, rebels, paramilitaries, and terrorists. Indeed, one of the central premises of the responsibility to protect (R2P) doctrine is that standing by in the face of mass atrocities is reprehensible. According to the R2P, the international community has a responsibility to protect threatened populations. Even if war and military intervention is not appropriate, doing nothing is not an option.

But what should states and other actors in the international community do instead of waging war and doing nothing? There are numerous potential measures, ranging from comprehensive economic sanctions, diplomacy, and positive incentives, to criminal prosecutions, non-violent resistance, and arming rebels. Although the options are several, each raises tricky ethical issues. Take, for instance, economic sanctions. On the one hand, sanctions avoid some of the direct harms of war—they do not involve bombing campaigns and military occupations. On the other, they can fail to address the situation and lead to significant hardship for civilians. They are also alleged to violate the Kantian prohibition on using innocent civilians as a mere means. By purposefully using the suffering of innocents to pressurize their governments, the argument goes, sanctions wrongfully instrumentalize the general population (Gordon 1999*a*). Alternatively, consider diplomacy. Various diplomatic measures can attempt to coerce aggressors, such as the cutting of diplomatic ties, naming and shaming, and expulsion from international bodies. However, when the state lambasting the aggressor does not practise what it preaches, such measures may be hypocritical. This might be thought to render such criticism impermissible since the hypocritical state lacks the entitlement to criticize others. Other measures also face notable challenges. What, if anything, can non-violent methods such as civilian defence and civilian peacekeeping do in the face of a ruthless opponent? Is it a serious concern that positive incentives can give aggressors a benefit that they do not deserve? Does providing arms to rebels render the supplying state complicit with abuses by rebels and, if so, does this mean that arming rebels is impermissible?

It is far from obvious, then, what should be done instead of military intervention (from hereon 'intervention') or doing nothing. Each alternative raises thorny ethical issues. However, these issues have not been properly considered in the existing literature. To be sure, it is widely held that war should be eschewed and that non-violent alternatives should be pursued instead. For instance, various pacifist approaches assert that war is impermissible and we should adopt non-violent alternatives. Just War Theory asserts that war should meet the comparative principles of last resort or necessity in *jus ad bellum*, which highlight to some extent the moral importance of considering the alternatives to war. However, although both pacifists and Just War Theorists typically assert the need to pursue alternatives to war, there has generally been a lack of systematic ethical analysis of these alternatives. As we will see, there are some exceptions (particularly in relation to economic sanctions), but these focus on the case for *particular* alternatives. They do not consider the case for the alternatives *as a whole*.

Accordingly, this book considers the ethics of the alternatives to war. It considers the leading measures, from sanctions to non-violence. The central aim is to provide a 'moral map' of the main alternatives to war. I will draw on five central moral considerations in political philosophy to highlight the issues that the alternatives raise, and to consider if, and how, we can navigate these issues. For those particularly interested in only one measure, one can read the chapters discretely. However, the full moral picture and the complex relations between the measures emerge only once we consider all the major alternatives.

To determine the moral justifiability of an alternative, we need to answer two seemingly obvious questions. The first is whether the alternative is superior to *not launching it*. The second is whether it is superior to *other measures*. To answer these questions, the book provides a framework for assessing all the alternatives—what I call the 'Pragmatic Approach'—and presents two overarching themes. The first is that there are several weighty moral considerations *in favour* of pursuing the alternatives, which are often overlooked in standard accounts of the ethics of war and peace. The second is that there are additional arguments *against* war. Overall, then, the book argues that the case for war is weaker and the case for many of the alternatives is stronger than commonly thought. When reacting to mass atrocities and aggression, I will argue it is, in general, morally obligatory to pursue the alternatives, rather than military force. Although I will ultimately reject pacifism and argue that wars are sometimes permissible, I will claim that these occasions are likely to be rare, given the case for the alternatives. To some extent, this will provide grist to the pacifist's mill.

The Pragmatic Approach will be outlined and defended in chapter 2. It will be used to assess the central alternatives to war and is pragmatic in three senses. First, it considers not simply necessary features, but also contingent facts about the contemporary international system. Second, it aims to reflect judgements in the currently nonideal international system, rather than being a purely idealized account. And, third, it gives significant weight to instrumentalist considerations—in particular the effectiveness of a measure at advancing basic human rights. But it is not fully instrumentalist. Rather, it holds that other values are relevant in the assessment of the alternatives (fairness, the distinction between *doing* and *allowing*, interceding agency, and desert), even if they are not as significant.

The rest of this chapter will set the scope for the ensuing analysis. In section 1.2, I will highlight the political and theoretical significance of considering the alternatives and outline the problems caused by the lack of clarity surrounding them. In section 1.3, I will make clear the scope of the analysis and outline the measures that I will focus on. Section 1.4 will provide a précis of the ensuing chapters.

1.2 SIGNIFICANCE OF THE ANALYSIS

The need to consider the ethics of the alternatives has been highlighted by the recent conflict in Syria. This started in 2011 in the context of the Arab Spring with a peaceful uprising against the Assad regime. In response to the Syrian government's brutal crackdown on the protesters, the conflict quickly spiralled into a complex regional war involving various international actors. According to the Syrian Network for Human Rights (2017), by March 2017 there were over 200,000 civilians killed (this excludes combatants—the overall death toll is more than double this). Many of these deaths have been due to the Assad regime's indiscriminate attacks, which, according to Amnesty International in their Annual Report (2017), amount to war crimes. Much of the public debate has been about the possibility of intervention against Assad. Yet it has been clear that it would be difficult to launch the size of operation necessary to remove the Assad regime, given its military capacity and Russian backing.[1] In general, there has been little understanding of what, if anything, the international community could and should do instead of war and, especially, the

[1] In April 2017, the Trump Administration ordered isolated missile strikes against the Shayrat airbase, after the Assad regime reportedly used chemical weapons in the town of Khan Shaykhun. Even after the strikes, the possibility of a full-scale military operation to fully tackle the crisis seemed remote.

ethical issues raised by potential alternatives.[2] For instance, the possibility of supplying arms to the supposedly 'moderate' rebel groups in Syria has sometimes been discussed and indeed has been tried by the US, UK, France, Qatar, Saudi Arabia, and other actors. However, the ethical challenges raised by using this method—such as that arming rebels might render one complicit—have been insufficiently understood in the public debate (and seemingly amongst policymakers). Similarly, it has sometimes been suggested that Assad could be offered exile (Wright 2015), but the understanding of the normative case for this—such as whether it is wrong to reward an aggressor with exile—has been weak. Economic sanctions have also been tried, but have seemingly made the situation worse (Moret 2015). And the attempts to secure a referral to the International Criminal Court (ICC) have foundered in the face of Russian and Chinese vetoes.

More specifically, there are three overarching reasons why it is important to examine the ethics of the alternatives to war. These are (1) to develop the R2P doctrine; (2) to have a fuller understanding of Just War Theory and, in particular, the requirements of last resort and necessity; and (3) to offer appropriate guidance as geopolitical shifts render the alternatives to war increasingly significant. I will now outline each of these points in turn.

1.2.1 The R2P and the Alternatives to War

In its 2001 report, the International Commission on Intervention and State Sovereignty (ICISS) argues that when a state is unwilling or unable to protect its citizens from the egregious violations of basic human rights, its sovereignty is suspended and the international community has a responsibility to protect. According to the ICISS, the international community's responsibility to protect involves the responsibility to prevent, to react, and to rebuild. States at the 2005 United Nations (UN) World Summit agreed that there exists a 'responsibility to protect' in cases of genocide, ethnic cleansing, crimes against humanity, and war crimes. The 2009 report, *Implementing the Responsibility to Protect*, by the then UN Secretary-General, Ban Ki-moon, helpfully frames the R2P in terms of three pillars. These are the domestic responsibilities of states (pillar one), the international responsibilities to assist states in living up to their domestic responsibilities (pillar two), and 'timely and decisive response' (pillar three). The latter involves the international responsibility to ensure that states fulfil their responsibilities to their populations when they are manifestly unable or unwilling to do so. Virtually all leading accounts of the

[2] This is clear from the insider account of the events in the UN Security Council presented by Hardeep Singh Puri (2016), the Indian Representative to the Security Council between 2011 and 2012.

R2P make clear that humanitarian intervention is only *one* option in response to mass atrocities under pillar three and that there are several international non-military or non-coercive options. Yet there has been little analysis amongst R2P scholars of the merits and drawbacks of the alternatives to intervention and, in particular, the ethical issues raised by these alternatives.[3]

The R2P has quickly become the central framework for considering responses to mass atrocities, so it is worth considering this point in more detail. The notion of the *international* responsibility to protect is widely accepted to be the most important and value-added element of the R2P. As Jennifer Welsh, the former Special Advisor to the UN Secretary-General on R2P, puts it, a core element of R2P is '*the international community's* remedial responsibility to act' (2014*b*: 126). That is, when states are unable or unwilling to protect their populations from mass atrocities, the international community has a remedial responsibility to assist them (under R2P's pillar two) or coerce them to do so (under R2P's pillar three). This international responsibility has emerged in practice to be understood as a 'duty of conduct' or 'responsibility to try' (Bellamy 2015*b*: 72; 2015*c*: 171; Welsh 2014*b*: 126). This is an accepted international responsibility to *attempt* to address or prevent mass atrocities. This notion rests on the premise that there is not one blueprint for appropriate action for *all* cases. Rather, states and other actors should try to address mass atrocities in other states by adopting an appropriate measure, rather than overlooking the crisis.

However, it is unclear what exactly we should view as an appropriate measure, given that the notion of the responsibility to try/duty of conduct is ambiguous. The worry with such ambiguity is that various actors in the international community can shirk their responsibility to protect. They can claim that they have done what they can and other actors cannot easily hold them to account since they cannot point to specific responsibilities upon which they have failed to act. To make the responsibility to try—and in turn the international responsibility to protect—much more determinate and potentially influential, we can—and should—flesh it out into various specific requirements. Thus, considering the alternatives to war is important to develop the R2P doctrine and especially (but not solely) pillar three. It can help, first, to provide a better understanding of what states and other actors should do when humanitarian intervention would be unjustifiable or unfeasible. It can help, second, to specify the precise responsibilities of the R2P. By gaining a better understanding of what specifically can be done, we can start to have a

[3] A potential exception is Alex Bellamy's (2015*a*) astute report for the Stanley Foundation. Given its policy focus, however, this report does not examine the alternatives in detail or consider the ethical issues fully. Also see the short briefing paper by Simon Adams (2016), Executive Director for the Global Centre for the Responsibility to Protect.

more determinate—and potentially more influential—account of what states and other actors should be doing.

Accordingly, a better understanding of the ethics of the alternatives to war can help to flesh out the responsibility to try and, more broadly, to fulfil the international responsibility to protect. Indeed, in his 2015 report, *A Vital and Enduring Commitment: Implementing the Responsibility to Protect*, Ban Ki-moon identified 'clarifying and expanding options for timely and decisive response' as one of the 'six core priorities' for R2P over the next decade.

1.2.2 The Ethics of War and Peace

Let us now turn to the second major element of the significance of the ethics of the alternatives to war: it is central for the assessment of the justifiability of *wars and military interventions*. To consider whether a war is justified, it is not enough to consider the case for the war compared to doing nothing. The case for the alternatives is crucial. This was apparent in the 2003 US-led war in Iraq, justified by the US and UK as necessary because of Saddam Hussein's supposed Weapons of Mass Destruction. There was a clear alternative: give diplomacy more of a chance. The UN Monitoring, Verification, and Inspection Commission, led by Hans Blix, had already visited many of the purported sites and not found any evidence of weapons. The failure of the US-led coalition to find Weapons of Mass Destruction subsequently vindicated the claims of those who argued that the war was problematic because it did not give the weapons inspectors enough time.

The importance of considering the alternatives to war is recognized in Just War Theory largely in the form of the *ad bellum* principle of last resort. There are various formulations of this principle, but it is widely understood *not* to require that war literally always be the last resort. Rather, it is understood to hold that war must be comparatively better, such as more effective or less harmful, than the alternatives to war (see section 10.4). Some recent work in Just War Theory frames this in terms of the principle of 'necessity', applied to the *ad bellum* period.[4] In short, war should be necessary, since the other options will cause more harm than good. Comparative assessments involving the alternatives to war are, then, crucial to assessing the justifiability of a war according to Just War Theory. However, such assessments are not straightforward. Sometimes the alternatives will be worse than going to war. This might be because they will lead to the deaths of more civilians, other things being equal. For instance, providing arms to

[4] See, for instance, Aloyo (2015) and Lazar (2016).

rebel groups may be worse than intervening directly, if the rebel groups will use the arms to target civilians. Various diplomatic measures, such as mediation and naming and shaming, may also be worse if they fail to tackle the situation properly. Moreover, assessing the comparative case involves more than simply counting the likely death tolls of the various options. Several other moral considerations might be relevant to the assessment. These include that sanctions might intend harm (see section 3.2.2), that diplomacy might be hypocritical (see section 5.2.2), that non-violent measures might reinforce privilege (see section 6.3.1), and that positive incentives might 'crowd out' intrinsic motivation (see section 7.3.3).

Consequently, the evaluation of the alternatives is complex, but vital to assessing the case for the justifiability of a particular war. To put it bluntly, we cannot know whether a war is just without understanding the ethics of the alternatives. By providing an account of the ethics of the alternatives to war, this book will therefore help to contribute to Just War Theory. This includes (1) the broader issue of if and when war is justified (compared to the alternatives) and (2) how we should understand the comparative Just War requirement of *jus ad bellum* (last resort or necessity), the prevailing accounts of which typically overlook the specific moral issues facing the alternatives.[5] Indeed, sections 2.2 and 10.4 will offer an account of this comparative condition.

Considering the alternatives to war is also important for pacifism. Pacifists challenge the case for war. If they do not wish to endorse simply standing by in the face of mass atrocities and serious external aggression, they need to assess what we should do instead. Yet, pacifists largely overlook this question and focus instead on providing critique.[6] Understanding the ethics of the alternatives is therefore crucial to developing a richer account of pacifism that goes beyond critique to offer positive, feasible policy prescriptions in response to ongoing or imminent crises.

[5] For instance, the leading works in Just War Theory by Bellamy (2006), Biggar (2013), Fisher (2011), Fabre (2012), Lango (2014), McMahan (2009), Orend (2013), and Walzer (2015) do not consider in detail the ethics of the alternatives to war. The main exceptions are Lango (2009*a*), which focuses on non-violent action in general, and the edited volume by Just War theorists Michael Gross and Tamar Meisels (2017), which considers several of the options of 'soft war' (although this collection for the most part does not focus on the same measures as covered in this book).

[6] This is true, for instance, of Atack (2012), Cady (2010), Cicovacki (2013), Fiala (2004), and Holmes (1990). A potential exception is chapter 8 of Robert Holmes' (1989) *On War and Morality*, where he defends disarmament, but Holmes does not generally explore the variety of the alternatives to war in detail. By contrast, Gene Sharp's *The Politics of Nonviolent Action* (1973) does consider 198 forms of different non-violent action (in *Part Two: The Methods of Nonviolent Action*). However, the vast majority of these are concerned with domestic action. In addition, Sharp's work does not focus on the ethical issues surrounding the various alternatives. In similar vein, Jackson (2017) argues that the critiques of counter-terror policy have failed to offer clear alternatives to violent responses to terror.

1.2.3 The Alternatives to War, Geopolitical Shifts, and the Rising Powers

The third broader reason for the importance of the ethics of the alternatives to war concerns the increasing political significance of these measures. It seems likely that it will be more difficult for major Western powers to wage large-scale wars in the future. To start with, the US and UK's misadventures in Iraq and Afghanistan have appeared to reduce public belief in the utility of large-scale war or humanitarian intervention (Davies and Johns 2016*a*). The significant public opposition to the mooted humanitarian intervention in Syria against the Assad regime in 2013 indicates that any Western leader is likely to have to face much resistant public opinion.[7] Moreover, in the wake of the financial crisis and neoliberal austerity measures, there have been significant cuts to military expenditure. This further reduces the ability of Western powers to undertake large-scale military operations abroad. (At the time of writing, the early days of the Trump Administration have suggested that there might still be high levels of military expenditure in the US, although it still seems unlikely that the impulsive Administration would sanction military operations on the scale of those in Iraq and Afghanistan.) Perhaps most significantly, in the future it will be more difficult to secure international support for major wars and military interventions, most notably from the UN Security Council, which is an important factor in their legitimacy and ultimately their effectiveness (Recchia 2017). It is widely expected that the 'BRICS'—Brazil, Russia, India, China, and South Africa—will rise in global influence, if not necessarily uniformly, and there will be a relative decrease in the power of the US and Europe. The BRICS are notoriously much more non-interventionist, at least in their rhetoric, and often define their foreign policy agendas in opposition to Western interventionism. The BRICS have opposed several potential and actual cases of humanitarian intervention, such as the Russian veto in the case of Kosovo, the Chinese support for the Sudanese government in the case of Darfur, and the Russian support for Assad's regime in Syria. More generally, there has been a long-standing opposition by China and Russia to democratic and human rights movements. Brazil, India, and South Africa have, at times, also seemed opposed to humanitarian intervention and R2P, and have strongly defended principles of non-intervention.[8]

[7] For instance, an Opinium/Observer poll found that the UK public opposed action against the Assad regime in September 2013 (Helm 2013). There was greater public support for the action against the Islamic State of Iraq and Syria (ISIS) (Agiesta 2015). However, this was not a humanitarian intervention—its main aim was counterterror.

[8] On the various positions of the BRICS on R2P and intervention, see, generally, the contributions in the special issue of *Conflict, Security, and Development*, 14/4 (2014).

To explain further, in the aftermath of the NATO-led intervention in Libya, the BRICS states claimed that NATO exceeded the mandate given to it by UN Security Council Resolution 1973. This was by allegedly focusing on regime change rather than on the protection of civilians, as well as by purportedly being inappropriate in its target selection, violating the arms embargo by transferring arms to rebels, and generally causing too much harm to civilians and civilian infrastructure.[9] It was also suggested that the UK, the US, and France acted bombastically and arrogantly in the UN Security Council, ignoring the reasonable concerns of other states (Evans 2012). The allegations led to a perception that the UN Security Council would be unlikely to authorize humanitarian intervention again in the future. For a while, there was a worry that this 'blowback' would derail the R2P. In this context, in 2011 Brazil presented the 'responsibility while protecting' (RwP) initiative (Brazil 2011*a*). According to Brazil (2011*b*: 16), this offers 'an additional conceptual step' and 'a new perspective' on R2P and the protection of civilians more generally. RwP is largely about humanitarian intervention: it calls, for instance, for extra care when using military force to protect civilians, for guidelines on humanitarian intervention, and for a new reporting mechanism by interveners.

At first, RwP was seen by the major Western powers as an attempt to block Western interventionism (Evans 2012; also see Luck 2012). However, as the notion mellowed,[10] it is more accurate to say that it proposes a restrictive approach that still allows for the occasional instance of humanitarian intervention, but that can make it harder to intervene militarily. Although RwP was subject to a significant amount of international attention in 2012 and 2013, interest in it fell away as Brazil did not do much to push the notion forward. Nevertheless, it seems that the central notion within RwP that states must follow a more restrictive account of humanitarian intervention is likely to be influential in the future, even if not framed in terms of RwP (Pattison 2016; Stuenkel and Tourinho 2014: 398). Indeed, in 2012, Chinese scholar Ruan Zongze, Vice-President of the Chinese Institute of International Studies that seemingly has links to the Chinese government, proposed the notion of 'Responsible Protection'. This was an even clearer attempt to delimit Western interventionism. Its conditions are stricter than those of RwP and following them would make it almost impossible to engage in humanitarian intervention (Garwood-Gowers 2016).

If proposals such as RwP and Responsible Protection are indicative of the doctrines and norms that will develop as there are shifts in global power, the alternatives to intervention will become increasingly important. This is because military intervention will become harder to carry out whilst in

[9] Lehmann (2012) also advanced some of these claims.
[10] Brazil dropped the requirement for strict chronological sequencing of the pillars of R2P.

conformity with the expected, restrictive standards of behaviour in the international community. Indeed, both RwP and Responsible Protection call for those undertaking humanitarian intervention to consider alternative measures. It seems likely, then, that any potential Western intervention will have to navigate carefully the positions of the BRICS and, if the BRICS oppose the intervention, potentially endure significant reputational and other political costs. Although there may still be some Western interventions, particularly on a smaller scale, it will not be so easy to intervene as during the 1990s and 2000s.

Although potentially less likely to engage in large-scale, direct military intervention, major Western powers will still attempt to secure their foreign policy goals by other means. These include several of the measures that I will consider in this book, including arming rebels, economic sanctions, and naming and shaming. However, the analysis will be pertinent not only for major Western states. On the contrary, it is particularly significant for smaller and middle powers, both Western and non-Western, that, for varying reasons (such as lack of lift capacity), cannot undertake large-scale military interventions, and so *already* must rely largely on the alternatives. Indeed, as we will see, less materially powerful states can use some of the measures, such as diplomatic criticism, to exert influence in excess of their material capabilities.

Considering the alternatives is also important to overcome policy paralysis in the face of deadlock in the UN Security Council. One of the notable limitations of humanitarian intervention is that the intervener typically needs UN Security Council authorization to be legal, unless there is consent from the target state. This hands much authority to the UN Security Council, whose permanent members may decide to block the potential humanitarian intervention (and other actions, such as sanctions or an ICC referral) for self-interested reasons (or other reasons, such as genuine disagreement). However, several (if not all) of the alternatives, such as the cutting of diplomatic ties, naming and shaming, non-violent resistance, accepting refugees, unilateral economic sanctions, and positive inducements do not require UN Security Council authorization. Both large and small powers can undertake these measures, even when the UN Security Council is stymied. Consequently, not only is considering the ethics of the alternatives to war important in light of geopolitical shifts, it is vital for understanding what smaller and larger states can and should do, when intervention is not politically possible because of Security Council deadlock.

1.3 SCOPE OF THE ANALYSIS

Having highlighted the broader significance of the ethics of the alternatives to war, I will now demarcate the scope of the book.

First, I will focus on international responses to two central types of circumstance: (1) mass atrocities and (2) serious external aggression. The former is the subject matter of the R2P doctrine, specifically genocide, ethnic cleansing, war crimes, and crimes against humanity. I use the latter—serious external aggression—as a catch-all term to cover international responses to serious threats to the responding state or to another actor, such as another state. The aggressor might be a state or non-state actor, such as a rebel group or terrorist actor. Serious external aggression includes, then, interstate conflicts, civil wars, and the international use of force by (and against) non-state actors. Accordingly, a state's response in cases of serious external aggression might comprise self-defence or might be helping others to defend themselves (e.g. in a counter-terror operation). It follows that I will consider both alternatives to humanitarian intervention under R2P (in cases of mass atrocities) and alternatives to defensive wars (in cases of serious external aggression). Note that many of the measures can be used in response to both mass atrocities and serious external aggression. But sometimes the measures relevant for tackling mass atrocities might not always be the same as those suitable for tackling serious external aggression. I will discuss the applicability of the different methods as we progress. For instance, civilian peacekeeping and ICC prosecutions are most relevant for R2P cases, whereas civilian defence and the cutting of diplomatic ties are most relevant for serious external aggression. It should also be noted that mass atrocities and serious external aggression are often interlinked—mass atrocities often occur in the context of serious conflict, although this is not always the case (Bellamy 2011).

Second, I will focus on alternatives to tackling *ongoing* or *imminent* mass atrocities and serious conflict. I will not consider longer-term, structural measures of prevention. There are numerous preventive measures, from developing early warning capacity, to education and disarmament. Thus, I will be concerned with, most clearly, the 'reaction' phase of R2P, which aims to address *ongoing* mass atrocities. That said, I will also be concerned with *some* of the 'prevention' phase of R2P, specifically the tackling of *impending* or *imminent* mass atrocities. This involves, in effect, the *pre-emption* of mass atrocities—pre-empting them when they are imminent—which is sometimes also called 'escalation prevention' (Sharma and Welsh 2015*a*) or 'direct' preventive efforts, which contrasts to 'root-cause prevention' (ICISS 2001: 23). This also reflects the language used to distinguish between preventive and pre-emptive self-defence, where the former concerns tackling a *temporally distant threat* and the latter concerns tackling an *imminent* one (Crawford 2005). This is not to deny that the longer-term prevention of serious external aggression and mass atrocities can often be more cost-effective and less harmful. I simply focus on tackling *ongoing* or *imminent* mass atrocities. I adopt this focus both to make the book manageable and because these are the circumstances in which wars could be potentially justifiable. That is to say, war and military intervention are generally viewed as permissible only in response to ongoing or imminent crises; the justifiability of preventive war and intervention is widely doubted, especially in concrete cases (as opposed to hypothetical scenarios). Ongoing or imminent mass atrocities and external aggression provide just cause for all of the measures that will be considered (they are the archetypical just causes for war). It is worth noting, though, that many of the alternatives may be justifiably deployed in many less serious circumstances as well, such as in cases of the more minor violations of human rights.

Third, I will be concerned with alternatives to war by *international* actors. I will not directly address what *internal* actors should do, that is, those in the state that is experiencing mass atrocities or serious conflict. This also raises several interesting issues, but I focus on international responses.[11] Although the analysis will sometimes focus on states, much of it will be relevant for other external actors, including regional organizations such as the European Union (EU), non-governmental organizations (NGOs), and international bodies such as the UN Security Council and ICC. Indeed, parts of the analysis will focus on these actors, most notably in chapter 6 (which will consider the case for non-violent intervention by NGOs) and chapter 9 (which will consider criminal prosecutions by the ICC).

Fourth, I will focus on seven sets of alternatives. These are selected thematically: economic sanctions, military sanctions, diplomacy, non-violent measures, positive incentives, military assistance, and measures that do not (for the most part) attempt to tackle the crisis directly but instead have other aims (i.e. prosecution and amelioration). More specifically, the book examines the following measures:

- Economic sanctions (chapter 3)
- Arms embargoes (chapter 4)
- Diplomacy (chapter 5):
  - Diplomatic criticism/naming and shaming (sections 5.1–5.2)
  - Dialogue (section 5.3)
  - Mediation (section 5.4)
  - The cutting and downgrading of diplomatic ties (section 5.5)
  - The denial of membership of an international or regional body (section 5.6)

[11] There is an emerging literature on the ethics of resistance and rebellion that considers some of the issues around what internal actors should do. Most notably, Part III of Michael Gross' excellent book, *The Ethics of Insurgency: A Critical Guide to Just Guerrilla Warfare* (2015), considers the alternatives to waging guerrilla war (the other parts of the book consider how guerrillas should wage war). Similarly, Christopher Finlay's (2015) book on *Terrorism and the Right to Resist: A Theory of Just Revolutionary War* applies Just War Theory to revolution and considers the most morally desirable strategy for revolutionaries, from those based on traditional accounts of *jus in bello* to strategic non-violence.

- Non-violence (chapter 6):
  - Civilian peacekeeping (sections 6.1–6.3)
  - Civilian defence (section 6.4)
- Positive incentives (chapter 7):
  - Economic and political inducements (sections 7.2–7.4)
  - Amnesties (section 7.5)
- Military assistance (chapter 8):
  - Military assistance to rebels (sections 8.1–8.3)
  - Military assistance to states (section 8.4)
- Prosecution and amelioration (chapter 9):
  - Actions by the International Criminal Court (ICC) (section 9.1)
  - Accepting refugees (section 9.2)
  - Humanitarian assistance (section 9.3)

Why do I focus on these measures? First and foremost, the book aims to be comprehensive. It aims to cover all of the central alternatives to war. By 'central' alternatives, I mean the following: (1) the measures that states and other actors have *frequently resorted to* in response to mass atrocities and serious external aggression (such as economic sanctions); (2) the measures that *public and academic discussions often raise* as potential options (such as arming rebels); and (3) the measures that have *significant potential merit* (such as positive incentives).[12] I do not consider measures that involve direct military action (or 'kinetic force'). These include most obviously war, but also direct military operations short of war, such as assassinations and targeted strikes, snatch operations, more coercive forms of peacekeeping, and the use of drone warfare. Such operations raise somewhat similar ethical issues to war, and analysis of them would detract from looking at the non-kinetic options.[13]

Although I frame them as alternatives, all of the options can also be *adjuncts* to war. They may remove the need for extensive military operations. In other words, they can replace *parts* of the military intervention. For instance, the use of civilian peacekeeping may remove some of the need for a more robust, coercive military operation in certain parts of a state. At other times, some of the measures may not replace any part of the war, but be purely an *addition*.

[12] For instance, they cover the main options listed in the highly influential ICISS (2001: 23–7; 29–31) report on the R2P as part of the direct prevention 'toolbox' and 'measures short of intervention'. They also cover the main non-military measures listed by former Australian Foreign Minister and Director of the International Crisis Group, Gareth Evans, in his account of the 'reaction toolbox' (2008: 107). In addition, they are similar to the accounts of the atrocity prevention toolkits by the Genocide Prevention Task Force (Albright and Cohen 2008: 61; 66), the World Peace Foundation (Conley-Zilkic et al. 2016), the Stanley Foundation (Bellamy 2011: 5), and the Task Force on the EU Prevention of Mass Atrocities (2013: 53), as well as the recent report on the Obama Administration's US mass atrocity prevention efforts by Alleblas et al. (2017: 33).

[13] These have also been discussed at length elsewhere (e.g. Aloyo 2013; Finkelstein et al. 2012; Lango 2009*b*; Strawser 2013).

For instance, naming and shaming may be in addition to humanitarian intervention to help delegitimize the target state's behaviour.

At times, the analysis will focus on the measures in isolation in order to simplify the ethical issues. However, it is important to bear in mind the various relations between the measures. First, the measures will often work best *when combined* (Hafner-Burton 2014: 276). For instance, section 7.4 argues that a mix of incentives and sanctions will often be most judicious, as this can ameliorate some of the resentment that occurs with purely coercive measures and avoid some of the risks of maintaining a purely non-coercive approach. Second, some measures *directly block* others. For instance, the cutting and downgrading of diplomatic ties can undermine the possibility for mediation, dialogue, inducements, and humanitarian assistance, as the diplomatic connections needed for these measures are incised (see section 5.5). Third, measures can also *indirectly block* other measures. This is, for instance, by their consumption of political will. Political will is valuable and finite, and politicians are likely to expend only a limited amount of effort on international matters. The crisis in question will also compete with other crises and issues on the international agenda of states, international organizations (such as the UN Security Council), and the global media. Pursuing a feasible and effective course of action is therefore vital. When states and other actors pursue a relatively ineffective or infeasible measure at the expense of measures that are more effective or feasible, civilians may die in the meantime. Fourth, and conversely, some measures can *enable other ones*. For instance, economic sanctions can enable positive incentives and vice versa (see section 7.4) and ICC actions increase the probability of economic sanctions (Appel 2018). More generally, the launching of one measure can increase the willingness of the international community to support another. The use of a less coercive measure first can show that it does not work, which can then enable a more coercive one. For instance, mediation may sometimes need to be tried politically before various international actors will support measures that are more coercive, such as targeted economic sanctions.[14]

1.4 THE ROAD AHEAD

I will now provide a précis of the road ahead. Chapter 2 explicates the Pragmatic Approach, the various factors of which I will defend throughout the book. It summarizes the relevance of the five central values, considers

[14] Of course, this might also be problematic if the measure enabled is unjustifiable, such as war. See section 3.3 on the worry that sanctions might lead to war.

objections and alternatives to this approach, and explores how we should weigh values.

Chapter 3 considers the case for economic sanctions, both targeted and comprehensive. It challenges the prevailing view on the morality of economic sanctions, which holds that sanctions (including to some degree targeted sanctions) are highly objectionable. To do so, it considers and replies to four central objections to economic sanctions. These are the 'Indiscriminate Objection', which asserts that sanctions are impermissible because of their apparent indiscriminateness, the 'Intending-the-Harm Objection', which holds that sanctions are highly problematic because they involve means that intend harms, the 'Instrumentalization Objection', which holds that sanctions wrongly use the suffering of innocents as a mere means, and the 'Ineffectiveness Objection', which holds that sanctions are ineffective. Having rejected the central arguments against sanctions, I go on to argue that sanctions are, in fact, favourable, in at least one respect: they are more likely to distribute fairly the currently inevitable harms to innocents of tackling aggression and mass atrocities. In doing so, this chapter further delineates the importance of fairness in the distribution of costs on the Pragmatic Approach.

Chapter 4 focuses on arms embargoes. The chapter first considers the idealized case for arms embargoes, which holds that they reduce the aggressors' access to weapons and frustrate their goals, whilst distributing the costs fairly and avoiding *doing* harm. Arms embargoes are, however, subject to a withering, nonideal critique in some of the academic literature. This highlights various problems such as that they are violated by sender states, that weapons are still obtained on the black market and through porous borders, and that they are used to avoid undertaking more effective action. However, I challenge this nonideal critique and argue that the idealized account is in fact largely correct: arms embargoes *do* often work once we adopt the correct measure of effectiveness (what I call 'morally valuable effectiveness'). In doing so, this chapter provides a defence of the importance and meaning of effectiveness—the central factor on the Pragmatic Approach.

Chapter 5 considers diplomatic measures, including diplomatic criticism (naming and shaming), dialogue and mediation, the cutting of diplomatic ties, and the denial of membership of an international body. The main part of the chapter focuses on diplomatic criticism, arguing that it can help to address the situation, contribute to morally valuable international norms, and even punish offenders. In doing so, I consider the objection that diplomatic criticism is too demanding and that states are not entitled to criticize others when they are being hypocritical. More broadly, the chapter establishes the moral importance of expressing condemnation and upholding morally valuable international norms.

Chapter 6 considers non-violent methods. In the first part of the chapter, I largely defend the case for civilian peacekeeping by groups such as Peace Brigades International and Nonviolent Peaceforce and, in doing so, delineate how this measure can be effective despite being unarmed. The chapter also highlights the limitations of civilian peacekeeping, including its small scale. The second part of this chapter considers civilian defence against an external aggressor. Although I argue that this may sometimes work, the chapter highlights one central limitation: it is unlikely to be effective against an aggressor that does not wish to occupy.

Chapter 7 considers the use of economic, political, and legal incentives. After presenting three notable reasons for using positive incentives—including the fact that they are not coercive—I consider several objections to their use. These include, centrally, the worry that they reward those who commit egregious wrongdoing and therefore are problematic in terms of desert. I also consider the potential moral hazard that such inducements will encourage others to commit wrongdoing and the potential for incentives to crowd out intrinsic motivation and to undermine morally valuable international norms and laws. Although I largely defend the case for positive incentives, I reject the case for amnesties.

Chapter 8 considers the case for military assistance to rebels and states, focusing mostly on the former. On the one hand, the chapter argues that it may be *exceptionally* permissible to arm rebels. In doing so, it rejects three considerations that one might think provide sufficient reason to uphold an absolute prohibition on arming rebels. These are that *rebels* are being armed, that *external* parties are supplying the arms, and that those supplying arms may be *complicit* in wrongdoing committed by the rebels. On the other hand, the chapter argues that arming rebels should generally be eschewed. It presents three objections: the 'Rebel-Risk Objection', which claims that it can be difficult to determine who the rebels are; the 'Escalation Objection', which holds that once arms are supplied to the rebel group, this will significantly escalate the conflict as other parties in the conflict will also seek arms or will escalate their response to the rebels; and the 'Diffusion Objection', which holds that it is difficult to ensure that the weapons stay in the possession of just rebel groups. The chapter also argues that many of these objections apply to arming *states*.

Whereas chapters 3 to 8 consider measures that *primarily* attempt to tackle the ongoing situation, chapter 9 considers measures that often do so only as a *secondary* aim: (1) criminal prosecutions, (2) accepting refugees, and (3) humanitarian assistance. I focus on the question of whether we should *frame* these measures as major policy options to tackle mass atrocities and serious external aggression. I argue that, on the one hand, we should see international criminal prosecutions by the ICC as a central part of the toolkit for responses to mass atrocities. This is despite worries about its politicization and linking it to R2P. On the other hand, I argue that we should not view accepting refugees and humanitarian aid as part of the R2P toolkit, in large part due to worries about buck-passing.

Chapter 10 considers the implications of the analysis, highlighting the two central themes: (1) there are several normative reasons in favour of the alternatives and (2) there are further objections to war. It goes on to consider the implications of the analysis, for pacifism, Just War Theory, and the R2P. I argue that, although the preceding analysis appears to strengthen the case for pacifism (since there is more to the alternatives than it often seems), it also poses a challenge to it. The chapter then outlines the implications for the *jus ad bellum* principle of last resort. I defend an account of 'Presumptive Last Resort', which holds that war should be *presumed* to be the last feasible option.

2

The Pragmatic Approach

How should we go about assessing the ethics of the alternatives to war, given the variety of the moral considerations that arise? It will help if we have a clear normative framework to guide us, which we can use to assess and to weigh the potential moral considerations that we will encounter. The aim of this chapter is to outline and to defend such a framework, which I call the 'Pragmatic Approach'. As we will see, this approach is pragmatic in that it is significantly instrumentalist and takes seriously the nonideal and contingent features of the contemporary international system. The Pragmatic Approach will help us to answer the two central questions necessary to determine whether a measure should be launched. The first is whether a measure is superior to *not launching it*. The second is whether it is superior to *other measures*.

The chapter will first delineate a series of tests that any moral theory should meet (section 2.1). I will then present the central features of the Pragmatic Approach in section 2.2, including the five central values on this approach. Section 2.3 will defend the Pragmatic Approach, showing how it meets the tests outlined in section 2.1. It will also delineate the links to Just War Theory, and especially the *jus ad bellum* principles of necessity and proportionality. I will go on to argue that the Pragmatic Approach is superior both to (i) three general alternative approaches (the 'Absolutist Approach', the 'Idealized Approach', and the 'Fully Instrumentalist Approach') and (ii) three different ways of treating values (lexical priority, a categorical approach, and threshold deontology).

The chapter will be more abstract and philosophical. It aims to show that the ensuing judgements about the alternatives are on a sure normative footing. For readers more interested in particular alternatives, it isn't necessary to read this chapter very closely, or even at all, given that the later substantive chapters are designed so that, as far as possible, they can be read in isolation. Notwithstanding, a complete understanding of the ethics of the alternatives to war will only become clear with an appreciation of the Pragmatic Approach outlined in this chapter. It should also be noted that the plausibility of the Pragmatic Approach and the importance of the five central values on it will become more patent as the book progresses. This is because I will only outline the importance of each of the five values in this chapter. I will defend their significance at greater length in the context in which they most arise.

2.1 FOUR TESTS

The Pragmatic Approach offers a moral theory of the ethics of the alternatives to war. But how should we judge what is an appropriate ethical theory of the alternatives to war and what is not? To that end, it helps to first consider more generally the requirements of a suitable moral theory in this context. I will argue that such a theory should do well on four tests. To do so, I will draw on leading accounts of the general assessments of moral theories, such as that offered by Mark Timmons (2013: 12–16).[1]

The first two criteria concern the need for a moral theory to be action-guiding. First, a theory should be *determinate*. For our purposes, it needs to offer clear normative prescriptions about the alternatives that could be adopted by states and other actors, or, more specifically, policymakers. Or, perhaps more likely, it needs to offer clear normative prescriptions that can be used to advise policymakers and, crucially, to hold them to account for their selection of measures (by interested parties, such as NGOs), and more generally to guide the public debate on the case for the alternatives. This might not necessarily need to involve clear prescriptions for every instance of mass atrocities or serious external aggression, which will depend to some extent on the particularities of the case. But a theory should offer guidance about the general case for each of the alternatives, which can be applied to particular contexts. Let us call this the 'Determinacy Test'.

Second, and related, a theory needs to be *relevant*. When considering the alternatives to war, it needs to be pertinent to current and future crises, and more generally to the contemporary international system, warts and all. A theory that offers guidance only for an international system that is far more developed and peaceful, or for political leaders somehow more wise and ethical, would be of little use for making judgements, here and now, about

[1] Other notable tests are offered by Hooker (2000: 4–29), Pollock (1988), and Valentini (2015: 737). The first and second tests are similar to what Timmons calls 'determinacy' and 'applicability' respectively. The third combines Timmons' standards of 'consistency' and 'intuitive appeal'. The fourth is closest to Timmons' criteria of 'internal' and 'external support'. Timmons also adds that a theory should have explanatory power—clearly explain why an option is right or wrong. I leave this aside to keep the section brief, but the Pragmatic Approach also meets this test since it assesses the leading options according to five central values. As such, there is a clear account offered as to why a measure will be justifiable or not, that is, it will score well or badly according to these five values.

how we should respond to crises in the unjust global order. Let us call this the 'Relevance Test'.

Third, a theory needs to be *plausible*. It needs to offer coherent and intuitively plausible prescriptions for when thinking about concrete cases. A theory that results in intuitively implausible or incoherent prescriptions should be revised, so as to be coherent with our considered moral judgements about cases. Let us call this the 'Plausibility Test'.[2]

Fourth, it is desirable if a moral theory has *wide appeal*. What I mean by this is that the approach could be endorsed by those who have differing but reasonable underlying world views. This is in the context of a somewhat pluralist world order, where states and individuals within them do not necessarily share the same view of how their own society and more generally the international system should be organized.[3] It helps, to that extent, if a theory relies on widely endorsed values. Let us call this the 'Appeal Test'.

The importance of wide appeal rests, first, on the need to recognize the potential fallibility of our own moral judgement. As the leading political philosopher of recent times, John Rawls (2005), puts it, there are 'burdens of judgement'. These arise from several factors, many of which are pertinent when considering the alternatives to war, from contested and complex empirical evidence, to the difficulties of making an overall assessment, and the influence of different political cultures. An upshot of the burdens of judgement is that there can be reasonable disagreement between actors in the international system about some of the central principles that should govern responses to mass atrocities and serious external aggression. Recognizing and reflecting reasonable disagreement can also help to ensure compliance with moral norms. Moral norms that are widely endorsed would appear far more likely to be complied with or at least can exert a greater 'compliance pull', that is, render the reasons to comply weightier, given the likely strength of the opprobrium if the norms are overlooked. This may make it harder for recalcitrant actors to ignore them. Accordingly, to ensure that moral norms have some influence in the international system, it may be sometimes better to seek consensus with other reasonable views. Sticking to one's own views could increase contestation and the ambiguity surrounding the norms, which could weaken their compliance pull. Moreover, an approach that has wide appeal is more likely to be comprehensible to a broad array of actors across the

[2] This is in order to be congruent with the method of reflective equilibrium (the predominant meta-ethical approach in contemporary ethics), which assesses our considered, intuitive judgements in particular cases, at various levels of abstraction, against our underlying theories and principles (see Daniels 2016; Rawls 1999*a*: 18–19, 42–5).

[3] This is in similar vein to Rawls' aims in his later works of *Political Liberalism* (2005) and particularly *The Law of Peoples* (1999*b*). Likewise, Sen's (2009) *The Idea of Justice* also calls for humility and a reflection of non-Western perspectives, as well as a more practical approach to justice.

international system. It can therefore help to meet the Relevance Test, helping to inform global public debate about the ethics of the alternatives to war in terms widely understood and values widely endorsed.

In what follows, I will argue that the Pragmatic Approach scores highly on these tests and fares better than potential alternative approaches. But to do this, I first need to delineate the Pragmatic Approach.

2.2 THE PRAGMATIC APPROACH

The Pragmatic Approach is pragmatic in three senses.[4] First, it is concerned with not only the *necessary* features of the various alternatives, but with their *likely* features and effects as well. In other words, it takes into account current contingent features of the alternatives, such as whether they are generally likely to be effective, even if they will not always be so. This differs from an approach that would focus on the 'deep morality' of the alternatives to war, in similar vein to the 'revisionist' approach to Just War Theory (e.g. Fabre 2012; McMahan 2009). (Revisionist approaches to Just War Theory often overlook current contingencies and focus largely on the 'deep morality of war', that is, only the first-order, *necessary* principles that should govern war. For instance, Cécile Fabre sees her account of the ethics of war as '[u]nearthing first-best principles' (2012: 12).) Although the necessary features are important, concentrating *solely* on these features of an alternative would provide an incomplete account of the case for a measure. For instance, chapter 7 will argue that one reason in favour of positive incentives is that they are non-coercive, which is a necessary feature of them. However, looking *only* to this feature would not help us to determine whether they are justifiable overall. This depends also on the likely effectiveness of incentives at tackling the situation in question, as well as whether they are likely to reward wrongdoers, both of which are contingent matters. To offer a fuller, more practically relevant account, the Pragmatic Approach therefore considers both the contingent and necessary features of the alternatives.

The Pragmatic Approach is pragmatic in a second, related sense. It offers an account of the ethics of the alternatives to war that is relevant not simply for ideal theorizing about the alternatives (although some aspects are relevant for this), but that is also relevant to the current, nonideal features of the international system.[5] This differs from a purely idealized account of the ethics of

[4] Note that the Pragmatic Approach does not depend on pragmatism in the philosophy of social sciences or pragmatism in ethics.

[5] See, further, Pattison (2018), where I present a similar case for focusing on the nonideal morality of war. I focus here on the need for a nonideal ethics *of the alternatives to war*.

the alternatives that is applicable only when circumstances are highly favourable. To explicate, Rawls (1999*a*) draws a helpful distinction between 'ideal theory' and 'nonideal theory'. Ideal theory (in the Rawlsian sense) is concerned with theorizing in circumstances of full compliance with the ideal moral principles and the existence of favourable circumstances in order to realize the ideal (such as favourable historical, economic, and social conditions). By contrast, nonideal theory is concerned with the lack of full compliance with the ideal moral principles and/or the presence of unfavourable circumstances, such as institutional and epistemic limitations. In one sense, *all* theorizing about addressing mass atrocities and aggression (including pacifism and Just War Theory) is an exercise in nonideal theory, given that it assumes that there will be non-compliance with *some* ideal moral principles. For instance, leaders will engage in aggressive wars against other states or murder their own populations. Notwithstanding, there still can be degrees of idealization in an account of the ethics of the alternatives, depending on how much one assumes compliance and favourable circumstances. A highly idealized account (akin to a 'revisionist' view of the alternatives to war) would largely overlook troublesome features of the current international system, such as that states often ignore moral considerations and that there is a lack of the resources to determine accurately the culpability of individuals. The Pragmatic Approach differs from this: it provides an account that considers not only idealized considerations, but also reflects likely non-compliance and unfavourable circumstances.[6] I will say more about this in section 2.3.

Third, the Pragmatic Approach is pragmatic in that it holds that the effectiveness of the measure is typically the most important consideration. The alternatives can be effective in various ways. They can fully tackle the situation immediately (such as by helping a government to defeat a terrorist movement) or can reduce its severity or duration. This might involve pressurizing belligerents into talks, encouraging them to have a break in hostilities, or incentivizing them not to commence or recommence force.

2.2.1 The Five Central Values

To answer the two central questions of whether a measure is superior to (i) not launching the measure and (ii) alternative measures, the Pragmatic Approach suggests that there are five central considerations. In addition to the (1) effectiveness of the measure, we should also look to the following considerations:

[6] As such, the Pragmatic Approach does not reject more idealized theorizing about mass atrocities and conflict. It is compatible with maintaining that the ideal *should* be strived towards.

(2) The likely *fairness* in the distribution of the costs and benefits of the option.
(3) How the option is likely to fare according to the distinction between *doing* and *allowing* (that is, whether it will *do* harm and, if so, to what extent).
(4) Whether it is likely that harm caused by the option is mediated by the *interceding agency* (or 'intervening agency') of others.[7]
(5) Whether the option will be likely to punish or benefit those who *deserve* to be punished.

Given that I will delineate each of these values in more detail as we progress through the book, I will only provide a précis of the value for now. To start with, (1) effectiveness concerns whether the measure can be reasonably expected to do more good than harm. Or, more precisely, it concerns whether the measure is likely to bring about more benefits than costs, compared to the counterfactual of the measure not being undertaken. On the account of 'morally valuable effectiveness' that I will develop, effectiveness should be measured primarily according to the effects on basic human rights, although other effects, such as on non-basic human rights, may also be relevant as a secondary concern. As I will argue, this is an account of *morally valuable* effectiveness, in that it is concerned with the promotion of something with a clear moral value—compliance with human rights—rather than whether the measure achieves the morally arbitrary foreign policy goals of a state. Note that, on this account of effectiveness, the aggregate effects on basic human rights are independent of the culpability of the individuals in question. This consideration instead comes in when considering (5) desert. As such, morally valuable effectiveness brackets the question of whether the individuals are liable, or deserve to be benefited or harmed; it simply focuses on the net effects in terms of the basic human rights of all those affected.

The second factor on the Pragmatic Approach concerns (2) how fair the measure is. Whereas the effectiveness of the measure relates to the *aggregate* effects of the measure on basic human rights, fairness concerns the *distribution* of costs and benefits. Although the costs should ideally be borne by those who are culpable (in proportion to the degree to which they are liable) and all benefits should accrue to those who are innocent, in the current nonideal international system it seems inevitable that innocents will have to bear some costs. This is either directly through the measure (such as a sanctions regime that harms innocents collaterally) or through a response that does not fully tackle the situation (such as an arms embargo that only partially reduces the

[7] I use the term 'interceding agency' (rather than the more common term, 'intervening agency') in order not to confuse the factor with other issues in the ethics of intervention discussed throughout.

severity of mass atrocities). In other words, I will argue that there is no perfect measure where we can be confident that only the culpable bear costs. What then is a fair distribution in this nonideal context? I will defend first the importance of assigning burdens to (i) those who *consent* to them. I will also argue that, when distributing burdens, one should look to (ii) those who have been *benefited* beyond their just entitlements. The placing of costs on the beneficiaries helps to move towards a more level playing field—or, more precisely, towards a situation where people receive their just entitlements. When it is too difficult to determine who, if anyone, agrees to the costs or to determine beneficiaries, I will argue that there should be (iii) the *sharing of the costs* of the action (or of inaction) between innocent individuals. Although the full realization of equal sharing is rarely likely to be possible, distributions that generally spread the costs may often be preferable. This is when costs would otherwise be concentrated on a few innocents.

The third consideration on the Pragmatic Approach concerns (3) the doctrine of *doing* and *allowing*. This asserts that it is worse to *do* harm (to innocents) than it is to *allow* it. To understand this difference, consider the following example:

> [i]n Rescue I, we can save either five people in danger of drowning at one place or a single person in danger of drowning somewhere else. We cannot save all six. In Rescue II, we can save the five only by driving over and thereby killing someone who (for an unspecified reason) is trapped on the road. If we do not undertake the rescue, the trapped person can later be freed. (Quinn 1989: 290)

It seems that in Rescue I we should save the five people, but in Rescue II it seems impermissible to save the five. This is because we should not *do* harm. It seems morally better if we *allowed* the other five to die. In the contexts of the alternatives, this means that we should favour measures that don't *do* harm, even if this would *allow* a somewhat greater harm.

This brings us to the fourth, related consideration, which is (4), the interceding agency of others. I will argue that the wrongness of an agent *doing* harm can be mediated somewhat by the interceding agency of others. The doctrine of doing and allowing concerns the causal relation that the agent has to the harm and, in particular, about the fact that it is directly connected to the harm. However, when others also have a close relation to the harm and, in particular, mediate it, the wrongness of the original agent doing harm is diminished, given that its relation to the harm is less direct. This means that we don't need to be so worried about the measure *doing* harm.

The final value is (5) whether the measure will punish or benefit those who *deserve* to be punished. Although it can often be difficult to determine desert given our epistemic limitations, which can limit the practical relevance of this consideration, it is possible to *sometimes* have a stronger understanding of the desert of those affected. Indeed, certain measures, such as targeted sanctions, amnesties, and international criminal prosecutions, target political leaders and senior military officials, and it does *sometimes* seem possible to get a better sense of their desert. They can be more accurately identified as culpable, and not only liable to defensive force, but also potentially deserving of punishment. Consequently, when such determinations are possible, desert can affect the justifiability of the measure.

Why these five values in particular? All five are widely viewed in political philosophy to be morally relevant considerations; they draw on underlying notions of beneficial aggregate consequences, fairness, agency, and desert. First, almost all leading accounts of contemporary ethics hold that (1) consequences matter, at least to some extent (key debates in ethics concern *how much* they matter and what are the agent-relative constraints on pursuing consequences). The importance and understanding of effectiveness will be a central theme of all of the chapters, but defended and outlined in most detail in chapters 3 and 4. (2) Fairness is central to debates in distributive justice, most famously Rawls' *A Theory of Justice* (1999*a*). The meaning and significance of fairness will be considered at greatest length in sections 3.4.2 and 9.2.1, such as when considering the fair distribution of refugees. The (3) moral asymmetry between doing and allowing harm is central to the Hippocratic Oath and is a key consideration in many accounts of individual self-defence, and more generally is a primary feature of most accounts of deontological ethics. If one holds that doing and allowing matters, which concerns how much one's agency is involved, it also seems to follow that it matters (4) whether harm is mediated by the interceding agency of others. The former (3) (the difference between doing and allowing) will be considered at greatest depth in chapters 3 and 4, and the latter (interceding agency) will be considered at various points, but most clearly when examining the problems of escalation that arise when arming rebels (section 8.3.2). Finally, (5) the relevance of desert is central to many retributivist accounts of punishment. Although its wider relevance in international ethics is often contested because of the epistemic and practical difficulties of determining what people deserve in many cases, it can be relevant in isolated cases when these problems can be overcome. I will explore desert at greatest length in section 7.3.2, which examines the issue that incentives can wrongly reward wrongdoers. To be sure, these are not the only moral considerations that I will explore. For instance, I will consider the issue that a measure (such as sanctions) may use people as a mere means (section 3.2.3), the wrongness of being complicit in injustice (sections 4.3 and 8.1), the wrongness of hypocrisy (section 5.2.2), and the intrinsic value of Habermasian dialogue (section 5.3). I will, however, largely reject the relevance of these other considerations or will argue that their importance stems from one of the five values of the Pragmatic Approach.

Thus, although the Pragmatic Approach gives significant weight to overall consequences of the measure, it is moderately instrumentalist. Rather than consequentialism, it adopts value-pluralism, in that it holds that there are different sorts of moral considerations (aggregate effects on human rights, fairness, whether the agent *does* harm, whether this harm is mediated, and desert).[8]

2.3 DEFENCE OF THE PRAGMATIC APPROACH

The Pragmatic Approach scores well on the four tests of a moral theory outlined above. Its taking into account the nonideal and contingent features means that it clearly passes the Determinacy and Relevance Tests. It can offer clear guidance about the case for the current leading alternatives to war, within the nonideal international system. In short, it is action-guiding.

Yet it might be objected here that the Pragmatic Approach is indeterminable and so it fails the Determinacy Test. Given the multiplicity of considerations and the messy circumstances of mass atrocities and serious external aggression, the objection is that there can be *no* way of assessing which factors have been met and, in turn, no reliable means of determining which measure will be suitable in a particular circumstance. It is, the objection posits, all about the context. However, this conclusion should be resisted. The context will, of course, determine some of the desirability of the measure. On the Pragmatic Approach, much will depend on how efficacious a measure will be in a particular situation. Yet the ensuing chapters will delineate a series of considerations that help to provide a guide to judge how effective a particular measure will generally be. For example, chapter 8 will argue that providing arms to rebel groups will typically be subject to the Rebel-Risk, Escalation, and Diffusion Objections. Providing such arms will therefore typically be ineffective. The ensuing chapters will also offer a guide to how the various alternatives will typically fare according to the other four considerations on the Pragmatic Approach. For instance, chapters 3 and 4 will consider whether sanctions and arms embargoes will generally distribute harm fairly and chapter 9 will argue that ICC actions are preferable in terms of desert.

The Pragmatic Approach also clearly passes the Plausibility Test. On the face of it, it seems plausible, first, that the most important consideration when assessing the alternatives to war should be the effectiveness of a measure at advancing basic human rights overall and, second, that there are other relevant considerations too which should inform the assessment.

[8] It might be claimed that these values could be incorporated into a complex account of consequentialism, whereby they are maximized. This might not be straightforward, however, since some of the values concern agent-relative considerations (such as *doing* harm oneself, compared to allowing it) and it is doubtful whether agent-relative considerations can be incorporated into consequentialism. See Brown (2011).

Of course, the plausibility of the Pragmatic Approach will be more clearly tested—and demonstrated—when we examine more closely each of the values in later chapters.

What about the Appeal Test? As noted above, all five values on the Pragmatic Approach are widely endorsed in political and moral philosophy, that is, draw on extensively defended, underlying notions of beneficial aggregate consequences, fairness, agency, and desert. Although these five concepts are clearly rooted in Western analytical philosophy, they also have broader appeal. The effectiveness of a measure is frequently cited in international debates about the merits of responses. Indeed, the debate is often framed *solely* in terms of the efficacy of the measure. Similarly, the measure of effectiveness that the Pragmatic Approach will adopt—the effect on basic human rights—is widely endorsed. States have universally signed up to various human rights declarations, and notions of human rights are found in major non-Western doctrines (Caney 2000). Notions of fairness and distributive justice are, likewise, endorsed in major non-Western doctrines, and non-Western states often lament the unfairness of the current global economic order.[9] States also often invoke other features of the Pragmatic Approach, such as the difference between doing and allowing in public debate. For instance, the Brazilian proposal of 'responsibility while protecting' (Brazil 2011*b*) and Chinese account of 'Responsible Protection' (Zongze 2012) (both amendments to R2P) endorsed principles similar to the 'first, do no harm' principle of the Hippocratic Oath, in response to the (perceived) bombastic NATO-led intervention in Libya in 2011. It seems, then, that the Pragmatic Approach passes the Appeal Test.

2.3.1 The Pragmatic Approach and Just War Theory

To demonstrate further the appeal of the Pragmatic Approach, it helps to consider its relation to Just War Theory. As noted above, to assess an alternative to war we need to know whether the alternative is superior to both not launching the measure and alternative measures. This parallels accounts of Just War Theory (most notably, Lazar 2016) that posit that the two central, underlying criteria for assessing the morality of a war is, first, whether it is superior to not going to war and, second, whether going to war will be better than the other options. These are fleshed out in terms of the *jus ad bellum* principles of *proportionality* and *necessity*. As such, we could view the question

[9] For instance, the Confucian notion of *yi* is, when concerned with justice, somewhat similar to notions of fairness and desert (Tsai 2005: 161).

of whether a measure should be launched in terms of whether it meets the requirements of proportionality and necessity.[10]

Let us first consider necessity. As noted in chapter 1, the principle of necessity *ad bellum* is often favoured by philosophers working on Just War Theory (those more practically driven focus on last resort, which I consider in section 10.4). Necessity is sometimes understood in narrow instrumentalist terms (e.g. Frowe 2011: 11–12), that is, as requiring only that the measure chosen be the most effective. But, recently, Seth Lazar (2012; 2016) has offered a more philosophically sophisticated account of necessity. Lazar argues that '[w]here an option *O* aims to avert a threat *T*, we determine *O*'s necessity by comparing it with all the other options that will either mitigate or avert *T*' (2016; also see Lazar 2012). Lazar notes that we should not limit this to simple aggregation: '[n]ecessity and proportionality judgements involve weighing harms inflicted and threats averted, indeed all relevant goods and bads' (2016). Lazar's account is helpful but substantively bare—he offers a formal account of the principle, but does not flesh out the various 'goods and bads' that should inform necessity.[11] This is offered by the Pragmatic Approach, which avers that there are five central considerations that should determine the necessity of an option. In other words, whether war—or an alternative—is morally superior depends on how it and the various leading alternatives fare according to the five values on the Pragmatic Approach. As such, necessity should be understood as follows: '*Whether a measure is morally superior to other measures*'. What determines whether a measure is morally superior is how it and the other options are likely to fare in terms of (1) effectiveness,

[10] To avoid misunderstanding: I do not mean to propose that we assess the alternatives according to the *legal* accounts of these principles in international humanitarian law. My point instead is that these principles should be understood *morally*, according to the values of the Pragmatic Approach. Also note that I do deny that there might be other criteria of Just War Theory. The point, rather, is that these criteria (such as just cause, legitimate authority, and last resort) can be derived from the *underlying* principles of proportionality and necessity (for example, a high bar for just cause can be explained by the importance of avoiding disproportionate costs, compared to doing nothing—see Heinze (2005); Pattison (2010: 20–4; 2016). For a defence of the centrality of proportionality and necessity in Just War Theory, and that other Just War criteria can be derived from them, see Lazar (2016), who argues that 'proportionality and necessity contain within them almost every other question in the ethics of war'. Also see Rodin (2011). Lazar (2012) in fact argues that necessity could include proportionality, but notes that this is a technical point.

[11] Lazar's account of necessity also differs from mine in that it compares options that have '*some prospect of averting or mitigating the threat*' (2016; emphasis added). I do not add this condition. A measure might have *no prospect* of averting the threat, but still be the best option. For instance, suppose that civilian defence would have no chance of tackling an invasion, but still provide the victims with a sense of empowerment and motivate others in other states to resist unjust aggression, and so do much more good than harm. It might be better than the other options, such as military force, because these options will face other problems, such as doing harm to innocents, even if these options have some (very small) chance of averting the threat.

(2) fairness, (3) whether the measure *does* harm, (4) whether any harm is mediated, and (5) desert.

Let us now turn to the *ad bellum* principle of proportionality. This requires that the measure be likely to do more good than harm, compared to not launching the measure. *Pace* Jeff McMahan (2013–14: 4), we should not judge the proportionality of an action compared to *doing nothing*. It makes more sense if the proportionality of an action is compared to *not doing it*. In this way, we can use proportionality to assess further actions (such as ICC actions) when we are already doing *something* (such as economic sanctions). That is to say, we need to know if when we are already undertaking one measure whether we should add a further measure. If proportionality focuses on doing nothing, it cannot answer this question. Moreover, proportionality is, like necessity, sometimes understood in purely instrumentalist terms (e.g. Fisher 2011: 73–6; Frowe 2011: 54–6; Lee 2013: 85–93). But this is unduly narrow, since it risks overlooking a host of non-instrumental considerations; it should be broadened out (see Lazar 2012; Rodin 2011). Thus, on the Pragmatic Approach, proportionality is as follows: '*Whether the measure is morally superior to not launching the measure*'. What determines whether the measure is morally superior is how it (and not launching the measure) is likely to fare in terms of (1) its effectiveness, (2) fairness, (3) whether the measure *does* harm, (4) whether this harm is mediated, and (5) desert.

Thus, in one sense, the Pragmatic Approach draws on Just War Theory and, in fact, indeed offers an account of it. That is to say, it offers an account of the *ad bellum* principles of necessity and proportionality in Just War Theory. More theoretically, it provides an account of how we should make these comparisons, based on the five values. More substantively, the analysis of the various chapters will provide an assessment of the leading alternatives to war and so flesh out these conditions of *jus ad bellum*, especially necessity (and last resort in section 10.4) so that we will be able to actually compare war with the leading alternatives, and so know whether it is comparatively justifiable. But the Pragmatic Approach is not *simply* an account of Just War. It is also relevant beyond considering war. It helps us to assess the alternatives when war is not a desirable or feasible option and, more generally, how states and other actors should assess responses to mass atrocities and serious external aggression. It is also relevant, therefore, more generally to the ethics of foreign policy. It draws on concepts central to Just War—necessity and proportionality—and offers accounts of them that are particularly relevant to the alternatives to war, but also applicable to war itself.

It is worth emphasizing two more points here. First, although I focus on the decision to *resort* to a measure here, much of the analysis is also relevant to ongoing decisions *during* the use of the measure. Periodically *during* the deployment of the measure, its justifiability should be assessed, including whether an alternative or addition would be better. For instance, a sanctions regime should be assessed to see whether it would be better to end it or whether an alternative, such as direct military action, should be launched instead (or alongside it). This is akin to the claim made in Just War Theory that the continuation of war should be subject to principles similar to that of *jus ad bellum* and be reassessed periodically.[12] Second, necessity (and proportionality) require not choosing between discrete options, but rather choosing between various packages of measures. As we will see in the next two chapters, for instance, economic sanctions and arms embargoes are typically launched alongside other measures.

2.3.2 Alternative Approaches

Thus far I have outlined the Pragmatic Approach, argued that it meets the four tests of a moral theory, and linked it to Just War Theory. But to more clearly see the case for the Pragmatic Approach, it helps to consider leading potential alternatives—and why the Pragmatic Approach is advantageous.

The first is the 'Absolutist Approach'. This holds that there are certain deontological considerations that are of absolute moral weight and so cannot be outweighed by instrumentalist concerns. For instance, it might be thought that it is always impermissible to *do* harm to innocents, even if this will allow for a much greater harm. The Absolutist Approach might be seen as a 'principled' approach, in contrast to the pragmatism of the Pragmatic Approach.[13]

The general problem, though, with the Absolutist Approach is that it clearly fails the Plausibility Test. It is mistaken to hold that the importance of deontological considerations cannot be outweighed. For instance, if one can save 100,000 lives by enforcing targeted economic sanctions that *do* harm to 100 innocent family members of the target regime, it seems that economic sanctions might be permissible, despite *doing* harm. Absolutism here would be clearly implausible. I will reject further instances of absolutist arguments throughout the book. It is worth adding here that deontological absolutism is now widely eschewed amongst leading moral philosophers. As Lazar notes, '[a]lmost all "practicing deontologists" recognize that rights can be overridden in extremis' (2017*a*: 585, n. 19) and, apart from one person, '[e]veryone . . . is a "moderate deontologist", who believes that intentionally killing the innocent is sometimes permissible, if the good achieved thereby is great enough' (2017*b*).

[12] See, for instance, Lango (2007), McMahan (2004: 713–14), Moellendorf (2008), and Toner (2010).

[13] To be sure, the Pragmatic Approach does endorse several principles. Indeed, the giving of significant moral weight to consequences is obviously a moral principle. The Pragmatic Approach also holds that there are several deontological principles, although these can be outweighed.

A second alternative to the Pragmatic Approach—the 'Idealized Approach'—is principled in a different sense. It offers an account of the moral principles (such as for when civilians can be held liable for economic sanctions) that should ideally govern the ethics of the alternatives to war, if circumstances would allow, most notably for determining accurately individual moral responsibility. As suggested above, this might be akin to a 'deep morality' of the alternatives to war, in similar vein to certain revisionist Just War Theorists' deep morality of the ethics of war (e.g. Fabre 2012; McMahan 2009). Although there is merit in considering the ideal principles that should govern the ethics of war and peace, such by providing a blueprint to strive towards, such an approach is radically incomplete.[14] There needs to be a nonideal account of the ethics of the alternatives as well. This is in order to reflect likely non-compliance and unfavourable circumstances of the current international system, where there are significant epistemic limitations, the lack of sufficient capacity, frequent attempts to abuse moral norms, and numerous unintended consequences. These include that targeted economic sanctions can still harm the innocent given the difficulties of determining culpability (see section 3.2.1), that there are insufficient civilian peacekeepers to be able to prescribe this measure (see section 6.3.2), that the use of incentives can be subject to moral hazard and extortion (see section 7.3.5), that it can be difficult to ensure, when arming rebels, that the rebels are fighting on the just side and unlikely to harm innocent civilians (see section 8.3.1), and that states can use the accepting of refugees and humanitarian assistance to pass the buck (see sections 9.2 and 9.3). An account of the ethics of the alternatives that overlooked such issues would either fail to be relevant, since it is not applicable to the current international system (and so fail the Relevance Test), or, if it is attempted to be applied, it could offer mistaken and counterproductive policy prescriptions, since it overlooks these features (and so fail the Plausibility Test).

The third approach is the Fully Instrumentalist Approach. This holds the effectiveness of the measure is the *only* consideration. Thus, to judge whether to launch economic sanctions, to engage in non-violent resistance, or to arm rebels, all that matters is how effective each measure will be in terms of advancing basic human rights. The obvious problem with the Fully Instrumentalist Approach is that it overlooks the other four considerations of the Pragmatic Approach. For instance, it ignores the intrinsic importance of a fair distribution of the benefits and burdens of implementing the measure. Although the import of this might be sometimes outweighed by effectiveness, it surely matters *somewhat* whether a distribution is fair. Suppose, for instance, that Option A (say, sanctions) and Option B (say, arming rebels) will harm

[14] I make this point in more detail in Pattison (2018).

those who are innocent. In the case of Option A, the harms will be borne by those who consent to them, whereas for Option B they would be borne by those who do not agree to them. If Options A and B are equally effective, it would seem odd to hold that we have no reason to prefer Option A. Even if Option B would be more effective, surely it matters to some degree that in Option A those distributed the burdens would agree to them. This is *one* reason in favour of Option A, even if not necessarily the most weighty one. The Fully Instrumentalist Approach would therefore fail the Plausibility Test.

2.3.3 The Case for Weighing Values

Accordingly, it seems that an approach that includes both instrumental and non-instrumental considerations should be adopted. When considering how the various values should be compared, the Pragmatic Approach, recall, adopts an approach that *weighs them*. This considers the various reasons for and against each of the alternatives, weighing the strength of these reasons, and typically holds that effectiveness matters most.

However, this is not the only method of treating these values. It might be objected here that a more straightforward method should be adopted, given that it might seem too tricky to weigh these values reliably. There are three leading alternatives to that adopted by the Pragmatic Approach.

First, *lexical ordering* ranks the values according to their importance. The values that are ranked higher are given lexical priority. What this means is that they are absolutely more significant than the values lower down the ranks. For instance, (1) effectiveness at improving compliance with human rights might be seen as lexically prior to (2) the fair distribution of harm. The values that are further down the ranking are relevant only when there is a tie between the options. For instance, suppose that (1) effectiveness is lexically prior to (2) the fair distribution of harm. Effectiveness would, in effect, be the *sole* factor in virtually all cases. It is only when measures are likely to be equally effective that they will be assessed according to (2) the fair distribution of harm.

The central problem with lexical ordering is precisely that it relegates the importance of the values further down the scale to being tie-breakers. It seems intuitive that they are more than that. They seem to be *countervailing* considerations to the importance of, for instance, effectiveness. For instance, distributive concerns are also important when deciding between two options that *differ somewhat* in their effectiveness. To see this, consider the following. In response to a serious threat posed by terrorists, Option A (e.g. war) will save a few more lives than Option B. However, Option B (e.g. an arms embargo) will be *much* better in terms of distributive justice (for instance, all of the costs will be borne by those who are global beneficiaries). Accordingly, Option B might be preferred. However, by lexically ranking effectiveness, one would insist that Option A is *always* better since there can be no appeal to fairness whilst there is a difference in effectiveness. Even if one holds that Option A should be preferred, it does still seem that we should consider distributive fairness in making this conclusion, rather than overlooking it completely, which is essentially what an account that adopts lexical priority would do.

A further, related problem for accounts that adopt lexical priority is that they fail to offer plausible responses to situations of risk, that is, where it is uncertain that the value will be present (Huemer 2010). For instance, suppose again that one holds that effectiveness is lexically prior to distributive justice. Suppose further that, on the one hand, in response to genocide there is a 1 per cent chance that Option A (e.g. war) will be more effective than Option B (e.g. sanctions) (and a 99 per cent chance that they will be equally effective). On the other, there is a 99 per cent chance that Option B will be significantly fairer in terms of distributive justice than Option A (and a 1 per cent chance that they will be equally fair). If one endorses lexical priority, then one would seemingly select Option A in this instance, given the trivial probability that Option A will be more effective. Yet this seems counter-intuitive, given that Option B in this case is likely to improve distributive justice significantly.

The second option is a *categorical approach* that requires a measure to do well on *all* of the five considerations. Thus, a measure, such as targeted sanctions, might be viewed as justifiable only if it is sufficiently effective, distributes harms fairly, does not *do* harm, and punishes those who *deserve* to be punished. Such an approach is sometimes found in Just War Theory (e.g. US Catholic Bishops 1992)—war can be justly waged only when all the criteria of *jus ad bellum* are met. The obvious problem with this approach is that this sets the bar extremely high for a permissible measure. It seems likely that in most cases *none* of the alternatives will do sufficiently well on *all* of the conditions. As I will argue in the ensuing chapters, there is no Goldilocks measure. The categorical approach could therefore end up prescribing doing nothing in response to many situations. In fact, it would not even prescribe that: even doing nothing will typically not meet these conditions, since it will not be effective, distribute harm fairly, or ensure that those who are culpable for the crisis receive their just deserts. So, the categorical approach risks policy paralysis.

The third option is *threshold deontology*. This holds that deontological considerations are the sole considerations up to a certain threshold but that, above the threshold, achieving good consequences becomes the sole consideration. In our context, this would mean that deontological considerations should determine which alternative should be adopted, until a certain threshold of sufficiently weighty consequences is reached. One might hold, for instance, that measures that avoid doing harm should be adopted, until a certain threshold of potential lives saved, when effectiveness then becomes the criterion.

There are several problems with threshold deontology. The most obvious issue is that it is notoriously difficult to offer a plausible justification of a particular threshold (Alexander 2000). Why should one, for instance, draw the threshold at 1,000 lives rather than 1,001 lives? Beyond this, there are two further problems. On the one hand, it seems that, *below the threshold*, effectiveness still matters. Even in less serious cases, the efficacy of the response is an important moral consideration, even if not the only one. But this is overlooked by threshold deontology, which holds that deontological factors are the only considerations below the threshold. To explicate, suppose that the threshold is set at 1,000 lives and there are two feasible options to save lives in response to a situation. Option A (e.g. civilian peacekeeping) would not *do* harm but would save only one life, whereas Option B (e.g. naming and shaming) would *do* a small amount of harm (such as impose some reputational costs on a handful of innocent politicians) but would save 999 lives. On threshold deontology, Option A would be preferred because it does not do any harm. But it seems intuitive that there is a much stronger case for Option B, given that it would save 999 lives. It seems clear, then, that *effectiveness matters below the threshold.*

On the other hand, threshold deontology wrongly excludes *deontological considerations above the threshold*. It holds that they are no longer relevant, once a certain degree of effectiveness has been reached. Suppose again that the threshold is set at 1,000 lives. Again, there are two options on the table. Option A (e.g. positive incentives) would *not* do harm and would save 10,000 lives overall. By contrast, Option B (e.g. sanctions) would *do* significant harm. It would cause 9,000 deaths, but would also be somewhat more effective—it would save 20,000 lives and so 11,000 lives overall. Now, it seems that there is at least a somewhat plausible reason for preferring Option A, given that it would not *do* harm. The fact that it won't do harm seems relevant to the choice, but is overlooked on an approach that adopts threshold deontology, given that this case is above the threshold for deontological concerns to matter. Even if one does not think that this is determinative, it is surely a *reason* against Option B that should be taken into account in the choice between options. It seems, then, that deontological considerations matter above the threshold.

To be sure, a more sophisticated version of threshold deontology may avoid this worry: it could allow for consequences to matter below the threshold and for deontological considerations to matter above it. It would hold instead that above the threshold consequences matter more (but are not the only consideration), whereas below it deontological considerations matter more (but, again, are not the only consideration). Such an account would be closer to the weighing account of the Pragmatic Approach. Still, the tricky (and perhaps insurmountable) challenge remains of providing a plausible justification for that threshold, without this being drawn arbitrarily.[15]

The case for the weighing method of the Pragmatic Approach is now clear. It does not relegate lesser values to tie-breakers (unlike lexical ordering), result in policy paralysis (unlike the categorical approach), or draw an arbitrary threshold (unlike threshold deontology). But how exactly are the values of the Pragmatic Approach to be weighed? I will now suggest that this can actually be straightforward.

2.3.4 Weighing Values on the Pragmatic Approach

In this section, I will present a more detailed account of the weightings that should be given to each factor and how they compare. The logic is simple: the Pragmatic Approach holds that all values are of equal import and simply looks to the likely *quantity* of the value at stake to make determinant judgements. This is a function of (i) how many individuals are likely to be affected and (ii) the likely magnitude of the effect on each individual. Looking to the likely quantity of the value at stake provides a clear and straightforward way of weighing the values, in the context of the ethics of the alternatives to war: the values likely to be in largest quantity are most weighty.

I want to make three caveats. First, by looking to the quantity, I do not mean to suggest that we can necessarily quantify *numerically* the values of the Pragmatic Approach. It will obviously be far too difficult in most cases to provide precise assessments of this. Rather, my point is that we should look to *rough*, general assessments about the amount of value that appears to be at stake. Second, our assessments about the importance of the amount of value should be tempered by our intuitions (i.e. our considered moral judgements about cases), under the method of reflective equilibrium. This might mean that we sometimes step away from a purely quantity-based view. Third, and related, my aim in this section is to defend one way of weighing values that seems plausible *in this context*. We need a straightforward, clear, and practicable basis for weighing the values, which looking to quantity offers. A more sophisticated account might consider both the *quantity* and *quality* of the value at stake. This would hold that values are not of equal import; some are more important than others.[16]

[15] See Alexander (2000) for a clear reputation of threshold deontology, largely based on this issue, and Lazar (2017*b*) for a rejection of a threshold approach to subjective permissibility in the ethics of killing. In similar vein to the Pragmatic Approach, Lazar (2017*b*) defends an approach that calls for the maximization of 'moral utility', which can incorporate several deontological values. Also see Lazar (2017*a*) and Portmore (2017).

[16] For a detailed exploration of the different ways in which values and reasons can be weighed, see Lord and Maguire (2016).

Let us consider an example to make clearer what I am proposing. Suppose that Pakistan is considering a response to a terrorist threat from Afghanistan. Option A—positive incentives—would be highly effective but would wrongly reward corrupt officials who are somewhat responsible for the threat. By contrast, Option B—criminal prosecution—would be less effective but would punish the corrupt officials. Which option Pakistan should undertake will depend on how much of the relevant values is at stake. That is, it will depend, on the one hand, on the difference in the degree of effectiveness of the measures and, on the other, how much Option A would reward the officials and Option B would punish them. If Option A is likely to be much more effective and only a handful of officials would be rewarded, it should be favoured. The likely size of the effect on basic human rights would be large, where the likely stakes in terms of desert would be small. If, however, the difference in effectiveness will only be marginal and several officials would be wrongly rewarded by Option A and rightly punished by Option B, Option B should be chosen. Then, the likely size of the effect on basic human rights would be trifling, where the likely stakes in terms of desert would be much larger.

Usually, the most important factor will be the effectiveness of the measure given that how relatively effective a measure will be will typically affect (i) a large number of individuals (ii) in significant ways—such as by improving the protection of their basic human rights. That is, the quantity of the value will often be large. I will argue this in more detail in the ensuing chapters. The important point to note for now is that the Pragmatic Approach is moderately instrumentalist because of the typically high stakes involved in the effectiveness of the various measures.

It is unlikely that so much will be at stake with the other four values (i.e. the amount of the value at stake will not be so large). To start with, (2) fairness will not be so important since there will typically likely to be (i) fewer individuals affected and/or (ii) the magnitude of the effect will be smaller. This is because the alternatives to war do not, of course, aim to be primarily distributive and, as such, are unlikely to have a large *positive* effect on numerous individuals. For instance, they do not aim to change the structure of the international system that renders the poor disadvantaged in the first place, such as unfair trade tariffs, odious debt, and the enforced liberalization of public services. That said, the measures might have a larger *negative* effect on fairness, such as by increasing the burdens on those who are already significantly disadvantaged.[17] In addition, whether (3) the measure *does* harm seems less important,

[17] This seems particularly the case for two measures. First, as we will see in section 9.2, accepting extremely large numbers of refugees can place very sizeable costs on states near to the crisis (such as Lebanon) and typically the already impoverished within the Global South. Second, wars and direct military interventions typically impose significant costs on those who are

since it concerns only the agency of the agent performing the action. The doctrine of doing and allowing, recall, permits the agent to give preference to their own agency, that is, to favour allowing over doing harm, since one would be doing harm oneself. But the doing of harm concerns only *your* agency, whereas the effectiveness of the measure may concern the basic interests of hundreds of individuals.[18] Moreover, even when it does harm, this harm might be reduced by (4) the interceding agency of others. This can reduce the weight that should be given to the wrongness of doing harm. Similarly, the importance of (5) desert will often concern only a handful of individuals in minor ways. For instance, an inducement to a culpable leader will wrongly reward only *one* individual, providing them with only a small improvement in their life (such as a reputational or financial gain). Again, the amount at stake will be much smaller.

I want to highlight two caveats to the moderate instrumentalism of the Pragmatic Approach. First, the relative difference in effectiveness between measures may not be that large; in such cases, the other values will be more important. Second, sometimes it will be difficult to determine the comparative effectiveness of measures, given nonideal epistemic limitations. It may be hard, for instance, for a foreign ministry with limited resources to determine whether economic sanctions or political incentives are likely to be more effective in response to mass atrocities. However, states may sometimes—and perhaps often—have a better sense of how measures will fare according to the other values (and, more specifically, how much value is at stake with each). Most obviously, it will often be clear that a particular measure (such as economic sanctions) will *do* much more harm, that a measure (such as political incentives) will wrongly reward those who are culpable, or that a measure (such as prosecution by the ICC) will punish those who are culpable. In such cases, when states are in the dark about the relative effectiveness of the measures, these other considerations should determine which measure should be undertaken. To be sure, we can often have a sense of the relative effectiveness of the measures; indeed, the ensuing chapters will examine the effectiveness of all of the measures and highlighted indicators of their likely effectiveness in

globally disadvantaged. This includes peacekeepers from developing countries, with rich Western states providing only a supporting role (Bellamy and Williams 2009) and the increased use of private military and security companies which employ 'third-country nationals' and locals to carry out many of the riskier roles (Pattison 2014*b*), who have been subject to several serious labour abuses (ACLU 2012).

[18] One complication concerns how we should treat collective agents that *do* harm, such as the US. It might seem that we should *treat all of the individuals* within the collective as doing harm; if so, this would mean that, for instance, 320 million individuals *do* harm when the US enforces a sanctions regime. This would make the concern of doing and allowing highly significant. However, it seems more intuitive to treat such actors either as a single agent or to focus on particular individuals within the agent, such as the US President, who decide to launch the action.

particular circumstances. My point is that (1) it might still nevertheless, on occasion, be hard to compare the efficacy of the measures and (2) it is possible to often have a stronger sense of these other considerations. It is clear, then, that they can play a significant role on the Pragmatic Approach.

2.4 CONCLUSION

This chapter has presented the Pragmatic Approach, which is pragmatic in the sense that it reflects nonideal considerations, is moderately instrumentalist, and considers contingent features. Section 2.1 proposed four tests of a moral theory. Section 2.2 presented the main claims of the Pragmatic Approach and the five central considerations on this approach, and linked this approach to Just War Theory. Section 2.3 defended this approach, highlighting how it fares well on the four tests and is superior to alternative approaches.

In what follows, the Pragmatic Approach will inform the assessment of the alternatives (although not in an overly methodical manner). Indeed, it is on the basis of the Pragmatic Approach that later chapters will argue that wars should generally be avoided and that the alternatives should be pursued—in fact, there is an obligation to consider and pursue them. As we will see, one does not need to endorse problematic principled (i.e. absolutist or idealized) approaches to reach this conclusion. Chapter 3 will examine what is often viewed to be the leading alternative to military action: economic sanctions. Although economic sanctions are often robustly criticized, I will argue that they are not as bad as often viewed.

3

Economic Sanctions

Economic sanctions are the most obvious of the alternatives to military intervention. At the end of the First World War, Woodrow Wilson, the then President of the United States, famously proclaimed that

> [a] nation boycotted is a nation that is in sight of surrender. Apply this economic, peaceful, silent, deadly remedy and there will be no need for force. It is a terrible remedy. It does not cost a life outside the nation boycotted, but it brings pressure upon the nation that, in my judgment, no modern nation could resist.
>
> (in Nincic 2011: 16)

Sanctions continue to be one of the central measures undertaken in the response to aggressive states, authoritarian governments, and states that are attempting to secure weapons of mass destruction (including nuclear weapons). The use of sanctions hugely increased after the end of the Cold War, reaching over 300 cases between 1990 and 1995 (Morgan et al. 2014: 549). They continue to be frequently used. For instance, between February 2014 and February 2015, the US introduced or amended twenty different sanctions programmes (Drezner 2015: 755). Although there has been a move away from comprehensive, multilateral sanctions, states still engage in unilateral or bilateral broad sanctions and multilateral, 'targeted' sanctions. The latter, sometimes called 'smart sanctions', include measures such as asset freezes, travel bans, and smart trade sanctions.

Sanctions are also widely seen as a tool to implement the responsibility to protect (R2P) doctrine. They are included in the report by the ICISS (2001) as a measure to realize the 'responsibility to react'. As the R2P has evolved, sanctions have continued to be seen as an important measure to realize the goals of the tackling and prevention of mass atrocities. For instance, the UN Secretary-General's reports in 2009 and in 2012 on R2P sees sanctions as a central element of the toolbox to implement 'pillar three' (Ban Ki-moon 2009; 2012). Indeed, UN Security Council Resolution 1970 concerning the situation in Libya in 2011 explicitly invoked the R2P and imposed various sanctions on Gaddafi's regime, such as a travel ban and an asset freeze, which Resolution 1973 later strengthened by adding an aviation ban (Popovski 2011).

Yet, despite their preponderance, sanctions have been widely criticized for failing to realize their policy goals (e.g. Pape 1997). They are also often criticized for being indiscriminate and for leading to widespread suffering, as well as for being disastrous for civil and political rights in target states (e.g. Peksen 2009). The comprehensive sanctions regime against Saddam Hussein's Iraq, in particular, was widely seen as morally reprehensible, and it has been (wrongly) claimed that it led to the death of 500,000 children under the age of five (Gordon 2010: 87).[1] Criticism of sanctions is so extensive that it is even suggested that war may be morally *preferable* to sanctions. The point is often made in the context of the discussion of the principle of last resort in Just War Theory. It is claimed that we should avoid a literal understanding of last resort, since war may be better than the alternatives and, in particular, better than economic sanctions (e.g. Fisher 2011: 73).

Over the next three chapters, I will consider the case for sanctions broadly conceived. In this chapter, I will consider *economic* sanctions, both comprehensive and targeted. In chapter 4, I will consider *military* sanctions, in the form of arms embargoes. In chapter 5, I will consider a further form of sanction—*political* sanctions, such as naming and shaming and expulsion from political bodies. The central objective of this chapter is to defend economic sanctions against several objections. My defence will be tentative and contingent. I will not mount a vehement defence of sanctions. Instead, I will show that they are (1) *sometimes* permissible, against absolutist arguments to the contrary, and (2) less vulnerable to the central objections than often claimed. To do this, I will reject what I call the 'Prevailing View', which is highly critical of them, found in much of the literature on economic sanctions. In providing this defence, I will explore the issue of fairness in the distribution of inevitable costs, which will also be relevant for later chapters as one of the central factors on the Pragmatic Approach, and suggest that sanctions are preferable when we consider fairness. Towards the end of the chapter, I will explore further the import of the difference between *doing* and *allowing* harm, which is another relevant consideration on the Pragmatic Approach.

3.1 ECONOMIC SANCTIONS INTRODUCED

Economic sanctions attempt to impose costs on receivers, often, but not solely, in order to realize political change in the target, by curtailing economic relations. Certain sanctions regimes may be *comprehensive* in that they ban *all* trade in goods. They may still allow for some import of food and medical

[1] The methodology underlying this statistic is now highly questioned (Moret 2015: 135, n. 4).

materials under a humanitarian exception. The Oil for Food Programme in Iraq, for instance, allowed Saddam Hussein's Iraq to sell some oil in order to buy food and other basic supplies, in order to alleviate the severe humanitarian suffering of the Iraqi people. (The proceeds of the sales of oil, however, were widely misappropriated, with much of the proceeds not reaching the suffering Iraqi people.) More likely, however, is that the sanctions are *targeted* at particular goods or assets, which I will discuss shortly.

Sanctions may be unilateral, bilateral, or multilateral. That is, the 'sender' may be by a single state, such as in the case of the US's ongoing comprehensive sanctions regime on Cuba.[2] Sanctions regimes may be bilateral (involving several states) or multilateral in the sense that they are broader still, such as the EU's sanctions on Russia, in light of its annexation of Crimea. Sanctions may also be multilateral in the sense that the UN Security Council authorizes them. In the 1990s, the UN imposed comprehensive sanctions on Iraq (in response to its invasion of Kuwait and attempt to develop weapons of mass destruction), Yugoslavia (during the civil war), and Haiti (after the overthrow of Jean-Bertrand Aristide). More recently, however, the UN Security Council has avoided such a comprehensive approach, particularly in light of the problems of the sanctions regime in Iraq. It has instead focused either on certain goods or on particular individuals. In fact, the UN has not imposed comprehensive sanctions since the 1990s (Eckert et al. 2016: 1).

This brings us to the next key feature, which concerns the target—the 'receiver'. Sanctions may be targeted at (1) the state in general or (2) particular individuals, such as leaders and their families, selected firms and business groups, political parties, non-state actors, such as insurgents or terrorists, or regimes, such as the Taliban (Biersteker et al. 2016*b*: 13). For instance, the EU or UN Security Council may freeze the bank account of a ruler or seize the assets of a suspected terrorist.[3] The labels of 'smart sanctions' or 'targeted sanctions' are often used to denote sanctions targeted at particular *goods* and/or particular *individuals* or *groups*. They include the following: *commodity* and *sectorial* sanctions, which restrict trade in specific commodities (such as diamonds and timber) and trade related to certain sectors (such as the oil industry); *travel restrictions*, which include travel bans for particular individuals and their families; and *financial sanctions*, which include asset freezes of particular individuals or governments, restrictions on access to banks, and suspensions of loans or aid (Biersteker et al. 2016*b*: 26–7;

[2] In 2016, the Cuban government estimated that the sanctions cost it $4.6 billion the previous financial year and $125.9 billion over the fifty-five years that the embargo has been in place (VOA 2016).

[3] The UN Security Council has, however, often recently avoided targeting leaders directly, in large part in order to overcome political difficulties in the Council and, in particular, Russian and Chinese opposition (Wallensteen 2016: 262).

Welsh 2015: 113).[4] The labels of 'smart' and 'targeted' sanctions can, however, be somewhat misleading. They can elide the targeting of particular *goods and assets* with the targeting of particular *individuals*, which can give the impression that smart or targeted sanctions do not harm innocents. However, as I will discuss further in section 3.2.1, sanctions on particular goods can still be hugely indiscriminate and cause significant suffering amongst individuals. (And even sanctions on particular individuals can harm those who are innocent.) The worry is that the labels of 'smart' or 'targeted' sanctions can downplay these negative effects, overlooking potential casualties. This is in similar vein to the worry that the language of 'smart bombs' and 'targeted precision' in war downplays the likely harms of 'smart' bombing campaigns, and ultimately potentially renders it easier to go to war.[5]

Although often painted as such, it is mistaken to hold that smart sanctions are a new development and that they have largely replaced comprehensive sanctions. First, although they are now much more widely used, measures that target particular individuals and particular goods were widely used prior to the 2000s, such as against apartheid South Africa. Indeed, they accounted for 60 per cent of the sanctions between 1945 and 1950 (Morgan et al. 2014: 552).[6] Second (and again as we will consider further below), there has been a recent drift back towards broader sanctions—the 're-comprehenzivation' of targeted sanctions—whereby 'targeted' sanctions are less discriminate. The reasons for this re-comprehensivization include the more distant memory of the humanitarian effects of sanctions on Iraq and the difficulty of implementing properly targeted sanctions (Biersteker et al. 2016*d*: 270–1).

3.2 DEONTOLOGICAL OBJECTIONS TO ECONOMIC SANCTIONS

Sanctions generally receive a bad rap. According to the Prevailing View on the morality of economic sanctions, which is found in much of the (relatively small) body of literature on the ethics of sanctions, broader and (to a lesser

[4] In what follows, I include financial sanctions and travel bans under 'economic sanctions', even though they may not technically be economic measures. I will discuss arms embargoes separately in chapter, 4 given that they raise particular ethical issues.

[5] See, further, Zehfuss (2011). To be clear, as we will see below *passim*, some of the relevant academic literature documents that targeted sanctions can have negative humanitarian effects.

[6] What is now seemingly unlikely is a comprehensive sanction regime that is authorized by the UN Security Council and is therefore multilateral, such as the sanctions regimes on Iraq, Haiti, and the former Yugoslavia in the early 1990s.

extent) targeted sanctions are highly objectionable.[7] For some, sanctions are morally impermissible or highly problematic, regardless of the merits and demerits of the alternatives (and sometimes even if there are exceptions in the sanctions regime for the provision of humanitarian necessities).[8] Indeed, proponents of the Prevailing View sometimes reject outright the permissibility of broader sanctions.[9] Others argue that it is conceivable that sanctions may be permissible if they meet certain conditions (particularly when they take the form of targeted sanctions), but generally hold that sanctions are objectionable because of their alleged indiscriminateness, wrongful intentions, use of innocents as a means, and/or ineffectiveness.[10]

Against the Prevailing View, I will argue that sanctions are not *necessarily* morally problematic and, in fact, *less* morally problematic than is often claimed by proponents of the Prevailing View. In what follows, I will reply to (1) what I call the 'Indiscriminate Objection', which asserts that sanctions are impermissible because of their apparent indiscriminateness. I will then consider and largely repudiate the claims that sanctions are highly problematic because they (2) involve means that intend harms (the 'Intending-the-Harm Objection'), and (3) wrongly use the suffering of innocents as a means (the 'Instrumentalization Objection'). Having considered three deontological objections to sanctions, I will then explore the instrumental objection that (4) they don't work (the 'Ineffectiveness Objection').

3.2.1 The Indiscriminate Objection

A central objection to sanctions by those who endorse the Prevailing View is what I will call the 'Indiscriminate Objection'.[11] In short, this holds that sanctions are impermissible because they are indiscriminate in that they impose significant harms on those who are not liable. Accordingly, on this objection, sanctions are morally problematic because, as Joy Gordon argues, they 'are inconsistent with the principle of discrimination from just war doctrine' (1999*a*: 124). More specifically, they appear to violate the principle of non-combatant immunity, which asserts that civilians should not be intentionally targeted in war. This is most obvious for comprehensive, multilateral sanctions, such as those against Iraq, where many of those who bore the brunt of the sanctions regime were children and the vulnerable. In fact, such is

[7] The main discussions of the morality of sanctions include Damrosch (1994), Ellis (2017), Fabre (2016), Gordon (1999*a*; 1999*b*; 2011; 2017), Lopez (1999), Pasternak (2009), Pierce (1996), and Winkler (1999).

[8] See, for example, Gordon (1999*a*; 1999*b*) and McGee (2003).

[9] See, for instance, Babic and Jokic (2000) and Gordon (1999*a*).

[10] See, for instance, Pierce (1996) and Winkler (1999).

[11] See, for instance, Gordon (1999*a*; 1999*b*; 2011) and McGee (2003).

the apparent lack of discrimination in sanctions that various scholars claim that they are similar or analogous to sieges, since they undermine the economy of a society and, in doing so, prevent the production or importation of necessities.[12] In addition, sanctions can result in increased repression, as governments frame economic sanctions as an external threat to unity and justify their repression against anti-regime groups critical of the government as necessary to maintain cohesion (Peksen 2009: 62–3). They can also decrease compliance with women's rights (Drury and Peksen 2014), worsen public health (Peksen 2011), and undermine press freedom and independent media, which are obvious targets as governments crack down on opposition in the face of the external coercion of sanctions (Peksen 2010).

In what follows, I will not completely reject the Indiscriminate Objection. Rather, I will argue that, although it may sometimes give us reason to oppose sanctions, it does not establish that sanctions are necessarily impermissible. To do this, I will start by considering two less convincing responses.

The first response is that those in the state who are subject to the sanctions are liable to them because they are collectively responsible for the unjust threat (e.g. Christiansen and Powers 1995: 106–7). However, it seems that an extreme and probably implausible account of collective responsibility would be required to hold that sanctions are generally permissible on this basis. Accounts of collective responsibility typically require that groups have representative decision-making procedures, that group members have common interests and shared solidarity, and/or that there exist shared attitudes between group members; yet the lack of these features often prompts the need for many sanctions regimes in the first place, including in cases of government repression against its population (Winkler 1999: 148).

The second response is to hold that 'smart sanctions' only harm those who are liable and so avoid the objection. This is mistaken. It is not only broader sanctions that fall foul of the Indiscriminate Objection; smart sanctions can too.[13] That is to say, targeted sanctions on particular individuals and sanctions of particular goods can also impose harms on those who are innocent. They can have several unintended consequences. This is in at least three ways.

First, 'smart' trade sanctions on particular industries, such as timber or oil, can damage an important sector of the economy and undermine the exports of the state and, as a result, weaken its ability to fulfil basic governmental functions (Gordon 2011: 326). For instance, the impact of the EU's decision

[12] See Babic and Jokic (2000), Gordon (1999*a*: 126), and Meisels (2011: 103). On the wrongness of sieges and blockades, see, for instance, Walzer (2015: 160–75).

[13] See Gordon (2011) and Rudolf (1998: 17). More generally, unintended consequences (both positive and negative) are found in 94% of cases of targeted UN sanctions, such as an increase in criminality and corruption (58% of cases), strengthening of authoritarian rule in the target state (35% of cases), and harmful effects on neighbouring states (19% of cases) (Biersteker et al. 2016*b*: 27–8; Eriksson 2016: 202–3).

to ban the import of crude oil from Syria was about $450 million per month (Eriksson and Giumelli 2011). The sanctions on Syria worsened an already dire situation by exacerbating the economic deterioration (including worsening unemployment, falling salaries, and the rising price of basic commodities) and by decreasing access to basic public health and clean water (Moret 2015: 129–30). Similarly, the EU's targeted sanctions on Iran, including restrictions on its central bank, an oil embargo, and trade bans on natural gas and metals, resulted in Iran's sharp economic decline and various negative humanitarian impacts, such as a reduction in the medical treatments that were available (Moret 2015: 120).[14]

Second, as the sanctions regimes in Iran and Syria indicate, 'smart' financial sanctions also have notable general effects. The freezing of a bank's assets can mean that several welfare and commercial activities are significantly damaged, with negative effects for the general population (Wallensteen 2016: 263). Moreover, the penalties by the US in particular for even accidental violations of targeted sanctions can be severe. One upshot is that private banks become very wary of trading with seemingly legitimate businesses even if there is only a slight chance that the money will be destined for actors associated with sanctions, for fear of accidentally violating the targeted sanctions and having to pay a huge fine to the US (Eriksson 2016: 198).[15] Targeted financial sanctions can therefore still significantly harm general trade and place notable burdens on those in the target state who own or are employed by firms that lose out. In addition, NGOs working in conflict zones may not be provided with banking services, given that banks are risk averse, with the result that NGOs are unable to provide humanitarian relief that is deeply needed to assist thousands of threatened individuals (e.g. it can become very difficult to pay workers in the field). This also means that NGOs have to spend time and resources on due diligence systems to ensure, as far as they can, that they do not accidently violate a sanctions regime. The money could, of course, be much better spent assisting threatened populations.[16]

Third, travel bans and asset freezes can be mistakenly imposed on those who are in fact innocent. Perhaps most notably, the Security Council Resolution 1267 imposed asset freezes on those only *suspected* of being terrorists. The process by which this Resolution was imposed has been widely criticized, including for its opaqueness and the lack of appeal, and ultimately for harming those who are innocent. Billions of dollars have had to be paid in compensation

[14] The sanctions regimes on Syria and Iran can be seen as part of the re-comprehensivization of targeted sanctions by the EU or 'de facto comprehensive sanctions' (Moret 2015: 120; also see Portela 2016). This is whereby supposedly targeted sanctions are in fact fairly comprehensive and can have similar effects to comprehensive sanctions.

[15] For instance, BNP Paribas were fined $9 billion by the US regulators for violating sanctions against trade with Sudan, Iran, and Cuba (BBC 2014).

[16] For an account of this issue, see Keatinge and Keen (2017).

to targets who did not receive proper statements of the reasons for their listing, as well as for wrongful listing (Eriksson 2016: 197, n. 21).

It is clear, then, that targeted sanctions do not avoid completely the Indiscriminate Objection. A better defence of targeted sanctions is that sanctions on particular individuals (and to a lesser extent on particular goods) are *less* likely to harm innocent civilians than several other measures. This admits that virtually all of the feasible responses to aggression and mass atrocities, from military intervention, to targeted sanctions, to doing nothing, typically harm those who are not liable. This is either *directly*, if the agent harms innocents when responding to the situation, or *indirectly*, if there is an insufficient response to the situation, which means that those currently bearing the harms must still bear them. Military action clearly almost always involves the imposition of harms on those who are not liable to them.[17] In the case of doing nothing, innocents who are currently subject to the threat of aggression and mass atrocities will have to continue to bear harms for which they are not liable.

It follows that there may be a lesser-evil justification for broader and targeted sanctions: given that no option can seemingly avoid the Indiscriminate Objection, we need to look to the option that results in the *least* harm to innocents, and sanctions may sometimes result in less harm than the alternatives. This depends on sanctions being sometimes the lesser evil, that is, on whether sanctions are in fact sometimes likely to result in less harm to innocents. This will depend in turn on the efficacy of sanctions at addressing the situation, compared to all the alternatives, including doing nothing, and the incidental harms that sanctions cause. As I will discuss further in section 3.3, both broader and smart sanctions seem likely at least *sometimes* to be effective. To reiterate, this is not to deny that the Indiscriminate Objection may still apply to economic sanctions or to hold that sanctions are often *likely* to be justified as a lesser evil. The point, rather, is that the Indiscriminate Objection does not provide a decisive objection to economic sanctions; it depends on the efficacy of sanctions.

3.2.2 The Intending-the-Harm Objection

A second major objection to sanctions is that they intentionally target innocents. I will call this the 'Intending-the-Harm Objection'. That is, it is alleged by critics of sanctions that sanctions intentionally target innocents so that their suffering will persuade the target state to change its policy.[18] In October 2011, US Republican Senator Mark Kirk, who was influential in the US

[17] In this regard, Allen and Lektzian (2013) find that, although sanctions harm, military conflict has greater negative consequences on health outcomes.

[18] See, for instance, Gordon (1999*b*), as well as Thomas (2005: 111).

sanctions policy in Iran, stated that it is 'okay to take the food out of the mouths of [Iranian] citizens from a government that's plotting an attack directly on American soil' (Moret 2015: 127). Similarly, US Democrat Brad Sherman, a keen supporter of sanctions in Congress, wrote that '[t]he goal... is to drive Iran's economy into a crisis to force its leaders to the negotiating table', adding that '[c]ritics... argued that these measures will hurt the Iranian people. Quite frankly, we need [them] to do just that' (Moret 2015: 127). Such statements may appear to contravene a central premise of the Doctrine of Double Effect that, when promoting a good end, any bad effects must be incidental side effects rather than intended. For instance, in Michael Walzer's formulation, '[t]he intention of the actor is good, that is, he aims only at the acceptable effect; the evil effect is not one of his ends, nor is it a means to his ends' (2015: 153).

The Intending-the-Harm Objection is mistaken. For one, its scope is limited. Many sanctions regimes do not rely on the suffering of innocents in the target state to push the government to change its policy. For example, commodity and sectorial sanctions instead involve bans on goods, such as oil, and financial sanctions freeze the assets of particular individuals, groups, or banks. In doing so, they harm innocents as a side effect.

The objection also does not have any purchase against sanctions regimes that *do* rely on the suffering of innocents in the target state to push the government to change its policy. The central problem with the objection is that the suffering of innocents should not be viewed as wrong *because it is intended.*[19] Consider the following scenarios:

> *Angola 1*: Angola has been sending its troops into the civil war in the Democratic Republic of the Congo (DRC) in order to gain favourable access to natural resources. South Africa imposes sanctions on Angola, knowing that the harm inflicted will cause a certain amount of suffering of innocent Angolans. It intends this harm, since the *pressure of this suffering* will, by internal uprisings, lead to the Angolan government ceasing its interference in the DRC, which is the central objective of South Africa. Overall, much more good will be achieved.
>
> *Angola 2*: Again, South Africa imposes sanctions on Angola, knowing that the harm inflicted will cause a certain amount of suffering on innocent Angolans. This time it does not intend the harm. Instead, it knows that the *embarrassment of being sanctioned* will mean that the Angolan government ceases its interference in the DRC (again, the main reason for the action of South Africa). The policy will be as effective and lead to the same amount of suffering as in *Angola 1*.

It seems that in both cases the sanctions are permissible. It would be odd to hold that *Angola 2* is permissible, but *Angola 1* is not because the harm in

[19] In other words, I am sceptical of the Doctrine of Double Effect on this issue of the intended means (the ensuing discussion will, in effect, briefly present an objection to this doctrine in the context of sanctions). See, further, Bennett's seminal discussion (1995: 195–224).

Angola 1 is *intentional*. In this context, it helps to consider the objection in terms of motives and intentions. Agents' intentions are their objectives or the purposes of their immediate action, whereas their motives are their underlying reasons for acting (or their ultimate goal). In general, agents' *motives*, and not their *intentions*, seem to matter non-instrumentally.[20] This is because what seem morally important are agents' *ultimate goals*; as far as is possible, these are what should be assessed non-instrumentally, given that they ultimately determine agents' actions, rather than their intentions, which are simply the objectives or purposes of agents' immediate action, designed to bring about their motives. In the case of sanctions, agents need to be (predominantly) motivated, for instance, by concern to reduce the suffering of innocents (such as in a humanitarian crisis). The sender should be assessed according to whether it has this concern. If the sender possesses such motives, it is unclear why it matters that some of its intentions are nefarious *when considered in isolation*, such as when they intentionally target innocents so that the suffering of innocents will persuade the target state to change its policy. What matters is that the intentions are ultimately formed in order to realize rightful motives, such as tackling the crisis.[21] In *Angola 1*, the motive is good: to help those in the DRC. The central intent is designed to achieve this motive: a sanctions regime to help those in the DRC. The imposition of the harms is intended, but only to fulfil the rightful motive. It therefore does not seem objectionable.

3.2.3 The Instrumentalization Objection

The third, related major objection to sanctions on the Prevailing View is what I will call the 'Instrumentalization Objection'. This is the claim that sanctions involve the instrumental use of the suffering of non-liable agents to achieve the greater good.[22] For instance, Gordon asserts that 'sanctions reduce individuals to nothing more than means to an end by using the suffering of innocents as a means of persuasion, thereby violating the Kantian principle that human beings are "ends in themselves"' (1999*a*: 124).[23] The Instrumentalization Objection is separate from (or in addition to) the concern that the sender *intends* harm to the receiver. It applies even when the sender foreseeably

[20] I defend this point in more detail in Pattison (2010: 154–68; 2014*b*: 38–41, 58).

[21] To be sure, this is not to deny that intentions are sometimes instrumentally important.

[22] See, for example, Gordon (1999*a*) and Pierce (1996: 110).

[23] To be clear, Gordon (1999*a*: 128) notes that this objection has a limited scope, not applying when the objective is the prevention of the deaths of innocents. This caveat takes almost all of the force out of her objection. In cases when the deaths of innocents are not at stake the action would already typically be ruled out by proportionality—the need to do more harm than good (it would be hard to achieve this when harming innocents without helping another set of innocents).

harms the receiver, using them as means to an end, that is, *regardless of the intent of the sender.*

This objection is subject to notable limitations. First, as for the Intending-the-Harm Objection, it will apply, at most, to only certain types of sanctions regimes. This is where the suffering of innocents in the target state is used to push the government to change its policy. The harms of the measures of targeted sanctions such as asset freezes and travel bans are often *side effects* of the coercive use of force against liable agents, rather than being instrumental to the success of the sanctions.

Second, the objection is not unique to sanctions. It can also apply to war and even doing nothing. Wars may use the suffering of innocent soldiers or of civilians in cases such as those involving terror bombing, where the suffering of innocent soldiers or civilians is used in order to demoralize the opposing forces and to persuade the opposing side to cease its efforts. Perhaps less obvious is that doing nothing may also use the suffering of innocents as a means. States may make the calculation that letting civilians in another state suffer will lead to a rebellion or to severe international opprobrium of the aggressor, and so be the means by which the aggressor changes its policy.

Third, even when sanctions do use the suffering of the population as a means, this is not always wrong. This is because what appears to be wrong when agents are used instrumentally is that they are shown an egregious form of disrespect. That is, they are not viewed in the agent's deliberations as separate persons worthy of respect, with fundamental rights and weighty interests. They are treated as objects or *mere* means, since their interests do not figure sufficiently in the sender's deliberations. However, the instrumental use of the suffering of innocents may not always treat innocents as *mere* means. For this, there must be a denial of respect. And sanctions may often not involve such a denial of respect; senders will not use innocents as mere means.

Why won't they? The sender may well be concerned about the interests of those they appear to 'use', such as the civilians whose suffering is used to pressurize the target governments. They may consider the suffering of the population in the deliberations, and include this as a notable reason against sanctions. However, they judge, all things considered, that it is more important that the sanctions be implemented because there are weighty reasons in favour of them, such as if they will help to tackle mass atrocities. Indeed, the sender may lament that there is no way to avoid imposing the costs of sanctions on the innocent party in order to help others. The sanctions policy may also not be reckless or negligent, since there is no reasonable alternative that would achieve the same end without causing such harm. Moreover, it is also conceivable—and perhaps sometimes likely—that a sender will use the suffering of those harmed as a means in order to assist *these same individuals.* For example, a sender may inflict some suffering on the people of an authoritarian state in order to pressure the government to change its policy towards these people. In such cases, the sanctions policy that uses the citizens as means may in fact be motivated by respect for these citizens.

This is not to deny that states sometimes might still use innocents as mere means when engaged in sanctions. They also sometimes use the suffering of innocents recklessly or negligently by failing to put in place an option that reduces the suffering of innocents. This is because, for instance, sanctions are more politically convenient for the government of the state and so they use the suffering of the sanctions regime in order to attempt to achieve policy change in the target. In such cases, the state's reckless or negligent instrumental imposition of harm shows insufficient attention to the interests of those affected. The Instrumentalization Objection may therefore still *sometimes* apply. My point is that (1) sanctions will not always instrumentalize others; (2) the Instrumentalization Objection may also apply to other options; and (3) using someone as a means *per se* is not wrong—what is wrong is using someone as a *mere* means—and sanctions may not involve the use of others as a mere means. As such, the force of the Instrumentalization Objection to economic sanctions is heavily circumscribed.

3.3 AN INSTRUMENTAL OBJECTION TO SANCTIONS: THE INEFFECTIVENESS OBJECTION

The fourth objection is that 'sanctions don't work' since they do not result in policy change in the target. The sanctions regimes against Syria and Sudan failed to stop the government-sponsored abuses. Likewise, the sanctions on Russia after it invaded Crimea seemingly resulted only in counter-sanctions and costs to innocent Russian citizens, rather than a return of the Crimea to Ukraine or an end to Russian interference in Ukraine. The objection, then, is that sanctions rarely, if ever, achieve what they set out to do.

Let us explore this objection in more detail. Johan Galtung (1967: 388) famously lambasts the 'naive theory' of sanctions, which has been more recently called the 'pain-gain' model. This is the view that the more pain experienced by the target, the greater the positive impact on policy. This pain-gain model overlooks a series of complicating, unintended consequences. Most notable is the 'rally-round-the-flag' effect. This occurs when even those in the receiver state who have serious reservations about the government or its agenda nevertheless rally behind it when it appears assaulted from abroad. Sanctions can thus result in the shoring up of domestic support for an aggressor, as those in the receiver state resent the sanctions even more than the government's aggression. Governments can also shore up political support by maintaining control of scarce resources and handing them to supporters. In addition, sanctions can weaken liberalizing elites in the receiver, who rely on external trade and more generally external relations to buttress their position (Peksen 2009: 63) and in turn strengthen nationalist and xenophobic politicians and groups. Receivers can also *adapt* and *evade*, in order to circumvent the cost of sanctions. For instance, receivers can obtain goods through black and grey markets or from certain states that do not comply properly with the sanctions regime. Receivers can also reduce the impact of sanctions by diversifying their trading relationships, by becoming more self-sufficient, and by decreasing reliance upon certain exports (Galtung 1967).[24] This is to such an extent that a recent study finds that 'for the most part, sanctions fail to put significant stress on the economic conditions of target countries' (Shin et al. 2016: 495).

On its own, the claim that sanctions are not effective would not necessarily preclude the case for their use. If they could be used without harming innocents or precluding other means of tackling mass atrocities, it might be worth *trying* them. However, the problem with economic sanctions is that they *do* harm in these ways. First, as the Indiscriminate Objection makes clear, economic sanctions are very costly for individuals in the sender and receiver states. Second, a potential worry of sanctions is that they are used instead to give the impression of doing *something* to tackle the crisis and therefore to avoid undertaking action that is more robust (Gordon 1999*a*: 142). Overall, the objection is that economic sanctions are highly likely to be disproportionate. On the one hand, they fail to achieve much good—they do not achieve their objectives. On the other, they cause significant harm, either directly (to the sender and receiver) or indirectly (by precluding more robust action to tackle the situation).

Is the Ineffectiveness Objection correct? It does seem that economic sanctions may often not succeed, at least in securing their stated objectives. Moreover, the negative humanitarian effects of economic sanctions are far less visible to domestic and international audiences than those of wars, which often patently maim and kill, such as through bombing campaigns. The somewhat concealed costs may render economic sanctions a far more politically feasible response to give the appearance of 'doing something' in response to a crisis and may go a long way to explain their continuing popularity. However, these costs are still hugely problematic and should often mean that sanctions are not launched.

Nevertheless, the Ineffectiveness Objection is not sufficiently strong to altogether preclude the permissibility of economic sanctions. The harms of targeted sanctions are often far less grave and are *sometimes* limited only to

[24] Evasion and coping strategies are present in 90% of the cases of UN targeted sanctions and include forged documents, front companies, denial inspection, reliance on family members, stockpiling supplies, diversion of trade with third countries, and disguising vessels (Biersteker et al. 2016*b*: 29).

those strongly suspected of being directly responsible for the mass atrocities or aggression. Sanctions can also avoid some of the rally-round-the-flag effect when they are targeted at individuals (Taylor 2010: 23). Moreover, even if they are ineffective, *properly* targeted (discriminate) sanctions may still be worth trying. This is because the costs are borne by those who are *liable*, which may even be seen as a reason in favour of this option, given that those who are culpable may *deserve* to bear some costs.

In fact, contra the Ineffectiveness Objection, according to recent data on sanctions use in general, it seems that sanctions *do* (as a whole) work *sometimes*, if not *often*. First, the HSE database demonstrates that the dominant view that 'sanctions don't work' is overstated, since according to this data sanctions work 34 per cent of the time, but this rises to 51 per cent for 'modest policy changes' (Hufbauer et al. 2009: 158).[25] Second, the most recent version of the Threat and Imposition of Sanctions (TIES) database (which includes both threatened and imposed sanctions between 1945 and 2005) shows that sanctions are successful in 37.5 per cent of cases in which there is data for the final outcome, which rises to 56 per cent when negotiated settlements are viewed as successful cases (Morgan et al. 2014: 546). Third, the data produced by the Targeted Sanctions Consortium shows that, overall, UN targeted sanctions work 22 per cent of the time, but are clearly *ineffective* at constraining only 56 per cent of the time and at signalling only 44 per cent of the time (Biersteker et al. 2016*b*: 32).

In similar vein, George Lopez argues that the success of UN Security Council authorized targeted sanctions has been 'rather high' (2012: 140). Although they failed in Sudan, Somalia, and North Korea, they worked, he suggests, in eight out of twelve cases.[26] For instance, he argues that, in the context of the Arab Spring in 2011, targeted sanctions by the UN, EU, and US played a major role in degrading the firepower of the Libyan regime and support amongst Libyan elites. He argues that

> [b]y cutting off nearly half of Qaddafi's usable monies ($36 billion was locked down in the first week of sanctions), the international community immediately denied the dictator the ability to import additional heavy weapons, to hire mercenaries, or to contract with elite commando units. These constraints

[25] This database is criticized by Robert Pape (1997) for overstating the effectiveness of sanctions (he judges the success of sanctions at only 5%) and there has been a series of subsequent methodological exchanges, which Drezner rightly notes 'produced far more heat than light' (2011: 99). Pape (misleadingly) excludes any consideration of effectiveness where there is a threat or use of military force (Biersteker et al. 2016*c*: 223). For a helpful overview of the debate about measuring the effectiveness of sanctions, see Brzoska (2013).

[26] These include in Liberia, Sierra Leone, the Democratic Republic of the Congo, Côte d'Ivoire, and Libya. Lopez could also add Iran, which at the time he was writing had not ended its uranium-enrichment programme, and so he views this case as a failure. Some of the cases he cites involve arms embargoes, the efficacy of which are discussed in chapter 4.

> meant that Tripoli... was not destroyed in an all-out battle. The humanitarian impact of sanctions was negligible, while without the sanctions the Libyan war would have been longer and deadlier. (2012: 144)

They worked, he argues, because they denied key individuals the resources that they needed to restart violence. Thus, Lopez concludes, well-defined, narrowly targeted sanctions are an 'ethical and efficacious instrument', even if they often need to be used alongside other measures and are not flawless (2012: 144–5).

It is important in this context to include economic sanctions' longer-term, expressivist, or 'symbolic' effects in the assessment of effectiveness.[27] As I will discuss in section 5.1, naming and shaming can help to condemn aggressors and advance morally important international norms over the longer term. This is by demonstrating commitment to these norms and advancing the sense that they set appropriate standards of behaviour that require conformity. This can help, in turn, to reduce some of the severity and likelihood of future incidents of aggression. This is not simply because the norms deter potential aggressors. It is also because the norms make it clear that mass atrocities and external aggression are not appropriate behaviour in the international system. However, it is not only naming and shaming that can play this role; sanctions can too. In fact, sanctions, in expressing condemnation, provide one of the clearest affirmations of the norm. This is because they show a clear commitment to the belief in the criticism being levelled, rather than simply rhetorical posturing. To be sure, this is not to deny that sanctions are, on occasion, launched in order to give the appearance of doing something and may only have minimal effects on prevailing norms.

3.3.1 Morally Valuable Effectiveness Introduced

This data and the inclusion of the longer-term effects on norms help to provide a buttress against some of the force of the Ineffectiveness Objection: they do seem to work sometimes. But we need to go further still. There is a larger methodological problem in much of the prevailing understanding of the efficacy of sanctions and, in turn, in much of the Ineffectiveness Objection (this is at least as far as our purposes here go—to assess the case for the alternatives to war). This is the prevailing focus on whether the goals of the sender are achieved, rather than the central effects of the sanctions regime. In what follows, I will explicate this issue. But, before doing so, I want to make

[27] See Addis (2003) for an account of the expressivist role that sanctions can play. To be clear, the label 'symbolic' is not meant to indicate that sanctions are *only* symbolic. They may often symbolize disapproval of the practice *and* have direct practical effects.

clear that this problem is not limited to economic sanctions. It affects many of the alternatives considered in this book, where the relevant literatures focus too much on goals rather than effects (I will discuss relevant examples in later chapters). All the options, from war to non-violent resistance, should be assessed according to their effects—and particularly their effects on basic human rights, measurable by indicators such as conflict intensity and duration. This is what I will call 'morally valuable effectiveness'. I will begin to present this notion below, but let us first get back to sanctions.

The pain-gain view of sanctions, recall, understands sanctions as about senders attempting to change the policy of the receiver by implementing a notable cost on them. One problem with this account is that it overlooks the other goals of sanctions. The Targeted Sanctions Consortium rightly criticizes this narrow understanding of sanctions. They argue that sanctions should not be judged simply by whether they effectively (1) *coerce* the receiver (on the pain-gain view), but also by how much they (2) *constrain* the receiver of the goods needed to carry out its policies and (3) *signal* disapproval (see Biersteker et al. 2016*a* and especially Giumelli 2016).[28] This is a welcome development in understanding the efficacy of sanctions, but it does not go far enough. The problem is that this account, like much of the literature, still ties the assessment of effectiveness to the *apparent goals of the sender*. That is, sanctions are effective if they achieve the senders' goals of attempting to coerce, constrain, and/or signal.[29]

Why is this a problem? First, it can be difficult to determine what the goals of the sender are. Public statements may not accurately reflect the actual aims. Determining the goals is particularly an issue for UN sanctions regimes, since the Security Council may not even publicly communicate its approach and in fact sometimes lacks a coherent conflict resolution strategy (Security Council Report 2013: 3).

Second, a sender may have multiple goals. The tripartite account of the Targeted Sanctions Consortium is an improvement on the pain-gain model that focuses only on one goal. Yet there are often many further goals of the sender; they are not simply to coerce, constrain, or signal. For instance, states can launch sanctions as part of great power games (Taylor 2010). Similarly, a goal of sanctions is often to appease domestic audiences, to show that something

[28] Also see Morgan (2015), who similarly highlights the need to consider alternative models to the coercion view, such as constraint (although he does not spell it out in these terms).

[29] A similar approach can be found elsewhere in the sanctions literature. For instance, the updated version of the TIES dataset has three measures of success: when the target partially or fully acquiesces; when there is a negotiated settlement; and when the goals of the sender and the target are met (Morgan et al. 2014: 546). To be sure, some of the literature (e.g. Hultman and Peksen 2017) does adopt an approach that focuses on the effects in its assessment of sanctions. Baldwin (1999) provides a similarly strong critique of the sanctions literature for focusing too much on goals, rather than costs.

is being done in response to the situation, or even to divert public attention. Should sanctions be assessed according to these goals? They would need to be if the achievement of policy goals is to be used to assess effectiveness, to the extent to which playing great power games and appeasing domestic audiences are often policy goals of the sanctions. However, assessing effectiveness according to these goals is not helpful for the central issue, which is whether sanctions *should* be used as a policy to tackle mass atrocities and serious conflict.[30] Central to this is not whether the various, often opaque political objectives of the sender are achieved. Rather, what is crucial is whether sanctions have a positive or negative impact on basic human rights.

Third, focusing only on goals wrongly leaves out the costs of the sanctions regime for the sender, receiver, and third parties (Baldwin 1999; 2000). A sanctions regime could be deemed as effective because it successfully achieves the goal of the sender, despite having terrible humanitarian consequences. Conceivably, this could be the case even if the goal of the sanctions regime is to tackle mass atrocities. Suppose that the goal of the sender is to tackle ethnic cleansing of 1,000 civilians in the receiver state. The sanctions are successful in tackling ethnic cleansing, but destroy the economy of the receiver, with the death of 10,000 civilians. Surely, it would be odd to label the sanctions as effective.[31]

The crux is this: for our purposes, sanctions should be assessed according to their effects in the context that they are used, not their various goals. In other words, the assessment of effectiveness should be focused on the effects of sanctions, rather than whether they achieve the *goals* of the sender. For '*morally valuable effectiveness*', the primary determinant of effectiveness should be the effects on basic human rights. In practice, this means that, for our purposes, sanctions should be assessed according to their effects on the intensity and duration of conflict, the level of mass atrocities, and any severe humanitarian consequences, which in turn will typically affect basic human rights significantly.

There are three related attractions of this way of conceiving effectiveness. The first is that this is much more appropriate for policy *prescription* (recommending what states and other actors should do, which is our focus), rather than policy *analysis* (assessing whether states achieve what they set out to). To know whether states should pursue sanctions (or other measures) in response

[30] To be sure, the Target Sanctions Consortium also acknowledges this point (see Biersteker et al. 2016*d*).

[31] This is not to deny that when senders possess certain goals, such as to tackle mass atrocities (and these goals can be reliably determined), achieving the goals *might* mean that the policy is more likely to advance human rights effectively overall. My point is that these goals should not be the *sole* test of the efficacy of the policy, when it may have *other* effects on human rights (both positive and negative), such as serious negative effects on health, in addition to any effects on mass atrocities.

to mass atrocities and serious external aggression, we need to know their expected effects on basic human rights.

Second, on this approach, any negative humanitarian effects of a sanctions regime are *internal* to the effectiveness of sanctions, rather than *external* to it. This differs from most accounts, which can judge sanctions effective even when they fail to tackle the crisis and have severe humanitarian effects, as long as the goals of the sender are achieved. Similarly, the internal costs of sanctions should be included in the account of the overall effectiveness of sanctions, unlike the goal-focused approach (Baldwin 1999; 2000).[32]

Third, this approach coheres with assessments of effectiveness in the parallel literature in the ethics of war. In recent important statements of Just War Theory (e.g. Hurka 2005; Lazar 2016; McMahan 2009), the effectiveness of achieving the belligerent's various goals is not widely viewed as fundamental to the justifiability of military action. Rather, the focus concerns *proportionality*, that is, whether the war will do more good than harm, compared to not launching war.[33] This is for an obvious reason: whether a policy will do more good than harm is crucial to its moral justifiability. Far less crucial, though, is whether the belligerent will achieve their goals. For instance, the military intervention in Libya should be judged according to whether it was likely to improve compliance with basic rights overall, rather than whether it was likely to stop the killing in Benghazi and overthrew Gaddafi (two purported goals of the NATO-led coalition).[34]

3.3.2 Morally Valuable Effectiveness and Sanctions

What are the implications of viewing the effectiveness of sanctions in this way? On the one hand, certain sanctions regimes may be deemed effective overall. This is because, although they do not achieve their policy goals, they may have a positive impact on basic human rights in the short term (such as by helping

[32] In similar vein, the Targeted Sanctions Consortium authors recommend in the future that, first, unintended consequences should be factored explicitly into analysis of the sanctions, given that they can overwhelm an effective policy outcome (especially given the broadening of UN targeted sanctions to encompass less discriminatory measures) and, second, costs to the sender and private sector institutions should be included (Biersteker et al. 2016*c*: 246). This would, they argue, 'provide a more accurate measurement of the utility of UN targeted sanctions as an instrument of global governance' (Biersteker et al. 2016*c*: 246).

[33] Sometimes a 'reasonable prospect of success' is included in the list of criteria for *jus ad bellum*. However, the principle of reasonable prospect of success can be subsumed under proportionality, that is, what matters is the reasonable prospect of achieving more good than harm overall.

[34] Some may still wish to hold that effectiveness should be judged according to the completion of the sender's goals and that proportionality should be used to denote the effects on basic human rights, rather than combining the two. Even if so, the key point is that proportionality is what matters *morally*, not effectiveness in achieving the sender's goals.

to reduce conflict intensity) and in the longer term by advancing morally relevant norms, such as by clearly expressing condemnation of the sanctioned behaviour.

On the other hand, some sanctions regimes may be judged ineffective overall, even if they appear to achieve their political goals. The inclusion of negative humanitarian effects in the assessment of effectiveness would render certain sanctions regimes ineffective. For instance, in the mid-1990s, the US was the main backer of the UN sanctions regime on Iraq and resisted pressure from other members of the UN Security Council to alter the regime (Drezner 2011: 98). The then US ambassador to the UN, Madeleine Albright, said in a *60 Minutes* interview that even if the sanctions would result in the death of half a million Iraqi children 'the price is worth it' (*60 Minutes* 1996). Suppose that the sanctions *had* resulted in the removal of Saddam Hussein (or had been effective at achieving other political goals), but resulted in these deaths. They should not be, on my account, judged effective, given their disastrous impact on basic human rights.

In sum, sanctions should clearly not be viewed as generally effective, but the strong repudiation of sanctions by the Ineffectiveness Objection is mistaken. They will at least *sometimes* bring about overall more good than harm. This is particularly the case for targeted sanctions on (1) particular individuals, where negative effects on human rights are minimal and the costs often borne by those who are liable or beneficiaries. Such sanctions may also help to express condemnation of the behaviour, without significant negative unintended consequences. However, comprehensive sanctions and targeted sanctions on (2) particular goods will often have significant negative humanitarian consequences, which mean that they will overall do more harm than good. Any positive expressivist effects may be small in comparison to the unintended harms of the sanctions regime. They are, then, far more likely to be ineffective overall.

But what about the other worry, which is that sanctions (allegedly) will reduce the likelihood of more robust action (for instance, since they are used to give the impression of doing something)? This should not be unduly worrisome. First, if sanctions *do* have this effect, this might not be morally problematic. If most wars are unjust, then the potential for sanctions to lead to fewer wars might in fact be morally *desirable*. Second, it is moot whether sanctions do in fact have this effect. On the one hand, sanctions are sometimes used often instead of war, such as by the US, in the face of hawkish domestic calls to undertake injudicious military action, such as against North Korea and Iran. The launching of the sanctions regime may be the only politically viable way of avoiding a catastrophic war. Moreover, sanctions diminish the capacity of the receiver, which reduces the likelihood of war between the sender and the receiver (McCormack and Pascoe 2017). On the other hand, sanctions also increase the likelihood that the target will face attack from *third parties* (not the sender), as the target state is delegitimized by the signalled criticism and the economy is weaker, making it less resistant to military attack (Peterson and Drury 2011). Indeed, in several cases, sanctions have been succeeded by military action, such as in the former Yugoslavia, Kosovo, Sierra Leone, and Libya (Welsh 2015: 116). There are, then, conflicting considerations and so it seems unclear overall whether sanctions are in fact likely to lead to war and whether this really is morally problematic.[35]

In summary, it seems that the criticism that sanctions don't work misses the point. What matters is whether they are proportionate—do more good than harm—not whether they work in terms of achieving the goals of the sender. Although they often face the costs highlighted by the Indiscriminate Objection, they might still sometimes have some positive impact on the enjoyment of basic human rights. This is by, for instance, coercing the aggressor, denying them what they need to succeed, and reaffirming that the behaviour in question is objectionable. All this is not to deny that it is important to be cautious when resorting to sanctions or to deny that comprehensive sanctions are often problematic.[36] However, at least the strong claims of the Prevailing View that sanctions are always impermissible should be rejected.

3.4 IN FAVOUR OF SANCTIONS: FAIRNESS INTRODUCED

Thus far, we have considered four potential objections to sanctions and, so, have rejected much of the case for the Prevailing View. In this section, we will consider reasons to favour sanctions.

First, should economic sanctions be launched to *punish* aggressors, such as insurgents, terrorists, or other states? The obvious problem with this is that

[35] It is worth highlighting that, like several of the other alternatives, sanctions may be more effective when they are combined with other measures. For instance, David Lektzian and Patrick Regan (2016) find that when sanctions are combined with military intervention the likely duration of conflicts is significantly shortened. Indeed, sanctions are typically undertaken alongside other measures. UN sanctions are *always* combined with other measures (Eckert et al. 2016: 9). They are used alongside negotiation (97% of cases), peacekeeping (60% of cases), military force (52% of cases), and criminal prosecutions (46% of cases) (Biersteker et al. 2016*b*: 30). See, more generally, Bentall (2016) on the relationship between sanctions and other measures.

[36] For instance, a recent study finds that the threat of sanctions can induce the receiver to increase violence before sanctions are imposed and, once they are imposed, sanctions can result in increased violence during civil conflicts (Hultman and Peksen 2017). Another recent study (Krain 2017) finds that sanctions do not have any effect on the severity of genocides and politicides (i.e. the number of people killed year on year), even when the sanctions are comprehensive, long in duration, and combined with other measures. That said, it also notes that sanctions may still have a positive effect on the *duration* of mass atrocities (Krain 2017: 103). Sanctions have also been found to be effective in shortening the duration of civil wars (Escribà-Folch 2010).

economic sanctions tend not to harm the aggressors and, instead, punish the general population. As a result, sanctions, when conceived as trying to punish aggressors, probably only end up collectively punishing the innocent. The exceptions are *fully* targeted sanctions, which impose costs on *only* those who are liable. This could, in principle at least, provide a retributivist reason in favour of targeted sanctions, to the extent that those who are culpable (and only those who are culpable) deserve to face punishment. However, as we have seen, this is not a blanket defence of targeted sanctions: in practice, they may also sometimes harm those who are not culpable.

Thus far, I have largely focused on the *aggregative* effects of sanctions, that is, whether they do more good than harm overall. I have suggested that we should look at the option that will be the lesser evil. I will now consider their *distributive* effects, once the aggregative effects are held constant. In other words, I will consider the *fairness* of sanctions. These distributive effects, I will argue, provide a reason in favour of them.

3.4.1 Fairness

In what follows, I will argue that sanctions are likely to distribute harms more fairly compared to both war and doing nothing. Before arguing this, however, it is worth replying to an immediate worry to the Pragmatic Approach: considering fairness in detail is redundant in the ethics of war and peace since those who are *liable* should bear all the costs. More precisely, one might think that a *fair* distribution of the costs has those who are *culpable* (or, on some accounts of liability (e.g. McMahan 2009), *morally responsible*) bearing all of the costs. Their wrongful action means that they should bear the costs. This could be fleshed out also in terms of the principles of distribution of burdens. Perhaps the most sophisticated discussion of fair distribution of burdens is found in the literature on the ethics of climate change (e.g. Caney 2005*b*; Caney 2010; Page 2008; Page 2012). This explores the fair distribution of the burdens of mitigating and adapting to climate change. A central principle in this literature is the 'Contribution to Problem Principle', which (on one of the most plausible versions) holds that those who are morally responsible for climate change should pay.

The problem, though, with holding that those who are liable should bear the costs is that this is unlikely to be feasible. There are significant epistemic and practical constraints on knowing who is liable and developing precise targeting measures, in order to ensure that no innocents have to bear costs.[37] It is

[37] This is a general worry with all accounts of the allocation of burdens which look to historical responsibility; it can be difficult to determine who was morally responsible and then to actually allocate responsibility to that agent. See Page (2012).

clear that war and various other measures, such as arming rebels, will typically harm those who are innocent. But so will doing *nothing*, which leaves vulnerable populations to their fate. The same is true for *all* measures that fail to tackle the crisis fully. Even if the measure is partially effective at tackling the crisis, some of those who are vulnerable will have to bear costs for which they are not liable. Thus, with all the options, there will still be some currently unavoidable harm to those not liable. It follows then that the question is this: how should we distribute these costs—the remainder—amongst *those who are not liable to them*?

In what follows, I will consider three leading ways of distributing fairly the remainder, that is, of the unavoidable harms to innocents of aggression and mass atrocities. My aim is not to defend one of these ways over the others *in general* or to rank them. My focus instead is on the relevance of these ways of assigning the harms of tackling mass atrocities and unjust aggression and their relevance for the case for and against sanctions vis-à-vis the alternatives. I will suggest that some—but not all—favour economic sanctions.

3.4.2 Consent

The first way of distributing costs is to assign them to those who *agree* to them. Although largely overlooked in the literature on the distribution of burdens (e.g. Miller 2001), consent is sometimes held to be relevant in the context of the permissibility of placing the burdens of sanctions on individuals. For instance, Lori Damrosch (1994: 73) argues that, when the objective is the empowerment of the civilian population, the international community should defer to the authentic judgements of leaders about the degree of hardship that the population is willing to suffer in a sanctions policy. If the leaders judge that the population is willing to suffer the burdens of sanctions, they can be permissibly assigned these burdens.

The importance of consent in this context captures much of the related notion that a target population must welcome the action. Let us call this the 'Welcoming Principle'. The Welcoming Principle is commonly invoked in the ethics of humanitarian intervention: the victims must approve intervention. According to Fernando Tesón, '[i]f the citizens whose rights are being violated do not wish to be rescued if they consent to their government then perhaps foreigners should not substitute their judgment for theirs' (2006: 107). In the context of economic sanctions, the Welcoming Principle would be as follows: the victims enduring the crisis that the sanctions regime aims to address should welcome the sanctions regime. The Welcoming Principle might be specified further. On the one hand, the principle could be narrowed so that the consent of only those who are innocent is sought (and so not those who are culpable, such as terrorist groups hiding amongst the civilian population). On the other, the principle could be broadened so that it includes not simply those in the target state. It might also include other innocent individuals affected, such as those working in extractive industries in neighbouring states that lose significant revenue due to the sanctions on a particular commodity.

The central reason in favour of the Welcoming Principle concerns the burdens that those who are subject to the measure have to bear. Those who are innocent should be able to choose if they have to bear significant costs. It matters, for instance, that someone has a choice in whether to undergo chemotherapy, given the impact that this can have on one's quality of life, even if it can extend it. What does much of the normative work here is individual autonomy. That is, (innocent) individuals' freedom of choice about whether to accept burdens should be respected, as far as possible. Consequently, consent is relevant *in general* to the permissibility of placing burdens on someone and the Welcoming Principle seems to be important when considering whether to impose sanctions, *compared to not imposing them.*

There is an obvious limitation, however, to the relevance of consent in the context of economic sanctions: consent is unlikely to be sufficiently free. This is because those who might consent to a sanctions regime typically do so under significant duress. Their options may often be as follows: (1) accept the sanctions regime, which will impose upon them significant burdens, or (2) do not have a sanctions regime and continue in the prevailing situation (such as civil war and mass atrocities). In other words, they are faced with a Hobson's choice: (1) endure a potentially very burdensome sanctions regime or (2) endure the suffering involved in the status quo. As such, their consent lacks a reasonable alternative. It therefore does not appear to provide a strong enough reason to burden them.[38] Although when in the position of having to choose between two egregious harms, individuals may choose the lesser harm (or can be expected to), this does not mean that they should be the ones to bear the burdens of the situation.[39]

There is a weaker version of consent (and, in turn, the Welcoming Principle) that avoids the problem of relying on explicit, free consent. This relies instead on the notion of individual preferences in the context of the distribution of inevitable harm. To that extent, I draw on Franklin Miller and Alan Wertheimer's influential 'fair-transaction model' (2010; 2011), which rejects the need for insisting on a strict view of consent. On the fair-transaction model, what is required is that A responds 'in a reasonable manner to B's

[38] The consent to the sanctions imposed on South Africa during apartheid might be thought to be an exception, although it would clearly fall short of more demanding notions of consent. Although the African National Congress (ANC) called for sanctions, it was faced with a Hobson's choice: the harms of apartheid or the harms of sanctions.

[39] It is not just the consent of those affected by the sanctions regime that should be taken into account. The consent of those affected by likely inaction should also be sought, given that they would have to endure aggression, civil war, or mass atrocities.

token or expression of consent or what A reasonably believes is B's token or expression of consent' (2010: 81). This model is relevant even in coerced choices. In such cases, there is still reason to respect the preferences of the affected individuals, despite them being in a coerced situation. To see this, suppose that Charlie is in a lifeboat and can save only one of Anna or Brenda. Anna loves Brenda and wants her to live at her expense, and so Anna gestures as best as she can whilst drowning that she doesn't want to be saved. By contrast, Brenda wants to live in order to look after her children. In the choice of who to save—of where to distribute the unavoidable costs of someone drowning—it matters that Anna has a preference not to be saved and Brenda does not have this preference. It follows that Charlie should save Brenda, that is, distribute the costs to Anna, as far as she can reasonably judge Anna and Brenda's preferences through Anna's hand gestures. Even though Anna is not *liable* in any way to these costs—to drowning—Anna's preference to take on the costs should be respected by Charlie. This is out of respect for her wishes when facing a forced choice. Thus, if those affected agree to a sanctions regime, even though it will burden them, there is reason to respect their wishes.[40]

Accordingly, a weaker requirement of consent and a form of the Welcoming Principle could, in principle at least, still be relevant for the fairness of the distribution of the costs of tackling the situation. Notwithstanding, it still seems often unlikely that consent will play a *major* role in determining the fairness of the distribution of the costs. This is because it can be tricky to determine reliably the wishes of the innocent enduring the crisis and other innocents affected about whether they want a sanctions regime (or indeed any other policy). The practical difficulties are patent: to determine accurately the wishes of those affected, one would need to conduct interviews, referenda, or detailed opinion polls, which are often not possible in the midst of civil war or mass atrocities. To be sure, there might be some less reliable measures which provide a general indication of the preferences of those affected, such as by speaking to diaspora, trusted intermediaries (such as certain NGOs), and the local media. These can sometimes provide a rough indication of the opinions of those affected, such as whether they are willing to take on the costs of the sanctions regime compared to inaction. When such information is available, it should be reflected in the distribution of costs. However, it seems unlikely that reliable information can generally be obtained about opinions on economic sanctions.

[40] Thus far, I have focused on comparing economic sanctions to inaction. But those affected may also have strong preferences about what sort of action should be taken to address the current situation. For instance, as committed pacifists, they might want non-violent intervention rather than war. Again, as far as possible, those responding to the situation should respect these wishes.

Lopez (2012: 147) argues that there need not be express consent: there would be hypothetical consent, he argues, since we can reasonably expect that repressed populations would consent to take on the burdens of sanctions. In his words, '[*w*]*e can morally argue for sanctions on some countries because history supports the contention that repressed people will consent to such*' (2012: 147). Yet, as already noted, such consent is unlikely to be free. It is also questionable whether the majority of individuals would generally consent to a sanctions regime, given the apparent prevalence of the rally-round-the-flag effect, where the sanctioned population support their regime when threatened from abroad. It appears from this that sanctions are generally unpopular with those in the target state, and so one should not assume that the 'repressed people' would consent to sanctions.

3.4.3 Benefiting

A second way of distributing costs is to look to those who are seemingly benefited by the action. This has affinity to the 'Beneficiary Pays Principle' in the literature on climate change (e.g. Caney 2005*b*; Page 2012), which holds that those who benefit from climate change (such as through industrialization) should be the ones to bear the cost of resolving it. In similar vein, Jeff McMahan (2010*b*) defends a form of this principle when considering the just distribution of harms between combatants and non-combatants in cases of humanitarian intervention. He argues that, other things being equal, those who are the subjects of humanitarian intervention should bear greater costs than bystanders or just intervening soldiers since they benefit from the intervention.[41] Similarly, it might seem that this provides a reason to burden those benefited by sanctions, that is, those in the receiver who will be benefited by the removal of their authoritarian leader or the halting of the mass atrocities.

However, being benefited in this way is not typically morally relevant. The problem is that those being 'benefited' might still be significantly disadvantaged. Those in the receiver are often in a very bad situation to start with, such as being under an authoritarian leader or under the threat of aggression by another state. Although their situation may improve, it will have often started at a very low level. Those who have not been 'benefited' by the sanctions regime may often be far better off. Consider, by analogy, the case of those who have had treatment to tackle a genetic disorder. They may seem to have been benefited by the treatment, but they would have been in a much worse situation to start with. Their treatment only brings them back up to the level

[41] I consider (and respond to) McMahan's arguments in Pattison (2014*a*). For a defence of the moral relevance of benefiting (from injustice), see Goodin (2013) and Goodin and Barry (2014). For a critique, see Huseby (2015).

of others. They should not be the ones to pay for all of their treatment. In fact, the converse may be true. If the treatment is itself burdensome, it may be that others should bear the burdens of paying for the treatment. This is because those 'benefited' have already had the significant misfortune of having to bear the costs of having a genetic disorder. Similarly, if many of those who must bear the burdens of mass atrocities or an authoritarian leader are not morally responsible for this situation, then, given that these individuals have already had to bear the costs of the mass atrocities or of having an authoritarian leader, others should bear the costs of tackling the situation.

That said, being benefited can be morally relevant to the distribution of costs once we understand this notion in a different way. This is once we take into account the starting position of those who are benefited. In particular, it matters that agents benefit when they are already in a privileged position, that is, they possess more than their just entitlements. In such cases, when those who are benefited bear the costs, this may decrease the unequal effects of their undeserved privilege. (This does not require that the beneficiaries be advantaged by the sanctions regime *in particular*. What matters instead is that they are beneficiaries *more generally of the global-economic system.*) Consider the following example of a British farmer given by Simon Caney (in the context of bearing the burdens to resistance):

> Suppose that the current system of barriers to trade in agricultural produce is unjust and that as a result she has more than her fair share because of this injustice. Suppose, however, that she does not play any causal role in maintaining these privileges. As such, although she is not a cause of injustice she has more than her fair share because of injustice. In such a case it seems entirely reasonable for resistors to take action that burdens her. Suppose that they engage in illegal trade (evading customs) and that by selling more goods they lower her profit margin. In this case she can have no cause for complaint. She is not being rendered worse off than she is entitled to be, for, *ex hypothesi*, she was receiving more than her fair share. (2015: 70)

When we focus on distributing costs between states, looking to the beneficiaries beyond their just entitlements will often mean that wealthy states would bear the costs of the policy.[42] This is because, on plausible accounts of just entitlements, most wealthy states do not have rightful entitlements to their resources. This is clearest on cosmopolitan egalitarian accounts, which emphasize weighty positive obligations (such as to give significant amounts of humanitarian aid) that largely go unfulfilled (e.g. Caney 2005*a*). Wealthy states fail in their positive obligations and so are not entitled to much of their wealth. But this is also true of accounts of just entitlements that emphasize

[42] This is somewhat similar to the 'Ability to Pay Principle' in the literature on distributing climate burdens. This holds that those most able should bear the costs (see Caney 2005*b*; Caney 2010; Page 2012).

obligations not to violate negative rights, that is, focus on an agent's entitlements being lost by their violations of negative rights (e.g. Hjorthen 2017; Pogge 2008; Wenar 2008). It seems that many states have obtained their wealth through practices which lead to rights violations (such as colonialism, unfair trade practices, and contributing to climate change). Again, they lack the entitlement to their wealth. Thus, once we understand benefiting as focusing on those receiving more than their just entitlements, being a beneficiary *does* provide reason to be distributed costs.

How does this apply to sanctions? On the one hand, it does not seem that benefiting in this way will *generally* be relevant to the context of economic sanctions since the receiver will typically be relatively badly off, compared to other states. For instance, at the time of writing, states subject to financial sanctions by the UK include Belarus, Burundi, Central African Republic, the Democratic Republic of the Congo, Egypt, Eritrea, Guinea, Guinea-Bissau, Iran, North Korea, Somalia, Sudan, Syria, Tunisia, Yemen, and Zimbabwe. It would be hard to claim that the average civilian in these impoverished states have more than their just global entitlements.

On the other hand, benefiting in this way is more relevant when considering the internal costs to the economies of rich senders. It is also relevant for targeted sanctions. As noted above, measures such as asset freezes and restrictions on travel potentially harm innocents, since those directly targeted may be in fact innocent and, even if they are not, their families will be affected. Nevertheless, certain targeted sanctions may still be preferable. This is because those who are burdened, even if innocent, can be those (the elite, such as family members of leaders) who do very well out of the current system—more than their just entitlements.

3.4.4 Sharing of the Costs

A third way of distributing costs is the sharing of reasonable and unreasonable costs. This is particularly relevant when we must assume that the affected individuals are in a roughly equal starting point because, for instance, it is impractical to determine whether a measure will receive consent or will help ensure just entitlements by burdening beneficiaries.

Why should *reasonable* costs be shared between innocent individuals? Most obviously, reasonable costs should be shared so that no one must bear *unreasonable* costs, that is, costs that they are not duty-bound to bear (nor liable to bear). By sharing costs, the amount that each has to bear will be lowered. Accordingly, each might (potentially) bear only the costs that they can be reasonably asked to bear, such as in their general humanitarian duty to tackle mass atrocities.

In addition, by sharing even otherwise *reasonable* costs, the overall burden that one individual has to bear will be lower. This may mean that their lives are much less likely to be affected by taking on the currently inevitable (but reasonable) costs of the situation. If one individual is required to bear *all* of the (otherwise reasonable) costs of the situation, they will be potentially disadvantaged compared to others who do not have to pay these costs. To see this, suppose that, in order to save a child drowning in a pond, it would cost an individual $1,000, which would be within the parameters of a reasonable cost for the individual to bear. If others cannot share in these costs, the individual can be reasonably asked to pay the entire amount. But now suppose that it is possible to share the costs between 1,000 agents so that each pays $1. The costs should be shared, even though it would be otherwise reasonable to require the one individual to pay $1,000. This is because, by sharing in the costs, the effect on one particular agent is massively reduced; the particular agent is not disadvantaged relative to others by, for instance, his or her random proximity to the pond. The brute bad luck of being in this situation is, in effect, shared across all parties, so that the agent is not unluckily $1,000 worse off. For instance, assume that bearing the $1,000 means that the agent would have to go to a less prestigious university compared to others, with the result that his or her future opportunities, although still good, are not as good as those who do not have to pay. But by everyone paying $1, everyone's future opportunities, relative to each other, are unaffected.

There may be cases where the overall burden of the situation is such that some innocents will inevitably have to bear *unreasonable* costs (costs that they are not liable to bear because of previous wrongdoing and cannot be reasonably asked to bear in the fulfilment of their duties). Like reasonable costs, unreasonable costs should also be shared in order to reduce the burdens on particular individuals. For instance, suppose that it is necessary to resort to the compulsory acquisition of private property to defeat an aggressor. It is better that the unreasonable burdens of the compulsory acquisition (such as the amount seized) be shared, as far as possible. This could be, for example, by increasing the number of those who are subject to the compulsory acquisition of private property and by reducing the amount seized from each individual. The reasoning is the same: spreading the costs will mean that the lives of those impacted are less negatively affected by taking on the currently inevitable costs of the awful situation. If one individual is required to bear *all* of the unreasonable costs of the situation, that individual will potentially be disadvantaged compared to others. Underlying the importance of sharing costs is, then, a concern for equality. According to Edward Page, on this view 'benefits and burdens pertaining to any human activity should be distributed so that inequality is minimised' (2008: 564).

Let us apply this to sanctions. Sanctions seem likely to be preferable to both war and intervention and doing nothing, since they better share harm, other things being equal (the net harm being of equal magnitude). More precisely, sanctions seem more likely to (but will not always) share the costs of the policy. First, sanctions seem preferable partly because they are more likely to share the *internal* costs of the response to the situation, that is, the costs that the party responding to the situation bears.[43] In the cases of military intervention and war, these costs are often borne almost *fully* by soldiers (and their families). By contrast, the harm of banning trade in certain goods with another state may not be unreasonable for those in the sender. As David Baldwin argues, in war

> costs fall disproportionately on males between the ages of eighteen and thirty. Within the United States the costs of the Vietnam War were borne disproportionately by the young, the poor, the nonwhite, the male, and the less well educated parts of the population. By comparison, the effects of President Carter's grain embargo were probably distributed much more fairly.
> (1985: 140–1)

And if the burdens do seem to be unreasonable for a particular sector of society (such as those who work in the boycotted industry), they could be compensated, and the costs of compensation shared amongst those in the society (Baldwin 1985: 288). This is obviously much harder for soldiers who will suffer significant injury or even death in tackling the situation.[44]

Sanctions are also likely to (somewhat) better share costs *externally*, that is, amongst those in the target state and those in third parties. Wars often involve the concentration of harms, with particular individuals and groups having to bear much greater costs (often physical injury or death) than others do. Similarly, doing nothing will typically lead to a concentration of harms, such as the persecution of those from certain ethnic, religious, or socio-economic groups. By contrast, the more diffuse nature of sanctions—given that they often involve general economic burdens—means that they are more likely to (although will not always) spread the costs to a greater degree among the whole society. Those working in particular parts in the economy (such as in the extraction of natural resources) may be more affected but, again, compensation may also be more easily realizable than for wars or doing nothing in such scenarios, and the costs of such compensation may be spread.[45]

[43] The internal costs of sanctions are detailed in Doxey (1996: 66–70).

[44] Of course, in the case of doing nothing, there are no direct internal costs, but there may be indirect costs, such as a loss of international reputation. Note that I limit my argument here to comparing sanctions to war and doing nothing. It is less clear that sanctions are likely to better share costs than other options, such as naming and shaming.

[45] All this is not to suggest that fairness provides a very weighty reason in favour of sanctions. On the contrary, recall that on the Pragmatic Approach, the importance of aggregate effects on basic human rights is in most cases greater than that of fairness, given the larger stakes normally involved.

3.5 SANCTIONS AND THE DOCTRINE OF DOING AND ALLOWING

Against my defence of the import of sanctions for reasons of fairness, it might be argued that it is wrong to redistribute harms, even if sanctions are fairer. For instance, it would be wrong to launch a sanctions regime that would impose harms on a *new set of individuals*—those in certain industries—even if this would be fairer—since they are beneficiaries. Harms should not be redistributed to those who are not liable to these harms since this involves *doing* harm. This invokes the difference between *doing* and *allowing* harm (the third factor on the Pragmatic Approach). That is, it is worse to *do* harm—bring it about oneself—even if this *allows* greater harm to befall others.

How weighty is this consideration? On one view, the distinction between doing and allowing has overwhelming weight. It follows that the standard response to cases of mass atrocities and aggression should therefore be *not* to redistribute harm, since at least then the state is not doing the harm itself, even if it allows a much greater harm or much unfairness. As such, sanctions are impermissible. However, this seems counter-intuitive and is out of kilter with the mainstream view in moral philosophy that the doing and allowing distinction is not of absolute moral import (e.g. McMahan 2010*a*; Quinn 1989; Scheffler 2004). That is, it can still sometimes be permissible to *do* harm, in particular when countervailing considerations in favour of doing harm (such as achieving very beneficial consequences) outweigh the import of the distinction.

On the more moderate view adopted by the Pragmatic Approach, it is generally impermissible to *do* harm to non-liable agents, but permissible when there are very beneficial consequences at stake (such as the tackling of 10,000 impending deaths by doing harm to 10 innocents). In other words, a significant decrease in the overall amount of harm can mean that considerations of doing harm are outweighed. This is because (as argued in section 2.3) of the much greater stakes—doing harm only concerns *your* agency, but the measure in question could protect the basic interests of 10,000 individuals. Similarly, securing a *fairer* distribution of harm may also outweigh the moral importance of the difference between doing and allowing. That is to say, it may be justifiable on occasion for an agent to bring about a fairer distribution of harms even if, when doing so, it does some harm itself. For instance, suppose that 10,000 non-liable citizens in the south of Gabon are being repressed by the Gabonese government. France launches a successful sanctions policy that halts this repression but, in doing so, harms 10,000 non-liable citizens in the north of Gabon. Assume that, unlike those in the south, those in the north clearly and freely consent to such harms, and are much wealthier, far more so than their just entitlements.[46] Such a redistribution—the *doing* of harm

[46] My rejection of consent above was largely that it is not likely to be free in the context of sanctions; for the sake of making the point clearly, I assume that it is free in this example.

to those in the north—seems permissible because it is a fairer distribution, even though the overall amount of harm to non-liable agents is the same in both cases.[47]

3.6 CONCLUSION

In this chapter, we have considered the case for economic sanctions. I have argued in defence of sanctions and, in doing so, have rejected much of the Prevailing View. First, I argued (1), against the Indiscriminate Objection, that sanctions may still sometimes be permissible as a lesser evil, (2) that the Intending-the-Harm Objection is implausible, (3) that the apparent instrumentalization of sanctions is of little moral concern, and (4) that sanctions may still be effective and, more broadly, that we need a better account of effectiveness—morally valuable effectiveness. Second, I argued that sanctions can be (somewhat) preferable because they more fairly distribute costs. In doing so, I have highlighted the importance of considering fairness. Nothing that I have said is meant to offer a blanket defence of sanctions; sometimes—and perhaps often—they are impermissible. Targeted sanctions on (1) particular individuals are more likely to be justifiable, but comprehensive sanctions and targeted sanctions on (2) particular goods or assets are more likely to do more harm than good. Notwithstanding, both broad and supposedly targeted sanctions, although often problematic, are less morally bad than is often claimed.

In chapter 4, I turn to consider what is often deemed a specific form of targeted sanctions: arms embargoes. As we will see, arms embargoes, like economic sanctions, are often severely criticized, which, I will suggest, is also largely mistaken.

[47] Moreover, some of the harms of economic sanctions may be mediated by the government of the receiver. To that extent, the wrongness of the fact that sanctions may involve the sender *doing* harm will be diminished by the 'interceding' (or 'intervening') agency of the receiver, since their doing of harm is more causally remote. For instance, Saddam Hussein's government foreseeably imposed many of the costs of the sanctions regime on to the Iraqi people. The receiver is therefore in significant part responsible for harm. To be sure, the sender should still be held responsible for bringing about foreseeable negative consequences (that is, in agent-neutral terms). My point is that the wrongness of doing harm is somewhat diminished. I consider the relevance of interceding agency in more detail in sections 4.3.4 and 8.3.3.

4

Arms Embargoes

Chapter 3 focused on economic sanctions, both targeted and comprehensive. In this chapter, I focus on military sanctions, in the form of arms embargoes. Arms embargoes have become a central tool of the response to serious conflict and mass atrocities. They have been used in response to many of the major conflicts and mass atrocities over the past twenty-five years, including in Yugoslavia, Rwanda, Liberia, Sierra Leone, the Democratic Republic of the Congo, Yemen, Libya, and Syria. For instance, in 2015, the UN Security Council approved an embargo against Houthi rebels in Yemen in response to the intensification of the civil war and deterioration of the humanitarian situation. Arms embargoes have also been used in response to challenges to global security, such as the threat of weapons of mass destruction (in Iran and North Korea), terrorism (Al Qaida and Afghanistan), and threats to states' authority (in Haiti and Liberia) (Fruchart et al. 2007).

Arms embargoes are widely seen as a plausible option in several policy-circles and amongst advocate groups. For instance, the 2009 report *Implementing the Responsibility to Protect* by the then UN Secretary-General, Ban Ki-Moon (2009: 25), includes arms embargoes as a potential measure under pillar three. In July 2016, several leading human rights, humanitarian, and peacebuilding organizations, including Amnesty International, Control Arms, Human Rights Watch, Oxfam, and Refugees International, wrote a joint letter calling on the UN Security Council to impose an immediate arms embargo on South Sudan. This was in order to 'reduce unlawful attacks on civilians' and to 'send a strong message that the international community will not enable those fighters who have shown a complete disregard for the laws of war easy access to weapons and ammunition with which they can rearm and commit or facilitate further abuses'.[1]

Yet, as we will see, much of the academic literature strongly repudiates arms embargoes. In the nonideal world, it is claimed that arms embargoes don't

[1] The UN Security Council later rejected a draft resolution, due to eight abstentions, with many of the states that blocked the embargo claiming that they failed to work in similar situations (UN 2016).

work. They are violated by sender states, which are keen to continue to sell their weapons. Weapons are also obtained on the black market and through porous borders, and the embargoes are rarely monitored and enforced. The instances of violation abound, from the British supplying of arms to Sierra Leone in the 'Arms-to-Africa Affair', various states supplying the apartheid South African regime, and Russia and China supplying Sudan. Arms embargoes are, according to the critics, simply a fig leaf, used to keep 'clean hands', to avoid being seen as complicit in or condoning the situation, and to avoid undertaking more effective action. What's more, if they *were* to be effective, they would create another central problem: they would block just rebel movements and just states from defending themselves from attack.

The central aim of this chapter is to defend the case for arms embargoes. To do this, I will first consider the prima facie, *idealized* case for arms embargoes in section 4.2. This seems straightforward: they can reduce aggressors' access to weapons and so frustrate their goals, whilst distributing the costs fairly, and avoiding *doing* harm. In section 4.3, I will outline the nonideal critique of arms embargoes. In section 4.4, I will challenge this critique. In particular, I will argue that arms embargoes *do* often work—they are often effective—once we have the correct measure of effectiveness ('morally valuable effectiveness') and more generally are morally justifiable. To that extent, I will argue that the prima facie, idealized case is largely correct.

Before beginning, it is worth briefly linking this chapter to chapter 8, where I consider the case for supplying arms to rebels and states. I will argue against the permissibility of arming rebels and states. The case against arming rebels and states will highlight the disproportionality of this option and that arming rebels can *do* harm. It does not immediately follow from this, however, that arms embargoes are the morally right option. This is because the case against arming rebels and states focuses on the wrongness of transferring *additional* arms. In the case of arms embargoes, by contrast, at issue is whether states should try to *reduce* arms. It could be, for instance, that it is wrong to both arm rebels *and* to implement an arms embargo because the latter would be counterproductive.

4.1 ARMS EMBARGOES INTRODUCED

Arms embargoes come in different forms. First, they can be *unilateral*, such as the US embargo on Vietnam, which was only lifted in 2016. They can be *regional*, such as the embargo by the EU on Syria. And they can be *imposed by the UN Security Council*, such as the embargo imposed on rebels in the Central African Republic in 2013.

Second, an arms embargo may be *impartial*, applying to *all* sides, such as the embargoes on the former Yugoslavia in 1991 and 1998, Somalia in 1992,

Liberia in 1992 and 2001, Rwanda in 1994, and Sierra Leone in 1997 (Tierney 2005: 647). Or they may be *partial*, applying to only one or some groups, such as those perceived to be acting unjustifiably. Notable examples include those imposed on the UNITA rebels in Angola in 1993, on the Taliban in Afghanistan in 2000, and on Iraq in response to its invasion of Kuwait (Tierney 2005: 647).

Third, and related to the above, arms embargoes can be focused on *rebels* or on *states*, or both.

4.2 THE PRIMA FACIE CASE FOR ARMS EMBARGOES

I will now outline the prima facie, idealized case for arms embargoes. This case is idealized since, as we will consider below, it is objected that arms embargoes do not enjoy these features in practice, given various nonideal problems such as, most notably, non-compliance with the arms embargo by the sender.

Four central features render arms embargoes prima facie attractive. First, and most straightforward, *on the face of it*, arms embargoes can reduce aggregate harm significantly and, in doing so, reduce the ferocity of the conflict and the extent of mass atrocities. This is by reducing the means by which combatants can inflict intended and unintended harms on innocent civilians (and other innocent combatants). Often, combatants will simply not be able to undertake as many operations or as extensive operations. Moreover, as I will discuss further in chapter 8, one of the central problems with military assistance is that weapons may stay long after a conflict has ended and be diffused throughout society, causing various problems (the Diffusion Objection). The limiting of arms transfers can, *seemingly*, reduce some of this problem. Arms embargoes can also reduce the *duration* of conflicts, pushing them towards a mutually hurting stalemate ripe for resolution. That is to say, by diminishing the capacity of one or both sides from obtaining arms, embargoes can make it more expensive and ultimately difficult to fight, leading to a stalemate and a decreased sense that victory is likely. This can encourage parties to negotiate and ultimately to an earlier end to the conflict.

Second, arms embargoes can be symbolically important. That is, they make it clear that the sender state does not condone the behaviour of the aggressor and, instead, condemns it (Brzoska 2008: 4). Like naming and shaming (considered in chapter 5) and economic sanctions (considered in chapter 3), this can help to contribute to maintaining global norms against the behaviour in question. They can also avoid complicity in the wrongdoing of the aggressor if, for instance, the weapons would otherwise be used in violations of basic human rights. To put this another way, arms embargoes help to *maintain clean hands*.

Third, the internal costs to the sender of arms embargoes are relatively small compared to measures considered in other chapters. As I will argue in section 7.2.2, lower costs to the sender matter because states have fiduciary *pro tanto* duties to reduce burdens borne by their citizens.

Fourth, the (relatively limited) costs of arms embargoes are more likely to be fairly distributed, at least as far as the *sender* is concerned. These costs are borne by those employed in the arms industry, shareholders, and those who reside in states that sell arms. How fair the distribution is depends in part on one's views of the global trade in arms. Let us consider two views.

On a strong view, the global trade in arms is an immoral trade that causes significant harm to innocents as arms are sold to repressive states, fuelling war and conflict. Those who freely participate in this trade act culpably, by contributing to this trade negligently or recklessly. On this view, employees should, when they can, choose to work in trades that do not lead to extreme harm to the innocent; failing to do so renders one culpable. The shareholders of arms companies are also culpable, on this view, given the reasonable foreseeability of the harms to the innocent of the arms trade. Moreover, the majority of those in the major exporting states are somewhat culpable for the maintenance of the global arms trade, such as for failing to sufficiently pressurize their states to trade more ethically and for failing to campaign against the arms trade. According to the strong view, then, (1) the costs of tackling mass atrocities and serious external aggression should be borne by those who are culpable for their role in this immoral trade and (2) those in the major exporting states are often culpable, as employees, shareholders, or passive citizens.

On a more moderate view, the global trade in arms is a mixed blessing, where it causes significant harm to innocents but also is currently necessary in order to maintain international stability.[2] On this view, those participating in the global trade in arms are not necessarily culpable. In part, this depends on which firm they work for and in which state, and how their weapons are likely to be used. Those who work for arms that (as far as it can reasonably be determined) are unlikely to be used to support despots and to fuel wars, but instead to support legitimate states, are not culpable.

However, even on this more moderate view, it seems clear that those who freely work in the arms industry and the shareholders of defence firms are often global beneficiaries. The major exporting states are the rich, powerful states. The biggest exporters are the permanent five members of the UN Security Council (Russia, China, the US, the UK, and France), plus Germany, Spain, and Italy (Sheffield 2016). They are also typically the beneficiaries of the global economic and political system. As argued in chapter 3, it is morally

[2] For an account of the ethical need for an arms trade, see Christensen (2015). Christensen bases his defence on states' need to protect individuals' basic security rights.

preferable that, if innocents have to bear costs, those who are global beneficiaries bear these costs, rather than those who do poorly out of the current international system. In other words, the globally privileged (beyond their just entitlements) should bear the costs.[3] Thus, even those who do *not* work in the sector, but reside in the state that exports many weapons, could rightly bear some of the costs of the arms embargoes, for instance, as the amount that their state receives in tax revenues from arms sales is reduced.

Consequently, on both the strong and moderate views, arms embargoes fairly distribute harms amongst the senders, either to those who are culpable or to those who are beneficiaries.

4.3 THE NONIDEAL CRITIQUE OF ARMS EMBARGOES

I have outlined, then, four reasons in favour of arms embargoes. Against this prima facie case for arms embargoes, a common critique of arms embargoes is that they are, in fact, counterproductive. One of the most forceful critiques of arms embargoes comes from Dominic Tierney. He argues that:

> Much of the impact of UN arms embargoes in civil wars can be summarised as irrelevance or malevolence. Virtually every case of a UN arms embargo applied to a civil war has been a failure. Much of the intuitive promise of arms embargoes in civil wars is illusory, and the increasing frequency of their adoption can be contrasted with their dubious record at ending or ameliorating conflict... Although arms embargoes are often seen as a wise middle option between doing nothing and military intervention, they can be the most problematic option. (2005: 661)

Others make similar claims. Alex Vines (2007: 1121) argues that UN arms embargoes did not generally stop weapons reaching Africa. Gordon argues that not only do 'arms embargoes in fact do little to actually reduce the flow of weapons', in fact 'they create a black market for weapons, with opportunities for higher profits than in the legal arms trade' (2015: 263). They are, she claims, 'generally ineffective and disappointing' (2015: 264). Likewise, the SIPRI report by Damien Fruchart et al. argues that 'UN arms embargoes... have not stopped the flow of [small arms and light weapons] and ammunition to embargoed targets, the continuation and spread of conflicts, the undermining of governmental authority by non-governmental armed forces, the

[3] Even if one adopts a restrictive view of just entitlements, which focuses on violations of negative rights, it seems clear that exporting arms is often likely to lead to rights violations. As such, the receipts from working in sectors related to the exporting of arms should not be viewed as part of one's just entitlements.

attempts of regimes to acquire [weapons of mass destruction], or international terrorist acts' (2007: 50).

More specifically, arms embargoes may appear to have the following significant flaws: (1) they are ineffective since they are not upheld (the 'Ineffectiveness Objection'); (2) they are used by states to avoid undertaking more effective measures (the 'Fig Leaf Objection'); (3) they restrict innocent individuals from fighting just wars against aggression (the 'Weakening of Just Movements Objection'); and (4) they are used by senders to avoid complicity and to avoid condoning wrongdoing, which is mistakenly prioritized over undertaking effective action (the 'Clean Hands Objection'). In what follows, I will consider each of these objections in turn.

4.3.1 The Ineffectiveness Objection

The Ineffectiveness Objection claims that arms embargoes do not work and can even be counterproductive. For instance, Tierney argues that 'with only a few partial exceptions, arms embargoes have failed' (2005: 646). The arms embargoes in Somalia, Rwanda, and Liberia between 1992 and 1995, he notes, were barely enforced. Even if states vote for an arms embargo, they may violate it soon afterwards, such as the French supply of arms to the Rwandan army after the 1994 embargo, some of which fell into the possession of the genocidal forces (Tierney 2005: 652).[4] Let us explore this objection in more detail.

Externally, the sender will often, the objection runs, fail to comply with the embargo. Senders may have an interest in propping up an ally. Alternatively, they may wish simply to sell arms for financial reasons. The internal costs, in terms of the financial harm to the arms industry, may make it preferable still to supply arms, particularly if this can be done covertly, out of sight of the international community. In fact, the presence of the arms embargo may make it more profitable to supply arms since the embargoed state will struggle to obtain arms from other states (Tierney 2005: 651). By arming the embargoed state, the sender can reap substantial economic and strategic benefits, which outweigh the consequences of the failure of the embargo for the state (Moore 2010: 595–6). The embargo may also be insufficiently monitored and enforced. States may face few penalties for failing to comply with it. As a result, states may insufficiently investigate and monitor the transfers of arms by defence firms based in their state and may even directly organize the transfer of arms themselves.

Internally, the receiver may still be able to obtain arms through porous borders, given that the states that are subject to mass atrocities and serious

[4] For a detailed discussion of the arms embargo on Rwanda, see Fruchart (2007).

external aggression often lack strong border controls (Erickson 2013: 170). What is more, the receiver can often obtain arms through the black market (Gordon 2017: 57). In doing so, states can unintentionally strengthen criminal elements, bringing them into the economic and political mainstream, and render public officials as criminals by forcing them to obtain weapons through illegal sources (Tierney 2005: 656–7). Moreover, there are often already significant stockpiles of weapons (Tierney 2005: 651) which can be used by states and rebel groups to continue fighting. In addition, local actors can sometimes replace imports with arms produced by the domestic arms industry. For instance, the arms embargoes against South Africa did not undermine its ability to wage war, since it instead built a formidable domestic arms industry (Tierney 2005: 651).

As such, the Ineffectiveness Objection poses a strong challenge to the case for arms embargoes, suggesting that they may even be worse than doing nothing. I will consider these claims further in section 4.4.

4.3.2 The Fig Leaf Objection

The Fig Leaf Objection is that states will use arms embargoes as a fig leaf to avoid undertaking more effective measures, such as military intervention. It gives the impression of 'doing something', thereby potentially quelling domestic demands for action in response to mass atrocities or aggression (Tierney 2005: 647), without necessitating costly action. For instance, the arms embargoes were used to quell the demand to do something in Rwanda and Yugoslavia, avoiding the need for Western military intervention on a large scale (Tierney 2005: 656).[5]

Is this objection plausible? It depends on the original measures, such as arms embargoes, being ineffective and in particular unjustifiable in themselves. It also depends on the possibility of more effective—and in particular more justifiable—action that is stymied by the use of arms embargoes. Although the Fig Leaf Objection may, on occasion, be right, in general it is not clear that the use of arms embargoes is ineffective (as I will shortly consider). Moreover, other, more coercive options may be more morally problematic. Perhaps most obviously, a full-scale war may fail to meet the requirements of *jus ad bellum*. If arms embargoes preclude this, it may in fact be a reason *in favour of* launching the embargo. In addition, there may be no other plausible,

[5] Similarly, the Security Council Report (2013: 16) suggests that sanctions have been used in cases such as Guinea-Bissau in order to *appear* to be doing something. As we will see in later chapters, this objection potentially applies to several of the alternatives to military intervention. For instance, in section 9.2, I consider the related issue that accepting refugees and humanitarian assistance can involve passing the buck.

feasible option on the table that has not already been tried. For instance, various diplomatic methods, such as naming and shaming, may have already been tried and an International Criminal Court prosecution may not be feasible because the aggressor has not ratified the Rome Statute and the situation is highly unlikely to be referred to the International Criminal Court by the UN Security Council.[6] The arms embargoes may therefore not in fact block the alternative.

Furthermore, even if there are other plausible, feasible options, the use of the arms embargo may not be the reason for the stymieing. For example, the reason that there is not an International Criminal Court prosecution might have nothing to do with the launching of the arms embargo, but rather the fact that the aggressor is not a member of the Rome Statute. Likewise, the reason that there is not a peacekeeping operation might not be because the arms embargo provides political cover for states, but simply because the target state has refused to consent to a peacekeeping operation.

Finally, and perhaps most notably, arms embargoes are widely used *alongside* options that are more coercive. Indeed, arms embargoes are typically used alongside various other measures. For instance, arms embargoes are used in 87 per cent of cases involving UN targeted sanctions (Biersteker et al. 2016*b*: 26, 30). It seems then that any Fig Leaf effect is likely to be minor.[7]

4.3.3 The Weakening of Just Movements Objection

This objection is that arms embargoes prevent legitimate states and just rebel movements from defending themselves in the face of unjust attack. In such circumstances, individuals need weapons to exercise the rights of self- and other-defence. The arms embargo can deny innocents the access to weapons that they need to ensure these rights. For instance, the arms embargo on the former Yugoslavia crippled the Bosnian government, denying the threatened population the weapons they needed to defend themselves. The Croats, by contrast, were able to purchase weapons from Eastern Europe, and the Serbs controlled the domestic arms industry and the national army (Tierney 2005: 658).

This objection, though, is not generally persuasive. First and foremost, where it is clear that there is a just side (such as arguably in the Bosnian case), the embargo can be partial. This will still enable the just side to fight. Second, a blanket arms embargo is sometimes not subject to this objection. This is because in many wars there will be no just side to supply arms to, which

[6] See, further, section 9.1 for analysis of the requirements for ICC prosecutions.

[7] This is not to deny that the Fig Leaf effect might still *sometimes* occur; my point is that it should not be generally presumed, given these considerations.

reduces the scope of the objection. Moreover, even when there is a just side, it does not always follow that it should have access to arms. As I will discuss in section 8.3, there are problems with arming even those fighting just wars. These include the risk of escalation, the problem of ensuring that the weapons remain in the hands of the just side, and the difficulty of determining which side is acting justifiably. There is still reason, then, to maintain blanket arms embargoes even when there is a just side, although sometimes this might be outweighed and it might be preferable that the embargoes are partial. The crux is this: instead of the focus being on ensuring that the just side wins or on assisting it to do so, it should be on improving the compliance with individual basic human rights by, for instance, minimizing harm to civilians. This may mean that, on occasion, it is necessary to have a partial embargo, but at other times it may be best to maintain a full embargo, even if this does frustrate the just side, since this will reduce harms to civilians and cut the flow of arms overall.

4.3.4 The Clean Hands Objection

The Clean Hands Objection states that embargoes are undertaken because the importance of avoiding condoning and avoiding being complicit in wrongdoing is mistakenly prioritized over undertaking effective options that save lives. There are two parts to the Clean Hands Objection. The first is a moral worry about overemphasizing the wrongness of condoning wrongdoing and contributing to wrongdoing. The second is the empirical claim that states unduly care about condoning wrongdoing and contributing to wrongdoing.[8]

The first part of the Clean Hands Objection is correct. The importance of avoiding condoning wrongdoing and being complicit in wrongdoing should not be given undue weight. More specifically, I will now suggest that the importance of avoiding condoning and being complicit is only *pro tanto* and, in the case of being complicit, is captured by other considerations. It is worth spending some time here establishing these points, since these issues will also arise with other measures, such as positive incentives and arming rebels.

Let us start with the moral importance of avoiding condoning. This is only *pro tanto* since it may still sometimes be all-things-considered permissible to act, even if one appears to condone a wrong. This is if the action undertaken

[8] Note that the Clean Hands Objection differs from the Fig Leaf Objection, which concerns cases when the more justifiable option is intentionally avoided for mendacious reasons (such as to avoid domestic costs). The worry with the Clean Hands Objection is that the arms embargoes are erroneously undertaken for what might seem to be morally valid concerns about avoiding condoning wrongdoing and being complicit in it.

will be the best possible means of improving compliance with basic human rights in the long term. For instance, in chapter 7, I will consider the case for the use of positive incentives. These might be directed at leaders culpable for aggression. Although this may appear to condone the wrongdoing, if the positive incentive is effective at improving compliance with basic human rights in the long term, such as by addressing the situation overall (and avoiding longer-term consequences), it may be justifiable. Similarly, it might be thought that negotiations and dialogue with aggressors condones their behaviour, but might be all-things-considered justifiable, if such negotiations bring to an end the conflict (and do not have problematic longer-term, symbolic consequences). What matters, then, are the *consequences* of condoning. Condoning will often exacerbate the situation and lead to further incidents of it. However, when the consequences suggest that condoning (or—more precisely—*appearing to condone*) is the best way of tackling the situation, then an act that appears to condone is not all-things-considered unjustifiable.[9]

What about complicity? At the heart of the notion of complicity is that it is wrong to 'contribute to *another's* wrongdoing' (Lepora and Goodin 2013: 41).[10] There are two leading accounts of complicity, non-causal and causal. First, on the non-causal account, one can be complicit even when one does not causally contribute to others' wrongdoing (Kutz 2007). You might be non-causally complicit because your attempt to contribute fails or others' attempt to harm fails, or because the agents would have acted anyway—you make no causal difference. However, the non-causal account is not relevant for our purposes since we are concerned with the potential wrongness of foreseeably contributing to others' wrongdoing and, on the Clean Hands Objection, the importance of avoiding doing so. Second, on the causal account of complicity, '[a]n accomplice is one who acts with the consequence or result that the principal commits the wrong' (Gardiner 2007: 141). More specifically, complicity involves increasing, through one's actions, the probability of others committing harm and/or the magnitude of the harm committed by others. One can cause others to commit harm through, for instance, knowingly enabling their harm.[11] Suppose, for instance, that your neighbour offers a lot of money for your gun. You know that he is a dubious character and appears

[9] I draw a distinction between behaviour *appearing* to condone and that *actually* condoning serious wrongdoing. I presume that the latter is always wrong, since it concerns the mindset of internally approving of mass atrocities or serious external aggression—agents should never judge this to be right. This point seems banal. Rather, what is actually at stake is whether agents should give the impression of *appearing* to condone.

[10] I focus here on what Lepora and Goodin (2013) refer to as 'complicity simpliciter'. They delineate meanings of complicity and, like my argument here, deny that being complicit in wrongdoing is necessarily impermissible.

[11] I focus on harms here, but it might also be possible to be complicit in other wrongs, such as by contributing to others' rewarding of injustice.

to be planning a violent armed robbery of rich footballers in your area. Regardless, you sell a gun to your neighbour and so are complicit in the violent armed robbery of rich footballers. What seems wrong with your complicity is that you knowingly enable your neighbour to engage in a violent act—armed robbery. What the notion of complicity usefully captures, then, is a specific type of wrongful action, where one brings about harm to innocents by causally contributing to *the wrongs by others*.

Why is complicity wrong? I now want to argue that the underlying wrongfulness of being complicit is not an additional moral factor. Rather, it can be captured by the importance of two other considerations—concerns about (1) increasing risks of harm and (2) doing and allowing harm. What is primarily wrong about being complicit is the bringing about of harm to innocents (or increasing its probability), such as to the rich footballers and their families in the case above. And the reason why, in turn, bringing about harm is wrong is, first, for an agent-neutral reason: simply, it is wrong to harm innocents. Being complicit is wrong, then, because one will increase overall harm by enabling or exacerbating harm (or increasing the risk of the harm), such as by supplying the gun used to rob rich footballers. Bringing about harm is wrong, second, for an agent-relative reason: when *you* enable or contribute to harm committed by others, you are *doing* harm.[12] In the case above, *your* supply of the gun to your neighbour *does* harm to the innocent footballer. This invokes the difference between doing and allowing harm (the third factor on the Pragmatic Approach), which, recall, is widely claimed to be morally important and holds that it is worse to do harm—bring it about *oneself*—even if this allows greater harm to befall others.

Against my claims here, it might be thought to stretch the distinction between doing and allowing too far. That is, it might be thought that one can only *do* harm if one is *the agent that actually commits the harm*. On this reply, then, it is only your violent neighbour who *does* harm—in selling the gun, you do not do harm to the rich footballer. We should reject this response. It seems to be too narrow a conception of doing harm, seeing it as a matter of all or nothing. Instead, there are different degrees of doing harm, depending on causal closeness to the harm. In the rich footballer case, your neighbour's actions are worse than your actions because his are causally closer, whereas your responsibility is slightly diminished because it was foreseeable, albeit unlikely, to you that your neighbour could have *not* engaged in the robbery. Both of you are causally implicated—your positive

[12] Complicity may also be seen as wrong because complicit agents possess the mental state of intentionally (in the sense of being motivated to harm), recklessly, or negligently bringing about harm. If so, this mental state—the *mens rea*—also explains why it is problematic. This also does not seem to be necessary, though: an agent could seem to be complicit if they merely foresee that their actions will lead to others harming.

actions are responsible for the robbery—but there are different degrees to which you *do* harm.[13]

Having argued that complicity can be captured by other moral values, let us now consider the wrongness of complicity. The importance of avoiding being complicit is only *pro tanto* and although one may be involved in bringing about a harm, the action may be all-things-considered justifiable. For instance, as I will discuss in chapter 8, although arming rebels may mean that one contributes to the harms caused by rebels, it can still be (exceptionally) permissible to arm rebels, since the arming of the rebels may bring about much better consequences in terms of tackling the situation. More precisely, the wrongness of being complicit is only *pro tanto*, first, because, although being complicit in others' wrongdoing might increase harm to *some* innocents, sometimes it might still reduce *overall* harm. In agent-neutral terms, bringing about some harm may be permissible—and even obligatory—if this will reduce overall harm. For instance, if supplying arms to a rebel group will enable it to kill *some* civilians, but will enable peace and prevent *thousands* more deaths of civilians, there is a weighty, agent-neutral consideration in favour of this action, despite it bringing about some harm.

Second, although being complicit in others' wrongdoing involves *doing* harm, this can be outweighed by achieving hugely beneficial consequences. As I argued in chapter 3, the moral prohibition against doing harm is not absolute—it can be outweighed by other considerations on the Pragmatic Approach. Moreover, since in cases of complicity your doing of harm is more causally remote, it is more easily outweighed. My reasoning is as follows. The reason why agents are allowed to maintain clean hands and *not* to do harm, even when this would allow for a much greater harm, concerns the 'agent-relative prerogative'. This holds that you can prioritize your own interests, projects, and agency, at least to some degree, since otherwise morality would be too demanding.[14] Crucially, *how much* your agency is involved determines the strength of the agent-relative prerogative. If you are to pull the trigger yourself, you would be more responsible, and so have a stronger justification for wanting to maintain clean hands. But when you are less causally involved, because the harm depends on others' subsequent actions, then your doing harm will be more causally remote. The harm is mediated by others' 'interceding' (or 'intervening') agency. You have *somewhat* less reason to avoid doing harm—to maintain clean hands. Suppose, for instance, that a murderer will not kill their victim if someone hits an innocent bystander with a large stick, thereby breaking the bystander's leg. You can rightly object to having to be *the person* who breaks the leg of the innocent bystander, given the

[13] Indeed, some argue that doing harm can include 'enabling harm', which is the removal of an obstacle to harm (see Hanna 2015).

[14] See Quong (2009) for an account of this prerogative in the ethics of self-defence.

agent-relative prerogative. It seems too demanding on you to have to be the one that delivers the harm and you can permissibly maintain clean hands. But suppose that you could easily supply the stick to someone who is willing to attack the innocent bystander. It does not seem too demanding that you supply the stick. On the contrary, supplying the stick, and being complicit in the harm, might be supererogatory (or even obligatory) since it will save an innocent life—if so, it would be impermissible to maintain clean hands. Thus, although still often wrong, being complicit in harm seems somewhat less bad than directly committing the harm oneself.

In the case of arms transfers, sender states will still typically do harm—by enabling, for instance, rebels to kill innocents—but this harm is mediated by the interceding agency of others—such as the rebels, who actually pull the trigger. This means that it is still wrong for them to *do* some harm by supplying weapons, but this is not as wrong as when they directly commit murder. Consequently, the Clean Hands Objection is largely right to be sceptical about the importance of avoiding condoning and being complicit in wrongdoing.

But what about the second part of the objection? Recall that this concerns the *empirical* claim that states are motivated too much by avoiding condoning wrongdoing or by avoiding being complicit. This is more dubious. In general, states do not seem to be unduly concerned about maintaining clean hands, given the numerous instances where they do not condemn wrongdoing. Many states often *do* condone it and *are* complicit in it. As such, it does not seem clear that maintaining clean hands provides a central reason why states continue to maintain arms embargoes. A more plausible explanation seems to be that states launch arms embargoes because, as Michael Brzoska notes, they are 'often seen as comparatively cheap in terms of costs for national economies and national governments' (2008: 4).

To be sure, some governments might still adopt the idealized view of arms embargoes as working, that is, as reducing the arms that can be used by aggressors to kill civilians. This suggests, then, that states seem to hold that arms embargoes work. This is implied in much of their rhetoric surrounding arms embargoes. This brings us to the next section, where I argue that they generally do work.

4.4 THE NONIDEAL CASE FOR ARMS EMBARGOES

The four objections above appear to challenge the nonideal case for arms embargoes. Together, they suggest that arms embargoes are not complied with (the Ineffectiveness Objection), harm just rebels and states (the Weakening of Just Movements Objection), and are used to avoid undertaking more robust justifiable action mendaciously (the Fig Leaf Objection) or mistakenly (the Clean Hands Objection).

This nonideal critique might have some purchase, *on occasion*, against arms embargoes. Like all of the measures, the case for them depends on the contingencies. However, on a strong version of the critique, these objections are *presumptive*. They should be presumed to apply in most cases. Against this, I will now argue that once we look more closely at the effectiveness of arms embargoes, drawing on recent studies, we can see that, in fact, arms embargoes are *generally justifiable*. This contravenes the common perception, noted above, of them as ineffective and morally problematic. That is to say, in most cases the four objections either do not apply or are not sufficiently forceful to preclude the case for arms embargoes. In doing so, I will largely reaffirm the prima facie case outlined in section 4.2.

4.4.1 Morally Valuable Effectiveness

Crucial to understanding the effectiveness of arms embargoes is to adopt a suitable measure of effectiveness. In particular, it is important to develop further the account of what chapter 3 called 'morally valuable effectiveness', which is a central factor on the Pragmatic Approach. Recall that morally valuable effectiveness holds that measures should be assessed according to their effects in the context that they are used, not their various goals. The primary determinant of effectiveness is, on this account, the effects on basic human rights.

The critics of arms embargoes sometimes consider their effectiveness according to demanding measures.[15] First, they consider whether arms embargoes lead to policy change in the target, as well as whether the arms embargoes achieve the stated aims of the embargo, which may sometimes involve lofty, ambitious (and potentially disingenuous) rhetoric. Second, the embargo is assessed according to whether it is effective at stopping arms; non-compliance renders it ineffective. As Brzoska argues, '[e]ven more so than in the... sanctions literature, the measure of success is often limited to the attainment of the full degree of intended output and impact, that is a stop of arms flows to target and/or the end of the target's incriminated policy... This sets a high

[15] For instance, Tierney (2005: 650) proposes five measures of effectiveness: whether they prevent or restrain the actors from accessing weapons, change the political positions of target groups, promote symbolic values, facilitate or undermine additional effective action, and have unintended consequences. On his account, to be a success, 'an embargo should significantly reduce the number of weapons possessed by target combatants, weaken their capability, and thereby at least partly achieve the embargo's political, humanitarian, or symbolic goals'.

standard for arms embargoes, higher than standards of success in other policy areas' (2008: 2).[16]

Both measures of success are very difficult to meet. First, it seems obvious that arms embargoes alone are unlikely to lead to significant policy change. An arms embargo will often only, at best, diminish the capacity for fighting. It may do little to offer positive or negative incentives to affect the belligerents' reasons for continuing to fight. Second, and as outlined above, *fully* stopping arms transfers is extremely difficult, given porous borders, the black market, and incentives to sender states to contravene the embargo. Given their demandingness, these measures seem to load the dice against the potential effectiveness of arms embargoes.

Crucially, these measures of effectiveness do not seem to capture what is important. That is, they appear to overlook the fact that arms embargoes can have a significant impact on basic human rights even without policy change and significant compliance. This is primarily by reducing arms flows and so reducing the intensity of the fighting. It is also conceivable that there could be a policy change and full compliance *without* having a major impact on the degree of violations of basic human rights. This could be if, for instance, the embargoed agents begin peace negotiations and there is full compliance with the arms embargoes, but the violation of basic human rights continues as the states or rebels use existing stockpiles to continue their violence. The problem with policy change and degree of compliance as measures of effectiveness, then, is that they are under-inclusive and do not focus on what is morally most pressing—the violations of basic human rights. The effects on basic human rights are the central measure of effectiveness on the account of morally valuable effectiveness. To reiterate the point made in chapter 3, effectiveness should be assessed by the *effects* of the measure, rather than the *goals* of the sender.

It is also worth reiterating here that a measure's effectiveness is not solely determined by its effect on *ongoing* rights violations. Its effectiveness also includes longer-term effects on basic human rights, such as by addressing the root causes of the conflict and putting in place norms and stable institutions in order to prevent *future* rights violations. For instance, helping to advance norms such as R2P and norms against aggression can help to improve compliance with individual basic human rights. Thus, seemingly symbolic effects can be an important part of effectiveness; what matters is whether and how much upholding and advancing the norm is likely to affect compliance with human rights and reduce the likelihood or intensity of future incidents of the violation of basic human rights. More precisely, morally valuable effectiveness will typically be a function of the following:

[16] Also see Brzoska and Lopez (2009) for a detailed critique of the over-demandingness of much of the literature on arms embargoes and the need for a broader notion of success.

(1) the likely effect on the crisis (how '*successful*' the measure is);
(2) the likely costs to the agent undertaking the measure (the '*internal costs*');
(3) the likely costs for those subject to the measure, such as collateral damage (the '*external costs*'); and
(4) the likely effects for third parties and the international system more generally, such as helping or weakening international norms (the '*broader effects*').

This account of morally valuable effectiveness is sufficient for our purposes here, but it is worth flagging up three complexities for the Pragmatic Approach. First, as I will discuss (in chapter 7) when I consider positive incentives given to leaders, some—such as those who commit genocide—may deserve not to receive any benefit and may even deserve to be punished. Positive effects on those who are highly culpable may therefore be excluded and potentially even treated as problematic, on a highly nuanced account of morally valuable effectiveness. However, there are often severe epistemic difficulties in determining culpability reliably when launching a response to mass atrocities and serious external aggression. Moreover, it seems that even many of those culpable still might be entitled to many increases in the enjoyment of basic human rights (after all, prisoners still have most human rights). As such, we can, as a rule of thumb or heuristic, view those affected as likely to be sufficiently deserving of the benefit. In other words, on morally valuable effectiveness, the effects on basic human rights are not dependent on the liability (that is, culpability) of the individuals in question. This consideration is bracketed and instead comes in when considering desert, which is the fifth factor on the Pragmatic Approach.

Second, the Pragmatic Approach focuses on the effects on *basic* human rights. Basic rights are the primary 'currency' of assessing the effectiveness of the alternatives. This notion draws on Henry Shue's (1996) influential accounts of 'basic' rights. Basic rights include the rights to subsistence (such as the right to adequate food, clothing, and shelter) and physical security (such as the right not to be subject to murder, rape, and assault). Such rights are *basic* because they are required in order to be able to enjoy all other human rights (Shue 1996: 18–20). They therefore should be privileged because they need to be established in order to enjoy human rights (Shue 1996: 20). For example, subsistence is needed in order to be able to enjoy the right to freedom of speech. However, other goods are relevant, beyond direct and indirect effects on basic human rights. In focusing, then, on the effects on basic human rights, I mean to suggest only that these are likely to be the *primary* determinant of morally valuable effectiveness. On the Pragmatic Approach, the effects on individuals' basic human rights should be seen as most weighty, given the importance of ensuring these rights. Morally valuable effectiveness will therefore largely turn on its impact on these rights. But it will also depend on the effect on other goods (such as effects on non-basic human rights), especially in marginal cases, again on a nuanced account of morally valuable effectiveness. For simplicity's sake, for the most part I will highlight the effect on basic human rights.

Third, effectiveness should be measured according to the counterfactual of the measure not being undertaken, that is, compared to the likely effects of not undertaking the measure. As such, the comparative likely impact of *other* measures on the situation does not determine the likely effectiveness of the measure in question. It follows that several measures may be effective. Amongst these measures, the one that is likely to be *most* effective should be favoured. Viewing effectiveness in this way avoids having to say, oddly, that a measure is ineffective, despite potentially saving thousands of peoples' lives, because another measure would be even more effective.

4.4.2 The Moral Significance of Effectiveness

Why does morally valuable effectiveness matter so much? To start with, it seems highly intuitive that effectiveness is a central consideration for the Pragmatic Approach. It seems crucial that, whatever measure is adopted, it will improve compliance with basic human rights. If a measure will not do this, it seems impermissible. Suppose, for instance, that targeted sanctions will overall worsen compliance with basic human rights in a particular crisis. It seems intuitively clear, then, that targeted sanctions should not be launched. This is also reflected in accounts of the *jus ad bellum* principle of proportionality in Just War Theory. This, recall, requires that war do more good than harm. If war will do more harm, it should not occur. This is also echoed in much of the discussion around the alternatives. For instance, as we have seen, there is debate about whether arms embargoes are effective. As we will see in later chapters, there are similar debates around most of the other measures, including naming and shaming, the cutting of diplomatic ties, civilian defence, civilian peacekeeping, positive incentives, and international criminal prosecutions. Regardless of one's view of the effectiveness of these measures, what the sides in these debates implicitly agree is that effectiveness is a central consideration for the justifiability of the measures. If they are not effective, they should not be undertaken; if they are effective, they perhaps should. It seems highly plausible, then, that effectiveness is a central condition for the alternatives' justifiability. More philosophically, it seems right that, in general, the likely consequences of action should play a significant role in the assessment of its justifiability. This might not be the only factor, but it is a major one. Indeed, leading deontologists such as John Rawls accept this; they do not deny that consequences matter, but rather simply add that there are weighty, non-consequentialist factors as well. Rawls, for instance, argues that: '[a]ll ethical doctrines worth our attention take consequences into account in judging rightness. One which did not would simply be irrational, crazy' (1999*a*: 26).

The Pragmatic Approach holds that effectiveness is a major determinant of which measure should be adopted. To that extent, when selecting between measures, each of which is effective (that is, will do *more good than harm*), it is typically the *most effective* measure (that is, will do *most net good*) that should be adopted. Again, this is intuitively appealing. When selecting between the measures, it seems immediately plausible that a central consideration is the degree of effectiveness of each of them. To see this, suppose that there are three options, each of which would do more good than harm and impose the same amount of costs on the innocent populations of the sender and receiver. Option A is targeted sanctions, which would tackle the ongoing mass atrocities to a *small* degree. Option B is an international criminal prosecution, which would tackle the ongoing mass atrocities to a *significant* degree, but not fully. Option C is a package of measures including an arms embargo, which would tackle the ongoing mass atrocities almost *fully*. Although all the options are better than doing nothing, it seems, when selecting between the options, there is a strong prima facie reason to choose Option C, given that it would tackle the mass atrocities almost fully. Its greater effectiveness intuitively matters.

Effectiveness matters so much because of what is at stake. As considered in section 2.3 (which explored how to weigh values), much more will be typically at stake when considering the comparative effectiveness of the measures than when considering the other four values on the Pragmatic Approach. The difference between Options A and C above, for instance, will be whether the measure tackles mass atrocities a little or almost fully. This could mean the difference between life and death for tens of thousands of individuals. It seems, then, that the effectiveness of a measure will typically affect a large number of individuals in significant ways—such as by improving the protection of their basic human rights. For instance, it seems generally unlikely that a measure would be able to make such a sizeable impact on the *fairness* of the harms that innocents have to face, given that existing inequalities will be likely to remain. Suppose, for instance, that in the above example Option A would much more fairly distribute harms than Option C. This is *a* positive reason in favour of A, but it is unlikely to make a huge difference in terms of the fairness of those affected, given that it is a one-off act. (*Ongoing* systems of distributive justice in the sender and receiver states are far more likely to determine overall fairness.)

Thus, it seems highly plausible that effectiveness—understood as morally valuable effectiveness—is a central determinant of the justifiability of the measure. On the Pragmatic Approach, it plays a central role in determining which measure is adopted. This is intuitive, coheres with approaches in other relevant domains, and can be rationally explained, given what is at stake—the effects on many individuals' basic human rights.

4.4.3 The Effectiveness of Arms Embargoes

Let us return to arms embargoes. On the account of morally valuable effectiveness I have presented, we should focus on the effects on basic human rights. Other measures of effectiveness, such as policy change and full compliance, may have little impact on basic human rights. Moreover, they may fail to take into account two notable, related effects that arms embargoes have on basic human rights. These are, first, a reduction in the intensity of the conflict and battlefield deaths and, second, the amount of arms flowing around the state. The relevance of the first is obvious; the second matters for basic human rights because, as I will discuss further in chapter 8, arms transfers (that is, arming rebels and states) can have a significant negative impact on basic human rights, beyond the immediate fighting.

Once we assess arms embargoes according to their effects on basic human rights and in particular on battlefield intensity and the availability of arms, we see that they are *typically* effective (even if not always so). Indeed, a recent spate of quantitative studies demonstrates this. First, in his study of seventy-four arms embargoes, Brzoska (2008: 10) finds that, although they affected target policies in only seventeen cases (including Angola, Burundi, Democratic Republic of the Congo, Haiti, Liberia, Sierra Leone, and South Africa), the success rate for reducing arms inflows is 39 per cent. When the focus is on UN sanctions, this rises to 57 per cent, including significant changes in Afghanistan, Angola, Ethiopia, Eritrea, Haiti, Iraq, Liberia, Sierra Leone, Sudan, and Yugoslavia (Brzoska 2008: 13).

In similar vein, in their assessment of African civil wars from 1989 to 2005, Lisa Hultman and Dursun Peksen (2017) find that arms embargoes in civil wars reduce battlefield deaths by 46 per cent, seemingly because of a reduction in the flow of arms. They argue that '[d]irecting an arms embargo against a country with a civil conflict might thus help alleviate the human cost of conflict by considerably diminishing the intensity of conflict' (2017: 1330). They give the example of Ethiopia, where the arms embargoes imposed in 1990 in response to the ongoing internal conflict resulted (along with other measures) in a significant drop in the intensity of the conflict and its ending in mid-1991 (2017: 1332). Even the generally critical SIPRI report by Fruchart et al. (2007) finds that, on their much more demanding notion of effectiveness, UN arms embargoes lead to improved target behaviour in 25.2 per cent of cases. This increases to 29 per cent when one removes cases dealing with weapons of mass destruction and terrorism, and climbs to 32.1 per cent and

36.4 per cent if one takes into account the extent to which the UN attempted to monitor the embargo and control borders.[17]

Why are arms embargoes somewhat and sometimes effective? First, despite some high-profile exceptions, states do tend to comply with arms embargoes. To that extent, Jennifer Erickson (2013) finds that, contrary to the claims that states violate arms embargoes, embargoes *do* generally repress exports of both small arms and light weapons (SALW) and major conventional weapons. This is despite incentives to export and the lack of penalties to ensure enforcement. She suggests that compliance may be because of normative or domestic pressures and security concerns (Erickson 2013: 168). Second, obtaining weapons from the black market is often costly and the weapons are of inferior quality (Moore 2010: 597). In addition, it is difficult for states to increase arms production because of the necessary capital investment (Moore 2010: 597). Third, there have been significant strides made in the monitoring of arms embargoes, and in the language used, so as, for instance, to cover dual-use equipment (Tierney 2005: 652–3; Vines 2007: 1110). There have also been improvements in cooperation and knowledge sharing within the UN system and beyond, and increased integration with peacekeeping operations (attempting to avoid UN peacekeepers looking the other way as arms dealers go about their business), more refined lists of items covered, and greater efforts to monitor compliance and criminalize sanctions busting (Brzoska and Lopez 2016: 74–5; Lopez 2012: 143).

Arms embargoes will clearly not work all of the time. However, there are various indicators for when they are most likely to be effective. This is when they are multilateral, which helps to reduce the flow of arms and strengthen the symbolic sense of disapproval (Brzoska 2008: 4–5). They also work best when used alongside other measures, such as comprehensive sanctions (Brzoska 2008: 15). In addition, they are typically more effective on non-state actors than on states, given that states can normally more easily counter the embargo (Brzoska 2008: 5).

Moreover, recall that the likely costs of arms embargoes will be low (and lower than many other measures). This is both for the internal costs and for those in the political community suffering the mass atrocities or conflict (the external costs). They clearly differ from measures such as comprehensive economic sanctions and military intervention, which are likely to impose significant costs. Of course, arms embargoes are not a risk-free measure, but are often worth trying, given that they are unlikely to *do* much additional harm. The major worries are that they preclude a just side from defending

[17] To be clear, Fruchart et al. (2007) generally highlight the ineffectiveness of arms embargoes (although they tend to highlight incidents of violation, rather than offering general trends). They also posit that it might be other factors, such as changes in leadership, which explain the change in target behaviour (Fruchart et al. 2007: 51).

itself, strengthen criminal elements, and preclude further, more robust action. However, when these effects are unlikely, arms embargoes should be adopted, even if it is unclear that they will be strongly complied with. They should be used, for instance, alongside other measures as a standard response.

4.5 CONCLUSION

The upshot, then, is that the prima facie case is largely correct. Arms embargoes often reduce aggregate harm. They also are relatively low cost for the sender, distribute harms more fairly (on both the moderate and strong views of the ethics of the arms trade), and often are symbolically important by helping to denounce the wrongdoing. To that extent, arms embargoes are a form of sanction that should be generally pursued.

5

Diplomacy

The previous two chapters considered economic sanctions and military sanctions (that is, arms embargoes) and defended both measures against their critics. This chapter turns to consider what, if anything, diplomacy can do to help to tackle mass atrocities and serious external aggression. It will consider diplomatic sanctions, such as naming and shaming and the cutting of diplomatic ties, as well as non-coercive measures such as dialogue and mediation.

Diplomacy might appear to be akin to doing nothing in response to mass atrocities and aggression, where significant economic or military coercion is required instead. Against this sentiment, I will argue that some forms of diplomacy can be efficacious. I will defend in particular the case for diplomatic criticism (or 'naming and shaming') as a response to serious external aggression and mass atrocities by insurgents, terrorists, or other states. In doing so, I will defend diplomatic criticism over other diplomatic responses and argue that cases where states fail to respond to mass atrocities, aggression, and other serious human rights abuses are problematic. These include the South African failure to criticize Robert Mugabe's Zimbabwe, the Australian failure in the 2013 Commonwealth Meeting to criticize the abuses of human rights by the Sri Lankan government, the failure of the UK (under Margaret Thatcher) to criticize General Pinochet's human rights abuses in Chile, and the British and American failure to criticize human rights abuses in Uzbekistan. In similar vein to what I will argue, in August 2014 Ed Miliband, the then leader of the Labour Party, criticized David Cameron for his 'inexplicable' silence on 'the killing of hundreds of innocent Palestinian civilians caused by Israel's military action' in Gaza (Boffey 2014). I will also argue that diplomatic criticism should often be undertaken *in addition* to other ways of addressing serious external aggression and mass atrocities. Thus, I will argue that states (and other actors) should often register diplomatic criticism of offenders both when they undertake other measures and when they do not (such as because military intervention would do more harm than good).[1]

[1] Interestingly, there is very little written on diplomatic measures from a normative perspective. As far as I am aware, the only exceptions are Bjola (2014), Bjola and Kornprobst (2013),

The chapter will proceed as follows. In section 5.1, I will present the case for naming and shaming. I will suggest that this stems from three bases: (1) efficacy at addressing the situation; (2) contribution to global norms; and (3) punishment. In section 5.2, I will consider (and largely, if not fully, repudiate) two leading objections to international criticism. The first—the 'Demandingness Objection'—is that it is far too demanding. The second—the 'Hypocrisy Objection'—is that states are not entitled to criticize others when they are being hypocritical. Sections 5.3 and 5.4 will examine the case for dialogue and mediation, particularly as an alternative to naming and shaming, which is sometimes referred to as 'megaphone diplomacy' by advocates of mediation. I will highlight the potential congruence between these measures as well as delineate the limitations of dialogue and mediation. Section 5.5 considers—and largely rejects—the merits of cutting and downgrading diplomatic ties, despite the possibility that this strategy could avoid the condoning of wrongdoing. Section 5.6 examines—and defends—the case for denying membership of an international or regional body.

5.1 THE CASE FOR DIPLOMATIC CRITICISM

5.1.1 Successfully Addressing the Situation

Let us first consider the potential positive reasons for engaging in diplomatic criticism. I will focus on three reasons. The first is straightforward: although the efficacy of diplomatic criticism is often understated (for instance, it is viewed as simply doing nothing in response to aggression), diplomatic criticism may often be at least somewhat successful at addressing the situation. This is because, in short, people try to avoid criticism. Why do we care about being criticized? Most fundamentally, as R. Jay Wallace argues, '[w]e are social creatures, and it matters to us deeply whether we are thought well of by our peers' (2010: 331).

More specifically, on constructivist accounts of International Relations, states are concerned with both the 'logic of consequences'—that is, maximizing their fixed interests and preferences—and the 'logic of appropriateness'—conforming to expected behaviour determined by the prevailing norms of the international system (Finnemore 1996; March and Olsen 1998). In regard to the logic of appropriateness, states seek (perceived) legitimacy. When states are criticized, challenges are posed to their reputations and their international standing. If the criticism is widely upheld, the subsequent loss of (perceived)

Gross (2013), and Toscano (2001). Gopalan and Fuller (2014) examine the case for shaming in international law and, in doing so, consider similar points to those examined in this chapter.

legitimacy might be significant not only for the state's interests (for instance, if it is barred from membership of international bodies and loses trade agreements) but also for its self-identity (for instance, if its view of itself as a force for good in the international system is challenged).[2]

Consequently, if we accept that states care about the loss of legitimacy, and that diplomatic criticism is important for leading to such a loss, states will sometimes be keen to redress the situation at hand in response to diplomatic criticism, or under the threat of such criticism. The potential impact of such criticism is missed on accounts of International Relations that focus on material interests and on enforcement only through economic or military measures. Although certain states may prioritize material interests or be less worried about international criticism (such as because they are already international pariahs), challenges to their international reputation do seem to lead to changes in certain states' behaviour.[3] International criticism, then, is not simply 'doing nothing'; rather, it can play an important role in leading to changes in the behaviour of states.

Even when states are already engaged in other ways of addressing the crisis, such as war or economic sanctions, diplomatic criticism can help to put further pressure on the aggressor. Moreover, it can help by providing a clear public justification of war and economic sanctions. Indeed, as I argued in chapter 3, the effectiveness of economic sanctions may depend in part on what they achieved symbolically, that is, by their expression of disapproval of the receiver. In doing so, they can contribute generally to existing international prohibitions on aggression and other practices. Crucially, to do this, they need to be accompanied by an account of the reasons why the regime is to be sanctioned.

This argument about the efficacy of diplomatic criticism can be stated more precisely by drawing on Thomas Risse's (2000) Habermasian account of communicative action. According to Risse, the logic of consequences (which, in effect, concerns the realm of rational choice where agents pursue fixed interests and preferences) and the logic of appropriateness (which, as we have seen, concerns the import of social structures in influencing and constituting agents)—should be supplemented with the 'logic of argumentation'. The logic of argumentation concerns the role played by individual agents in influencing others' interests or preferences. Actors will not always have fixed interests or preferences; these will be up for negotiation.

At times, all the actors in question will be open to persuasion. This seems unlikely, however, for states reacting to serious external aggression or mass

[2] Criticism is also important for getting the situation onto the international agenda (Risse 2000: 20), such as mass atrocities that have not been previously discussed by the UN Security Council.

[3] See, for instance, the cases of Indonesia and Morocco discussed by Risse (2000: 29–30).

atrocities. Rather, *one* set of actors is more likely to be open to persuasion. That is to say, the audience will often encompass not simply the actors directly involved—the critic and the agent subject to the criticism—but also the international community more generally, including world public opinion. By providing an account of external aggression or mass atrocities and, in particular, by stating its empirical claims about the violations and asserting its normative claims about the wrongness of the violations, the critic is putting forward an argument that the subject of their criticism should amend their behaviour or face international opprobrium. The audience—the international community—is open to persuasion about the case at hand and will assess the case presented by the critic, as well as the responses of the alleged wrongdoers, such as that they are 'fighting terrorists'. Although the situation may not match the requirements of the Habermasian Ideal Speech situation (which requires no coercive influences), the force of the better argument may still prevail.

Once persuaded, for instance, of the facts of the case, the relevant audience—actors in the international community—may repudiate the wrongdoer for failing to conform to the required normative standards of the international system. In order to fend off the opprobrium of the international community, the norm-violating government may make rhetorical concessions and cease denying the validity of or contesting human rights or related norms (Risse 2000: 32). This may open them up to further criticism about their failure to live up to norms that they in fact endorse and, ultimately, may lead to a shift in the perceived preferences and interests of the norm-violator, and a shift in behaviour, in order to be consistent (Risse calls this 'self-entrapment' (2000: 32)).

What goes on in such cases cannot be *solely* explained by the logic of consequences or the logic of appropriateness. This is because the interests or preferences of the relevant audience are not fixed (so cannot be explained by the logic of consequences). It is also because it may not be clear that the behaviour violates what is deemed appropriate or, more generally, what may be deemed appropriate may not be yet determined (and so cannot be explained by the logic of appropriateness). It may not be clear that the behaviour violates what is deemed appropriate because of the lack of information, for instance, about the situation. Rather, the matter is more complex. On the one hand, the critic is engaging in the logic of consequences: it is using what Risse calls 'rhetorical action' in order to realize its fixed but normatively valuable preferences or views, which are not up for negotiation. It does so by persuading *others* in the global public sphere, who are subject to the logic of arguing, that the wrongdoer *should* be subject to a loss of legitimacy—in effect, by the logic of appropriateness. Thus, diplomatic rebuke can be effective since the critic presents an argument in order to persuade the international community of the wrongness of the violation, which can lead to the delegitimation of the wrongdoer.

An upshot of this argument is that diplomatic criticism should often be *public*: the critic needs to denounce publicly the wrongness of the violation in order to persuade the international community that the wrongdoer *should* be rebuked. Quiet diplomacy will not achieve this. The efficacy of international criticism by states appears to be supported by the recent quantitative literature on naming and shaming, carried out by NGOs, the international media, and international organizations. Central pieces in this literature hold that, although naming and shaming by these actors might make little difference in redressing lesser human rights violations and could potentially be counterproductive (Hafner-Burton 2008), it can be important for helping to decrease the severity of genocides and politicides (Krain 2012; Krain 2017) and government killing (DeMeritt 2012). The case presented in this literature for the efficacy of naming and shaming is similar to my defence of the efficacy of diplomatic criticism. For instance, in explaining his findings that naming and shaming works, Matthew Krain (2012) posits that this is because naming and shaming can inform about abuses, frame perpetrators as pariahs, damage their legitimacy, activate powerful bystanders who can impose costs on them, and ultimately lead to changes in policy.[4]

An example of successful diplomatic criticism was the criticism in the Fowler Report of sitting African heads of states for violating sanctions on UNITA, the Angolan rebel group, which shot down a UN plane in early 1999 and was in large part responsible for the extremely bloody civil war that ravaged Angola for three decades. This report created a storm of protest, given the UN's normal passivity, but helped to publicly shame the violators of the Chapter VII UN Security Council Resolution, with the result that sanctions effectively disrupted UNITA's supply lines and ultimately led to negotiations and the demilitarization of UNITA in 2002 (Biersteker et al. 2016*c*: 234).

To be clear, I am not claiming that there will always be such effects; some regimes may still ignore the criticism of the critics and not be significantly influenced by a loss of legitimacy. Alternatively, they may be already significantly delegitimized (such as the Assad regime and North Korea) and so further repudiation of them will exert very little pressure. However, others are often more influenced by reputational concerns. This is shown in part by their working hard to cover up abuses, such as by expelling the international media. For instance, in 2009 the government of Sri Lanka reportedly

[4] To be sure, the focus of this literature is on naming and shaming by NGOs, the international media, and international organizations. There is not, as far as I am aware, a quantitative study of the impact of naming and shaming *by states in general* (the focus of this chapter). (Franklin (2008) does consider the impact of criticism by states (and other actors) of human rights abuses, finding that it reduces repression, but he focuses on the Latin American case.) For a recent collection of largely qualitative essays on naming and shaming, which does consider shaming by states, see Friman (2015).

threatened to expel the international media in order to reduce coverage of its abuses in its campaign against the Tamil Tigers (Ramesh 2009).

5.1.2 Contribution to Global Norms

Beyond the tackling of the immediate situation in question and the exertion of international pressure on the norm violator, international criticism can play an important role in the establishment and the upholding of morally valuable international norms and laws. By criticizing others—and in particular by *publicly* criticizing others—states may express their view that there are certain norms in the international system and that these have been violated by the aggressor. This helps to reinforce the claim that the norm against the transgression exists, in addition to any action in support of the norm (such as economic sanctions)—it makes it clear that the action is in support of the norm. This matters in turn because strong norms can improve the compliance with basic human rights, as states and other actors feel bound to comply. For instance, the US's strong rebuke of the use of chemical weapons by the Assad regime in Syria and Barack Obama's assertion that their use would cross a 'red line' appeared to strengthen and even advance the norm and laws against the use of such weapons. Subsequently, in September 2013 the UN Security Council passed Resolution 2118, which was lauded by the then US Secretary of State, John Kerry, as 'declaring together, for the first time, that the use of chemical weapons... [is] also a threat to international peace and security' (2013).[5]

To put the point more precisely, in constructivist accounts of International Relations, actors that develop and propagate new international norms are referred to as 'norm entrepreneurs' (Finnemore and Sikkink 1998: 896). Actors that help to establish further existing norms are 'norm carriers' (Heinze 2009: 124). The aim is to achieve a 'norm cascade' whereby the norm becomes adopted by states because of international socialization (Finnemore and Sikkink 1998: 902). Once cascaded, norms can become internalized within the actors so that conformity becomes almost automatic (Finnemore and Sikkink 1998: 904). International criticism can play a role in norm entrepreneurship and development. When criticizing others, states can assert that the practice contravenes what *should* be viewed as a widely held

[5] Of course, the subsequent failure to intervene militarily in response to the crossing of the red line may be claimed to have weakened the taboo against using chemical weapons (for instance, given the apparent use of them subsequently by the Syrian and Sudanese governments). On the other hand, the renewed diplomatic effort and attempted destruction of the weapons may show that the norm violation did in fact motivate a clear, robust international response. The same could be true of the Trump Administration's strikes on Syria after the Assad regime used chemical weapons in Khan Shaykhun in April 2017.

norm. They may then go on to defend their own, more detailed account of the norm, or help to cascade existing emerging norms.

A potential example of the former is the Brazilian rebuke of the NATO-led bombing campaign in Libya in 2011 for (allegedly) going beyond the mandate of Resolution 1973 and then its subsequent development of the RwP ('responsibility while protecting') concept. As noted in section 1.2, RwP emphasizes that those considering undertaking humanitarian intervention need to consider alternative measures first, that interveners need to take extra care when using military force to protect civilians, that interveners should report continually to the UN Security Council, and that there are guidelines for humanitarian intervention (for the UN Security Council). Although RwP has not been formally adopted, the import of this contribution in terms of clarifying and developing R2P for future instances of military intervention has been widely noted (e.g. Stuenkel and Tourinho 2014) and RwP might be seen as Brazil engaging in norm entrepreneurship (Benner 2013).

The contribution to global norms seems particularly relevant for emerging norms—norms that are not fully established—such as some of the R2P (specifically, the precise requirements of the international remedial responsibility to protect).[6] However, it may also be relevant for international law, insofar as a central element of customary international law is *opinio juris*—the belief amongst states that certain norms are legally binding. The public expression of criticism may be expressed legally (such as if the state in question is criticized for having violated international law with their transgression of state sovereignty) and therefore helps to provide an important assertion of *opinio juris*. When the international law is contested, the statement might be influential and help to establish or to uphold the view that a certain morally valuable law *is* law. This may have highly beneficial long-term consequences for the international system.[7]

This point can be taken further. States need to avoid condoning the aggressive behaviour of other states since failure to register rebuke could give the impression that the state agrees with the behaviour in question, such as ethnic cleansing. Not only can this undermine the potential reputational costs imposed on the aggressor in the case at hand, it can undermine the

[6] The R2P involves the international remedial responsibility to protect, the details of which are emerging, as well as norms concerning pillar one (the protection responsibilities of states) that are well established, such as in international law.

[7] To reiterate, I focus here on naming and shaming, but other measures may help to advance morally important global norms, particularly when clearly in support of the norm. When accompanied by a clear justification in support of the norm, they can show commitment to it and reinforce the sense that it is binding on states. This might include economic sanctions and military intervention, as well as ICC prosecutions. Indeed, as I will consider in section 9.1, one of the arguments for ICC prosecutions is expressivist.

norm against the behaviour as the sense that it is an expected standard of behaviour is reduced. For instance, Brazil's failure in 2014 to condemn Russia for the annexation of Crimea not only reduced some of the reputational costs on Russia, it also weakened the sense that annexation of another state's territory is perceived as impermissible.[8]

In fact, when states fail to register rebuke of those engaged in aggression, such as insurgents, terrorists, or other states, they might potentially be complicit in future situations of aggression (as well as of the current situation). The complicity may stem from the fact that their silence can be reasonably foreseen to be perceived by other parties, including the aggressor, to be an act of condoning the continuation of the aggression under consideration or future aggression of a similar nature.[9] This can help to enable new forms of aggression or the continuance of the current aggression. As argued in chapter 4, complicity is a useful notion to capture the fact that one can act wrongly despite the harm being committed by others.

5.1.3 Punishment

Third, those who engage in egregious wrongdoing should be punished—and in particular receive what they deserve (the fifth factor on the Pragmatic Approach). The international system is, however, fairly devoid of means of punishment. International criminal tribunals and the International Criminal Court (ICC) provide means of punishment for *some* of those engaged in external aggression and mass atrocities, such as insurgents, terrorists, or other states. But (as we will see in section 9.1) the powers of the ICC and such tribunals are limited.

This does not mean, however, that there is *no* punishment available in the international system. Certain forms of targeted economic sanctions, such as asset freezes and travel bans, can punish leaders responsible for egregious crimes. Similarly, diplomatic criticism, such as in the form of widespread opprobrium, can punish decision-makers (who should be the focus of punishment) since they face reputational loss.[10] The reputational loss that stems from such sanctions may not be *all* that such leaders deserve—they might deserve, for instance, life imprisonment. Notwithstanding, it seems that such leaders deserve *at least* international opprobrium and the accompanying reputational loss.

[8] See Stuenkel (2014) for analysis of the reasons why Brazil failed to condemn Russia.

[9] See section 4.3.4. Beversluis (1989) presents a similar argument in the context of economic sanctions.

[10] I focus here on the retributivist case for punishment. I will delineate further in section 7.3 why desert is an important consideration on the Pragmatic Approach.

Consider, for instance, the general tarnishing of the reputation of Tony Blair and George W. Bush after their War on Terror and War in Iraq. This was established by the widespread critique of their policies and (it seems to me) was deserved. And, even if leaders *are* subject to other forms of punishment, such as targeted economic sanctions, they may deserve reputational loss *as well.* To be sure, decision-makers may suffer a loss of legitimacy simply by the tacit rejection of their policies in the global public sphere. However, it seems that this is more likely with the public, explicit rejection of their policies, which can come with a clear public denouncement of their actions.

5.1.4 Two Further Considerations

I have thus far presented three reasons in favour of engaging in diplomatic criticism. I now want to present two further considerations that help to buttress this case.

First, diplomatic criticism is likely to be preferable to several of the measures considered in terms of external costs imposed on innocents and, in particular, preferable to war and economic sanctions. Although diplomatic criticism may sometimes cause *some* harm to innocents (such as if the criticism delegitimizes the state and in turn harms its trade, leading to economic hardships (Gopalan and Fuller 2014)), the magnitude and likelihood of harm to innocents on both sides in war and economic sanctions will typically be much larger. The internal costs to the warring or sanctioning party are also likely to be much greater for war and sanctions than if they were engaged in only diplomatic criticism.

Second, diplomatic criticism can be undertaken by many states. In contrast, only a few states may permissibly launch a war, given the costs involved. Wars and interventions can generally be undertaken effectively only by states with significant military capabilities. For instance, in most (but not all) cases of humanitarian intervention and other defence, states would require hugely expensive air- or sea-lift capacity in order to intervene in other states. Accordingly, in response to many cases of external aggression and mass atrocities, there are few states (and sometimes no states) that could wage war against insurgents, terrorists, or other states effectively, by doing sufficient good to outweigh the harms of the use of force. Given that Just War Theory requires that action be likely to be effective under a principle of proportionality, it would follow that most states should not wage war, because of the likely disproportionate costs of war. Yet diplomatic criticism can be pursued not simply by the potentially warring parties as an alternative or addition to war or economic sanctions, but also by less materially capable states that do not have war or economic sanctions as a feasible option. Since the costs to innocents are generally much lower with diplomatic criticism, the launching of diplomatic criticism need not be likely to achieve as much good in order to outweigh such harm, compared to war or economic sanctions. Diplomatic criticism also seems to be a measure that less materially powerful states can use to exert influence in a manner that is much greater than their material capabilities. This is because they may have the better arguments and so influence international public opinion to exert pressure on the wrongdoers in a manner that exceeds their capabilities, and potentially have much more influence than more militarily powerful actors whose hypocrisy or entrenched interests may remove some of the influence of their critique. Indeed, rather than from powerful states, such criticism may come best from an ally, such as the Australian condemnation of the Indonesian atrocities in East Timor in 1999 (Conley-Zilkic et al. 2016: 16).

5.2 OBJECTIONS TO DIPLOMATIC CRITICISM

Thus far, I have presented the case for international criticism as an alternative and addition to other means of addressing mass atrocities and external aggression by insurgents, terrorists, or other states. I will now consider two potential responses.

5.2.1 The Demandingness Objection

The first response is that international criticism is extremely demanding. By engaging in such international criticism, states may, for instance, lose important trade deals. As such, even if diplomatic criticism will address the situation, and be the best response under comparative Just War conditions such as last resort, it would not be permissible. This is because it would be disproportionate, given the excessive internal costs borne by the criticizing state. Overall, these costs could mean that it would be worse than doing nothing.

The worry about demandingness can, however, be largely defused by making two related points. First, as noted above, diplomatic criticism is often much less costly than other measures to address mass atrocities and serious external aggression. Second, even though there is reason to give some greater weight to internal costs (see section 7.2.2), common-sense morality appears to hold that the internal costs that states may be asked to bear in terms of the tackling of egregious human rights violations is quite high. This is as long as the measure is effective *overall* (that is, do more good than harm overall). It is widely held that, in certain cases, states have a moral duty to undertake military intervention in order to tackle egregious violations of human rights (see, generally, ICISS 2001; Pattison 2013). This is despite the fact that the financial costs of intervention are often very significant.[11] This is also despite the fact that there may be casualties when doing so (although in certain states, such as the US, there seems to be less of an acceptance of casualties). Hence, *if* we accept that efficacious military intervention to respond to mass atrocities may be morally justifiable, despite its costs, it would seem that efficacious diplomatic criticism that could similarly tackle mass atrocities might also be morally justifiable, despite its costs.

Moreover, when responding to aggression against one's own state, citizens may be willing to accept even greater burdens than those which they can be required to bear in the tackling of mass atrocities. This may mean that it is permissible for states to take on even greater costs when engaging in self-defensive measures. The costs of forthright criticism in response to external aggression therefore seem unlikely to exceed the level of costs that states can permissibly take on in response to external aggression. Accordingly, even seemingly high internal costs would not rule out diplomatic criticism as a disproportionate option.

5.2.2 The Hypocrisy Objection

The second objection to diplomatic criticism is that states are not entitled to criticize others in many cases. This is, in particular, when they are being hypocritical. That is, when states have previously engaged in the same or a similar practice, they lose their entitlement to be able to criticize others for engaging in this practice.

The objection about hypocrisy is one of the most common objections levelled against those who engage in diplomatic criticism. It is used by those engaging in morally problematic behaviour to deny that the agent criticizing them has the right to do so. For instance, in response to US criticism of its human rights record, in 2012 the Russian foreign ministry issued a fifty-page official report cataloguing American violations of human rights, including rendition, police discrimination, and drone strikes (Weir 2012).

The scope of this objection may appear to be very broad. Nearly all states in the international system face *some* human rights problems internally or have previously engaged in or supported aggressive action. For instance, the coalition for the (in my view, aggressive) 2003 War in Iraq was made up of forty states, roughly one in five of the states in the world. More broadly still, the Amnesty International Annual Report (2017) discusses human rights issues in over 150 states. Hence, if we give much weight to the wrongness of hypocrisy, very few, if any, states in the international system could potentially be able to

[11] For instance, the costs of the Kosovo intervention, including post-war reconstruction, is estimated at $46 billion in the ICISS (2001: 71) report on R2P.

engage justifiably in international criticism of other states over aggression and/or abuses of human rights, if we also view the Hypocrisy Objection as having a wide scope (I consider the objection's scope below). On such a view, diplomatic criticism is likely to be generally wrong and potentially impermissible.

Why is hypocrisy wrong? And why might it establish the impermissibility of diplomatic criticism? Most fundamentally, at the interpersonal level, hypocrisy seems wrong because, as Wallace (2010) argues, it appears to deny the equal moral standing of other agents. At the individual level, we think that the denial of equal moral standing, such as between sexes or races, is a form of disrespect. If we were to say, for instance, that men are not required to give a percentage of their earnings to international charities but women are, we would think that this denial of equal moral standing is baseless and potentially disrespectful of both men and women. Thus, Wallace argues that 'hypocritical moral address' is 'inherently objectionable' and 'a significant moral fault' since it 'offends against the commitment to the equality of persons' (2010: 308).[12]

At the international level, the worry is similar. When a state criticizes another, but engages in the same practice itself, it is effectively asserting that the same standards do not apply to *it*. The implicit claim is that it is exceptional—and superior—to other states. Similarly, if we hold at the international level that certain political communities are subject to the rules of the international system but others are not, there seems to be a morally problematic denial of equal moral standing. Hypocrisy, then, including at the international level, seems morally wrong because it denies the equal moral standing of those who are being criticized.

Hypocritical criticism also seems problematic instrumentally since it can weaken the impact of the hypocrite's (even correct) critique since it is perceived to lack credibility (Mor 2012: 394). The critic, when the hypocrisy is public, may be regarded with suspicion and dismissed. In terms of Habermasian communicative action, one of the three key 'validity claims' for speech acts is concerned with the truthfulness and authenticity of the speaker (Risse 2000: 9–10). When the speaker is seen as hypocritical, the force of their argument is reduced, as this aspect is weakened.

In addition, hypocrisy may be problematic because of its effects on the international community. It can undermine the practice of an appeal to international norms by means of, for instance, diplomatic criticism, since such appeals are viewed cynically and sceptically, especially in regard to the motives of the state that is making the criticism. The state may not take

[12] In fact, there is, according to Wallace, a double denial of equal standing. Not only are you, the hypocrite, elevating your own interests above those whom you criticize, you are also elevating the interests of the victims of those whom you criticize above the interests of the victims of those whom you yourself wrong. You fail to treat both sets of individuals equally; you attach greater import to the claims of the *victims of those whom you criticize* then the claims of your *own victims* (Wallace 2010: 330).

seriously the requirements of the norm itself and may not believe that, regardless of its rhetoric, conformity is in fact morally or legally required by it. To that extent, hypocrisy is a worry because it can undermine the status of norms as requiring conformity. It appears to show that the norms or laws governing international society are in fact weak or non-existent since they do not compel action for all. Instead, hypocrisy appears to reaffirm a Realist view of the international system whereby states are simply motivated by narrow material interests and norms have little influence. Accordingly, hypocrisy is a worry because it can undermine the status of norms as requiring conformity. Thus, Daryl Glaser notes, when the US behaves hypocritically, it subverts 'the authority of words used to describe desirable goals such as democracy and human rights' (2006: 265).

5.2.3 Replies to the Hypocrisy Objection

Despite these considerations, the force of the Hypocrisy Objection is severely limited. The overarching reason why hypocrisy *seems* to matter independently is that one fails to act when one should. For instance, the US's hypocrisy in criticizing Russia matters because of its own violation of rights in Guantánamo Bay. But what is the central problem here? It does not seem to be the hypocrisy *in itself*, but rather the substantive failure to meet the requirements of morality. What is *mainly* wrong with the US criticizing Russia is not the sense that the US sees itself as superior but rather that *it has violated rights in Guantánamo Bay*. In fact, hypocrisy seems to be of small independent moral wrongness. This is because it is attitudinal in that it concerns the attitudes that we hold about others' moral standing—the mindset of being superior to others. Although this mindset *is* objectionable, it seems far more important that agents live up to the substantive demands of morality. Indeed, such mindsets seem generally of little independent moral import when it comes to considering matters of international politics. For instance, the independent moral import of an agent's motives seems small when considering the much larger harms involved in wars and mass atrocities in Just War Theory.[13]

To see this more clearly, it helps to isolate the weight of the independent moral wrongness of acting inconsistently and, specifically, the denial of equal moral standing. To that extent, it helps to consider a case where acting consistently requires going *against* the substantive demands of morality. Consider that the UK ignores the role that its arms play in Saudi atrocities in Yemen, but then criticizes Russia's bombing campaign in Syria. Of course, it

[13] See Pattison (2010: 156–61; 2014*b*: 26–36).

should ensure that it plays no role in Saudi atrocities in Yemen. But, if it does so, it seems better that it be hypocritical (and, implicitly, deny equal moral standing) and still criticize Russia's campaign in Syria than not to. Although failing to criticize in the case of Syria would be treating all equally, it seems that states should treat *some* well rather than *all* equally badly. The independent moral import of acting consistently, then, seems to be clearly outweighed by the importance of going some way towards meeting the substantive requirements of morality, even if this enacts the agent's problematic, hypocritical mindset (and the denial of equal moral standing). As such, states can permissibly—and perhaps should—criticize, even on pain of hypocrisy (and the denial of equal moral standing), when doing so asserts that a particular group should not be subject to mass atrocities.

In addition, hypocritical criticism may sometimes still be efficacious. First, the criticism may play an educative role, in helping to establish facts about the case unbeknownst to other agents. It may, for instance, help to highlight how serious the ongoing mass atrocities are. Second, the criticism may add to the cacophony of voices that condemn the action and the hypocrisy may have little negative instrumental impact on international norms. That is, the criticism may play a larger role in tackling the crisis than the hypocrisy does in weakening the case. Third, if hypocrisy is the homage that vice pays to virtue, then hypocrisy can, on occasion, help to reinforce norms. This is particularly when the hypocrisy is unexposed (Glaser 2006: 262). It may also apply when it is exposed. The hypocrite, in effect, says the following: one is morally required to perform a certain action. I am too weak of will and/or self-interested to perform the action myself (and even can—and perhaps should—be rightly rebuked for it). But others can be rightly rebuked for their failure not to perform the action. Fourth, in asserting and potentially strengthening the norm, hypocritical criticism provides a means by which others can criticize the hypocrite, when the hypocrisy is exposed. In short: they should practise what they preach. Fifth, states often claim that their action conforms to the norm and *deny* the allegations of hypocrisy. Hence, even if they are acting hypocritically—and it is obvious that they are doing so—states will still assert that the norm is binding; this may strengthen the norm. Indeed, hypocritical states may be affected by their hypocritical justifications for action and amend their behaviour accordingly in order to be more virtuous, in large part due to concerns about their reputation. Indeed, it seems that this has already happened in certain cases of humanitarian intervention. Ryan Goodman (2006) argues that, even when states present a case for humanitarian intervention mendaciously, they become entangled in the humanitarian justifications that they present, which can pacify the situation to some extent. The humanitarian framework that they adopt renders interstate disputes less likely to escalate and enables additional opportunities for conflict resolution (Goodman 2006: 116). To be clear, these considerations may not repudiate fully the negative consequences of hypocrisy. Nevertheless, they show that some of the instrumental worries surrounding hypocrisy may not always be serious.

Moreover, although the scope of the Hypocrisy Objection is, at first sight, broad, it is in fact quite small. G. A. Cohen notes, in discussion of the related issue of '*tu quoque*' ('you too') criticism, that '[f]ew of us think that no one can call the kettle black who has committed *sin* of any kind' (2013: 134). He considers two alternative views (2013: 135–7). On the 'quantity view', it is appropriate to criticize only when your sin is *less* than the sin committed by those whom you are criticizing. On the 'quality view', it is appropriate to criticize only when your sin is of a different *kind* to the sin committed by those whom you are criticizing.

Like Cohen (2013: 140), I think a combined account, whereby the sin needs to be of the same kind and seriousness, is the most intuitively plausible account of hypocrisy. On this combined account, when the sin is of a different kind (such as killing compared to the denial of freedom of expression), the state is not acting hypocritically when it criticizes others. Similarly, when the sin is of a lesser quantity, such as when killing one person in a bundled, mendacious police operation, but not mass killing, the state is not acting hypocritically when it criticizes others.[14]

Two further considerations reduce the scope of the Hypocrisy Objection. First, it seems that the agents accused of hypocrisy (or other lapses) still need to be committed to or engaged in their wrongful action. If they subsequently denounce and apologize for their wrongful action—they show that they no longer have the problematic mindset—it does not seem that they can be rightly rebuked for being hypocritical, since they no longer deny others' equal moral standing. For instance, it seems that one could not rebuke modern-day Germany for hypocrisy for, on the one hand, Nazi policies in the 1930s and 1940s and, on the other, its recent criticisms of other states' human rights records. Similarly, changes of government (such as in US administrations) can often mean that allegations of hypocrisy are problematic, since the new government may no longer deny others' equal moral standing.

Second, for criticism to be hypocritical, it needs to concern wrongful action in the first place. If the initial action was in fact morally *justifiable*, the criticism is not hypocritical. Even though it may involve, for instance, some unavoidable harms to innocents, these harms should be put in the context of the all-things-considered permissible action. For instance, a state may engage in a bombing campaign in humanitarian intervention that unavoidably leads to civilian casualties, but helps to save thousands. If that state goes on to rebuke

[14] Criticism of a different scale or kind may, like hypocrisy, also deny the equal moral standing of other agents. But it would not be hypocrisy *per se*; it would be a different sort of moral failing. See, further, Wallace (2010: 336).

others for engaging in a bombing campaign that *unnecessarily* leads to civilian casualties, its critique is not hypocritical.

All this is not to deny that states should not be hypocritical. They should act rightly—and not engage in internal or external aggression themselves—and should possess the attitude that others are morally equal. But their failure to do either—to act rightly or to have the right attitude—does not foreclose the possibility of permissible diplomatic criticism that is hypocritical. It will often be preferable that they engage in diplomatic criticism despite the apparent hypocrisy than not criticize.

5.3 DIALOGUE

Let us now consider the case for dialogue. It might be thought that, rather than engaging in diplomatic criticism, states should instead engage in dialogue with those involved in serious external aggression and mass atrocities—insurgents, terrorists, or other states. This is because diplomatic criticism may be viewed as preaching or 'monologue'—or, more colloquially, 'megaphone diplomacy'—and so viewed as unlikely to be effective. It might make it difficult for those criticized to save face and step back from a policy quietly, for fear of appearing to be weak, compared to a private rebuke which might have more purchase on occasion, since it can allow the aggressor to avoid humiliation. Moreover, the central premises of the notion of 'public diplomacy' are relationship building and dialogue, which are claimed to be more likely to achieve the broader, long-term aims of diplomacy.[15] The sharing of understandings and listening to others' complaints and viewpoints, the argument goes, is much more likely to lead to a shift in behaviour than the strong rebuke of offending agents. For instance, criticizing China's human rights record might seem unlikely to lead to a shift in policy. Engagement and long-term dialogue might be viewed as what is required to lead to such a shift. Monologue may be viewed as moralizing, perhaps leading to the entrenchment and potentially illicit but influential accusations of hypocrisy.

[15] I will not offer a definition of public diplomacy here since there is very little agreement on what exactly it involves in the literature on the topic, bar the need for relationship building and dialogue. Influential accounts of public diplomacy include Cowan and Arsenault (2008), Cull (2008), Fitzpatrick (2007), Gilboa (2008), and Nye (2008). Interestingly, Berridge (2010: 179–82) argues that public diplomacy is in effect simply propaganda. To that extent, it may be viewed as more similar to monologue than the dialogue emphasized by other scholars of public diplomacy (for Berridge, public diplomacy is aimed at the population of the target state, rather than at the international community more generally, which, as noted above, is the main audience of diplomatic criticism). By contrast, Mellison (2013: 440) claims that the main difference between propaganda and public diplomacy is that the former is generally uninterested in relationship building and dialogue. Also see Sharp (2009: 270–5).

By contrast, by giving all the parties a voice, dialogue might offer opportunities for engagement and, in turn, increased positivity towards opposing viewpoints and potential acceptance of political outcomes as fair (Cowan and Arsenault 2008: 19). This may not only tackle the immediate problems of mass atrocities or external aggression, but may also lead to a shift in approach of the actors so that they do not engage in such behaviour in the future. In a somewhat similar vein, Paul Sharp (2009: 10–12), in his account of a 'Diplomatic Theory' of International Relations, argues that 'thinking diplomatically' privileges the maintenance of relations and that 'diplomatic understanding' suggests 'quietism'. He notes that one of the implications of the Diplomatic Theory of International Relations is 'the morality of suspending judgement' (2009: 299). This, he suggests, stems not only from the import of continued dialogue and retaining ongoing relations, but also from moral scepticism stemming from a pluralistic international society and the resultant epistemic uncertainty about purported moral universals, such as those that give rise to calls for humanitarian intervention.[16]

In addition, it might be claimed that dialogue is intrinsically valuable. Thus, some accounts of public diplomacy assert that states should engage in relationship building and dialogue with other states not simply in order to tackle mass atrocities and external aggression. Rather, one should understand the case for public diplomacy as depending in part on the intrinsic value of listening to and debating the issues—in short—the interaction (e.g. Cowan and Arsenault 2008: 19; Fitzpatrick 2007: 208).

How strong is the case for dialogue over monologue? It seems clear that dialogue may *sometimes* be better than preaching. Sometimes states should not engage in public, international criticism, given that it might be counterproductive (e.g. foreclose actors from stepping back from their aggression quietly). However, an outright rejection of monologue would be mistaken. First, the case for monologue—diplomatic criticism—is stronger than is often perceived. We should judge monologue not simply by the efficacy of tackling the immediate situation, but also by the other considerations in favour of criticism that have been discussed above. For instance, if the argument above about the contribution to international norms is correct, there is a longer-term, countervailing consideration in favour of such criticism. This is often missed with the defences of dialogue. That is, the aim of diplomacy should not be simply to persuade the state in question to refrain from its abusive action—which is the goal of dialogue—but also to persuade *other* states to refrain from being abusive.

Second, although dialogue may sometimes succeed, we should be realistic about its success and the comparative success of diplomatic criticism. In many

[16] To be sure, Sharp is generally at pains to point out (e.g. 2009: 308) that the moral claims of the Diplomatic Theory of International Relations may be disputed.

cases, both will fail to tackle the immediate crisis or longer-term abuses. For instance, China might not listen to the proclamations of certain states about its human rights record. Yet it also seems unlikely that dialogue on this issue will achieve much success either. In this context, Katrin Kinzelbach (2014: 2) argues that the secretive EU–China Human Rights Dialogue has delivered little; there remains continued disagreement and there has been little long-term influence on China's compliance with human rights. On the contrary, the EU–China Human Rights Dialogue has, according to Kinzelbach (2014: 197), diluted international pressure on human rights, relegating and isolating human rights concerns from high-level political discussion. Dialogue is therefore no panacea and the likelihood of success should be judged accurately, rather than the actors holding false hope of agreement.[17]

Third, the independent value of dialogue at the international level seems weak. To return to Risse's account of communicative action discussed above, dialogue would involve both the critic and the wrongdoer negotiating about the alleged serious external aggression or mass atrocities. The preferences and interests of both actors would not be fixed: both actors would be open to be persuaded. The worry, however, is that in the sorts of cases that this book is primarily focused on—external aggression or mass atrocities—it would not be *morally desirable* for the critic to be persuaded that external aggression and/or mass atrocities are justifiable. A reasoned consensus that reaches this conclusion would be morally bankrupt. Dialogue may only be appropriate, then, for the empirical question of establishing the facts of the case, but even then, evidence that the critic possesses may be incontrovertible and so they should *not* be persuaded to accept the unacceptable. Dialogue may seem more valuable when the normative case is ambiguous; reasoned consensus may then be of value. But any value of such consensus will not stem from the process of dialogue *itself*. As Risse (2000) notes, dialogue in the international system is far from the Habermasian Ideal Speech situation given, for instance, entrenched inequalities. As such, it seems implausible to hold that international dialogue is intrinsically valuable, even if the better argument does win through.

Fourth, and perhaps most importantly, dialogue and diplomatic criticism are not necessarily incompatible. Rather, as some advocates of public diplomacy (e.g. Cowan and Arsenault 2008; Gilboa 2008) note, they are appropriate for different contexts. In the longer term, dialogue can build trust and friendly relations that can be used to persuade states to shift their outlook and not to engage in mass atrocities or external aggression. In the short term, when mass atrocities or external aggression is impending or ongoing, it seems that monologue will often be preferable, since there is not the time required for

[17] This is not to deny that such dialogue should often be tried, compared to doing nothing; my point is that it should not foreclose the case for more robust critique.

relationship building and persuasion. In addition, dialogue and monologue may run continuously, so that the state or other body both publicly repudiates and tries to persuade privately at the diplomatic level. And, on occasion, dialogue may have been tried and have failed, and so it becomes necessary to resort to monologue. To that extent, dialogue can often be seen as a plausible option of 'Best Resort' (see section 10.4), that is, a (longer-term) option to be tried before resorting to war or other more coercive options. This is still consistent with holding that diplomatic criticism should also often be launched on occasion before more coercive options, and even sometimes instead of dialogue, when dialogue is unlikely to be successful.

5.4 MEDIATION

Mediation involves the engagement of the belligerents by a third party, who listens to grievances and explains how interests and identities may be realized by changing the behaviour to avoid the impending action, as well as, on occasion, offering incentives and the threat of political (and other) sanctions.[18] Notable successful mediation efforts include the African Union-led mediation effort in Kenya in 2008 in response to the violence after the election, the mediation in Kyrgyzstan in 2010 by the UN Regional Centre for the Preventive Diplomacy for Central Asia after intercommunal violence, and efforts by the African Union and ECOWAS (Economic Community of West African States) to resolve the conflict in Guinea in 2009–10 (Welsh 2015: 105). Conducting diplomacy quietly through mediation gives states a means of changing their behaviour without losing public face. Mediators, G. R. Berridge (2010: 236) argues, need to be impartial in the dispute. Being a public critic of one of the parties would seem to potentially undermine this impartiality. This might seem to undermine my case for diplomatic criticism.

Yet, in similar vein to the point made above about dialogue and monologue, mediation and criticism may be compatible. Where appropriate, it may be that mediators should *threaten* to criticize publicly (along with other potential incentives and sanctions). This gives the offending state(s) a chance to redress their behaviour before they face the criticism. To that extent, mediation is rightly seen as part of the toolkit of preventive diplomacy, to be considered before crises develop (although may still sometimes be used in the midst of them, such as the mediation efforts in Kenya in 2008 after post-electoral violence). Indeed, it might be viewed, like dialogue, as a plausible option of

[18] Mediation concerns third-party involvement and therefore differs from negotiation, which concerns the encounter between parties attempting to resolve their dispute (Welsh 2015: 104).

Best Resort to generally (if not always) be tried before resorting to war or other more coercive options.

To be sure, mediation also faces challenges. It can be difficult to find an acceptable mediator who is perceived as sufficiently impartial, belligerents sometimes may not be willing to enter into negotiations just yet because, for instance, they see it as more profitable to continue fighting, and it can be difficult for the mediator to maintain impartiality in the face of the belligerent that has committed mass atrocities (Welsh 2015; also see Evans 2008: 106–11). In addition, although mediation is often framed as non-coercive, effective mediation may often require significant levels of coercion of the belligerents. For instance, in Kenya, domestic actors were threatened with visa bans and cuts to aid, and even with force (Welsh 2015: 112).[19]

5.5 THE CUTTING AND DOWNGRADING OF DIPLOMATIC TIES

Let us now consider the case instead for the significant downgrading and severance of diplomatic ties with the state engaged in mass atrocities or external aggression.

There are, on the face of it, two immediate, potential attractions of cutting and downgrading diplomatic relations. First, by distancing oneself from the offending state, states can make it clear that they view the wrongdoing as illegitimate. This could seemingly help in furthering some of the central reasons to engage in diplomatic criticism: it might be thought to increase pressure on the wrongdoers by delegitimizing them and to make it clear that the wrongdoing contravenes morally important international norms. Second, and related to the above, cutting ties may be thought to remove any potential complicity in the wrongdoing. The sanctioning state cannot be said to condone or enable the wrongdoing. By contrast, if states maintain their presence within aggressors (and vice versa), the wrongdoing may be perceived to be condoned. To the extent that such presence provides aggressors with a veneer of legitimacy, those who maintain such presence may be viewed as enabling the maintenance of the wrongdoing (which withdrawal would redress) and so be complicit in it.

However, there are notable countervailing worries with the cutting and downgrading of ties. On the one hand, diplomatic criticism *already* makes it clear that the wrongdoer should be delegitimized and morally important norms have been violated. The cutting and downgrading of ties seem likely to contribute little in this regard. Indeed, Krain finds that these measures do

[19] See, further, Brahimi and Ahmed (2008) on the 'seven deadly sins' of mediation, which need to be avoided by mediators.

little to make things better 'and under particular conditions may even make things worse' (2014: 46–7). Krain posits, in similar vein to my point here, that diplomatic disengagement fails to work because it does little to raise the costs for wrongdoers, beyond the implicit threats and the delegitimation that already comes from naming and shaming.

On the other hand, the cutting and downgrading of ties may be counterproductive in terms of addressing the immediate wrongdoing. The withdrawal of ambassadors and the cutting of diplomatic ties can lead to a loss of intelligence and could reduce the ability of the sanctioning state to communicate to the aggressor the complaint that they have and to make it clear what needs to be done in order to redress or prevent further wrongdoing. This is because one of the primary roles of an embassy is to communicate between the sender and the target state, in order to explain decisions and to forge relationships (Maller 2010: 66; see further Berridge 2010: 103–24). For instance, Tara Maller (2009) argues that the US cutting and downgrading of ties in Afghanistan and Sudan in 1989 was counterproductive for its counterterrorism policy. In the case of Afghanistan, the decision to cut democratic ties weakened the US's ability to achieve accurate decision-making in response to the rise of Osama bin Laden and the Taliban, and missed the chance to strengthen the moderate sectors of Afghani society (Maller 2009: 517–25). In the case of Sudan, diplomatic disengagement led to a lack of sufficient reliable intelligence on Sudan and ultimately to the misguided Al Shifa strikes that strengthened anti-US feeling amongst radicals (Maller 2009: 525–9).

Moreover, the cutting and downgrading of ties may also have longer-term implications for the relations between agents, making it harder to achieve changes in the wrongdoer to avoid future instances of mass atrocities and serious external aggression. In other words, diplomatic disengagement can undermine the potential for dialogue, which, as noted above, may be beneficial in the long term. As Maller (2009: 513) argues, diplomatic ties provide a means by which a state can engage in public diplomacy to project a positive image of the state abroad and to provide channels of communication to work out differences and to resolve conflicts before they escalate. Continued engagement is required for a clear articulation of interests, as well as to enable parties to humanize each other, to build trust, and to foster greater understanding (Maller 2009: 530).

5.6 THE DENIAL OF MEMBERSHIP OF AN INTERNATIONAL OR REGIONAL BODY

The final diplomatic measure to consider is the expulsion or suspension of an aggressor from membership of an international or regional body. For instance, in 2002 the Commonwealth suspended Robert Mugabe's Zimbabwe because of its human rights abuses. In 2011, Syria was suspended from the Arab League. Similarly, Libya was suspended in 2011 from the Human Rights Council, following a vote in the General Assembly. A variant of this measure is to refuse candidate membership of an international or regional body. For instance, in October 2016 states voted against giving Russia a seat on the Human Rights Council because of its role in Syria. This was the first time that a permanent member of the UN Security Council had been denied a seat.

The denial of membership of an international body can harm the perceived legitimacy of the suspended state (ICISS 2001: 31), making it clear that it is viewed as disreputable in the eyes of the international community or at least the relevant organization. It makes it clear that the international community or organization disapproves strongly of the state's behaviour and signals that it needs to amend this in order to be a full member of international society. Expulsion can also undermine the target state more materially, as it loses technical and financial assistance (ICISS 2001: 31).

There are some concerns, though, with this measure. In his account of the history of expulsions, Louis Sohn (1964) argues that they have had little positive effect. This is in part, he argues, because the expelled states were often still included in international society in other ways and so were not fully isolated and delegitimized. Moreover, the expelled regime may *already* be isolated and delegitimized, and perhaps become insulated. According to Gareth Evans, the expulsion of Mugabe from the Commonwealth 'left Robert Mugabe profoundly unmoved' (2008: 112). There is also the possibility that the suspension or expulsion will, like the cutting of diplomatic ties, undermine key means of communication.

However, these concerns are not grave. Lines of communication might still be maintained on a bilateral basis. And, apart from exceptions when a state won't be delegitimized or is already delegitimized, denying membership of an international body does seem to be an exceptionally clear and obvious way that an international body can register its disapproval of the regime and pressurize it. And even if denying membership won't isolate or delegitimize a state further, it can more broadly reinforce relevant norms in the longer term, such as around mass atrocities. Denying an international stage to abusers and aggressors is important if the international community is to uphold norms against mass atrocities and aggression. For these reasons, then, the denial of membership should often be pursued.

5.7 CONCLUSION

This chapter has considered the case for diplomatic measures to tackle mass atrocities and serious external aggression. I have defended the case for diplomatic criticism, in order to criticize offenders in order to tackle the situation at hand, to contribute to the relevant global norms, and to punish. The cutting and downgrading of political ties should generally (if not always) be eschewed, although the denial of membership of an international body is often justifiable. Dialogue and mediation may sometimes be appropriate, but this does not mean that international criticism is inappropriate. Indeed, the case for such criticism is stronger than it may first appear, since the instrumental case for dialogue also faces problems, the non-instrumental case for dialogue seems weak, and monologue may be compatible with dialogue and mediation.

The practical recommendations that follow from this analysis are clear: states and other actors should publicly denounce external aggression and mass atrocities much more than they do. To that extent, diplomatic criticism is a central means of helping to fulfil the R2P and for tackling serious external aggression by states and non-state actors. Along with the other forms of sanctions defended in the previous two chapters—particularly some targeted sanctions regimes and arms embargoes—diplomatic criticism is often a plausible and desirable alternative and addition to other measures.

6

Non-violent Resistance

The previous chapters have defended three forms of sanctions: economic sanctions (especially targeted economic sanctions), military sanctions (in the form of arms embargoes), and diplomatic sanctions (specifically, naming and shaming). This chapter moves away from sanctions to consider non-violent measures. It will focus on two measures: civilian peacekeeping and civilian defence. Whilst civilian defence comprises various non-violent measures to oppose external aggressors, civilian peacekeeping involves civilians attempting to tackle human rights abuses and even mass atrocities. The most notable method of civilian peacekeeping is 'international protective accompaniment' by groups such as Peace Brigades International and Non-violent Peaceforce. This involves unarmed bodyguards protecting potentially threatened groups or individuals by deterring abuses, or if abuses occur, reporting them.[1]

My aim in this chapter is straightforward: to defend civilian peacekeeping and, to a lesser extent, civilian defence. Although both measures have sizeable limitations, I will argue that they can play *some* role in tackling conflict, human rights abuses, and mass atrocities. Notwithstanding, I will also make it clear that these non-violent options should not generally be undertaken *at the expense of* more coercive ones, such as traditional peacekeeping and military defence, but instead sometimes used *in addition to* these methods. To that extent, in contrast to some of the defenders of civilian peacekeeping who are highly critical of military peacekeeping or humanitarian intervention (e.g. Carriere 2010; Wallace 2017), I do not deny the need for traditional peacekeeping and intervention (and national defence) *as well.*

The chapter will proceed as follows. Section 6.1 will delineate civilian peacekeeping. Section 6.2 will present the prima facie case for civilian peacekeeping

[1] These two measures are frequently seen as non-violent. However, other measures we will consider (such as positive incentives, humanitarian aid, and accepting refugees) may also be viewed as non-violent, given that they may often not be significantly, directly harmful. Also recall that I focus on *international* non-violent methods; for a recent analysis of the ethics of domestic non-violence, see Parkin (2017).

by considering the relative advantages of civilian peacekeeping over humanitarian intervention and traditional forms of peacekeeping. In section 6.3, I will consider three objections to civilian peacekeeping and will argue that, if civilian peacekeeping were upscaled, it could face several problems, which would resemble some of the problems facing military peacekeeping and humanitarian intervention. In section 6.4, I turn to consider the case for civilian defence. In doing so, I will consider the objection that this measure fails to work in response to a ruthless opponent, but suggest that this does not repudiate fully the case for civilian defence.

6.1 WHAT IS CIVILIAN PEACEKEEPING?

Civilian peacekeeping is 'the prevention of direct violence through influence or control of the behaviour of potential perpetrators by unarmed civilians who are deployed on the ground' (Schweitzer 2010: 9). The most frequently undertaken activities in civilian peacekeeping are international protective accompaniment and observing and reporting human rights abuses (Janzen 2014). As noted above, international protective accompaniment involves 'unarmed bodyguards, often spending twenty-four hours a day with human rights workers, union leaders, peasant groups, and other popular organizations who face mortal danger from death squads and state forces' (Mahony 1997: 208). Other activities include inter-positioning between fighting forces, negotiation and dialogue with the relevant actors, relationship building, solidarity actions, rumour control, early warning, and training (Nonviolent Peaceforce 2014: 3; Schirch 2006: 31–40; Schweitzer 2010: 11–12).

Civilian peacekeeping differs *somewhat*, but not *altogether*, from UN peacekeeping and from the roles played by other non-state actors before, during, and after conflict, such as certain journalists, human rights advocacy groups, and humanitarian organizations. On the one hand, unlike many of the more well-known contemporary manifestations of UN peacekeeping, which have received a Chapter VII mandate from the UN Security Council to use coercive means to militarily ensure the protection of civilians, civilian peacekeeping is non-military and comparatively non-coercive. It clearly differs, for instance, from the UN's 'Intervention Brigade' in the Democratic Republic of the Congo, which has a mandate to use force to coerce spoilers. However, although the UN's more coercive peace operations, such as in the Democratic Republic of the Congo, attract much more attention, there are still several UN peace operations, such as the missions in the Western Sahara (MINURSO), the Israel–Syria border (UNDOF), and Cyprus (UNFICYP), which do not involve the direct use of military force. These are somewhat similar to civilian peacekeeping and several of the arguments I present for civilian peacekeeping will also apply to them. Similarly, several of the roles played by humanitarian organizations and human rights advocacy groups can resemble that of civilian peacekeeping. For instance, the presence of humanitarian aid workers in a refugee camp may help to deter attacks on the camp. These may be unintended but welcomed effects of these organizations' main objectives or secondary, subsidiary ones. Unlike for civilian peacekeeping organizations, however, protective accompaniment is not their *primary* intention.

Thus far, civilian peacekeeping has been on a relatively small scale. According to Randy Janzen (2014), the exact numbers of civilian peacekeepers is difficult to determine, but around fifty organizations have engaged in unarmed civilian peacekeeping since 1990, with a significant recent rise. Civilian peacekeeping is also largely new. It mostly developed in the 1980s, largely in Latin America with the work of Peace Brigades International, the best-known organization. Founded in 1981, Peace Brigades International focuses on non-partisan protective accompaniment and it has served in Nicaragua (1983), Guatemala (1983–99; 2002–present), El Salvador (1987–92), Sri Lanka (1989–98), North America (1992–9), Haiti (1992–2001), Colombia (1994–present), Mexico (1995–present), Indonesia (2000–11), Nepal (2005–present), Kenya (2013–present), and Honduras (2013–present).

There are differences between civilian peacekeeping organizations, such as variations in the importance given to being non-partisan, avoiding interfering in the situation, and obeying the law (Coy 2012). For instance, Christian Peacemaker Teams and the International Solidarity Movement are much more partisan in their interventions: in addition to international protective accompaniment, they engage in solidarity activities, such as by rebuilding destroyed homes, dismantling barricades and blockades, organizing demonstrations, and even engaging in civil disobedience (Coy 2012: 971). Note that I will focus on *international* civilian peacekeeping. Protective accompaniment may also be provided by local organizations (or have a local element to it), but my focus is on the international element (as with the other measures considered thus far).

Civilian peacekeeping has had some notable successes. For instance, Tim Wallis (2010: 30), the former Executive Director of Nonviolent Peaceforce and International Secretary of Peace Brigades International, documents the success of protective accompaniment in Nicaragua during the 1980s. The mission began when several US citizens went to border towns in Nicaragua to investigate the effects of the Reagan Administration's funding of the Contras. They found that, contrary to what they had expected, there were no attacks on civilians. The villagers told them that as long as 'you're here they are not going to attack us'. The Americans reportedly responded, 'oh, if that's really the case, then we'll stay here and we'll get more people, and we'll stop them attacking you!' Subsequently, over the next seven years, Witness for Peace (a civilian peacekeeping organization) sent thousands of US citizens to Nicaragua.

The presence of these Americans meant that the Contras could not attack due to the risk of killing American citizens, given that they were being funded by the US. So, they stopped attacking the villages. More generally, many organizations have noted that there have been immediate shifts in the treatment of human rights activists once civilian peacekeepers have been deployed (Janzen 2014). Indeed, in 2004, Peace Brigades International reported that *no* human rights activist accompanied on a one-to-one basis by one of their civilian peacekeepers had been killed in the last two decades (Schirch 2006: 57).

How is civilian peacekeeping—and particularly international protective accompaniment—successful in the face of violence? As Christine Schweitzer, one of the founders of the International Balkan Peace Team, notes, '[m]any people find it hard to understand what an unarmed peacekeeper can achieve in a violent environment... [T]hey cannot shoot and kill attacking perpetrators... Unarmed peacekeepers do, however, have their own sources of power' (2010: 13). These include the moral authority that comes with using non-violent methods in the face of violence. More precisely, protective accompaniment works by changing the perceived costs of using violence, since aggressors 'typically see a higher political cost in using violence around foreigners' (Mahony 1997: 210). These costs include the reporting of international misdeeds globally, which can lead to direct or indirect repercussions, including pressure on the supporters of perpetrators (Schweitzer 2010: 13). It is important to highlight here that what matters is the *perception* of such costs: '[i]f they believe foreign witnesses will produce international political consequences, then any foreigners may play some protective role, whether or not they can really produce such consequences' (Mahony 1997: 212). Beyond affecting strategic calculations, international civilian peacekeeping can also help with long-term stability by emphasizing the potential role played by non-violence, such as by developing cultures of peace (Janzen 2014).

More generally, non-violent methods often work and, contrary to much popular opinion, often work *better* than violent ones. This has been documented recently in the influential work of Maria Stephan and Erica Chenoweth (2008) on civil resistance movements (also see Chenoweth and Stephan 2011). They find that major non-violent campaigns are *six* times more likely to be successful than violent campaigns facing repression. The reasons they give include non-violent movements' increased legitimacy and, in turn, participation rates. They also include the fact that regime violence against non-violence can lead to higher costs for the regime, such as increasing solidarity with the resistance movement, defections, and external support for the opposition.[2]

[2] To be sure, the success of non-violent movements since 2010 has fallen, seemingly because oppressors are increasingly recognizing the power of them and so doing more to counteract them, including violence, counter-movements, and infiltration (Chenoweth 2017). They are still much more successful, though, than violent movements, whose success rate has also fallen.

This builds on the work of Gene Sharp (four-times nominated for the Nobel Peace Prize), who, in his three-volume *The Politics of Nonviolent Action*, catalogues 198 non-violent measures, outlines how these can be used successfully, and defends the case for non-violence.[3] A central notion is what he calls 'political *jiu-jitsu*' (1973: 657–97). This concerns the process by which non-violence deals with violence. When violence is met with violence, there will often be little uproar as there is relatively little international sympathy for the fate of the belligerents. Violent responses can also often harm innocents and disenfranchise those who do not want to risk harming their fellow citizens. By contrast, violence used against non-violent groups is much more likely to delegitimize the oppressors. Both international audiences (and supporters) and members of the oppressor group are more likely to dissent. The use of violence against non-violent groups can also lead to the victims' cause being viewed more favourably. As a result, there can be increased domestic support, as sympathy and resolve from others leads them to join or support the cause. Thus, '*[t]heir nonviolence helps the opponent's repression to throw him off balance politically. The nonviolent group is also able to gain far more support and power than if it had met violence with violence*' (Sharp 1973: 658). As violent groups become aware of these effects, they may become less willing to use force in the first place, for fear of repercussions.

6.2 THE PRIMA FACIE CASE FOR CIVILIAN PEACEKEEPING

To show the prima facie case for civilian peacekeeping, and particularly protective accompaniment, this section will outline how it appears to be comparatively advantageous to military peacekeeping and humanitarian intervention on the Pragmatic Approach.[4]

First, humanitarian intervention and military peacekeeping often harm innocents. This is sometimes through the direct use of force, such as through bombing campaigns that cause collateral damage, or through indirect effects that can arise with the presence of an intervening military force, such as prostitution rings, human trafficking, and dramatic changes to the local economy and cost of living. The worry in both cases is not simply a consequentialist

[3] An updated list of methods to include digital forms of non-violent resistance has been compiled by Mary Joyce and Patrick Meier, available here: digital-activism.org/projects/cr20/.

[4] Some of the objections to humanitarian intervention are presented by Roland Paris (2014) as the 'structural problems' of humanitarian intervention that, he claims, ultimately render the R2P doctrine as 'fated to flounder'.

one about the foreseeable problematic, unintended effects of humanitarian intervention and military peacekeeping. It is also deontological in that the intervening parties *do* harm. That is, even if they are effective all things considered, they still *do* harm. By contrast, given that it does not involve any violent methods, protective accompaniment seems to do no harm, or at least do no *direct* harm using military force. Recall that, an important (if not unduly weighty) consideration for the Pragmatic Approach is how the measure fares according to the difference between doing and allowing of harm. Thus, there is some reason to favour protective accompaniment.

Second, both military peacekeeping and humanitarian intervention can face unrealistic expectations about what can be achieved by the operation on the part of those enduring the current crisis and of the international community more generally. Intervening forces are often expected to make significant, visible increases in civilian protection across vast areas, yet lack sufficient troop numbers or equipment to be able to achieve this. They are also often judged according to much more ambitious political goals, rather than whether they contribute to improving civilian protection. Moreover, situations can deteriorate further whilst intervening forces are in the field. Although such operations may still be effective (indeed, I think they are—see Pattison 2010), this is often only counterfactually—the situation would have been even worse without the intervening forces. Establishing their effectiveness can therefore be difficult. This leads to significant contestation about humanitarian intervention and ultimately weakens support for the measure, which probably in turn influences its likely actual effectiveness (the central consideration, recall, on the Pragmatic Approach).

By contrast, the apparent success of international protective accompaniment can be more easily demonstrated. It depends, in part, on whether the specific individuals accompanied have been killed or subject to various abuses, which is easier to establish than showing that human rights abuses have been prevented across vast areas. To be sure, counterfactual assessments may be required to prove, in reality, that protective accompaniment was in fact successful, given that the protected individual may not have been killed. However, even if the counterfactual judgement is questioned, protective accompaniment is not simply about tackling *objective* threats to individuals and groups, but also about improving *subjective* perceptions of security. That is, civilian peacekeepers can reduce the subjective perceptions of insecurity of such individuals and groups that can lead to them being too fearful to engage in their human rights activism. As Liam Mahony (1997: 210) argues, international protective accompaniment provides encouragement to engage in activism, regardless of whether the accompaniment actually protects people from anything—it helps them overcome the long-term fear installed by statist terror.

Third, troop-contributing countries often contribute troops to UN peace operations only for financial reasons. It may also be that the particular soldiers involved agree to such operations only out of purely self-interested reasons, such as those related to financial incentives. By contrast, it seems that civilian peacekeepers are *more likely* to be motivated by altruistic reasons *in the overall balance of reasons* than regular soldiers.[5] There may be exceptions where regular soldiers may overall be better motivated (or even solely by altruism) and there may be civilian peacekeepers who are motivated largely by self-interest. But even if both civilian peacekeepers and regular soldiers possess mixed motives, it seems that altruism is likely to be a weightier reason, in the overall balance of reasons, for civilian peacekeepers. For instance, members of Witness for Peace and Christian Peacemaker Teams have been reported to be motivated out of a spiritual desire to confront violence non-violently, and other groups have cited their members' humanitarian motives and the desire to help people in need (Schirch 2006: 82). Similarly, Matthew Eddy's (2011) study of the International Solidarity Movement highlights the import of volunteers' construction of a cosmopolitan identity.

Fourth, it is sometimes claimed that humanitarian intervention and peace operations rely on soldiers who, even if not conscripts, have signed up to risk their lives only to provide national defence, not to protect the lives of those beyond the borders of the state (Cook 2000). Such operations are therefore a form of conscription in that they require soldiers to fight wars to which they have not agreed. Although this argument is overstated, since many regular soldiers do seem to sign up to fight in peace operations (Baker and Pattison 2012), a few still might not. By contrast, *all* the members of civilian peacekeeping forces are volunteers (in the sense that they are not conscripted and fully agree to the risks; some are paid) and often from states where they have several other reasonable options, rendering their consent sufficiently free. As such, civilian peacekeeping may distribute fairly its internal burdens, since those facing these burdens clearly consent to them (as argued in section 3.4.1, placing burdens on those who consent to them can be fair).

It seems, therefore, that there is a strong prima facie case for protective accompaniment. It appears to have several potential, notable advantages over military peacekeeping and humanitarian intervention.

[5] This is relevant on the Pragmatic Approach the extent to which having individuals rightly motivated means that civilian peacekeeping is likely to be effective, that is, the extent to which motives are instrumentally justified. The importance of this might be best seen in the negative: measures that rely on individuals with problematic motives might be likely to run into several issues, such as those faced by the reliance on mercenaries or private military and security companies, including that those involved will commit human rights abuses and refuse to obey the relevant authority when this contravenes their interests (see Pattison 2014*b*).

6.3 OBJECTIONS TO CIVILIAN PEACEKEEPING

Thus far, I have painted a rosy picture of civilian peacekeeping. I will now consider three potential objections to it.

6.3.1 The Privilege Objection

The first objection, which I will call the 'Privilege Objection', is that protective accompaniment is premised upon, and reinforces, privilege, potentially including racism. The objection stems from the fact that 'outsiders are often seen as more effective peacekeepers than insiders because of the power of their Western passports, their white skin, and/or their ability to be impartial' (Schirch 2006: 52). To that extent, Patrick Coy (2011) discusses the example of 'George', a veteran of multiple Peace Brigades International teams, who responds to the question, 'if there is violence all around, who is going to protect you?' Coy reports that '[w]ithout missing a beat he raised the bare underbelly of his forearm to the group, and with his other hand he pinched a gathering of the pale skin there to highlight it and said simply, "My white skin"' (2011). The privileged status of civilian peacekeepers is also often influential in obtaining access in the first place (Boothe and Smithey 2007: 46). In addition, civilian peacekeeping may be claimed to reinforce prejudice (which gives rise to privilege to the beneficiaries) and, in particular, racist attitudes by highlighting that white skin renders one immune from attack and darker skin renders one more dispensable.

Given these sorts of concerns about relying upon and reinforcing prejudice (and in turn privilege), Coy (2011) notes that many members of Peace Brigades International felt extremely uncomfortable. The issue is not limited to Peace Brigades International, however. Coy (2011) suggests that this has been a problem for *all* international accompaniment organizations in the past and will be in the future. This is because such organizations 'can never operate completely outside the prevailing dynamics of race and privilege that still permeate the social and political systems within which accompaniment is applied' (Coy 2011). That is, where there are white Westerners performing protective accompaniment, or simply even Western organizations employing civilian peacekeepers, the underlying dynamics of race are likely to be present, often through colonial legacies or the systemic privilege of the West.

Although the Privilege Objection is potentially serious, it is not as worrisome as it may first seem. First, some of the reliance on racist attitudes and privilege more generally has been reduced (if not eliminated altogether for all organizations). This is because many organizations, including Peace Brigades International, are now much more ethnically diverse and use uniforms, rather than simply their white skin colour, to demarcate themselves (Coy 2011). They also employ more local staff. For instance, Nonviolent Peaceforce (2014: 7) report that 41 per cent of their staff are from the host state.[6] In addition to those who come from the host state (such as South Sudan), many of the internationals are from developing countries in Africa and Asia.

Second, as Coy (2011) documents, some members of Peace Brigades International argue (quite plausibly) that international protective accompaniment subverts status quo relations because white people become the escorts, rather than the stars of the show. This is particularly the case for non-partisan groups such as Peace Brigades International, given that they do not direct any of the activism. The protective accompaniment is often based on solidarity rather than usurpation (Boothe and Smithey 2007: 42).

Third, even if reliant on racist attitudes (or privilege more generally), international protective accompaniment may be morally justifiable on occasion if there are much greater benefits achieved overall. International protective accompaniment may not reinforce racism (or privilege) and may do much to undermine it in the long run, even if it is somewhat reliant on racist attitudes to do so in the first place. Indeed, protective accompaniment often attempts to protect human rights activists who defend moral equality and this may be much more important in challenging racism and other prejudices (Schirch 2006: 57).

6.3.2 The Supererogation Objection

The second objection, the 'Supererogation Objection', is that civilian peacekeeping—and in particular international protective accompaniment—cannot be defended as anything more than supererogatory. This is a worry because it may be wrong then to claim that this is a policy that *should* be put in place, as an alternative or addition to other means of tackling human rights abuses. The objection, in brief, is as follows: (1) International protective accompaniment largely relies on, in effect, people willing to be human shields. (2) Individuals cannot be morally *required* to be human shields since this seems far too demanding. They are in the field without any weapons to defend themselves. (3) Protective accompaniment therefore relies on supererogatory action and, as a result, cannot be prescribed.

To be sure, prescriptions may still be made whilst there are sufficient volunteers. For instance, we can say that various actors in the international community should try to encourage and support the volunteers as far as

[6] The issue may still not be resolved though. Boothe and Smithey (2007: 51–2) claim that, despite some improvements, certain organizations pay insufficient attention to the role of privilege in their training of staff.

possible. But, if protective accompaniment is to be expanded, it will need many more high-quality volunteers, which the organizations may find difficult to obtain. The issue could be resolved by significantly incentivizing protective accompaniment. At the moment, some civilian peacekeepers are paid a wage; this could be significantly increased. Yet this risks protective accompaniment facing many of the problems that arise with the use of financially motivated private actors in a conflict zone, such as that of mercenary motive (see Pattison 2014*b*).

Alternatively, civilian peacekeepers may be conscripted. On the face of it, this may seem abhorrent. Yet, it is widely thought (e.g. Galston 2003; Klosko 2005; Rawls 1999*a*) that conscription for wars of self-defence may be, on occasion, morally permissible, if absolutely necessary. It also seems that it may be occasionally permissible to use conscription for humanitarian intervention (Baker and Pattison 2012; Lefkowitz 2011; Pattison 2013). If individuals can be conscripted permissibly to defend fellow nationals, it may also seem that they may, on occasion, be conscripted to defend those beyond their borders. Even when conscripted, soldiers will be subject to notable risks, states and—more generally—third parties may still be able to permissibly subject their soldiers to such risk. This is if they will be able to save a much greater number of innocent individuals, such as when using a conscripted army to halt a genocide. Suppose, for instance, that in 1994 François Mitterrand could have used France's conscript armed forces to intervene militarily much earlier and more effectively that it did in response to the Rwandan genocide (and suppose that the French conscripts would not have given their consent to the operation). Even if the humanitarian intervention would have been very costly for some of the soldiers (for instance, death was likely for some), Mitterrand still could have permissibly ordered the intervention (and perhaps was obliged to do so). In such cases, any fiduciary obligations owed by a leader to his or her soldiers are outweighed by the greater moral import of saving a large number of lives by using the conscript army.

Hence, the consent and interests of soldiers should not be given overwhelming weight in a leader's deliberations when they decide whether to order intervention. It may seem that similar arguments provide the case for conscription for protective accompaniment. That is, the consent and interests of potential civilian peacekeepers should not be given *overwhelming* weight in third parties' deliberations in the case for protective accompaniment. Note, though, that the form of conscription differs. Conscription for civilian peacekeeping would not force individuals into becoming *combatants*. The civilian peacekeepers would still be civilians since they would not engage in combat. As such, the risks to them will often not be likely anywhere near as high as they are when individuals are conscripted to be soldiers. In other words, the potential conscription would not be *military* service, but rather would be compulsory *civilian* service, albeit international and somewhat risky. Moreover, Randy

Janzen (2014) finds that the fatality rate for UN peacekeeping mission staff is more than twelve times higher than that of civilian peacekeepers. This may be because political *jiu-jitsu* works or, instead, because civilian peacekeepers tend to operate in situations where they are less likely to be subject to attack.[7]

There is, however, an obvious worry with the case for conscription for civilian peacekeeping: the potential benefits of protective accompaniment seem to be of insufficient weight to render permissible conscription. There will not be enough vulnerable people protected to outweigh the wrongness of forcing individuals to be civilian peacekeepers, who are potentially at significant risk and, even if not, are forced to give up their own pursuits and take on significant hardships in the field.

Could instead the second premise of the Supererogation Objection be disputed? That is, could it be denied that being a civilian peacekeeper is only supererogatory? On the one hand, it may seem that being a civilian peacekeeper could, on occasion, be morally *required* if we hold that individuals are under an enforceable duty to protect vulnerable populations, when this can be done at relatively small cost. This may mean that they are required to even volunteer to be a human shield, if this is not too costly. (Note that by 'human shield', I simply mean someone whose presence deters an attack on another. It is a further question whether the individual consents to being a human shield or whether they are used by state or non-state actors.) Consider the following case:

> *Human Shield*: Alan is trying to kill Barbara. Christine can save Barbara by placing herself in front of Barbara, since she knows that Alan would be very unlikely to attack her. He has always had a crush on her and would not want to be violent in front of her.

One might think that Christine has a duty to act as a human shield, given that the risks to her are quite small. This might even be the case if there are *some*, albeit small risks, to Christine, such as if Alan has been drinking heavily and there is a small risk that he may become violent. To that extent, individuals may be morally required to be human shields on occasion.[8]

However, there are two countervailing problems with applying this to protective accompaniment. The first is that the costs to particular peacekeepers do seem likely to be often much greater than the peacekeepers can be reasonably required to bear. In addition to the risk of harm (even if the risk is not actually that high), there is significant bravery required, in addition to

[7] To be sure, there are more attacks on civilian peacekeepers perceived to be partisan, such as members of the International Solidarity Movement (see Coy 2012).

[8] For a defence of the (exceptional) permissibility of using human shields in war, see Fabre (2012: 256–67). Much of Fabre's case depends on the chances of the human shields living a minimally decent life being improved by this use. By contrast, my point here relies simply on human shields' duty to rescue. Also see Gross (2014) for a defence of the use of human shields.

discomfort, and cost borne by civilian peacekeepers. For protective accompaniment to be effective, it is vital that peacekeepers maintain their presence in the face of danger—this is in order to show the inefficacy of intimidation or violence in halting civilian peacekeeping (Schirch 2006: 47). In addition to risks in the field, being a civilian peacekeeper can involve quite significant hardship. Coy (2011) reports that Peace Brigades International members had to pay their own travel expenses, and received only limited health care and a stipend of $50 per month; in return, they put themselves at physical risk whilst working in a stressful, demanding job, living together with foreign nationals in a building that also doubled up as an office. (That said, and as noted above, many civilian peacekeepers are now paid a wage.)

The second problem is that, even if there is a duty to be a civilian peacekeeper, this does not seem to be a duty that could be permissibly enforced, at least at the moment. This is because there are not currently the accompanying institutional structures to render this permissible. NGOs are not appropriate agents to force individuals to be peacekeepers. States, for various reasons, can sometimes legitimately use coercive measures, but do not tend to engage in civilian peacekeeping. Even if they did, they would be morally required to develop institutional structures to render conscription for civilian peacekeeping permissible (such as a lottery to determine who is required to be a peacekeeper, in similar vein to jury service). They would also be required to show that alternative measures to increase the number of civilian peacekeepers, such as those considered below, would not render the resort to the draft redundant.

Hence, it seems that the Supererogation Objection is largely valid and can, at best, only be ameliorated, at least for the foreseeable future. The following steps might be taken to ameliorate the problems. More volunteers could be encouraged by, for instance, publicizing civilian peacekeeping and the need for volunteers. More expenses could be paid to cover training and travel. Civilian peacekeeping could also become more professionalized, increasingly being seen as a career option, even if it is not directly incentivized with high wages or other similar benefits. Other costs to volunteers could also be reduced as far as possible, such as risks in the field and lengths of service in the field, so that volunteers are encouraged and, in time, civilian peacekeeping may become morally required of individuals.

6.3.3 The Limited Use Objection

The third objection, which I will call the 'Limited Use Objection', is that civilian peacekeeping cannot achieve much. It is limited only to cases, first, when governments do not reject the presence of civilian peacekeeping. Access may often be revoked when, for instance, the state is repressive. Second, it is unlikely to work in situations of major conflict, where belligerents have few scruples about using force against international peacekeepers. In such situations, civilian peacekeepers may be killed indiscriminately, along with those whom they are trying to protect. Thus, Lisa Schirch (2006: 98–9) notes that there are no recent examples of successful civilian peacekeeping where there is high-intensity, widespread, decentralized fighting with massive numbers of troops and large-scale weaponry.

Is the Limited Use Objection correct? On the one hand, these limitations clearly demonstrate that protective accompaniment may not always work and cannot fully replace more coercive options, most notably humanitarian intervention. As I will reiterate further below, even though civilian peacekeeping is desirable, humanitarian intervention and military peacekeeping may still sometimes be morally permissible (and required). On the other hand, such limitations should not be overstated; they may sometimes not apply.

First, civilian peacekeepers can work without the express consent of the government (even if civilian peacekeepers still seek it) and are often better placed to negotiate access. This is because governments may not perceive them to be a major threat, given that they are unarmed, and so find less reason to oppose them than a military presence by peacekeeping or intervening forces.

Second, although civilian peacekeeping may not work in areas where there is major, ongoing fighting, it may still work in areas where there is still conflict but at a lower level of intensity. For instance, Nonviolent Peaceforce has operated in South Sudan, despite the ongoing, brutal civil war, with tens of thousands being estimated to have been killed. Nonviolent Peaceforce report that they provided international protective accompaniment for vulnerable civilians, such as women at risk of sexual violence and for internally displaced persons, and stayed on even whilst many humanitarian organizations pulled out (and provided protection for them) (Easthom 2014: 11). They also report that they have protected 31,160 children at risk, extracted 33 civilians from areas where mass atrocities were ongoing, saved the lives of 'dozens of civilians' who were at imminent risk of being killed in an ethnically mounted attack, helped 60,000 internally displaced persons at risk of being raped, attacked, or killed (which apparently were common occurrences when they were not present), and even negotiated with gunmen to stop them shooting women and children (Easthom 2014: 11). As the latter case shows, belligerents can, in certain cases, still be influenced by the various tactics of civilian peacekeepers.

6.3.4 The Upscaling Issue

A related problem to the Limited Use Objection, as already alluded to, is that civilian peacekeeping is currently on a small scale. However, Rachel Julian and

Christine Schweitzer (2015) suggest that Nonviolent Peaceforce and other civilian peacekeeping organizations set themselves the goal of deploying enough peacekeepers to be comparable to military peacekeeping. If civilian peacekeeping were to be used more widely, which seems attractive given the benefits outlined above, it might run into some notable problems of upscaling. These problems, I will now suggest, would mean that it could face some of the similar real and perceived problems of military peacekeeping and humanitarian intervention, although, like these two options, it would still sometimes be morally permissible and perhaps even morally required in the future.

If civilian peacekeeping organizations were to become larger, they might become much more dependent on funding from particular streams. This might mean that civilian peacekeeping organizations might lose some of their independence, which is easier to maintain as a smaller organization. Decision-making might also become increasingly influenced by political concerns—even if ultimately for the greater good—and this could lead to accusations of improper motive and selectivity, as often faced by humanitarian interveners. In fact, according to Schirch (2006: 71–2), the latter is an issue that civilian peacekeepers already face. In addition, if there were more civilian peacekeepers in the field, occasional mistakes might be more likely. Mistakes could include shows of strong partisanship, which could make redundant a whole civilian peacekeeping mission that depends on non-partisanship (such as by Peace Brigades International), as a government takes a different stance and views them as activists rather than simply protectors. In addition, if there were many more civilian peacekeepers in the field, this would raise the probability of peacekeepers *doing* harm, even if unintentional, such as by distorting local practices. For instance, as Mahony notes, there is already a worry that, '[w]ith accompaniment, activists might perceive their available space as far exceeding the real space. That is, they may risk dangerous activities because of accompaniment's encouraging function' (1997: 211). A much larger presence could also mean that peacekeepers face unrealistic expectations, as various actors in the international community and those who are vulnerable think that civilian peacekeeping could achieve much more than it can. Civilian peacekeepers could also become expected—and relied upon—to do much more than they would have the ability to do.

Do these potential issues mean that civilian peacekeeping should remain on a small scale? No, since some of these potential problems may be avoided or at least minimized by careful management of expansion. For instance, an increased professional ethos being taught could reduce the risks of occasional shows of partisanship and a repeated public reiteration of the limits of civilian peacekeeping may limit some of the risks of peacekeepers being given roles beyond their capacity. And, even if these risks were to apply, they would not necessarily preclude justifiable civilian peacekeeping. To see this, it helps to note that similar problems are not, all things considered, sufficiently weighty to render impermissible humanitarian intervention and military peacekeeping that will be highly effective at improving the enjoyment of basic human rights. Indeed, military peacekeeping or humanitarian intervention may still, on occasion, be morally required because they are likely to make a significant improvement in tackling the mass violations of basic human rights, compared to doing nothing, and will be much better than any other option, including civilian peacekeeping. As already suggested, this seems particularly likely in situations where there is significant ongoing conflict. In such cases, despite some negative effects that they cause, such as risk to intervening soldiers, military peacekeeping or humanitarian intervention will *sometimes* do a lot more good overall by tackling the mass violation of basic human rights (Pattison 2010). (The efficacy of UN military peacekeeping is supported by a recent quantitative study by Lisa Hultman, Jacob Kathman, and Megan Shannon (2014). They found that UN peace operations led to a 73 per cent reduction in battlefield violence (where there is at least a 10,000 troop deployment).)[9] The same replies would be open to defenders of civilian peacekeeping, if it were to face these issues. Despite the more complex moral picture that might develop if civilian peacekeeping were upscaled significantly, it might still be morally permissible and even potentially a duty (if sufficient civilian peacekeepers could be recruited). Although civilian peacekeeping might face several further alleged problems, some of these might be only illusory and other problems might be outweighed by much greater improvements in the overall enjoyment of basic human rights.

In summary, civilian peacekeeping has several attractive features, but is unlikely to be able to replace fully the more violent options of military peacekeeping and humanitarian intervention. In more conflict-laden situations, military peacekeeping or humanitarian intervention may be the only suitable option. In situations where there are mixed levels of conflict, it may be appropriate to carry out both military peacekeeping or humanitarian intervention (in the more conflict-laden areas) *and* civilian peacekeeping (in the less conflict-laden areas). Although protective accompaniment may appear to be required in less conflict-laden situations *instead of* military peacekeeping or humanitarian intervention, this cannot yet be prescribed given the Supererogatory Objection and the fact that civilian peacekeeping is currently only on a small scale. As such, in all levels of conflict, civilian peacekeeping cannot yet be seen as a major alternative, given the Supererogatory and Limited Use Objections, even if combined with other alternatives. If it were upscaled, civilian peacekeeping might be able to take on more cases where there is lower-level conflict, but military peacekeeping or humanitarian intervention might still be required where there is more intense conflict.

[9] Also see quantitative studies by DeMeritt (2015) and Krain (2005), which defend in part the effectiveness of humanitarian intervention.

6.4 CIVILIAN DEFENCE

Let's now turn to consider civilian defence. Whereas civilian peacekeeping is most apt for responding to mass atrocities and human rights abuses, civilian defence is more appropriate for tackling external aggression. Gene Sharp provides the most influential account of this option and its potential in his monograph *Civilian-Based Defense*. According to Sharp, civilian-based defence can both deter aggressors and, even if deterrence fails, make it much harder for them to achieve their ends.[10] First, the deterring of attack involves the building of capacity of civilian-based defence, which can in turn affect the potential aggressor's perception of the society's capacity to defend itself (Sharp 1990: 87). Second, resistance involves challenging an occupying force by various means of non-cooperation and defiance (Sharp 1990: 6). Measures include boycotts, strikes, protests, paralysing transportation, economic shut-downs, denial of legitimacy, and general inefficiency (Sharp 1990: 89). This form of resistance draws on Gandhi's famous insight that 'no Government can exist for a single moment without the cooperation of the people, willing or forced, and if people suddenly withdraw their cooperation in every detail, the Government will come to a standstill' (in Miniotaite 1996: 21). If aggressors use repression against the non-violent protest to silence them, this can back-fire, resulting in political *jiu-jitsu*, to the extent that the repression increases support amongst the resistors, which in turn makes it harder for the aggressors to implement their policies (Sharp 1990: 59).[11]

Advocates of civilian defence cite examples of resistance to Nazi occupation by Danish and Norwegian citizens, Czechoslovakian resistance to the Soviet occupation in the late 1960s, and Gandhi's campaign for Indian home rule (Cady 2010: 95–6).[12] One of the clearest cases occurred in Lithuania in 1990–1, in the context of its attempt to gain independence from the USSR (Alexandra 2003). In January 1991, troops killed 14 and injured 702 people who were attempting to protect a television tower in Lithuania, but this did not result in wider reprisals. Instead, it led to the continuation of the non-violent movement and the protection of the Supreme Council from the threat of imminent attack. Reportedly, '[m]ass walls of people were able to defend strategically important objects, such as the buildings of the Supreme Council and a transmission and radio center in Kaunas' (Miniotaite 1996: 25). In late 1991, the USSR withdrew its troops and international recognition was granted to Lithuania.

[10] Sharp's focus is on both foreign invasions and internal usurpations.

[11] For an overview of the influence of proposals for civilian defence, see Roberts (2009: 10–12).

[12] Sharp (1990: 14–16) offers the examples of the German attempt to defend against the Franco-Belgian invasion in 1923 and Slovakian resistance to Soviet occupation in 1968–9.

In addition to tackling the immediate situation, advocates of civilian defence offer a second reason in favour of this measure: the move away from regular militaries and increasing civilian defence would result in fewer wars and acts of aggression in the first place, as the process of disarmament and demilitarization would engender better relations with other states. By contrast, they argue, the presence of current militaries often exacerbates tensions (such as by undermining trust and increasing security measures) and leads to arms races (Alexandra 2003: 603; Sharp 1990: 144). As Duane Cady nicely puts it, 'a country trained in and dependent on nonviolent civilian defense, a country without massive conventional and nuclear weapons and armies, is far less likely to be feared by other countries as a potential invader, and thus far less likely to be targeted by them' (2010: 90).

A third reason in favour of civilian defence concern the worries with relying on military defence and in particular that the military may prey on the society that it is meant to protect (Sharp 1990: 145). As detailed in the literature on civil–military relations, the military may undertake coups and attempt military rule, drain resources in the attempt for even greater strength against the enemies of the state, involve the state in conflicts contrary to the interests or expressed will of societal leaders, and refuse to be subject to civilian rule (Feaver 1999). Even in less serious cases, it might still influence the political process, display public opposition to the civilian rule, and refuse to comply with civilian orders (Feaver 1999: 217–22).

A fourth reason for civilian defence is that this could avoid several of the major issues that arise with fighting *wars*. These include the death of morally innocent non-combatants and combatants, destruction of infrastructure, and the poisoning of societal relations for generations. By contrast, Cady (2010) argues, non-violent civilian defence can be much more conducive to peaceful relations within the society in the long term and help to begin to create the internal order necessary for genuine peace.

The four central arguments for civilian defence are, then, that it (1) can be successful by deterring attack and resisting oppression, (2) can lead to fewer wars, (3) avoids reliance on the dangerous regular military, and (4) avoids the harms of war.[13] Of course, for their full enjoyment, the latter three reasons depend on disarmament and the full-scale reliance on civilian defence. Notwithstanding, these benefits may still be enjoyed by a *partial* reliance on civilian defence and a weakening of the centrality of the military, as (2) the military begins to be seen as less dangerous internationally, (3) is less

[13] A list of further potential benefits of civilian-based defence is presented by Sharp (1990: 143–8). This includes a potential reduction in nuclear proliferation, the development of a more ethical foreign policy, a reduction in the size of government, a reduction in violence, fewer casualties, a reduction in international military aggression, and less dependence on other states for defence.

dangerous internally, and (4) wars are not relied on to such an extent for national defence.[14]

6.4.1 The Problem of the Ruthless Aggressor

There is an obvious objection to national civilian defence: it will not work in the face of a ruthless aggressor. To that extent, in the afterword to *Just and Unjust Wars*, Walzer (2015) argues that the success of civilian resistance depends upon the nature of the regime it is used against. It might work in cases of a constrained ruler, such as the case of Lithuania, where the USSR was undergoing the processes of 'glasnost' and 'democratization', and global public opinion was deeply sympathetic to the goals of self-determination of the Lithuanians (Miniotaite 1996). However, it will not work against more ruthless regimes, who make opponents of the regime disappear and 'who send out squads of soldiers to kill civilian leaders', who arrest and torture suspects, establish concentration camps, and exile people to remote parts of the country (Walzer 2015: 332). Walzer argues that '[n]onviolent defense is no defense at all against tyrants or conquerors ready to adopt such measures' (2015: 332). In similar vein, Barack Obama remarked in his speech accepting the Nobel Peace Prize that '[a] non-violent movement could not have halted Hitler's armies. Negotiations cannot convince al Qaeda's leaders to lay down their arms' (2009).

But what about the resistance to the Nazi occupation cited by defenders of civilian defence? Brian Orend (2013: 278–9) counters that non-violent movements in Sweden, Norway, and Denmark were not really successful, since they happened after Hitler had conquered these lands, and the fact that they were not crushed by the Nazis might have been because the Nazis did not consider them a serious threat to their control. Although the resistance did cause some problems for the Nazi rulers, according to Orend it ultimately was not significant in the rolling back of aggression, which depended on *military* action by the Allies.

On the other hand, as advocates of civilian defence (e.g. Alexandra 2003: 603) rightly point out, the flaws of non-violent defence also apply to *violent* responses, which also have often failed in the face of a ruthless, powerful

[14] An example might be thought to be Costa Rica, which does not have an official army. This was abolished in 1948 (although it does have militarily trained forces). In the case of war, the US has agreed to offer assistance and Costa Rica is a signatory of the Inter-American Treaty of Reciprocal Assistance, which is a collective security arrangement. However, in this case, non-violent national defence is not doing the work of protecting the state; rather, it is the military capacity of other states that does this. For analysis of the process of demilitarization in Costa Rica, see Høivik and Aas (1981), who suggest that the rhetoric of demilitarization may not fully match the reality.

aggressor (such as French defences against the Nazi Blitzkrieg attacks in World War II). In addition, although military force was ultimately required to liberate the occupied states, civilian defence was *partially* successful in reducing *some* of the atrocities committed by the Nazi regime (Summy 1994). For instance, in the Nazi puppet regime of Vidkun Quisling in Norway, teachers successfully resisted the attempt to implement a fascist curriculum (Summy 1994: 19). In Denmark, non-violent resistance helped approximately 7,000 Danish Jews to flee to neutral Sweden (Summy 1994: 20).

In fact, rather than the *ruthlessness* of the aggressor, the more significant consideration is the *degree of dependence of the regime on the acquiescence of the governed* (Summy 1994). Even a ruthless aggressor may be dependent on the cooperation of the ruled, given the extreme difficulty of ruling simply by force.[15] However, when an aggressor is not dependent on the cooperation of the general population, civilian defence seems to be of very limited utility. This is because, recall, the case for civilian defence largely revolves around resisting and disrupting cooperation. Most clearly, civilian defence is far less likely to be successful when the aggressor does not wish to occupy. The aggressor may instead have other goals, such as annexation of territory, securing economic resources (such as access to natural resources), or the removal of the current head of state. It seems unlikely that civilian defence, on its own, in such cases would result in aggressive forces halting their mission, given that there would not be any occupying government to resist. It follows that, in cases where acquiescence and cooperation are *not* required, such as where occupation is not necessary, protecting the rights of civilians requires other measures.

There are two further problems with civilian defence. First, it can appear to reward interstate aggression by failing to mount a sizeable challenge to it (Orend 2013: 280). The claim here is that a robust response is required in order to maintain the norm in international society that aggression is not appropriate behaviour, and therefore to deter future instances of aggression (and so to protect future individuals from facing aggression). Of course, measures such as naming and shaming and economic sanctions can go some way to assert this norm. But perhaps the clearest measure in this regard is robust national defence, vocally supported by the rest of the international community, which makes it very clear that the attacked state has a right to resist.

Second, civilian defence might be ineffective in the sense that it does more harm than good. It might actually *increase* the costs on civilians, as they are subject to increased attacks by a ruthless aggressor, without any compensating benefit in terms of significantly frustrating the goals of the aggressor. Thus, Walzer (2015: 323) argues that civilian defence potentially asks too much of

[15] Summy (1994: 28) argues that even apparently Hitler recognized this point.

civilians to sustain the battle. It, in effect, faces the Supererogation Objection endured by civilian peacekeeping: it is too demanding of civilians to be prescribed. Indeed, Walzer argues that 'nonviolence, under extreme conditions, collapses into violence directed at oneself rather than at one's murderers' (2015: 332).[16] This claim has empirical support: although non-violent movements attract less of a violent response than violent movements, since 1955 governments have still committed mass killings against about 20 per cent of non-violent movements and, since 2007, 92 per cent of non-violent movements have faced lethal repression from security forces (Chenoweth 2017).[17]

Notwithstanding, even if national defence is sometimes required, there is still a case for non-violent national defence *in addition* to military action. When necessary, military action can defeat the ruthless aggressor, make clear there has been a robust response, and avoid unnecessary civilian sacrifice. However, at other times, particularly when the opponent is an occupying force and is more sensitive to international public opinion, civilian defence can reduce some of the internally and externally dangerous reliance on the military and on war.[18]

To be clear, there are risks with a mixed defence policy. Sharp (1990: 136) cautions, in particular, against the addition of violent measures to ongoing non-violent measures. This can lead to violent repercussions against non-violent protesters and lead to the delegitimation of the non-violent movement. By contrast, the addition of non-violent measures to violent ones may help to achieve the goals of the violent measures at lower cost to innocent bystanders. What seems most plausible, then, is not the blanket mixing of approaches, but the selection of methods according to the situation, depending on the characteristics and likely responses of the aggressor. This conclusion is consistent with Sharp's powerful and persuasive account of this option in *Civilian-Based Defense*. Sharp is clear that the case for civilian defence is not dependent on pacifism (1990: 4). He is also careful not to exaggerate the potential for civilian defence to work in the extreme cases of mass atrocities and territorial aggrandizement (Sharp 1990: 85), where military action might still be required sometimes.

Despite the sizeable limitations faced by civilian defence against an external aggressor, it is worth reiterating that civil resistance, in response to *internal* repression, can be highly effective. The effectiveness of internal civil resistance is likely to be higher because the leaders are more likely to be influenced by reputational pressures to treat their own citizens well, such as by direct links to

[16] There is also a related feasibility worry, Walzer (2015: 33–4) suggests, since civilians cannot be expected to offer any more than brief or sporadic resistance.

[17] Chenoweth's focus is on domestic uprisings.

[18] Similarly, Swiss defence policy has advocated, in the case of failure to repel foreign aggressors, both armed resistance and nonviolent action (Sharp 1990: 134).

those affected and for fear of the delegitimation of the regime. By contrast, those engaged in external aggression are less likely to be so concerned by reputational pressures, as they often will not need to govern the population that is subject to the aggression and have already presumably disregarded international reputational concerns by engaging in their aggressive action.

6.5 CONCLUSION

This chapter has considered the case for non-violent resistance. I have argued that both civilian peacekeeping and civilian defence can play *some* role in tackling mass atrocities and serious external aggression, even if both are limited. They should, I have argued, be seen often as potential responses alongside more violent ones, although violent responses are sometimes necessary. The case is clearest for civilian peacekeeping: international protective accompaniment can play a role in protecting vulnerable populations, despite its relatively small scale. The case for civilian defence is more moot, but seems most viable when used against aggressors that are dependent on the acquiescence of the population.

7

Positive Incentives

Most of the responses to mass atrocities and serious external aggression that we have considered thus far are at least somewhat coercive. Even civilian peacekeeping relies somewhat on a degree of coercion, namely, the threat of various reputational and financial costs on the aggressors. By contrast, this chapter will explore the ethical case for using positive incentives to help to tackle mass atrocities and serious external aggression. These measures include economic incentives, such as aid and investment in a state, political incentives, such as recognition, and legal incentives, such as amnesties or exile for leaders. Such incentives have been used widely (and somewhat successfully) to limit nuclear non-proliferation in cases such as Argentina, Brazil, Kazakhstan, South Africa, South Korea, Sweden, Taiwan, and Ukraine (Haass and O'Sullivan 2000: 167). They have also been used to try to bring to an end conflicts within and between states, including in Bosnia, Burundi, Israel/Palestine, Northern Ireland, Papua New Guinea, South Africa, Sri Lanka, and Yemen.

The use of such incentives raises the obvious worry that they reward those who act wrongly, such as those who commit mass atrocities. In the summer of 2015, the possibility of offering exile to Assad was frequently mooted in the public debate about potential ways of resolving the conflict in Syria. Would it be wrong to grant the Assad regime exile given that it has been implicated in crimes against humanity? Similarly, is it justifiable to offer political recognition to groups that have been involved in or linked to terrorist activities, if this will help to end a conflict? For instance, was it right for the US to grant a visa to Sinn Féin leader Gerry Adams in 1994, given that, as David Mitchell (2008: 52) suggests, this provided the catalyst for the Republican movement to move away from militarism? There are also notable worries about the use of incentives that stem from other fields, most notably health and education, such as a concern that using incentives will undermine moral motivations and in fact encourage the very behaviour that these incentives attempt to discourage. Consider, for example, the Mo Ibrahim Prize, worth $5 million for ten years and $200,000 annually thereafter, which is given to democratically elected African leaders who step down peacefully and show good governance. Do rewards such as this prize corrupt leaders' motivations, when they should be intrinsically motivated to comply with human rights obligations?

Given these sorts of worries, the use of positive inducements in general is largely criticized in the literature on the ethics of incentives in domestic political philosophy (e.g. Grant 2012; Sandel 2012) and their use in the context of the gross violation of human rights is seen by David Cortright as 'inappropriate' (1997*b*: 279).[1] In contrast, the aim of this chapter is to defend the ethical case for using positive incentives to help to address mass atrocities and serious external aggression. I will argue that they should often be considered when responding to these situations. More specifically, I will suggest that they are generally preferable to using *solely* coercive measures. Notwithstanding, I will also argue that some of the potential drawbacks of positive incentives mean that they should often be partnered with the threat of coercive measures, rather than being used on their own.

The chapter will proceed as follows. I will first consider the meaning and use of incentives in more detail in section 7.1. Then I will present the prima facie case for the use of incentives in section 7.2. This will highlight three features that mean their use should be favoured, including their non-coercive nature and their potential success. Section 7.3 will consider the case against the use of incentives. This involves the deontological objection that they are impermissible because, even if they are effective, they wrongly reward those who are culpable, as well as the instrumental worries that they will lead to the 'crowding out' of intrinsic motivation, moral corruption and moral hazard, and extortion. Section 7.4 will go on to consider when exactly incentives may be appropriate and how they should be used. Section 7.5 considers a form of incentive that raises particular ethical issues: the offer of immunity from prosecution for leaders and others suspected of mass atrocities and aggression. I will reject the case for this form of incentive.[2]

A quick clarification: incentives are often offered with a clear *quid pro quo*. However, sometimes they may be offered simply to improve relations, such as goodwill gestures aimed at encouraging moderate voices within the receiver and promoting cooperation.[3] Such incentives are typically more suitable for the longer-term development of peaceful relationships and the longer-term

[1] To be sure, Cortright generally defends the use of incentives in international politics, apart from in cases of the gross violation of human rights.

[2] The field of International Relations has for the most part paid much less attention to the use of positive incentives as a measure to address mass atrocities and serious conflicts, focusing much more on coercive measures. See Baldwin (1985: 11), Drezner (1999: 189), and Nincic (2006: 322; 2011: 46–57) on this point. Moreover, the (comparatively small) literature that does consider the use of positive incentives in International Relations does not examine in detail the ethical issues that their use raises. As already noted, there is a literature on the ethics of the use of incentives domestically (e.g. Grant 2006; Grant 2012; Sandel 2012), but this has not considered their international application.

[3] See Nincic (2006) for a discussion of these, which he calls 'catalytic carrots'.

prevention of mass atrocities. For this reason, I will focus primarily on incentives where there is a conditionality attached. The next chapters will consider two forms of assistance that do not have such a clear *quid pro quo*: military assistance to rebels and states (chapter 8) and humanitarian assistance (section 9.3).

7.1 THE USE AND MEANING OF INCENTIVES

Positive incentives ('incentives' from hereon) are offers given to improve the position of the receiver. This is compared to the counterfactual of the receiver's situation without the offer. Incentives differ from threats that, by contrast, would worsen the receiver's situation, compared to what can be reasonably predicted to have happened without the offer.[4]

Sometimes an incentive may be simply the offer of ending coercion. Perhaps the most notable example is the lifting of sanctions. Consider the following (hypothetical) example. South Africa proposes to the leaders of Burkina Faso that it will lift ongoing sanctions on Burkina Faso if the latter halts the mass killing of its citizens. This would still be a positive incentive. This is because it improves the situation of those in Burkina Faso. What is important here is that the sanctions were *already* present before the offer is made. Now suppose that there are no ongoing sanctions on Burkina Faso. But South Africa informs the leaders of Burkina Faso that it will launch a *new* sanctions regime unless that country halts its mass killing. If Burkina Faso were to halt the violations, then it would not be subject to the new sanctions regime. This is not a positive incentive, but instead is a threat because the sanctions regime is *not currently ongoing*. The sanctions would worsen the situation of Burkina Faso, compared to the lack of any further interference.

David Baldwin, in his seminal account of incentives, clarifies the relationship between sanctions and incentives. He notes that situations in which the threat of punishment is withdrawn can be described

> as ones in which [the sender] uses negative sanctions (the punishment) to lay the groundwork for the subsequent use of positive sanctions (the promise to withdraw the punishment if [the receiver] complies). What [the sender] is doing in such situations is using the stick to shift [the receiver]'s baseline so as to make the subsequent promise of a carrot more attractive. *A*'s offer to stop tipping the boat if B will row is unlikely to be perceived by *B* as a carrot unless *A* is actually tipping the boat at the time the offer is made. (1971: 25)

[4] Various synonyms are used for incentives, including 'inducements', 'engagement', 'offers', 'carrots', 'positive sanctions', 'rewards', 'cheque-book diplomacy', and 'linkage'. I will use some of these terms interchangeably.

Baldwin (1971: 23) also helpfully points out that whether something is an incentive depends on subjective perception. He argues that some interactions can appear to be positive sanctions but are not, such as giving a bonus of $1,000 to an employee who expected $2,000. In order to distinguish between rewards and punishments, we need to look at the perceptions of the receiver. In particular, we need to look at their baseline of expectations at the moment that the influence attempt begins. This is defined 'in terms of [the receiver]'s expected future value position, i.e., his expectations about his future position relative to the things he values. Positive sanctions, then, are actual or promised improvements in [the receiver]'s value position relative to his baseline of expectations' (Baldwin 1971: 23). By contrast, negative sanctions 'are actual or threatened deprivations relative to the same baseline' (Baldwin 1971: 24). Of course, introducing the subjective element means that establishing the baseline empirically is sometimes tricky. The senders may see themselves as using carrots when the receiver sees them as using sticks (Baldwin 1971: 24–5).

Notwithstanding, some offers do contain threats. Suppose, for instance, that, in the example above, South Africa informs the leaders of Burkina Faso that it will lift its ongoing sanctions if Burkina Faso halts its mass killing but will extend the sanctions regime if Burkina Faso fails to do so. This is both a threat and an offer—a 'throffer' (Steiner 1974–5: 39). The leaders of Burkina Faso would be better off if they took up the offer but worse off if they did not. It is worth noting that throffers are common since states use both carrots and sticks at the same time to achieve their foreign policy ends.

What form do incentives take? First, economic incentives include offers of humanitarian aid, the prospective purchase of goods or assets, prospective debt relief, potential investment, and the offer of preferential trade deals, such as tariff reductions, 'most-favoured-nation' status, and subsidies for exports or imports (Baldwin 1985: 42; Griffiths and Barnes 2008: 13). For instance, the carrots of a comprehensive aid package and closer economic association with the EU were used by the EU and NATO to secure the Ohrid Agreement to end the inter-ethnic violence in Macedonia in 2001 (Evans 2008: 115).

Economic incentives may be seen as bribes, depending on the definition of 'bribery', such as if bribery is defined broadly as offering financial rewards to persuade agents to do what you want them to do. This has a notable negative connotation since bribery is often seen as inducing someone to act immorally. Yet leading philosophical accounts of bribery (e.g. Philips 1984; Pritchard 1998; Turow 1985) often accept that bribery may be permissible when certain conditions are met.[5] Most notably, the bribe might be used to induce agents to act morally. Take, for instance, a case where a well-meaning citizen pays a lazy government official to examine pollution of the local river, which the official

[5] That said, bribery is sometimes seen as inviting a person to violate their duty (e.g. Grant 2006: 32) and therefore impermissible.

would otherwise not do despite its being within their remit. Alternatively, if 'bribery' is defined narrowly as to denote the offering of financial rewards to persuade officials to act immorally, many economic incentives would not be bribes since they may not be targeted at officials or may not encourage them to act immorally. The connotation of bribery, then, should not prejudge the ethical assessment of economic incentives; depending on the account, bribery might be permissible or the economic incentive may not be a bribe.

The second type of incentive is political. Political incentives include offers of prospective seats on international bodies (such as the EU). For instance, in response to a prospective war within Romania (where over one million Magyars reside) in the early 1990s, and potentially a war between Romania and Hungary similar to that seen in the former Yugoslavia, the US and the EU offered Hungary and Romania the huge carrot of joining the EU, in addition to significant direct economic incentives.[6] Political incentives also involve the offer to a party of inclusion within a potential power-sharing agreement, such as between a rebel movement and an incumbent government, the prospective recognition of the party as a state or as the 'sole legitimate representative of the people', and the offer of official visits and receiving representatives. Other kinds of political incentive include the offers of withdrawal of military forces from a territory previously occupied and normalizing relations and ending isolation (Griffiths and Barnes 2008: 13). They can also involve holding prestigious positions. For instance, in May 2015 the Swiss government reportedly asked Sepp Blatter, the former president of FIFA, to offer the President of Burundi, Pierre Nkurunziza, a role as an international ambassador in return for stepping down peacefully rather than pursuing a controversial third term (O'Grady 2016). Nkurunziza turned down the offer; significant unrest ensued as he went on to hold a third term.

Third, legal incentives include amnesties and immunity from prosecution for leaders or various other officials. An offer of amnesty or exile can be viewed as positive incentives when they would halt a prosecution that would otherwise occur. Since they raise particular ethical issues, I consider them on their own in section 7.5, where I am much more sceptical about the case for their use.

Who are the receivers of incentives? They include not only political leaders, but also more generally state and non-state actors. For instance, the state may be offered significant investment. Other prominent individuals, such as rebel soldiers or members of particular groups, may also be the receiver of the

[6] The US provided over US$330 million to Romania and US$94.2 million to Hungary, and the EU provided €816 million to Romania and over €787 million to Hungary. The prospect of joining the EU offered further huge economic benefits, but required that aspirants resolve border issues and the problematic treatment of minorities. The relations between Hungary and Romania stabilized considerably and the treatment of the Hungarian minority within Romania improved, in large part due to the incentives offered. See Blanchard and Ripsman (2013: 50–64).

incentive. For instance, in the 2003 War in Iraq, the US tried to bribe Iraqi generals not to resist the invasion (Buncombe 2013; Parchomovsky and Siegelman 2009: 179). The receivers can also be third parties. For instance, they might be other states that have significant influence over those directly involved. Incentives can also be offered to those who could potentially respond to the crisis, such as in order to encourage other states to take part in a sanctions regime, peacekeeping operation, naming and shaming, or war against the aggressor.

7.2 THE PRIMA FACIE CASE FOR INCENTIVES

I will now outline the prima facie case for incentives. Three potential features of incentives render them attractive. Together, these help to show that the use of incentives may often be more justifiable than (1) doing nothing, that is, using them is likely to meet the requirements of morally valuable effectiveness, as outlined in chapters 3 and 4 (in short, do more good than harm, compared to the counterfactual of no action). These reasons also help to show that incentives may often be better than (2) purely coercive options, such as economic and diplomatic sanctions, as well as military intervention.

7.2.1 Incentives as Non-coercive

The first potential advantageous feature is that the incentives are not coercive. That is, there will be *fewer costs borne by the receiver* than with other measures. As outlined at the start of the chapter, they differ from other measures in this regard. But why does it matter morally that they are not coercive on the Pragmatic Approach? After all, other measures may intentionally coerce those who are *liable* to coercion, such as targeted sanctions on culpable leaders.

This matters, first, because (in agent-neutral terms) incentives are less likely to impose significant costs on innocents (that is, lead to fewer external costs). Although not often intentional, other measures, such as economic and political sanctions, sometimes unintentionally coerce innocent civilians.[7] This is in part because there is often epistemic uncertainty about which agents are liable and, even when not, coercive measures, such as economic sanctions, are notoriously blunt tools and so will typically cause collateral harm to those

[7] The measure may be justified, all things considered, because, for instance, the sanctions regime will help to bring a resolution to the conflict. But it is still morally preferable that innocent civilians are not *forced* to behave in a certain manner, if there is another option that avoids coercion and that will achieve similar results.

who are innocent. Since incentives do not risk *directly* coercing the innocent, they are not subject to these risks, at least to such an extent. As such, incentives are more appropriate in response to situations where there is a lack of clarity around which agents are liable and the exact nature of the crisis. To the extent that, in cases of aggression and mass atrocities, there will often be epistemic limitations and it will often be difficult to precisely target those who are liable, incentives should often be the option of first choice.[8] Of course, the use of incentives may face similar issues. But the risks are far lower, since the result would only be that the wrong agents are *rewarded*, not *harmed*. On the face of it, it seems far less problematic to wrongly *reward* someone than it is to wrongly *harm* them.

There is also an (agent-relative) reason to prefer incentives: they seem to fare better with regard to the doing/allowing distinction. Recall that this distinction holds that, other things being equal, it is worse to *do* harm than to *allow* it. Since incentives are not coercive, they are less likely to *do* harm to innocent civilians, at least directly.

Admittedly, incentives may still *do* harm to innocent civilians, albeit more indirectly. First, this may include other forms of harm, most notably manipulation. For instance, the sender may mislead the receiver about the value of a potential reward or promise a reward but fail to deliver on it (suppose, for instance, that because of the successful manipulation, the receiver fails to secure morally valuable goods from elsewhere). Second, an incentive can also lead indirectly to coercion, although not caused directly by the incentives themselves.[9] Suppose, for instance, that a warring rebel party is offered a role in a power-sharing agreement, which would bring to an end a conflict that has resulted in the death of millions of civilians. The inclusion of the party would, however, mean that it is likely to increase the low-level oppression of a minority group within the rebel-held territory. The incentive therefore leads to some coercion. Nevertheless, any coercion caused by the incentive will typically be further down the causal chain, depending somewhat on the degree of the interceding agency of others (how much other actors, such as the rebel group, are also responsible for bringing about the harm). This differs from measures such as war and intervention, and perhaps some economic sanctions, where the harms are often more direct.

In reply to this potential advantage, incentives might be thought to be *directly* coercive. Suppose, for instance, that Brazil offers Paula, a rebel in another state, several thousand dollars to give up her weapons. Paula would

[8] To be sure, incentives may cause unforeseen or incidental harm. But they do not coerce and they often will cause less harm than other measures, at least directly.

[9] Indeed, several of the objections to incentives considered in section 7.3 highlight that incentives can lead to perverse consequences, albeit indirectly. The Rewarding Evil Objection highlights that incentives can directly lead to a bad thing—the rewarding of wrongdoing—although this is not a harm.

otherwise struggle to feed her family. Her situation is therefore not one of free choice. Is the offer coercive? In short, no. It is not the *incentive* that is coercive, but rather the *situation in which she finds herself*. This may be caused by the unfair distribution within Colombia or, more generally, the unjust global economic system. The incentive in fact *increases* her potential options by offering an alternative that was not previously available to her. To that extent, incentives *increase* freedom, within a general context. Notwithstanding, an incentive may still not be sufficient to render the receiver's choice sufficiently free. The receiver may have little reasonable option but to accept the alternative. The alternative offered may also be insufficient to remove the receiver from their coerced situation. For instance, the money offered to Paula may be enough to enable her to feed her family, but not enough for her to look after her own basic needs.

In addition, an incentive may still be exploitative. If the agent who offers the incentive is aware of the coerced situation of the receiver, and uses this information in order to secure their own ends by offering a lower amount than they would have otherwise done (without this knowledge), the incentive may exploit the receiver's unequal bargaining position. Nevertheless, the exploitative incentive may still be permissible because, for instance, it will be likely to lead to highly beneficial consequences, such as leading to the end of a severe humanitarian crisis.

An important caveat here is that an incentives programme that depends first on the coercion of economic sanctions or other forms of coercion does not possess fully the advantage of being not coercive, *when the incentives programme is broadly conceived* (that is, in combination with the preceding coercion).[10] This includes the offer of lifting sanctions and the offer of immunity from prosecution. Consider, for example, the lifting of the ongoing sanctions on Iran in 2015, which led it to commit to give up its nuclear weapons programme. These sanctions are reported to have cost Iran more than $160bn in oil revenue since 2012 and the lifting of the sanctions will enable it to receive more than $100bn in frozen assets overseas (BBC 2015). The incentive offered to Iran depended on the preceding highly coercive sanctions programme.[11] Considered *holistically*, the interaction was highly coercive. Nevertheless, considered *in isolation*, an incentives programme may not be coercive. For example, on its own, the incentive of lifting the sanctions regime on Iran was not coercive since it improved the situation of

[10] The reliance on preceding coercion may also mean that the incentive does not enjoy some of the other advantages considered below. For instance, like sanctions, it may endure some of the problems that stem from the 'rally-round-the-flag' effect as resentment towards the sender is entrenched.

[11] Similarly, the carrot of potential lifting of sanctions after the conflict in the former Yugoslavia meant that some parties were more willing to enter into agreements and to establish normal conditions, resulting in the Dayton Accords (Eriksson and Wallensteen 2015: 1396).

Iran at the time of the offer of the lifting of the sanctions, given that the sanctions were already in place. Thus, what matters for whether an incentive programme is coercive is at what point in time the incentive is being assessed. To put this another way, the sanctions regime, at t_1, is coercive and the overall interaction, from period t_1–t_3, may also be coercive, but the offer to lift sanctions at t_2 is an incentive and not coercive.

It is worth making two further points about this feature of incentives. First, many cosmopolitans are generally much more sanguine about the use of more coercive options to address mass atrocities and serious external aggression by insurgents, terrorists, or other states. Indeed, cosmopolitans (e.g. Tesón 2003; 2005) have often provided the most powerful and influential (and sometimes most persuasive) defences of humanitarian intervention. Yet the advantages of not being coercive highlighted above, as well as the next two reasons, provides a reason for non-coercive options often to be favoured over coercive ones on a liberal cosmopolitan position. Second, the non-coercive nature of incentives means that the case for them is likely to have a broader appeal, including for those who are less sanguine about the use of more coercive options to address mass atrocities and serious external aggression than many cosmopolitans. This may be because they have less confidence in the coercive options (which may also be true of some cosmopolitans), they endorse a strong form of international pluralism in which communal self-determination and sovereignty are highly prized, or they are more sceptical about universalist ethics and, in particular, about using coercion in defence of universalist ethics. The fact that incentives are consensual should ameliorate or even abrogate several of these worries. However, as we will see in section 7.3, incentives may face several other worries.

7.2.2 Incentives and the Costs for the Sender

The second feature focuses on the costs *for the sender*. Wars and economic sanctions can be very costly for the sender. By contrast, incentives can be much cheaper, especially over the long run. This is not only in terms of economic costs, but also of other costs, such as political costs and cost in lives. For instance, even a seemingly large financial reward may be less harmful to the sender's domestic economy than engaging in long-term economic sanctions and much cheaper than waging a military operation. As Gideon Parchomovsky and Peter Siegelman pointedly put it, '[u]sing a $250,000 bribe that produces the same overall effect as a $1 million cruise missile effects a saving of $750,000' (2009: 180). Moreover, other forms of incentive come with very little economic cost for the sender.

Part of what often renders incentives less costly for the sender is that, because they are not coercive, they are not subject to retaliation by the receiver.

Economic sanctions may result in counter-sanctions, such as Russia's retaliatory sanctions on the EU in response to EU sanctions on Russia after its annexation of Crimea. Naming and shaming may result in the criticized state ending trade deals with the critic. And wars and interventions can result in the offender launching significant counter-offences. Baldwin puts it well: '[h]e who uses negative sanctions is more likely to have negative sanctions used on him. He who lives by negative sanctions is likely to die by them' (1971: 35).

Why do senders' costs matter morally? As noted in section 4.4, internal costs are an important determinant of effectiveness on the Pragmatic Approach—lower internal costs mean that the measure is more likely to do more good than harm, other things being equal. In fact, it seems that there is reason to give internal costs some degree of *extra* weight when considering effectiveness overall. Most obviously, internal costs seem to matter somewhat more because states have (limited) fiduciary obligations to citizens. This means that they are morally required to promote their states' interests, whilst still leaving scope for some limited positive cosmopolitan obligations. This moderate view coheres with most accounts in international ethics: it is widely accepted that states have weightier duties towards their own citizens whilst having some positive obligations to those beyond their borders—perhaps derived from humanitarian duties—and more stringent negative duties not to harm those in other states. The reason why states have weightier duties towards their own citizens need not detain us at length here, given that it is hardly controversial and there is an overlapping consensus amongst the leading accounts of international ethics on this issue.[12] But they include reasons that are contractual (such as that citizens consent to the state's authority on the promise that it will promote their interests), communitarian (such as that states are required to promote the valuable lives of the community), and cosmopolitan (such as that the best way to promote individual interests is to have them promote their own citizens' basic human rights).

In addition to this point about internal costs, there are two nonideal reasons worth highlighting why it is important to care about costs to the sender. The first is that, because of domestic political pressures, most governments have limited scope to act upon cosmopolitan requirements, given electoral pressures to spend on domestic ends and the preponderance of neoliberal governance that insists on cuts to government expenditure. They therefore need to use the international budgets that they do have as best as they possibly can. When economic and political investment is used to tackle mass atrocities and conflict, it cannot be used for other morally valuable ends, such as tackling global poverty, the effects of climate change, and human rights, at least directly.

[12] See, for instance, Buchanan (1999; 2004), Caney (2005*a*), Goodin (1988), Miller (2007), and Nagel (2005).

Ensuring value-for-money expenditure on tackling mass atrocities and conflict is therefore required for cosmopolitan reasons, in order to ensure that it is not subject to worries about opportunity costs—that is, that the money could have been better spent elsewhere (see Valentino 2011).[13]

Second, governments face competing, legitimate demands to improve domestic public services. They are likely to face domestic (and perhaps international) political constraints on how much economic and political investment they can make in providing public services, given, again, the preponderance of neoliberal governance and the electoral unpopularity of significantly increased taxation. When economic and political investment is used to tackle mass atrocities and serious external aggression, it cannot be used for morally worthwhile domestic ends (and which the government has a fiduciary obligation to ensure), such as improving schools, welfare, and care for the elderly, which may significantly impact inequality domestically and save lives. It is therefore morally important, for both cosmopolitan and domestic reasons, that incentives are a cost-effective measure to tackle mass atrocities.

Daniel Drezner doubts the cost effectiveness of incentives. He argues that '[t]he key difference between the carrot and the stick (be it economic or military) is that the stick is expensive when it fails, whereas the carrot is expensive when it succeeds' (1999: 200). This is because a 'successful threat of coercion is costless' since those threatened acquiesce before the threatened measure needs to be implemented, whereas a successful incentive is costly since the receiver gets the reward (1999: 200). Conversely, failed attempts at coercion are costly since the sender must implement sanctions or intervention; failed attempts at offering carrots are costless. Accordingly, Drezner argues, if both carrots and sticks are likely to succeed, senders will prefer sanctions—or, more precisely, the threat of sanctions—over carrots because the former will be more likely to be cost-effective.

This might be true, but it also follows that if both sticks and carrots are unlikely to succeed, or the chances of success are moot, senders should prefer carrots because they will be more cost-effective since they do not risk having to implement the threatened sanction. Waging war or putting in place economic sanctions often costs more than offering economic or political incentives. In addition, posing threats—even if successful—is not cost-free. It can lead to or exacerbate an adversarial relationship, and undermine any potential goodwill between the states. Moreover, some types of incentives, such as trade and technology, provide gains for both the receiver and sender, whereas sanctions are almost always costly for both parties (Cortright 1997*a*: 8; Dorussen 2001: 253). It therefore seems that incentives will generally be more

[13] Opportunity costs are also more generally important, that is, for assessing which crises the alternatives should be used to address.

cost-effective than coercive measures, particularly when coercive measures are used on their own.[14]

7.2.3 Incentives as Successful

The third feature is related and is again straightforward: incentives can sometimes, but not always, be successful at helping to tackle or ameliorate the crisis (which increases their chances of being effective overall—do more good than harm in terms of basic human rights). For instance, various political and economic incentives helped to bring to an end the twelve-year civil war in El Salvador and secure a peace agreement in 1992. This included, most significantly, the prospect of recognition of the FMLN (Farabundo Martí National Liberation Front) from the US in 1991, which played a crucial role in the FMLN deciding to end the war (Thale 1997).

Several of the objections considered in section 7.3 will challenge the efficacy of incentives. But before we examine these claims, it is worth considering why it is that incentives *can* be successful. In addition to the broader, more obvious point that incentives can provide the receiver with a weighty reason to stop mass atrocities or conflict, there are two specific points worth highlighting. First, incentives can play a key role when a leader wishes to comply but faces a recalcitrant domestic constituency. The promise of, for instance, large amounts of money can help to calm potential discontent and so render feasible a peace agreement. For example, in the aftermath of the first Gulf War, the US offered significant economic incentives to Jordan to conclude a peace treaty with Israel, including a grant of US$1 billion, debt forgiveness of US$4.3 billion, and foreign aid (Blanchard and Ripsman 2013: 37–49). The incentives in this case enabled the King of Jordan to buy off domestic opponents. The outcome was the Washington Declaration, which led to a formal peace treaty between Israel and Jordan in October 1994 (Blanchard and Ripsman 2013: 49).

Second, incentives have a notable comparative advantage over sanctions. As we saw in section 3.3, a common objection to sanctions is that they will make the population—and particularly leaders—even more recalcitrant and result in a 'rally-round-the-flag' effect.[15] This effect occurs when those who have serious reservations about the government or its agenda nevertheless rally behind it when it appears assaulted from abroad.[16] More generally, coercive

[14] Nevertheless, incentives may *appear* to be more costly because they appear on the budget line as clear expenditure for states, whereas the costs of a sanctions regime are generally over the longer term and are filtered through private companies who may have to bear the costs of not trading in the first place. On this point, see Cortright (1997*a*: 8).

[15] See, for instance, Dorussen (2001: 253) and Nincic (2006).

[16] See Nincic (2006: 323).

options can lead to significant resentment and unwillingness to do what those coercing want them to do, even if doing so would otherwise be rational (that is, in their self-interest). According to Miroslav Nincic, 'sticks often are counter-productive, as the renegade regime's authorities, seeking above all to secure their domestic position, find that it may be bolstered by external confrontations' (2006: 338). Put bluntly, those whose families, colleagues, friends, and co-nationals are being starved through sanctions or bombed in a war are unlikely to be willing to do what the agent coercing them wants them to do. This is both because they are being coerced—and resent this—and because they are the demands of the *coercing agent*.

By contrast, incentives do not tend to erode the willingness to conform. Positive inducements from external actors can appear less threatening and reduce the extent of the 'rally-round-the-flag' effect when combined with coercive measures (Nincic 2006: 327). They also do not have a 'scar effect'—unlike some coercive measures—which limit future relations (Dorussen 2001: 253). On the contrary, they can have positive spillover effects for other areas by increasing cooperation (Newnham 2004: 166).[17] The fact that incentives create less resentment can also mean that communication can be clearer and more precise, and as a result negotiations to secure peace may be more likely to succeed, whereas the message delivered by coercive measures may often become clouded by bitterness (Cortright 1997*a*: 8).

7.3 THE CASE AGAINST INCENTIVES

I have presented three features that suggest why incentives should be favoured. These are that they are non-coercive, can be comparably less costly, and can be more successful than other options. Together, they provide a prima facie case for the use of incentives. However, the moral picture is more complex; I will now consider five potential objections to their use. In their strongest form, these objections would deny the permissibility of the use of incentives in all cases.

7.3.1 The Rewarding Evil Objection

The first objection is the 'Rewarding Evil Objection'. This is the worry that incentives wrongly reward those who are engaged in mass atrocities and serious external aggression. According to Thomas Milburn and Daniel

[17] This is particularly the case for more open-ended incentives. Incentives with conditionalities attached may still be seen as external interference and be subject to some resentment (although probably less than more coercive measures).

Christie's study of the psychology of offering incentives, '[s]ome regard communication with adversaries during periods of high tension as intercourse with the devil. The very idea of rewarding the devil is to them obscene and a kind of blasphemy, no matter how effective it might be as a means of influence' (1989: 632). This worry is found, for instance, within certain factions of the policy community of the US, which view incentives not only as counterproductive but also as morally wrong (Nincic 2006: 322). Indeed, incentives may be difficult to implement because of domestic political constraints. For example, Congress blocked Henry Kissinger and Richard Nixon's attempt in the early 1970s to offer the Soviet Union political and economic incentives in return for restrained behaviour (Haass and O'Sullivan 2000: 178–9).

The Rewarding Evil Objection, then, concerns both a moral worry about the wrongness of rewarding wrongdoing and a political worry about the feasibility of using this measure in the face of likely opposition. The political worry can more easily be repudiated. Inducements can be offered covertly and may be able to be defended by skilful politicians. The worry also applies much more to particular states, where the retributivist bent is strong. Moreover, it is not clear that incentives are in fact unpopular amongst the public. Graeme Davies and Robert Johns' (2016*b*) survey of domestic opinions of incentives vis-à-vis other measures finds, on the one hand, that, when unsuccessful, incentives are more unpopular than coercive measures amongst the public because they can mean that states lose credibility, reward bad behaviour, and perhaps strengthen the target regime. On the other hand, Davies and Johns also find that the public does not reject inducements outright. When they are successful, the public is as favourable towards incentive regimes as it is towards coercive options. What is crucial, Davies and Johns argue, is the success of the measure. This is despite the complexity of policies based on incentives, compared to more straightforward coercive strategies.

7.3.2 Desert

The moral worry is less easily dismissed, however. It can be fleshed out more precisely in terms of a worry about the moral importance of desert (the fifth value on the Pragmatic Approach). That is, those who do not deserve to be benefited receive a significant reward for their wrongful behaviour. In fact, not only do they deserve *not to be benefited*, they deserve to be *punished*.

To explicate further, in his seminal account of desert, *The Geometry of Desert*, Shelly Kagan (2012) distinguishes between 'non-comparative' and 'comparative' desert. The former—*non-comparative desert*—concerns what an individual deserves regardless of what others get. For instance, it seems that Charles Taylor deserves to face imprisonment for his role in the mass atrocities in Sierra Leone and Liberia, even if other leaders, such as Assad and his regime, do not receive what they deserve because of the political difficulties of punishing them. By contrast, *comparative desert* concerns what an individual deserves compared to what others receive and, as such, is akin to fairness. As Kagan puts it, 'if I am just as deserving as you are (just as virtuous), then I should be doing as well as you (no matter how well you are doing). Similarly, if you are more virtuous than I am, then you should be better off than I am (no matter how well off I am)' (2012: 349).

Both non-comparative and comparative desert play a role in the Rewarding Evil Objection. First, in terms of non-comparative desert, the giving of an incentive seems wrong because, straightforwardly, it rewards those who act wrongly and who in fact should be punished, regardless of what happens to others who commit similar crimes (such as if others are punished or offered incentives). This evokes the retributivist notion that it is important, *in itself*, that certain individuals should be punished because they acted wrongly, independent of the consequences of doing so. According to Kagan, it is

> an *intrinsically* good thing, other things being equal, if people get what they deserve. So just as most of us would be prepared to insist that it is an intrinsically good thing, other things being equal, if people are well off... and just as many of us would be prepared to insist as well that equality is an intrinsically good thing, other things being equal... I think we should also accept the view that there is intrinsic value in people getting what they deserve... it is *intrinsically* better when people are getting what they deserve. (2012: 16)[18]

Of course, accepting this claim does not mean that non-comparative desert is the *only* value. Nor does it mean that the wrongdoer who deserves to be punished should *always* be punished. There may be countervailing considerations that contravene this. For instance, the current system of punishment may not ensure a fair trial and so may have a high risk of accidently punishing an innocent individual. In other words, one can be a pluralistic retributivist who accepts that non-comparative desert—and in particular the importance of punishing wrongdoers—is one moral value amongst many (Kagan 2012). I will consider *how much* weight this value has shortly. For now, it is sufficient to note that the Rewarding Evil Objection gives it *significant* weight. On this objection, non-comparative desert provides a very weighty reason to oppose positive inducements, given that they can reward wrongdoers.

The Rewarding Evil Objection also posits that positive incentives are problematic because of comparative desert. This is because those who do *not* commit abuses can claim that they have been treated unfairly. They conform to moral requirements but are not provided with financial rewards. Consider the following case.

[18] To be clear: desert can also have instrumental value. For instance, rewarding virtue and punishing wrongdoing can provide an incentive for people to behave morally, which may produce better consequences overall (Kagan 2012: 15).

Two similar, extremely poor states—say, Liberia and Sierra Leone—face significant internal uprisings. The Liberian government speaks to the leaders of the uprising, negotiates with them, and tries to address their grievances where they are legitimate. The government of Sierra Leone engages in a purge of the rebel leaders and significantly exacerbates the situation. A civil war results and the government of Sierra Leone agrees to a negotiated end to the conflict only when there is significant financial investment offered by India, some of which is used by some governmental officials of Sierra Leone to buy expensive luxury goods. The Liberian government is now in a weaker position—it lacks this investment—despite its doing what it ought to have done. It could rightly claim that, if there were to be investment, *it* deserves the investment, not Sierra Leone. On the Rewarding Evil Objection, then, the use of incentives is problematic because they go against what whose who act wrongly deserve, relative to those who act rightly.

Is the Rewarding Evil Objection right? It is correct to point to the wrongness of rewarding aggressors in terms of both comparative and non-comparative desert. However, this wrong is outweighed by countervailing considerations. Certainly, it *does* matter that wrongdoers get what they do not deserve. Although in some (and perhaps even most) contexts it is very difficult to determine what people deserve, it seems obvious that the leaders of aggressive regimes, rebel groups, and terror organizations do not deserve rewards. However, desert is only one consideration amongst many on the Pragmatic Approach and it will often be outweighed in the context of addressing mass atrocities and serious external aggression. In particular, this consideration is outweighed by the importance of minimizing harm to innocents.

To see this, suppose, for instance, that in the case above for the use of positive investment by India would significantly reduce the overall amount of harm faced by civilians in Sierra Leone, as they are subject to far fewer intentional and unintentional attacks by government forces and rebel groups. The positive investment is also used, however, by some governmental officials to buy luxury goods, for instance on expensive shopping trips to Paris and Dubai. Intuitively, the reduction in the overall amount of aggregate harm to the innocent seems to clearly outweigh the wrongness of seemingly rewarding a few governmental officials. Giving a few what they do not (non-comparatively) deserve seems to be outweighed by the importance of addressing mass atrocities and protecting many civilians from attack. The amount of value—the stakes—involved with the reduction in serious harm to many individuals is much greater than involved with giving a few officials what they do not deserve.

Moreover, the use of incentives in such cases can *increase* the extent to which individuals receive what they (non-comparatively) deserve. If incentives are successful at helping to tackle the situation, they will reduce the harms that civilians have to bear. Paying the government to stop the war would ensure that thousands of civilians would not have to bear significant costs that they do not deserve. It would therefore increase non-comparative desert: even though the use of incentives means that a handful of leaders now receive a benefit they do not deserve, stopping the war would mean that thousands of innocents would no longer have to bear costs that they do not deserve.[19]

It might be replied that there is an asymmetry, namely that it is worse to reward wrongdoers than it is to harm the innocent, and this buttresses the Rewarding Evil Objection against this response. But, if there were an asymmetry, it would surely go the other way. As the case above suggests, intuitively, it seems far worse when innocents bear costs for which they are not liable than when those who are culpable are seemingly rewarded, when other things are equal.[20] Indeed, this is widely reflected in legal systems that maintain a high level of proof required to secure a conviction, in order to avoid punishing the innocent, even if it means that some guilty individuals are not convicted and enjoy the benefits of their crime.

But what of the worry of incentives in terms of comparative desert? Those who do not receive the rewards yet act appropriately still have a legitimate complaint about the unfairness, such as in the case of Liberia resolving an internal uprising peacefully in the example above. Nevertheless, the worry about comparative desert does not foreclose the permissibility of the sender offering an incentive. The importance of this consideration can be outweighed by other considerations, most notably the successful tackling of the situation. Again, this seems intuitive. In the case above, India is doing what it can to minimize rights violations in Sierra Leone. Although it may reduce comparative desert, this wrong seems to be outweighed by the import of addressing mass atrocities or serious external aggression by insurgents, terrorists, or other states.

This intuition can be somewhat explained by the fact that the *receiver* is in part responsible for the decrease in comparative desert. Thus, the interceding agency of the receiver reduces the wrongness of the sender's actions. Let me elucidate. As I will consider further in section 8.3.3, the interceding agency (or intervening agency) of others matters *somewhat* and so mediated harms are partially discounted in proportionality calculations. This is because interceding agency affects the causal relation to the harm. If one holds that the difference between doing and allowing harm has *some* moral force, it also matters when another's agency intercedes. This is because you are not *directly*

[19] We need to be wary of double-counting reasons here. On the Pragmatic Approach benefits to those who deserve them are already included in effectiveness, which focuses on benefits and costs to the innocent (or those we have to presume are innocent).

[20] I add 'seemingly' since the incentive-giver in these cases does not intend to reward the wrongdoing; rather, they intend to tackle the situation, which can result in certain culpable individuals receiving a net benefit. This may give the impression that they have been rewarded, even if this is not the intention.

causing the harm; your action—like when allowing harm—is more causally remote. This point can be applied to the case of incentives.[21] Although some of the responsibility for the unfair outcome lies with the sender, far more responsibility lies with the receiver. This is for two reasons. First, by using morally problematic methods, the government of Sierra Leone has put itself in an advantageous position. Second, by failing to redress the effects of its morally problematic methods, the government of Sierra Leone compounds its original wrongful behaviour. The government of Sierra Leone is morally required to give up its undeserved benefits (which it has obtained through injustice), which it fails to do.[22] Its failure to disgorge—such as by not sharing the reward—is also a cause of the decrease in comparative desert. Thus, the interceding agency of the *receiver* diminishes the degree of the *sender's* responsibility for any reduction in comparative desert. This makes it less likely that the sender would act impermissibly by offering the incentive, since it would only be in part responsible for bringing about this wrong.

All this is not to deny that seemingly rewarding injustice is a wrong that counts against incentives; the Rewarding Evil Objection is right about this. My point rather is that, on the Pragmatic Approach, such a wrong can be outweighed by the moral importance of reducing harms on innocents. This reply depends on the success of incentives at achieving good consequences. This brings us to the next objection.[23]

7.3.3 The Crowding-Out Objection

In the literature on the use of incentives in general, such as in healthcare (e.g. Gorin and Schmidt 2015: 34; Klein 2014), one notable worry is 'crowding

[21] Although the incentive in this case does not bring about harm, the wrongness of the sender *doing* an action that brings about a wrong—an unfair outcome—is reduced by the interceding agency of the receiver. Also note that interceding agency could reduce the wrongness of an agent *allowing* a wrong, such as if a state allows genocidal actions to go on within a state within its region, but other, better-placed states also fail to address the situation (the harm is mediated by both the genocidal actions of the government and others' failure to act).

[22] On the ethical case for disgorgement in the case of innocent beneficiaries, see Goodin (2013). Note though that this case is even clearer, since Sierra Leone is a *culpable* beneficiary.

[23] Incentives might appear to condone wrongdoing. But paying someone to cease problematic behaviour does not mean that one condones it. On the contrary, it demonstrates a resolve to tackle the behaviour. As I argue below, it may reinforce the R2P norm that something must be done to tackle the situation. It might also be thought that the use of the incentive renders one complicit in the wrongdoing of the receiver if, for instance, the money from incentives is used to repress a minority. But, as I argued in section 4.3.4, it is unclear what exactly is wrong with being complicit; it helps to be more specific in identifying the wrong involved. What matters is that the incentive is *all-things-considered justified* and, in doing so, that any harms that will result are factored into the assessment of their proportionality. The fact that an incentive may enable some wrongdoing may be outweighed by the larger, positive effects of the incentive.

out'.[24] This is the worry that incentives provide extrinsic motivation for compliance and this 'crowds out' any intrinsic motivation. The intrinsic motivation will no longer be present as the agent becomes reliant on the incentive. For instance, if individuals are offered money to adopt a healthier lifestyle, this may come to dominate any intrinsic motive that they have to be healthy.

Crowding out is worrisome because, without the incentive, the agent may return to their original behaviour, such as smoking or unhealthy eating. For instance, in 2011 *The Times* alleged that Italy secretly paid Taliban insurgents in the Sarobi district of Afghanistan not to fight (Coghlan and Bone 2011). When France took over the area, it was unaware of the bribes and, as a result, seriously underestimated the threat level, and ten French soldiers were brutally killed by insurgents no longer in receipt of the income.

The incentive may have a longer-term negative effect of removing any lingering intrinsic motivation. For instance, Michael Sandel remarks that '[p]aying kids to read books might get them to read more, but also teach them to regard reading as a chore rather than a source of intrinsic satisfaction' (2012: 9). The result may be that they soon stop reading, once the incentive is removed. Likewise, incentives to take part in the peace process in Bougainville, Papua New Guinea, led to the development of the perception of the unlimited availability of funds and that involvement in the peace process was all about financial gain (Regan 2008: 47). The incentives offered by Australia, New Zealand, and the UN in this case led to a norm whereby people became reluctant to take part in the process without some form of recompense (Regan 2008: 48).[25] In the context of mass atrocities and aggression, crowding out is also worrisome if one accepts the Kantian notion that agents should be predominantly motivated by the right sorts of reasons—intrinsic ones—to comply with moral norms, rather than extrinsic rewards. The worry is that incentives encourage agents to be motivated by rewards, rather than by the moral requirement not to engage in or facilitate mass atrocities and serious external aggression.

However, despite some exceptions, the Crowding-Out Objection is less worrisome in the context of responding to mass atrocities and serious external aggression than in other fields. First, even if incentives *do* crowd out internal motivation, this is not particularly problematic. The import of having individuals motivated by the right sorts of reasons is outweighed by the much greater import of tackling the mass violations of basic human rights or serious

[24] See Frey and Jegen (2001) for a detailed account of this phenomenon in economics and the underlying psychological reasons. Also see Sandel (2012: 43–91).

[25] Similarly, one of the worries surrounding the use of incentives in the context of nuclear proliferation is that they might encourage states to uphold non-proliferation standards only in return for tangible rewards (Cortright and Lopez 2005: 19).

external aggression. Individuals should not possess mercenary motives, but in the grand scheme of war, conflict, and mass atrocities, the worries about particular individuals' motivations seem far less weighty. It simply matters much more whether a measure is effective at addressing a crisis, or distributes harm fairly, than that the individuals involved are rightly motivated.[26]

Second, it is not clear that the use of positive incentives *does* crowd out intrinsic motivation in this context. There may sometimes be no good motive to crowd out—agents that are involved in the commission of aggression and mass atrocities may often lack any intrinsic motivation to comply in the first place. For instance, leaders may be driven economically or ideologically to engage in their aggressive behaviour and may not possess any intrinsic desire to cease their actions.

Third, and conversely, incentives can in fact help to 'crowd-in' motivation (Frey and Jegen 2001: 595), that is, help to realize an intrinsic motivation, such as by removing external obstacles to their fulfilment. For example, Jonathan Wolff suggests that incentives can act as a 'rationalization', that is, allow 'an individual to justify his or her behaviour to a peer group that would not otherwise accept the motivation as a justifying reason. On this understanding, cash payments allow individuals to act on non-cash motivations they already have. Under these circumstances, payments are not corrupting. On the contrary, they can be liberating' (2015: 29). He gives the example of a child who secretly likes reading but whose peer group scorn it and so uses a financial incentive to rationalize reading to the group, pointing to the fact that he receives $2 a book (Wolff 2015: 29).

The same may apply to certain states: they can use incentives to rationalize to their constituents their behaviour, where they would not accept the leader's real reason otherwise. As noted above, incentives can help to persuade a recalcitrant domestic constituency. The use of extrinsic motivation may also help to develop a habit of the desired behaviour and so continue after the ending of the incentive. The agent may become used to conforming to moral norms. Its own domestic constituency and international audience may also expect it to continue to conform and it may set up institutional mechanisms that will ensure continued compliance.

7.3.4 The Corruption Objection

Another notable worry posited in the literature on incentives is what I will call the 'Corruption Objection'. This is the worry that incentives corrupt society. Rather than rendering compliance with moral norms as something that

[26] For further analysis of the moral import of motives in war and the wrongness of a mercenary motive, see Pattison (2014*b*: 36–46).

should be expected because we should do the right thing, compliance becomes something that should *be paid for*. Thus, the economic motive may become predominant *in general* (rather than for a specific issue, which was the worry posited by the Crowding-Out Objection). Individuals may comply only when it is in their own self-interest and in general the moral force of relevant norms will erode. This will lead to the moral corruption of society, as individuals no longer play an altruistic role in communal life. For example, incentives may jeopardize the judgements about the kind of reasons that people have about health, seeing the reasons in simply economic terms and viewing their relations with health professionals purely economically. This corrupting influence on individuals can have a detrimental effect not only by leading to poor health, but also by corrupting people's characters, values, and relationships with others (Gorin and Schmidt 2015: 35). In *Strings Attached*, Ruth Grant calls this the 'spillover effect':

> [i]f you pay your child to mow the lawn, he or she is less likely to willingly do the dishes for free. Relying on incentives in one area can affect attitudes and behavior in other areas. By introducing payments in a family setting, you introduce the norms of the commercial domain, or the market, into a realm previously governed by different, more cooperative norms of family or community responsibility. (2012: 116)

In the context of mass atrocities and aggression, states and other actors will not see compliance with morally desirable norms as something they should do simply because they *ought* to do it, but because they will be *paid* to comply. Consequently, the use of incentives could erode compliance demanded by norms such as R2P and non-proliferation.

The Corruption Objection can be made more precisely. The worry is that it will reduce the sense that the international community demands conformity with moral norms. Moral norms can exert compliance pull on states when they are viewed as expected standards of behaviour by a sufficient number of states and other actors. The compliance pull stems from the fact that, for various reasons, states care about their perceived legitimacy amongst their peers. The Corruption Objection posits that the compliance pull of norms will be weaker as states no longer expect conformity without the offer of an incentive. Compliance will become seen as something that states should be *paid for*, such as by rich states. When there is no incentive on offer, non-compliance will not be viewed as illegitimate and so aggressors will not be subject to various reputational and other costs.

The potential effects highlighted by the Corruption Objection are unlikely to be significant, however. Perhaps most notably, the potential undermining of norms surrounding non-engagement in mass atrocities and aggression seems unlikely. There are numerous reasons why states and other actors do not engage in these activities. These include the moral repulsion against doing so, the pressure of international norms, worries about potential international responses, as well as internal opposition. Any effect on potential international norms of R2P and against aggression by offering the occasional incentive is likely to be minimal. The international community will still typically demand compliance with norms of R2P and against aggression, without the sense that this should be paid for. The use of incentives is unlikely to undermine a general moral repulsion against engaging in mass atrocities and aggression.

In addition, if the Corruption and Crowding-Out Objections are taken to provide absolute, strong reasons against the use of positive incentives, they could also rule out altogether the use of *coercive* measures. This is because coercive measures such as economic sanctions also rely on extrinsic motivation, on the threats or direct coercion to secure compliance. The threat of punishment may undermine intrinsic motivation to comply or corrupt society more generally, as agents are not motivated by non-prudential reasons to comply with moral norms. Yet it seems patent that the threat of coercion is on occasion permissible, despite the reliance on extrinsic motivation.

7.3.5 The Moral Hazard Objection

A fourth worry is about moral hazard. This is that the use of incentives, for instance, to attempt to secure healthy outcomes will lead healthy people 'to engage in unhealthy behaviors in order to become eligible for incentives' (Gorin and Schmidt 2015: 34). The same may be thought to occur with states—and particularly with poorer ones—which could engage in human rights abuses and aggressive behaviour in order to obtain rewards.[27]

Yet the likelihood of moral hazard occurring in this context seems small. Again, there are numerous reasons why states and other actors commence mass atrocities and serious external aggression.[28] They include historical grievances, the geopolitical situation, the personal character traits of leaders, and the political utility of committing the crimes for leaders. These reasons seem likely to be much more significant than the prospect of a reward.[29]

[27] The worry is noted by Cortright (1997*b*: 278) in the context of nuclear proliferation and offering North Korea incentives to denuclearize. The concern was that the prospect of a reward would encourage other states to secure nuclear weapons.

[28] There is a huge body of literature on this. Seminal works include Levy and Thompson (2010) (on war) and Valentino (2000) (on mass atrocities). For a rejection of moral hazard arguments about R2P, see Bellamy and Williams (2012). They argue that moral hazard theory 'reduces the complex sources of genocidal violence to a series of simple calculations' and so overlooks several causal factors (2012: 557).

[29] To be sure, *once commenced*, the offers of a reward to cease fighting or committing mass atrocities may become far more influential (because, for instance, of financial or political hardship following conflict).

Moreover, even if there is occasionally a moral hazard or the moral corruption of society with incentives used widely, this may be outweighed by the (numerous) occasions when incentives would play an important role in helping to tackle mass atrocities and aggression. Similarly, in the context of health incentives, Scott Halpern, Kristin Madison, and Kevin Volpp (2009: 515) argue that any effects on promoting monetary values and corrupting non-monetary values 'must be balanced against their more likely effects on curtailing the injurious social norms of smoking and overeating' (2009: 515).

7.3.6 The Extortion Objection

A fifth concern about incentives is the 'Extortion Objection' and it runs as follows.[30] Rather than stopping mass atrocities or serious external aggression, those who are rewarded will continue—or threaten to continue—their problematic behaviour in order to secure future rewards.[31] They will use the willingness of potential senders to secure more rewards. Ceasing completely and forever the problematic behaviour will end their potential income. Even if they do temporarily cease their behaviour, they will maintain the *threat* of restarting their behaviour in order to extort further rewards. Thus, the worry is that costly incentives will continue to have to be paid, even if it initially seems that one incentive may be sufficient. Indeed, incentives are sometimes seen as unsuccessful by policymakers because they can render oneself vulnerable to future extortion (Dorussen 2001: 253).

A related worry is that the incentive simply will not work because the aggressor will take the reward but not change their behaviour. This is especially the case when it is hard to monitor compliance. For instance, in the Iran–Contra affair, the US offered carrots to Iranian moderates who claimed to have influence over Lebanese militias that were holding the American citizens; however, the link between any pressure and the actual release of the hostages was not observable, meaning that the Iranians could claim that the terms of the deal were being met without many hostages actually being released (Drezner 1999: 193). Another related concern is that incentives will strengthen adversaries, providing them with resources that allow them to engage in mass atrocities or aggression to a greater extent.[32] For example, economic incentives may be used to fund arms or to resist the pressure of an ongoing sanctions regime.

[30] A form of this worry is highlighted by Cortright (1997*a*: 5).

[31] This phenomenon has been observed in the use of international environmental incentives. See Chang (1997).

[32] This worry is raised by Haass and O'Sullivan (2000: 165).

These worries about extortion and strengthening adversaries are somewhat valid. They point to the need to be cautious and careful in *how* incentives are offered and show that incentives will not always work. But they can be mitigated. Important in this regard is ensuring that the incentives are structured in such a way that they depend on future compliance.[33] That is, they are not all offered upfront, but are staggered or held back until compliance is achieved, and the incentives are ongoing (and so can be discontinued). This provides reason to prefer some incentives to others, such as those that are ongoing and able to be halted. Indeed, incentive regimes are often already structured in this way. For instance, the 2015 agreement to lift sanctions on Iran stated that Iran would not see sanctions lifted until the International Atomic Energy Agency confirmed that Iran had followed through with its end of the agreement. If Iran were to fail to live up to the terms of the deal, the UN sanctions would 'snap back' into place for ten years, with the possibility of a five-year extension (BBC 2015). The close monitoring of compliance can also help to ensure that the incentives are efficacious. In addition, the risks of extortion are mitigated if the use of incentives is widely publicized as a potential first response to a crisis, with the threat of coercive options if the incentives do not work. Any attempt at extortion may therefore risk a coercive response.[34]

7.4 INCENTIVES: WHEN AND HOW

In their strongest form, which denies absolutely the permissibility of incentives, all of the five previous objections are highly unpersuasive—incentives are sometimes permissible. But when viewed more moderately as highlighting some of the potential drawbacks of incentives, none of the previous five objections completely fails. The effects that they highlight may sometimes not apply or they may be overcome by countervailing considerations, but this will not always be the case. As such, my defence of the use of incentives is tentative. Accordingly, I will now turn to consider when and how exactly incentives should be used.

Central is that their use will be effective—in short do more good than harm. As noted in section 4.4, this is a function of the costs to the receiver, costs to the sender, and effectiveness at tackling the situation (as well as the broader

[33] However, this may lead to the 'Incentives Delivery Dilemma'. See section 7.4. On occasion, it may also be difficult for political incentives to be structured in this way.

[34] The threat of coercion can further mitigate the worry about moral hazard. If coercive options are still on the table, states are unlikely to engage in bad behaviour in order to seek a reward.

effects). I have suggested that incentives will often be effective. But this is not always likely. For instance, the offer of political support could be used mendaciously by a government to shore up its authoritarian position, rather than to change its aggression or support of mass atrocities. Or the government may accept a financial incentive but be too weak to deliver its side of the bargain. So, when are incentives likely to work? They are more likely to be efficacious when the following circumstances obtain.

First, the receiver needs to be in a position to accept the incentive and to respond as requested. Some leaders may not have the ability to change the behaviour of their constituents. In this context, in *Economic Statecraft and Foreign Policy*, Jean-Marc Blanchard and Norrin Ripsman (2013) argue that a government's compliance with incentives depends on its degree of 'stateness', that is, its ability to construct policies despite domestic opposition, its ability to perform basic functions, and the public's acknowledgement of the leader's right to rule. On their account, when leaders are unwilling to capitulate to the demands of the sender, incentives will be more effective when the receiver has lower levels of stateness (it lacks ability to resist the request). But when leaders are willing to go along with the demands of the sender, incentives will be more effective when the receiver has higher levels of stateness (when it is able to overcome domestic opposition).

Related to this, incentives seem particularly likely to be efficacious when leaders can use the incentive to realize a latent intrinsic motivation to comply—when they help to 'crowd in' motivation—and, in doing so, help the state's leaders to overcome an obstacle to compliance, such as domestic opposition. However, they are less likely to be successful when the receiver does not possess an intrinsic motivation to comply that is being blocked or when the receiver is unlikely to be motivated by the various incentives that could be offered. For instance, a receiver may not be interested in financial gain because it is motivated purely by political aspirations (Griffiths and Barnes 2008: 12) and does not need financial resources (for instance, because it is pilfering its population's resources or already receives significant external support). In fact, in such cases the offer of an economic reward to give up long-term political values may be interpreted as a bribe and so be seen as offensive (Griffiths and Barnes 2008: 12). This also points to the need to tailor the *form* of incentive to the political reality. Political incentives, such as recognition, are likely to be more efficacious when groups are uninterested in economic rewards and have strong political ambitions. In *Ending Wars*, Feargal Cochrane (2008) argues that violence should be seen as a tactic, rather than as a goal, and those who use it will stop when they see a more viable political alternative. If this is right, the offering of a political incentive may have a large role to play in addressing conflicts.

Who can offer incentives? The receiver of the incentives may not trust an adversary to deliver upon the offer. Indeed, the history of incentives has been littered with examples of grand promises being made that never materialized. More generally, without trust, the incentive will not work since the aggressor may simply refuse to change its behaviour. This takes the form of what I will call the 'Incentives Delivery Dilemma'.

> The Incentives Delivery Dilemma: On the one hand, the sender does not trust the receiver sufficiently to amend its behaviour and is therefore unwilling to deliver the incentive until after the receiver has changed its behaviour. On the other, the receiver does not trust the sender sufficiently to deliver the incentive. It is therefore unwilling to change its behaviour until it has received its incentive.

The Incentives Delivery Dilemma highlights that incentives may struggle to be efficacious when the exchange is between two adversaries. It also highlights that those offering the incentive need to be seen as sufficiently trustworthy for the incentive to be effective. This means that agents with good reputations and those with close relationships with the receiver are best placed to at least head up the offer. Beyond this dilemma, there are further reasons why it is important that the agent offering the incentive does not have an adversarial relationship with the receiver. Being seen as an adversary can mean that they are unlikely to be successful because the receiver may not want its perceived enemy to achieve its ends, even if this is in the interests of the receiver. In addition, the motives of an adversary may be viewed as suspicious by the receiver (Cortright 1997*b*: 281; Milburn and Christie 1989: 631).

Accordingly, certain states or individuals may be better at being the figurehead of the incentive offer than others, even if those who are seen as less trustworthy ultimately provide the resources. Alternatively, there needs to be a trusted intermediary to reduce the worry that the sender will not deliver. Trusted intermediaries, such as the UN or certain personalities, between the receiver and sender can help to reduce suspicions about a lack of compliance (Kriesberg 1981: 44). It is also important that there be coordination of donor efforts, so that the donors are not played off against each other and potentially undermine any peace process. In this context, the experienced diplomat Alvaro de Soto (2008: 28) proposes that the UN play the role of a clearing-house where understandings can be reached about who deals with what. As he puts it, '[w]e ought to avoid wildcat diplomacy, which doesn't do any good' (2008: 28). In fact, unlike most other measures, incentives may actually work better if offered *unilaterally* (Cortright 1997*a*: 8; Cortright 1997*b*). This is because the sender can more clearly specify the *quid pro quo*, which can be confused when the incentives are offered multilaterally, with different actors giving conflicting messages and offering different goals.

Compliance with the terms of the incentive needs to be closely monitored, such as by a UN observer mission, in order to avoid the aggressor receiving the reward without changing its behaviour. Without follow-up and supervision, the level of compliance may be lower. The incentives should, as far as possible, be ongoing rather than immediate, in order to avoid the risk of extortion. In other words, the potential rewards need to be staggered (Cortright 1997*b*: 278).

Although I have generally defended the case for the use of incentives over more coercive measures, they should *not* always replace options that are more coercive. The threat of coercion is sometimes necessary in order to avoid the risks highlighted by the Extortion and Corruption Objections. As Richard Haass and Meghan O'Sullivan (2000: 174–5) emphasize, positive incentives often require the threat of sticks if they are to be effective. To be sure, this is not always the case. Incentives may be sufficiently effective on their own. Much will depend on the appropriateness of coercion (sometimes all the coercive options may be unjustifiable and incentives are one of the few permissible options available), on whether the moral hazard and extortion will occur, and on whether the incentive will be likely to have a positive effect. Sometimes incentives will be effective even on their own, particularly in difficult cases when no coercive measures would be justifiable, given that in these cases positive incentives provide recalcitrant leaders, states, and domestic constituencies with a reason to comply with human rights norms and laws against aggression. This might not fully tackle the situation, but it might help to reduce some of its ferocity. Of course, when used alongside coercive measures, the policy as a whole would not fully enjoy the advantages of not being coercive that I have highlighted. But these advantages would still apply to the inclusion of incentives in the part of the policy. This brings me to the next point.

When coercive options, such as economic sanctions, are used, an incentive should be offered *alongside* them (rendering it a throffer). This will help to avoid or mitigate some of the resentment that purely coercive options can create and they may be much more likely to secure compliance, especially in the long term. The incentive should be targeted at the local population to reduce some of the hostility towards the sender and the 'rally-round-the-flag' effect. Inducements can help to make it clear to the general population that they are not the target.[35] Thus, when used alongside more coercive measures, incentives can help to augment the effectiveness of these measures. They might be seen as akin to a 'force-multiplier' for these measures. The offer of a carrot can make the stick less painful and reduce some of the resentment that comes with it. It is less clear, though, whether they can be used in conjunction with naming and shaming, since the public offer of an incentive could

[35] One drawback of a mixed approach, though, is that it may be more costly than using solely carrots or solely sticks, since (1) compliance will require paying the reward and (2) non-compliance will require carrying out the threat. That said, as noted above, some incentives may not be costly at all (such as recognition) and others may in fact be beneficial (such as trade deals). A mixed approach may also, on occasion, be less costly since it reduces some of the potential ramifications of a purely coercive approach and ensures that the incentives are efficacious, removing the need for further measures to be explored.

seemingly undermine the strict condemnation of the behaviour. But there can be ways around this: the incentive could be offered covertly; another agent could offer the incentive; or the rationale for the incentive may be offered whilst making it clear that the agent completely rejects the behaviour in question.

My point, then, is that strategies that use solely incentives may be better than strategies that rely solely on coercion; if coercion is required, it is often better to *also* use incentives. Nevertheless, a mixed approach will sometimes be better than a strategy that relies solely on incentives. Often, the key decision will be how much the strategy should rely on positive incentives relative to negative ones. In fact, almost all successful interactions involve some degree of positive incentive. As Cortright (1997*b*: 280) points out, it would be rare for a state to propose a *completely* coercive policy that attempts to destroy its adversary and, even if it were to do so, its proposition would probably not be morally justified. He notes that successful diplomacy often requires the presence of both sanctions and incentives, even if the incentive is only the ending of the coercive measure, such as the lifting of the sanctions.

As we have seen, there is often a close interlink between positive incentives and coercive measures. This is most obvious with the ending of economic sanctions, which draws on the previous coercion to offer an incentive. Conversely, positive incentives may provide opportunity for future coercive measures. An obvious example is the threat to end ongoing economic aid. After economic aid (potentially as an incentive), the subsequent threat of ending economic aid can provide a clear show of disapproval and sometimes play a significant role in helping to end conflicts and mass atrocities (Cortright 1997*b*: 293). This provides a further reason to offer a positive incentive, such as aid. It offers states and other agents leverage over the recipients—there is another stick that they can use if the recipient looks to engage in morally problematic behaviour again. Thus, incentives add more to the toolkit of responses to serious external aggression and mass atrocities than simply themselves.

To a lesser extent, this reasoning also provides a rationale for launching and maintaining coercive measures such as economic sanctions. It offers the possibility of their future lifting, which can be used as a positive incentive. Without the preceding sticks, states and other agents would not have this carrot to offer. Of course, whether this is morally justifiable depends on the nature of the sanctions regime and on the other morally relevant considerations, which as I suggested (in chapter 3) may count against the use of sanctions. The general point is that offering both incentives and sanctions provides future leverage, which adds to the general case for using them (which will be determined overall by several considerations).[36]

[36] One final point: it might conceivably be possible to justifiably offer a receiver an incentive to engage in what seems like a morally illegitimate purpose. For instance, financial incentives

7.5 AMNESTIES

I will now consider the most controversial form of incentive, which raises particular ethical issues. This is the use of amnesties and the offer of *de facto* immunity from prosecution. Leaders and other individuals may continue their problematic behaviour because of the fear that, if they step down, they will be prosecuted. They may not be willing to step down unless they receive guarantees that they will not be punished.[37] Indeed, amnesties have played important roles in helping to end conflicts peacefully, most notably in South Africa during the transition from apartheid. Leaders may also be offered exile in other states. For instance, Charles Taylor received exile in Nigeria after his role in mass atrocities in Sierra Leone and Liberia, and Idi Amin lived out the rest of his years in Saudi Arabia after ordering mass atrocities in Uganda and attacking Tanzania. As noted above, the possibility of exile has also been widely mooted for Assad, as a means of achieving regime change and ending the conflict in Syria. Exile was also offered to Saddam Hussein (to Bahrain) and to other leading officials by the US on the eve of the 2003 invasion of Iraq (Scharf 2006: 340). If Saddam Hussein had accepted, hundreds of thousands of lives might have been saved, including his own. In addition, Gaddafi reportedly rejected a proposal of exile prior to being indicted by the International Criminal Court (ICC) (Dancy and Montal 2017).

However, in this section I will argue that the use of international immunity from prosecution for leaders is, for all intents and purposes, absolutely impermissible. The position I endorse is what can be called a '*de facto* absolutism' for current circumstances: the offer of immunity for leaders from prosecution is impermissible in feasible circumstances. It therefore should not be used to help to end mass atrocities and external aggression.[38] In defending *de facto* absolutism, I accept that (1) there might be *conceivable* circumstances when the use of immunity for leaders is permissible, such as offering a leader exile, which stops the mass killing of ten million civilians. My focus is on *feasible*

may be offered to prospective rebel soldiers in order to fight against their state in what would be an unjust war, but which would lead both sides to the negotiating table. Or, a multimillion-pound bribe may be paid to a general to stop fighting, with full awareness that she would use this money in a morally problematic manner, such as spending it on heavy-polluting SUVs or setting up a small-scale criminal enterprise. Rather than looking to whether the recipient is being incentivized to behave justly *themselves*, we should look instead to the *justifiability of the sender offering the incentive*. On occasion, but probably only rarely, this may mean that it is justifiable to offer an incentive to behave in a morally problematic manner because this will be best at effectively addressing the situation.

[37] For a defence of amnesties (and rejection of international prosecutions), see Snyder and Vinjamuri (2004).

[38] This is in similar vein to the position of the UN Secretariat, which has asserted that immunity 'can never be permitted to excuse genocide, war crimes, crimes against humanity or gross violations of human rights' (Freeman 2009: 148).

cases, applicable to here and now, rather than thought experiments. I also accept that (2) it might be permissible to offer immunity for those not in major positions of authority, in part because of the difficulty of prosecuting absolutely everyone. I also do not deny (3) that domestic amnesties might be politically necessary and morally justifiable. I simply focus here on the international case.[39]

What is wrong with offering legal incentives? As we have seen, economic and political incentives can be problematic to the extent that they reward wrongdoers or have unintended effects, but are generally justifiable responses. Legal incentives—immunity or exile—can also endure these problems. There are also additional countervailing reasons in favour of prosecuting wrongdoers which preclude legal incentives. These points—and responses to them—will be considered in more detail in section 9.1, where I examine the case for international criminal justice as a tool for tackling mass atrocities and aggression. I will only briefly note them now.

The first reason is the importance of expressing moral outrage at the behaviour of the aggressor. This can help in the establishment of international norms against the crimes in question. A second, and related, reason is that prosecution is important in order to avoid future instances of the problematic behaviour. One of the central arguments for the ICC and other international tribunals is that they deter potential violators from engaging in problematic behaviour, with the potential for punishment (this is primarily through 'positive complementarity'). Offering immunity may undermine any potential deterrent effect by showing that, if a leader abuses her population, she will not necessarily be punished. The offer of immunity in a particular case will have to do enough in terms of the halting of the violations of basic human rights and the stopping of serious external aggression to outweigh any potential negative effects on the deterrent features of (international) law.

To be sure, much depends on *who* will be offered immunity from prosecution. The offer for those lower down the ranks may face far fewer negative ramifications than when immunity is offered to political leaders. The expressive condemnation of the violation may still be present by the prosecution of those in greater positions of power and the effect on the deterrence may be small as few see the immunity as being generally likely to occur in other cases. As noted above, it is also *conceivable* that it be permissible to offer a legal incentive of immunity from prosecution to leaders. However, it is currently not feasible that this will be the case for two reasons.

First, the stakes need to be high—the situation needs to be very bad—and the benefits (in terms of the likely ending of the violation of basic human

[39] A key issue in international criminal justice concerns whether the international community should respect domestic amnesties. See Wellman (2008) for a discussion of the ethics of this issue.

rights) need to be very likely to materialize and to outweigh the likely detrimental effects on international criminal law. Such cases seem very unlikely, in part because the human rights abuses can continue even without the presence of the leader. For instance, Uganda experienced a bloody civil war after the removal of Amin in which several hundred thousand people died. In virtually all cases, then, leaders should be prosecuted. This prompts the question: if a leader such as Omar al-Bashir in Sudan is offered exile, could this in fact make matters *even worse*, if those who are part of his regime take over that are more ruthless or bloodthirsty?

Second, cases of potentially permissible international amnesty seem unlikely because, in cases where immunity could be offered to leaders, there is no ongoing, international threat of prosecution. There is therefore no *incentive* offered to the leader. We have seen that an offer of immunity from prosecution is only an incentive if there is a pre-existing threat of prosecution. This threat needs to be likely for the offer of immunity to be an incentive. Immunity is usually granted at the domestic level, rather than the international one. Internationally, the scope for immunity to be offered is small. To be sure, international criminal tribunals applicable to the conflict or the ICC may decide not to prosecute. The ICC, for instance, can choose not to launch a prosecution if prosecuting will harm the 'interests of justice', which is meant politically, such as if a prosecution will undermine a peace process. However, the ICC's use of the 'interests of justice' is not an offer presented to perpetrators; rather, it is an internal decision made by the Office of the Prosecutor. Thus, it seems highly unlikely that the ICC would offer immunity from prosecution to leaders.

The offer of international exile may appear more feasible. However, the offer of exile would seemingly need to be to the leader of a state that has not ratified the Rome Statute. If the state has, it would be duty-bound to attempt to arrest the leader if the ICC has issued an arrest warrant. Even if it did not plan to do so, a leader is highly unlikely to seek exile in a signatory state, given the risk that they could be transferred to The Hague. Since over 120 states are State Parties to the Rome Statute, there are not that many states in which leaders can seek exile. Moreover, the rise in international criminal justice has meant that leaders will probably be much more sceptical about any exile agreements being upheld.[40] A significant precedent was the arrest and trial of Charles Taylor, who agreed to exile in Nigeria in 2003. The warrant for his arrest, issued later in 2003 by the Special Court for Sierra Leone, was enforced and has 'reinforced the principle of no safe haven' and, in doing

[40] There might still be exceptions, though, such as the exile agreement reached for Yahya Jammeh, the former authoritarian President of Gambia in January 2017 (for exile in Equatorial Guinea). Yet Jammeh, although authoritarian, had (seemingly) not yet engaged in the level of human rights abuses that would render him potentially subject to an ICC action.

so, has meant that exile arrangements have come to generally be seen 'as illusions—as traps for naive and foolish leaders' (Freeman 2009: 121). Thus, the potential incentive of exile is unlikely to be accepted by leaders.

7.6 CONCLUSION

In this chapter, I have offered a cautious defence of the use of positive incentives. The use of positive incentives enjoys the advantages of being not coercive, as well as being less costly and potentially successful. However, there are notable worries about their use. The worries about rewarding wrongdoers (the Rewarding Evil Objection), crowding out intrinsic motivation (the Crowding-Out Objection), the corruption of international society (the Corruption Objection), and moral hazard (the Moral Hazard Objection) are less of a concern, since they may not apply or be outweighed by the benefits of using positive incentives. Yet the worry about extortion is of greater concern, although it may be possible for it to be avoided by the careful structuring of incentives.

More generally, the chapter has highlighted that the use of positive incentives is not a cure-all. The chapter has also highlighted that there are important differences between types of incentives. Legal incentives in the form of international amnesties and offers of exile are particularly morally problematic. Economic incentives face fewer ethical issues, but may make little difference and can be perceived as insulting. Political incentives have most going for them but, again, whether they are likely to be efficacious will depend on the characteristics of the receiver.

The use of positive incentives is often preferable to a purely coercive strategy. Yet we have also seen that a strategy based on purely positive incentives can often be limited. Indeed, the chapter has stressed the close relationship between coercive and non-coercive incentives. The threat of coercion may sometimes be required in order to mitigate some of the drawbacks of the use of incentives, such as the worries about extortion. On the other hand, one of the notable attractions of the use of incentives is that they remove many of the hard edges off coercive strategies. To that extent, the partnering of coercive and non-coercive measures is often the best way of tackling mass atrocities and serious external aggression.

Coercive strategies often dominate the public and policy debates about responses to mass atrocities and serious external aggression. At the very least, this chapter highlights that non-coercive measures should be considered alongside coercive strategies and sometimes instead of them.

8

Military Assistance

Chapter 7 focused on positive incentives that have a clear *quid pro quo*. In this chapter, I turn to consider assistance often without conditionality, focusing in particular on military assistance and especially military assistance to rebel groups. This is one of the most notorious ways that states attempt to realize their foreign policy goals. The arming of rebel groups was particularly patent during the Arab Spring. After the uprising in Libya in 2011, various states provided lethal and non-lethal arms to the forces opposed to Gaddafi's regime. This included material and financial support from the Libya Contact Group, as well as arms from France, Qatar, and the UK (Corten and Koutroulis 2013: 90). In Syria, the arming of the various parties by external actors became one of the central dynamics of the conflict. On the one hand, Qatar and Saudi Arabia (and others) supplied arms to the Free Syrian Army (FSA), the UK and France provided it with 'non-lethal support', and the US and Turkey facilitated and coordinated the supply (BBC 2013). On the other hand, Russia and Iran supplied weapons such as missile systems, mortars, and rockets to the Assad regime. In 2012, the UK even secretly drew up plans to train and equip a 100,000-strong Syrian rebel army abroad, which would then strike at the Assad regime in a manner similar to the 'Awe' and 'Shock' strikes on Iraq in 2003 (Hopkins 2014). And, in 2017, despite the objections from its NATO ally Turkey, the Trump Administration decided to arm Kurdish rebels with heavy machine guns, anti-tank weapons, and other weapons, in order to help them take on the Islamic State of Iraq and Syria (ISIS) in Raqqa (Schmitt 2017).

There are two main reasons why arming rebels may be preferable to direct military action. First, it is often far less costly for the sending state, in terms of both the lives of military personnel and financial resources (Salehyan 2010: 503). (This has led some to refer to the arming of rebels as 'intervention-lite' (Barnes-Dacey and Levy 2013: 2).) Second, the arming of rebels can more easily be carried out covertly, that is, out of the public gaze and without the widespread knowledge of the international community. The upshot is that states have often supplied arms to rebels, most infamously under the Reagan Doctrine, which aimed to support anti-Communist insurgencies. Notorious examples include the US arming, training, and financing of the Nicaraguan Contras against the Sandinista government (including the covert funding of the Contras without congressional approval in the Iran–Contra affair); the British arming, in contravention of a UN arms embargo, of Sierra Leone through Sandline, a UK-based private military and security company (the Arms-to-Africa Affair); and the Russian supplying of arms to various pro-Russian separatist rebels in former Soviet states (including, recently, Ukraine). There have also been numerous cases of the arming of rebels in potentially more morally justifiable cases. These include the supply of arms by the US and some Islamic groups to the Bosnian Muslims during the break-up of the former Yugoslavia, and Soviet and Cuban military support for anti-apartheid forces in South Africa.

This chapter argues that arming rebels should be generally eschewed as an alternative to war, but may occasionally be morally justifiable. More specifically, I will argue that arming rebels can be a permissible alternative to war (even when the rebels are engaged in unjust wars), but only exceptionally since this is generally problematic. The former, far more permissive claim will be established in the first part of the chapter. The latter, more restrictive claim will be established in the second part of the chapter. In doing so, I will also consider—and also largely repudiate—the case for arming *states* against non-state actors engaged in aggression and mass atrocities, such as supplying arms to the Iraqi state in its fight against ISIS.

Some clarifications are necessary. To start with, by 'arming' rebels, I mean the provision of military equipment to rebel groups. That said, some of the analysis may also be applicable to other forms of support to rebels, such as when states train and finance them, or provide them with other apparatus, such as non-lethal equipment (such as radars, body armour, medical supplies, and communications equipment). By 'rebels', I mean those who are in armed opposition to their established government and possess political objectives. These objectives may be to supplant the current government (such as the various uprisings during the Arab Spring) or to secede (such as the Kosovo Liberation Army's attempt to secede from the former Yugoslavia). Other objectives that rebels might possess, which all take the form of resisting or challenging the government, include securing a (potentially greater) role in a power-sharing agreement, achieving changes to a particular policy of a state, and improving the human rights situation (such as the Zapatista rebellion in Mexico).

Second, arming rebels should be (and in policy circles *is*) seen as an alternative to war. To start with, it is an alternative to states *waging wars in other states*. That is, even if there is already a civil war going on in which the rebels are participating, arming rebels avoids a further war—an *inter*state war—such as between the external party and the repressive state. Indeed, during the public debate on Syria, the sending of arms was widely viewed as an alternative to war by the West against the Assad regime.[1] It was defended by those who were more optimistic that it would help to remove the Assad regime and therefore remove any purported need for direct Western military intervention. Notwithstanding, although arming rebels is sometimes an alternative to war and direct military intervention, it is sometimes carried out *alongside* war and direct military intervention. For instance, not only did the West arm the Libyan rebels, it also intervened militarily in support of them.

Third, it is worth linking this chapter to the case presented for arms embargoes in chapter 4. I argued that, in general, arms embargoes should often be pursued because they reduce aggregate harm, are relatively low cost for the sender, distribute harms fairly, and often are symbolically important by helping to denounce wrongdoing. But, although arms embargoes are generally permissible, this does not foreclose the question of whether it is morally acceptable to arm rebel groups and states. Most obviously, an arms embargo might not be in place. And, even if it is, it might be partial, applying to only one side of the conflict, leaving open the question of whether the other side should be offered military assistance. Thus, whereas chapter 4 focused on the case for *denying* arms to belligerents, typically supplied by third parties (such as other states and arms dealers), this chapter focuses on a different question: the case for *directly supplying* arms to rebels and states.[2]

8.1 THE BLANKET BAN VIEW AND THE CASE FOR ARMING REBELS

Let us first consider the view that arming rebels should *never* be adopted as a measure to tackle mass atrocities and serious external aggression. After all, on the face of it, it seems a highly controversial measure, far more so than the other measures we are considering, with a very dubious history, and potentially always wrong—and perhaps even worse than military intervention.[3] On this view, then, there should be a blanket ban on arming rebels.

[1] See, for instance, Vilmer (2012).

[2] It is also worth noting that, despite the popularity of arming rebels as a foreign policy option, there is very little, if any, detailed engagement with the ethical issues surrounding the practice. There is a growing literature on the ethical issues surrounding civil wars and, more specifically, the conditions for engaging in just rebellion (e.g. Buchanan 2013; Dobos 2012; Fabre 2012: 130–65; Gross 2015). However, the focus of this literature is largely on the question of the justifiability of the *rebels* engaging in civil war and of their conduct when doing so, rather than the permissibility of the arming of rebels by *other agents*. As I will argue below, in section 8.2, these are two separate questions (that is, I will argue that it can be justifiable to arm rebels who are engaged in an unjust civil war).

[3] I compare in detail the case for arming rebels with the case for military intervention in Pattison (2017).

Why should this blanket-ban view be rejected and it be at least *occasionally* morally justifiable to arm rebel groups? First, it seems intuitively plausible that arming rebels may sometimes be justifiable. Indeed, there have been real-life cases where it seems that it was all-things-considered justifiable to arm rebels. An obvious example was the British supply of arms to the French Resistance.

Second, and more substantively, the permissibility of arming rebels can be a corollary of the right to self-defence. If we hold that individuals have a right to self-defence, and that the only way that they can fulfil this right is by being supplied arms because, for instance, they have no other means of defending themselves against a brutal dictator, then their rights of self-defence require the transfer of arms. For instance, if Amy has a right not to be killed by Brenda, who is unjustly threatening her, Chloe could permissibly provide Amy with a means of defending herself, such as a gun. Similarly, if a group of citizens has a right not to be killed by their state, an external party could permissibly provide the citizens with weapons in order for them not to be killed by their state. Although the right to self-defence is limited by proportionality constraints (for instance, so that several innocents are not harmed in the exercise of this right), on occasion the supplying of arms may conceivably not pose any harm to innocents (for instance, Amy may harm only Brenda then destroy the gun). The permissibility of arming rebels can also stem from other rights, such as the right to self-determination. For instance, it might be permissible to arm rebels attempting to realize the self-determination of the group, if the rebels meet the requisite criteria. They might, for instance, need to be sufficiently authorized by the population of the group.[4]

It therefore seems that arming rebels might be justifiable *on occasion*, providing that they meet the relevant conditions. I will not flesh out all the conditions here, but they are similar to the well-rehearsed Just War criteria found for engaging in humanitarian intervention. They include, most notably, necessity (arming rebels must be superior to other options) and proportionality (arming rebels must be superior to not arming rebels).[5]

However, three considerations might be thought to provide sufficient reason to uphold an absolute prohibition on arming the rebels: (1) the fact that those being armed are *rebels*; (2) the fact that *external* parties are supplying the arms; and (3) the fact that those supplying arms may be *complicit* in wrongdoing committed by the rebels. Yet, these reasons do not seem strong enough to justify an absolute prohibition on arming rebels.[6]

[4] It is also possible that rebels can be armed to provide *other* defence, that is, to help defend threatened members of the group.

[5] To reiterate: I will later argue that it is *generally* unlikely that arming rebels will do more good than harm, given the empirical evidence on the effects of arming rebels; my focus here is on when this is *not* the case and whether arming rebels might be permissible in such (rare) instances.

[6] To be sure, I will later suggest that there are some plausible reasons (such as the importance of state control) for holding that it is more likely to be permissible to arm legitimate states than it

The fact that (1) *rebels* are being armed is not sufficient to ground an absolute prohibition because rebels may act permissibly. Indeed, the right of rebellion (when certain conditions are met) is widely endorsed.[7] Given this right, it seems that third parties might be able to assist others to secure their right to rebel. Moreover, it is widely held that states can be permissibly armed; if this is right, it also seems that it may be justifiable to arm rebels. For instance, if it is justifiable on occasion to arm legitimate states, why is it not justifiable to arm rebel groups who are trying to establish legitimate states? To deny this would be to maintain an unduly strong and implausible distinction between the permissibility of arming rebel groups and the permissibility of arming states. Such an asymmetrical, absolute prohibition seems unfair. This is because it would be based on a morally arbitrary feature of the threatened party, that is, *who is threatening them*. More specifically, it would depend on the status of the oppressed as being attacked by their *state*. But those who have the status of being attacked by *rebels* could permissibly obtain assistance from statist forces.

To see the unfairness, suppose that, in the Democratic Republic of the Congo (DRC), Abena is unjustly threatened with death by government forces. Unless she takes up arms against the forces of her government, she will be killed along with her children. She is supplied these arms by South Africa, which wants to overthrow the government of the DRC in order to halt its rights violations. Suppose further that, also in the DRC, Binah is unjustly threatened with death by a rebel group. Unless Binah takes up arms against the rebel forces by joining or assisting the state's army, she will be killed along with her children. She is supplied these arms by France, which wants to defeat the rebel forces in order to halt their rights violations. Why should we treat Abena any differently to Binah? Both women take up arms to defend themselves and their families. The actions of others determine whether Abena and Binah are deemed as rebels or government forces. Abena and Binah are simply defending themselves. To that extent, the status of Abena as a rebel fighting the government and Binah as part of a statist force fighting a rebel force seems a matter of luck (as far as they are concerned) and so it is morally arbitrary. Fundamentally at least, it seems morally irrelevant to whether it is justifiable to arm them.

Similarly, the fact that (2) the rebels are armed by an *external* party is not sufficient to ground an absolute prohibition. It seems clear that there could be the justifiable *internal* transfers of arms to the rebels from the domestic supporters of the rebels. For instance, during the Arab Spring, it may have been justifiable for the Libyan population to transfer arms to the Libyan rebels.

is to arm rebel movements. However, these reasons are not sufficiently strong to ground an a priori prohibition on arming rebels.

[7] See Buchanan (2013) and Finlay (2015) for two recent influential analyses.

However, if this is the case, it seems that *external* parties could also permissibly transfer arms, such as from the UK or France to the Libyan rebels. Why does it matter that the parties are *external*? To be sure, it might matter that the party is external for grounding a *general presumption* against arming rebels, but this does not seem to be strong enough to justify an *absolute* prohibition against arming rebels. This is because, in general, the relevance of being an external party—and the potential violation of state sovereignty—is not thought to offer a decisive reason to preclude support. Most notably, the literature on the ethics of humanitarian intervention widely accepts that it may be justifiable for *external* parties to intervene militarily in support of rebel movements. If we hold that being an external party in the case of direct military intervention is not sufficient to ground an absolute prohibition, the same seems true of arming rebels. The fact that an external party is transferring arms to the conflict therefore does not seem to provide sufficient reason to uphold an absolutist prohibition.

Indeed, the case for arming rebels is somewhat analogous to the case for the exceptional permissibility of humanitarian intervention. As with humanitarian intervention, what justifies the (exceptional) right to arm the rebels is a broad and serious threat to the enjoyment of basic human rights. Most clearly, this might consist of helping rebels to overthrow an oppressive regime, to secede from a repressive majority, or to reduce the extent of government repression. Like the arming of rebels, humanitarian intervention sometimes bolsters a particular side, albeit with the ultimate, predominant aim of promoting basic human rights in the affected political community. My point, then, is that if one supports the permissibility of humanitarian intervention, which may require intervening in support of a particular side, then there exists a prima facie case for arming rebels, perhaps albeit very rarely.

Indeed, as with humanitarian intervention, the importance of upholding the principle of state sovereignty, as traditionally conceived, does not provide sufficient reason to preclude the permissibility of arming rebels in all situations. One of the central, and largely uncontroversial, claims of the R2P doctrine is that state sovereignty implies responsibility for its population; if a state is manifestly failing to protect its population from mass atrocities, then the international community has a remedial responsibility to protect this population. As a corollary, humanitarian intervention is widely thought to be sometimes morally justifiable—and even sometimes morally obligatory—because of the potential for intervention to do more good than harm, despite the various risks that humanitarian intervention poses to international stability and its seeming contravention of the principle of non-intervention. The same might be true of arming rebels. When understood as a responsibility, sovereignty is not a bar to arming rebels if the state in question is manifestly failing to protect its population from mass atrocities. In such cases, worries about the effects of the violation of the principle of non-intervention may be outweighed. Indeed, arming rebels may conceivably not lead to much international instability. It may in fact conceivably improve stability by helping to put in place a more stable regime. Or arming rebels may enable the rebels to achieve sufficient good (e.g. by tackling the mass violation of basic human rights), thus outweighing any harms.

Let us now consider (3) the suggestion that arming rebels is unjustifiable since those supplying arms will be complicit in wrongdoing committed by rebels (or others).[8] Suppose, for instance, that Iran supplies arms to rebels in Yemen. It is reasonably foreseeable that some Yemeni rebels will use these arms to commit atrocities and, in addition, some of the weapons will be used after the conflict to support low-level criminal activity in the region. Iran is therefore complicit in the wrongdoing. Does this *necessarily* render Iran's supplying of the weapons to Yemeni rebels impermissible? It seems not. The potential complicity in wrongdoing involved when arming rebels does not seem sufficient to maintain an absolutist prohibition. Most obviously, sometimes—if perhaps only very rarely—there may be no wrongdoing committed by the rebel groups (or by others who will foreseeably use the weapons) for those providing the arms to be complicit in. For instance, the rebels might use the weapons only defensively and proportionately, and then destroy them.

Much more likely is that there will be *some* wrongdoing by the rebels or other groups (especially given the Rebel-Risk Objection and Diffusion Objection presented in section 8.3). However, although supplying arms may involve some complicity in wrongdoing, it might still—but perhaps only rarely—be all-things-considered permissible. As such, one may act complicitly but potentially still permissibly. As argued in section 4.3.4, acting complicitly is *pro tanto* wrong, but this does not mean that the action is all-things-considered impermissible. It concerns (i) the wrongness of *doing* harm, which can be outweighed by achieving much greater beneficial consequences, or concerns (ii) the bringing about of some harm, which can be outweighed by the fact that the option reduces more aggregate harm. Suppose that Iran's arming of the Yemeni rebels in the case above would help the rebels to halt a government-sponsored mass killing of several thousand civilians and so achieve extremely beneficial consequences. Suppose, further, that the foreseeable harms of supplying rebels are comparatively much smaller. For instance, suppose that only 5 per cent of the arms would be stolen and sold on the black market to criminals and a handful of rogue rebels would use the weapons in revenge attacks against civilians. It seems that Iran's supplying of arms would still be justifiable, despite the apparent complicity in wrongdoing, given the extremely beneficial consequences achieved. To be sure, achieving such extremely beneficial consequences

[8] For instance, the US received reports that the CIA-trained Syrian rebels had summarily executed prisoners and committed other notable violations (Mazzetti et al. 2017).

is likely to be very rare; as I will argue in section 8.3, arming rebels will generally be likely to lead to disproportionate costs.

8.2 THE JUST REBELLION VIEW AND ITS EXCEPTIONS

Having rejected the claim that it is always wrong to arm rebels *per se*, I now want to consider a seemingly more moderate view: it is always wrong to arm rebels *fighting unjust wars*. This is what I will call the 'Just Rebellion View', which holds that for it to be justifiable to arm rebels, they must be fighting a just war—one that meets the conditions of *jus ad bellum* and *jus in bello*.[9] If the rebels are fighting an unjust war, then the state supplying the arms acts wrongly. In what follows, I will reject the Just Rebellion View. I will argue that there may be exceptions when it is justifiable to arm even *unjust* rebels. To understand this, it helps to consider two questions. First, is the use of force by the rebels justifiable? Second, is it justifiable to arm them? I will argue that the answer to the second question does not depend on the answer to the first. Although the rebels may not meet requisite conditions for their war to be just, arming them may still be justifiable.

As has been noted in some of the literature on revisionist Just War Theory (e.g. McMahan 2004: 713–14), wars are subject to different phases and may involve different causes, and the same is true of wars fought by rebels. Although a rebellion may start out as a response to a just cause, such as remedying gross violations of human rights, it may later come to support an unjust cause, such as securing access to valuable natural resources. For instance, it might have been justifiable to arm the more moderate rebels fighting for freedom in Syria in the early stages of the conflict, before it morphed into a sectarian war with some of these groups changing aims and others being subsumed into groups fighting for more problematic causes.[10]

In addition to the possibility of there being different phases of a rebellion, there could also be different elements of it. For instance, a civil war may be unjust overall because its main aim is to overthrow a democratically elected leader and impose an authoritarian ruler, but it may have tangential elements that are justified, such as fighting for the greater redistribution of resources in particular areas. The arming of rebels in support of the just element may be justifiable, even if the overall war is unjust. For instance, it may be justifiable to

[9] This view is implied, for instance, in Havemann's (1998: 243) brief remarks on applying Just War Theory to UK arms exports. It is also defended by Christensen (2015: 37).

[10] Similarly, Buchanan (2013: 314–15) argues that the justifiability of intervention depends on the current situation, rather than on the previous impermissible acts of the revolutionary movement.

arm rebels who are justifiably protecting a refugee camp from attack by government forces, even if the main war waged by the rebels is unjust.

Moreover, it may be justifiable to arm rebels fighting an unjust war *throughout*. This seems to apply most clearly to unjust rebels who are fighting against other unjust parties. In particular, it seems most apt when rebels are fighting a *somewhat* morally problematic war (such as a rebellion that is fought for material gain, with very little representation) against parties whose war is *even worse* (such as other rebels who are fighting a brutal war of extermination or a ruthless, tyrannical state). Perhaps most notably, arming rebels may strengthen them and result in the conflict becoming a stalemate. The provision of arms, most notably major conventional weapons, by an external party, could significantly augment the strength of a rebel group, allowing it to engage directly with governmental forces rather than only with individual governmental personnel on a more ad hoc basis (Moore 2012: 335). And, in general, when rebels are strong, conflicts tend to be shorter because governments have incentives to compromise (Clayton 2013; Moore 2012: 335) and negotiated settlements are more likely. Both sides give up the hope of victory and negotiate a settlement that ends the brutal conflict (Hultquist 2013). By contrast, when rebel forces are weak, governments are less willing to negotiate because they do not want to encourage other insurrections and because living with a weak rebel force may be less costly than making concessions or trying to eradicate them.[11] Thus, Govinda Clayton notes that, according to his findings, 'it appears that the support and development of rebel forces is a viable approach to speed the resolution of civil war' (2013: 620). Indeed, equalizing the sides was one of the rationales offered in the public debate about arming rebels in Syria and attempting to force the Assad regime to negotiate.[12]

Accordingly, even though one may arm unjust rebels, this is not necessarily in order to assist them to achieve their (unjust) aims. Rather, the goal may be to frustrate the opposing side. For example, the rebels may have little or no hope of victory; indeed, the state supplying arms would not be aiming to help the rebels secure victory or realize their political vision. On the contrary, the final peace agreement may be different from that advocated by any of the belligerents. Hence, what matters is not the justifiability of the *rebels'* war,

[11] Although Moore notes this, he generally finds that increasing the provision of major conventional weapons increases the severity of civil wars (see section 8.3).

[12] Barnes-Dacey and Levy (2013: 3) discuss this argument in more detail. Also see Biggar (2013: 398–9), who argues that the Syrian rebels met most of the Just War conditions, but were not legitimate. Nevertheless, he calls for 'a more even balance of military forces—and therefore increased Arab and Western support of the rebels' so that the regime and its supporters 'become convinced that military victory over the rebellion is beyond reach and that political compromise is the only way forward'.

but rather the justifiability of *the state's arming of the rebels*, which will be determined in part by the foreseeable consequences of providing such arms. Of course, it is likely that the foreseeable consequences of arming just rebels will generally be much better than arming unjust rebels.

Although the justice of the rebels' war is not a necessary condition for arming rebels, it is important to emphasize again that this is only in exceptional cases and that potential benefits are often unlikely to be realized.[13] For instance, if one accepts the 'new wars' thesis (e.g. Kaldor 2012), victory is not always sought by belligerents since they may profit from the conflict itself. On this view, belligerents are not striving to defeat a clear opponent, but fight for a variety of complex—and seemingly contradictory—political and economic reasons. Therefore, the acceptance of a stalemate by such belligerents will often be unlikely. Moreover, even when stalemate is likely, the probability of arming (unjust) rebels leading to a stalemate that could do enough good—such as securing peace and ending the mass violation of basic human rights—to outweigh the harms that will be considered in section 8.3 seems small. Although there may be exceptions, in most cases the conflict can be expected to last longer as the rebels' incentives to back down are reduced.

8.3 GENERAL OBJECTIONS TO ARMING REBELS

Thus far, I have argued against two absolutist views: (1) that arming rebels is always wrong and (2) arming unjust rebels is always wrong (the Just Rebellion View). As such, arming rebels is at least *sometimes* a legitimate part of the toolkit to respond to mass atrocities and serious external aggression. I will now consider whether arming rebels should *generally* be seen as part of this toolkit. I will argue that we should be highly sceptical of the likelihood of arming rebels being *generally* morally justifiable, even when their wars are justified (as well as when their wars are unjustified). That is, arming rebels is only *exceptionally* justifiable. To do this, I will present three general objections to arming the rebels. In doing so, I will repudiate a counterpart claim to the Just Rebellion View, which, again, might appear plausible at first sight—that *just rebels can generally be armed*.

[13] To be clear, this does not mean that there are no such cases and that this is purely hypothetical. For instance, although the facts are contested, it might have been all-things-considered permissible for the US to arm the Croat forces during the Bosnian war, despite Tuđman's unjust war. The arming of the Croat forces may be claimed to have been beneficial overall, despite the forces' war crimes in Krajina, since it frustrated the Serb attempts to establish a Greater Serbia.

8.3.1 The Rebel-Risk Objection

The first objection—the 'Rebel-Risk Objection'—raises an epistemic problem: it can be difficult to determine who the rebels are. More precisely, it can be difficult to determine whether they are fighting with regard to the principles of *jus ad bellum* and *jus in bello* (for instance, the principles of the Just Rebellion View) and, if they were to get into power, whether they would be likely to be better than the current government. These risks were a frequently cited danger of the arming of the Syrian rebels (Carpenter 2012). That is to say, one of the central objections to arming the Syrian rebels was that it was unclear who the rebels were and whether they would potentially be even worse than the Assad regime.

Another important concern of the Rebel-Risk Objection is that it is difficult to determine whether arming rebels will ensure that only those who are liable to harm will be subject to it. For instance, the supplying agent may not possess sufficient information about the liability of those against whom the rebels will use force (or the liability of the rebels themselves). And even if it did have this information, it may lack sufficient control over the rebels to ensure force is only used against those who are liable. Thus, the Rebel-Risk Objection also posits that there are major risks concerning those subject to force by the rebels.

To help flesh out this point, we can frame it in terms of the contingent pacifist objection to revisionist Just War Theory (e.g. McMahan 2009). This objection runs as follows: the waging of any wars is likely to involve harms to those who are not liable to such harms, such as innocent civilians. On a revisionist approach to Just War Theory, there are likely to be many non-liable parties. This is because, on this view, not only is it wrong to target innocent *non-combatants*, it is also wrong to target innocent *combatants*, such as those who fight justly on the just side and even those who make just contributions to otherwise unjust wars. It is difficult to ensure that those waging war will target only those who are liable, since it can be difficult both to determine who is innocent and to ensure that there is no harm to innocents. Given the worries about *doing* harm to innocents (rather than simply *allowing* it), the risks of waging war are too great. As a result, some (e.g. Lazar 2010; May 2011) endorse contingent pacifism or argue that revisionist Just War Theory leads to contingent pacifism.

Such risks are even higher when arming rebels because those supplying arms will typically be in a worse position to determine who is liable, and must rely on those to whom they supply arms to make these judgements. Furthermore, whereas a state can exert *some* degree of control over its armed forces and have a series of mechanisms to try to ensure that only liable agents are subject to harms (such as training in international humanitarian law and court martials for soldiers), it typically lacks such control over rebels. The suppliers rely on a different actor, with its own set of interests and agenda, which they often have little means of influencing, bar the ceasing of funding or military support. Another way of putting this is in terms of the principal–agent problem: the principal (the supplier) has relatively little control over the agent (the rebels) in this context and few mechanisms to avoid, for instance, shirking international humanitarian law.[14] Moreover, the agents supplying arms are *doing* harm (and not simply allowing it) since their supply of arms helps to produce the harm—it is an action, not an inaction.

8.3.2 The Escalation Objection

The second major objection is what I call the 'Escalation Objection'—that is, that the arming of rebels could significantly escalate hostilities if, in response, other parties in the conflict also seek arms or intensify their response by clamping further down on any opposition groups. In this scenario, many more innocents are likely to be subject to serious harms. Thus, even though I noted above that the possibility of a stalemate might *potentially* be a reason to arm unjust rebels, there is a notable countervailing concern—that arming rebels will lengthen and intensify the conflict. The obvious upshot is that many more innocents are likely to be subject to serious harms.

Indeed, plenty of evidence shows that such escalation is likely. For instance, during the Sri Lankan civil war, the flow of arms prolonged the war and led to an escalation in fighting, as both the Tamil Tigers (LTTE) and the government imported arms in large quantities (Sislin and Pearson 2006).[15] The likelihood of escalation is also documented in a study by Matthew Moore (2012). He finds that in the 114 civil wars between 1946 and 2002 where at least 900 people were killed, no rebel group was transferred major conventional weapons without the government also receiving arms from another source. In general, he finds that arming rebels (and governments) creates more bloodshed and does not end a conflict any quicker.

8.3.3 Interceding Agency

The Escalation Objection provides further reason to be extremely cautious about arming the rebels. It is a major concern when making proportionality

[14] For in-depth analysis of the principal–agent problem in regard to proxy war, see Salehyan (2010).

[15] Sislin and Pearson (2006: 143) also find that arms acquisitions correlate 'with subsequent escalation', although they note that there are some variations in degrees of escalation, which might be explained by differences in the weapons being supplied, as well as other factors. They also note that some arms races 'might actually be beneficial to the termination of an ethnic war', since situations when neither a government nor rebel group can win or lose may be 'particularly conducive to producing favorable negotiations'.

calculations about whether arming rebels will be likely to escalate the conflict and so do more harm than good. One further complicating issue concerns the interceding agency (or 'intervening agency') of other actors in arming the opposing groups (the fourth factor on the Pragmatic Approach).

It seems that the interceding agency of others in a causal chain should be viewed as reducing or removing the responsibility of agents for harm earlier in that causal chain (most clearly, for their *doing* of harm). Thus, it might be held that the state supplying the rebels should not be viewed as responsible if escalation occurs. This is because it is the *other* party that is responsible for the escalation, since it provides arms to the statist forces. On this view, the state supplying the rebels should still be viewed as acting permissibly, since the harms caused by other parties are discounted. Suppose, for instance, that Turkey is considering arming a just rebel movement in Sudan. In response, it is reasonably foreseeable that the statist forces will obtain arms from China, which will significantly escalate the conflict, with the result of a much bloodier conflict in which many more innocents will die. Turkey may still be viewed as acting permissibly since it is, on this view, China—and not Turkey—that is responsible for the escalation of the conflict; Turkey has done nothing wrong.

Consequently, considerations of interceding agency might be thought to reduce the force of the Escalation Objection. But *how much* do they discount the worries of escalation? An extreme view gives the interceding agency of others huge weight. On this view, in the example above, Turkey would not have *any* responsibility for the harms caused by escalation in Sudan. In this vein, Ned Dobos (2012) argues that mediated consequences do not matter for rebels and, further, that there is no good reason for thinking that they should matter for intervening parties either. They do not matter for the rebels, he suggests, since those 'citizens facing violations of their basic human rights still retain their right of self-defense, irrespective of how others will react to the exercise of that right' (2012: 339).

However, this is too strong. Agents should still be generally held responsible for the foreseeable consequences of their actions at least *to some extent*. This is because it seems plausible that the interceding agency does not matter that much when assessing the case for the permissibility of states providing arms to rebels, and therefore the Escalation Objection still largely applies. In the hypothetical case of Turkey and Sudan, we should consider Turkey as acting wrongly because of the foreseeable negative effects.

Moreover, there is an obvious explanation for this intuition: reasonably foreseeable consequences matter morally when we are assessing what agents should do. Agents should, as far as is reasonably possible, attempt to promote good consequences and avoid bad ones, although certain, non-absolute deontological constraints (such as against doing harm) act as a check on this. This is not to deny that the permissibility of arming rebels is somewhat affected by the fact that the agency of others intercedes when they supply arms to opposing forces. If one holds, as on the Pragmatic Approach, that the difference between doing and allowing harm is morally relevant, it should matter when another's agency intercedes. You are not directly causing the harm; your action—like when allowing harm—is more causally remote.[16]

Thus, on the Pragmatic Approach, the foreseeable harms of escalation caused by the interceding agency of others seem to be *somewhat*—but not *fully*—discounted. If this is correct, this would reduce some of the force of the Escalation Objection, particularly in marginal cases where arming rebels before the interceding agency of others does much good but overall does marginally more harm, largely due to the reactions of others. Of course, most cases are unlikely to be marginal; consequently, the Escalation Objection will still tend to apply. That is, in most cases, it is likely that the arming of rebels will do significantly more harm than good, even if due to the interceding agency of others. In such cases, it is impermissible to arm rebels.

8.3.4 The Diffusion Objection

A third major objection—what I call the 'Diffusion Objection'—is that it is difficult to ensure not only that just rebels are armed, as in the Rebel-Risk Objection, but also to ensure that the weapons are delivered to or stay in the possession of the just rebels.[17] The weapons may become seized by other, unjust groups as the just rebels lose battles or their stockpiles are raided. More broadly, the weapons—particularly small arms—are unlikely to be destroyed after the conflict and may be sold on the black market or retained by former combatants.[18] The worry is that there will be a proliferation of arms, which would lead to significant problems, most obviously higher homicide rates, more violent crime, and further conflict. Thus, even if the supply of arms to rebels may appear to be justified in terms of tackling the immediate crisis, it is possible and indeed likely that such arms will enable significant wrongdoing in the longer term as arms are diffused in the affected society and beyond.[19]

[16] For a similar view, see McMahan (2013–14). The view that interceding agency matters *somewhat* is, I think, the predominant position in recent Just War Theory. See, for instance, Hurka (2005: 47–50). Tadros (2016) also makes this point, but generally offers a critique of the relevance of interceding agency. (Tadros' rejection (pp. 127–8) of the causal account of interceding agency (the account on which I rely) is essentially that it is not intuitive; I disagree.) Other important explorations of interceding agency include Attfield (2009), Bazargan-Forward (2017), and Zimmerman (1985).

[17] For instance, it was reported that airdrops of arms meant for Kurdish fighters near Kobani were obtained instead by the ISIS rebels that they were fighting (MacAskill and Chulov 2014).

[18] See, further, Hartung (2001).

[19] Note that the Diffusion Objection is broader than the concern that the rebels' war may change to be unjust and the weapons cannot be easily retracted if it does (this is the central objection to arming rebels posed by Christensen (2015: 37–9)). The Diffusion Objection, by

Accordingly, the Diffusion Objection asserts that states should not supply arms even to just groups because it is foreseeable that there will be the diffusion of arms that will lead to rights violations.[20] Of course, the black market may mean that rebels and other groups are able to obtain arms anyway (especially small arms), and that this is a key means of diffusion. However, this does not repudiate the objection, since the worry is that the supplying of arms will lead to even greater diffusion, that is, provide another means *in addition* to the black market supply of arms.

The upshot of the three objections is that arming rebels should generally be eschewed, even if the rebels are fighting a just war. Together, these objections show that arming rebels is likely to lead to significant harms to innocents, and therefore will typically be ineffective—that is, significantly decrease compliance with basic human rights.[21] In Syria, the attempt to arm and train Syrian rebels reportedly cost the US $1 billion over four years, but achieved very little, with the gains made by the Nusra Front prompting the Russian intervention on behalf of the Assad regime (Mazzetti et al. 2017). Donald Trump cancelled the programme in summer 2017, lamenting that 'massive, dangerous, and wasteful payments to Syrian rebels fighting Assad' and weapons that 'ended up in the hands of "Al Qaeda"' (implying the Nusra Front) (Mazzetti et al. 2017).

To be sure, the arming of rebels might still *exceptionally* be effective (understood as morally valuable effectiveness). This is because, first, the three key objections might not apply, or might not apply to a significant degree. For instance, the Rebel-Risk Objection might not be serious when much is known about the rebels, when the rebels are highly likely to fight justly for just causes, and when there is significant control over them. Second, even when the objections do apply, arming rebels might still be effective because the situation is so awful that the risks are worth taking, such as potentially the Bosnian and South African cases noted at the start of the chapter. Furthermore, when the arming of rebels is the only feasible means of responding to mass killings, the risk may also be worth taking. Although this *might* result in numerous harms to innocents, the alternative is certain: it *will* result in numerous harms to many innocents. Therefore, there may sometimes be a lesser-evil justification for providing arms, even when there is a notable risk to innocents.

Yet, it can be expected that these instances will be rare and that arming rebels will generally be ineffective, and so impermissible on the Pragmatic

contrast, asserts that there is still reason to worry about the diffusion of weapons, even if the justifiability of the rebels' war does *not* change.

[20] Again, the interceding agency of others may be thought to reduce *some* of the wrongness of supplying arms since the diffusion is largely the fault of other actors.

[21] This claim is corroborated, interestingly, by the CIA, which in a classified study (seemingly requested by Barack Obama) found that supplying arms to arm and train rebel groups 'rarely works' (Mazzetti 2014).

Approach.[22] First, it seems that the three objections will *generally* apply: it will generally be difficult to determine who the rebels are, arming rebels will generally escalate the conflict, and arms will generally diffuse.[23] Second, it is unlikely that arming rebels will do enough good to outweigh these likely harms. For instance, any increase in the fighting capacity of the rebels, and in their potential ability to achieve a just end, is likely to be matched by an increased fighting capacity of the government to oppose the rebels, and there will be further problems of rebel risk and the diffusion of weapons after the conflict.

8.4 ARMING STATES

I have argued that, although arming rebels might exceptionally be justifiable, even when fighting just wars, in general this measure should generally be eschewed, even when the rebels are fighting a just war. How does this apply to arming states?

On the one hand, supplying arms to states might be called for in the face of an unjust attack by a rebel group, under R2P's pillar two. That is, it might help to assist states to look after their populations, in the face of unjust rebellion by rebels or attacks by terrorists. Alternatively, supplying arms to a state might help it to fend off unjust aggression by another state. Moreover, there are Hobbesian (moral) reasons for maintaining that governments—and not rebels—should be able to obtain military supplies. This is to uphold a monopoly on the use of force so that there can be some degree of stability within the state, which is ultimately necessary for legitimate governance and to reduce the overall levels of conflict within both the state and the international system (for instance, so that armed rebels do not destabilize neighbouring states).

On the other hand, the three central objections to arming rebels provide some (if not decisive) reasons to be sceptical about the general permissibility of arming *states*. First, as for the Rebel-Risk Objection, there is a risk that governments may misuse the weapons supplied, it can sometimes be hard to judge the justifiability of the state and its various organizations, and there may be a lack of control over how government forces will use the military resources supplied. Second, as for the Escalation Objection, there is a worry that arming a state can foreseeably escalate the conflict because other parties will then arm

[22] There might be further negative costs associated with arming rebels that add to its likely disproportionality and render it particularly unsuitable for R2P cases. For instance, rebel groups with foreign sponsorship are more likely to target civilians since they do not require a civilian base for support. See Salehyan et al. (2014), Weinstein (2007), and Wood (2014).

[23] More generally, Sawyer et al. (2017) find that military support to rebels decreases the chances that a civil war will end.

the rebels and because there will be increased incentives for the government not to settle (Moore 2012).[24] Third, as for the Diffusion Objection, the arming of even legitimate states can be difficult to control. For instance, in his study, Thomas Jackson (2010) finds that one of the central ways for rebels to obtain their weapons is to steal them from government stockpiles.

It seems, then, that rebels and *some* governments should be precluded from being armed. That is, there should be a prohibition on arming *certain* states. But which states should be banned from receiving arms? To start with, I want to propose two straightforward tests. The first is when states are likely to violate the basic human rights of their citizens. This might be determined by examining the human rights records of states as documented by the World Reports of Human Rights Watch, as well as perhaps the Democracy Index of the Economist Intelligence Unit. The second is whether any negative effects of arming states are likely to be significant and so outweigh any benefits. Adopting these tests mean that one can accept the concerns about arming states but not fully preclude doing so, which could render it too hard for legitimate states to maintain their justified monopoly on force. This is because states would be reliant simply on the weapons that they can produce themselves, which leaves them vulnerable to rebels who obtain major conventional weapons through the black market. Yet it also accepts that there are serious worries with providing arms to states, as well as to rebels.

Is it permissible to arm states in other cases? Perhaps the trickiest case is whether it is permissible to supply arms to governments that are not legitimate but unlikely to engage in mass atrocities or foreign aggression. For instance, they might be what Rawls (1999*b*), in *The Law of Peoples*, identifies as a 'benevolent absolutism'. Although a benevolent absolutism rules without political participation, it does not engage in aggression against its own people or against others. It is not a member of full standing in international society but does, on Rawls' account, have the right to self-defence. This contrasts to what Rawls calls an 'outlaw state' (which is aggressive). Examples of benevolent absolutisms might include Tito's Yugoslavia, Lee Kuan Yew's Singapore, and Brunei (until the recent introduction of sharia law).

If such states face an uprising, it *might* be justifiable for them to use force to contain it. However, much depends on the character of the uprising. If the uprising is nationalist, extremist, or potentially extremely destabilizing, the use of force by the government might be legitimate and indeed even necessary to avoid mass atrocities and civil war. Yet, if the uprising is democratizing and liberalizing, and unlikely to throw the country into chaos, the use of force by the government would seemingly be impermissible. One tricky challenge facing the supplier is to estimate the character of the uprising and its effects,

[24] Also see Mearsheimer (2015), who highlights the risks of escalation in his opposition to arming Ukraine.

before supplying arms. Perhaps even trickier, the supplier needs to consider the potential for the supplying of arms to be problematic *itself*. Given the dangers of arming states, in terms of escalation and diffusion, there should be significant caution in providing arms to such states even if an uprising is likely to be legitimate. In general, then, the presumption should be that arms are not transferred to regimes with questionable human rights records, given that such regimes may well use these arms against its population.

8.5 CONCLUSION

This chapter has considered the case for military assistance as a means to help rebels and states facing mass atrocities and serious external aggression. It has argued, on the one hand, that it can be exceptionally justifiable to supply arms to rebel groups. This can even mean that it is exceptionally justifiable to arm unjust rebels, if the supply would be overall effective. This highlights the importance of separating the questions of the (1) justifiability of the actions of those being supported and (2) the justifiability of supporting them. I also argued that, on the other hand, it is generally impermissible to provide arms to rebel groups. This is because of the risks to innocent civilians, the problems of escalation, and the diffusion of arms. These problems, I suggested, also provide reason to be highly cautious in supplying arms to states.

Overall, then, military assistance should *not* be viewed as a central mechanism to help fulfil the R2P and to tackle serious external aggression. Despite the popularity of this measure, states and other actors should generally seek alternative means of addressing the situation. The crux is this: they should not be blinded by the potential exceptional permissibility of supplying arms to rebel groups and certain states into viewing that it is generally justifiable to do so. Even arming just rebels (and states) can be hugely problematic. As argued in chapter 4, the case for arms embargoes is generally strong. But even when there is not an arms embargo, states and other actors should generally refrain from supplying arms to rebels and many states.

9

Secondary Measures

Prosecution and Amelioration

Thus far, I have considered six sets of measures: economic sanctions, arms embargoes, diplomacy, civilian peacekeeping, positive inducements, and military assistance. All of these measures aim to coerce or persuade the aggressor to cease its behaviour, at least in part if not fully. In this chapter, I consider three additional means: (1) actions by the International Criminal Court (ICC), (2) accepting refugees, and (3) humanitarian assistance.

Unlike the other measures considered thus far, these measures do not always *primarily* attempt to tackle mass atrocities or external aggression. For the most part, they aim to directly tackle mass atrocities as a *secondary* intention. The main aim of (1) international criminal prosecutions is often to put on trial those who commit mass atrocities. It is post hoc, rather than an attempt to tackle *ongoing* abuses. (Notwithstanding, as I will argue shortly, it can still affect abuses, even if this is not the primary aim.) The objectives of (2) accepting refugees and (3) delivering humanitarian assistance are to ameliorate the crisis. These measures can still protect the potential victims from ongoing abuses.[1]

The occasional moral permissibility of these three measures is not subject to much dispute. Most scholars agree that international criminal prosecutions, accepting refugees, and humanitarian aid are *sometimes* morally desirable (although, as we will see, certain prosecutions by the ICC can still be controversial). However, there is much more contestation about *whether* and *how much* they should be seen as part of the toolkit of responses to mass atrocities and serious external aggression. For instance, one worry is that if they are

[1] That said, ICC actions are increasingly being seen as a means to tackle mass atrocities. They might then *sometimes* be primarily motivated by the desire to stop the ongoing crimes, which was arguably true of the Sudanese and Libyan situations, and perhaps the attempted referral of the situation in Syria. In such circumstances, ICC actions may be more akin to the measures considered in the preceding chapters.

seen as a key part of this toolkit, states and other actors will engage in these measures in order to avoid taking more robust action and that linking these measures to the R2P is counterproductive. Accordingly, this chapter will focus on two related issues. The first is how much of a role these options should play in response to serious crises. The second is to what extent they should be framed as major policy options. This is what I will call a matter of 'framing justice'.

I will first consider international criminal justice (in section 9.1). I will argue that, despite worries about it being counterproductive and politicized, and concerns about linking it to R2P, international criminal justice should be seen as a central part of the toolkit of responses to mass atrocities. Section 9.2 considers the role of accepting refugees. In contrast to international prosecutions, I will argue that worries about legitimate and illegitimate buck-passing mean that accepting refugees should *not* be seen as a central part of the toolkit of responses to crises (although still should be carried out). Section 9.3 will argue, for similar reasons, that humanitarian assistance should also not be seen as part of the toolkit of responses to crises (again, although still should be carried out).

Before beginning, it is important to note that these three measures are less relevant for serious external aggression (which does not also involve ongoing or impending significant violations of human rights). This is because aggression may not always lead to significant refugee flows or a humanitarian crisis, and international criminal justice may not be applicable. Although from 2017 the ICC's jurisdiction could have covered the 'crime of aggression', which included 'manifest' violations of the UN Charter, at the time of writing this has not yet come into force. Even when it does, the powers of the ICC will be limited, given that the violations must be 'manifest', that State Parties can opt-out, and that its remit does not include non-state actors (apart from referrals by the UN Security Council). Moreover, many crucial aspects of the jurisdiction remain contested (Koh and Buchwald 2015). For instance, it is still unclear how the 'manifest' requirement will be interpreted exactly and which states will be covered. As such, it is still unclear if and when the ICC will be able to play a major role in response to serious external aggression.

9.1 PROSECUTION: INTERNATIONAL CRIMINAL JUSTICE

The ICC can, though, prosecute in response to mass atrocities. Its jurisdiction covers genocide, war crimes, and crimes against humanity, in the territory of a state that has ratified the Rome Statute (a 'State Party'), by a national of a State Party, or when a case is referred to it by the UN Security Council. In addition to referrals by a State Party and the UN Security Council, the Prosecutor may initiate investigations *proprio motu*, that is, on her own initiative. The Prosecutor is tasked with analysing the prospective case and deciding whether there is a reasonable basis to proceed—the 'preliminary examinations'. The Prosecutor is also tasked with considering whether the situation is within the jurisdiction of the ICC, whether it is admissible (that is, whether the situation is being, or has genuinely already been, investigated by the state in question and whether the situation is sufficiently grave), and whether the case would be in the 'interests of justice'.[2]

At the time of writing, there have been twenty cases in ten situations appearing before the Court. The situations in Uganda, the Democratic Republic of the Congo, the Central African Republic, and Mali were referred by the states themselves (they are all State Parties). The situations in Darfur and Libya were referred by the UN Security Council (Libya and Sudan were not State Parties). The situations in Kenya, Côte d'Ivoire, and Georgia were investigated by the Prosecutor proprio motu. The ICC is also making preliminary examinations about the situations in Palestine, Ukraine, Iraq, Afghanistan, Colombia, Guinea, and Nigeria. It has sought prosecution of several rebel leaders, such as Joseph Kony, and current and former heads of state, such as Laurent Gbagbo, Omar al-Bashir, Uhuru Kenyatta, and Muammar Gaddafi.[3]

ICC prosecution, and steps towards it, such as through preliminary examinations, can help to both ameliorate and prevent mass atrocities. Most straightforwardly, the ICC can help to reduce *ongoing* abuses. The seemingly most obvious mechanism is by prosecuting—and imprisoning—the main offenders. Although the relatively small numbers of prosecutions might appear to mean that the likelihood of prosecution is low, for certain individuals, such as states and rebel leaders in African states, the chance of international prosecution is sizeable (Hillebrecht 2016).[4] Importantly, the greater

[2] This is understood, in a 2007 policy paper by the Office of the Prosecutor, as dependent somewhat on the facts and circumstances, so not possible to be clearly delineated (2007: 1). The 'interests of justice' are seen as exceptional and different to the 'interests of peace', that is, not about 'issues related to peace and security' (2007: 8).

[3] Although I will focus on the ICC, there are other forms of international criminal justice, such as ad hoc tribunals and prosecution through the principle of 'universal jurisdiction'. This principle holds that, for certain egregious crimes, states can prosecute perpetrators even when the mass atrocities do not occur within its territory and the perpetrator or victim are not citizens of the state in question (Mills 2015*a*: 78). The most high-profile case was the arrest of Augusto Pinochet on his visit to the UK in 1998.

[4] After the trial of Thomas Lubanga for using child soldiers in the Democratic Republic of the Congo, UN and NGOs officials began to refer to the 'Lubanga Syndrome' about militia leaders changing their behaviour to avoid prosecution, such as by hiding or expelling child soldiers from the militia (Saxon 2015: 148). Moreover, the number of states that will host war criminals is diminishing; for instance, in 2015, Senegal tried Hissène Habré, the former Chadian dictator, who had been in exile (Hillebrecht 2016: 624).

the actions undertaken by the ICC, the greater the threat of prosecution (Hillebrecht 2016: 632).

What is also crucial here is that prosecution might not be only by international actors, such as the ICC or other international tribunals. Central to the ICC's prosecutorial strategy is '*positive complementarity*', which aims to prompt otherwise reluctant or incapable *domestic* legal institutions into launching their own prosecutions, particularly after the launch of preliminary examinations. For instance, according to Kirsten Ainley (2015: 49), the ICC and US put pressure on the Colombian government to reform its domestic legal institutions. This in turn resulted in seemingly impressive results, due to the incentives offered and threats made by the ICC (also see Saxon 2015: 139). Thus, positive complementarity, along with the threat of international prosecution, increases the potential threat of prosecution, which decrease both *ongoing* abuses and potential *future* abuses as perpetrators worry about facing imprisonment.

Penal costs are only one part of this limited deterrent effect: there are also reputational costs that can be raised by an ICC action. These include what Benjamin Appel (2018) calls '*domestic costs*'. For instance, an accusation of committing war crimes can severely weaken the reputation of a government or a rebel group in the eyes of the domestic public. The reputational costs also include *international audience costs*. For instance, ICC actions may isolate and delegitimize certain groups, such as the Lord's Resistance Army, which can decrease international support and in turn accelerate peace negotiations.[5] The ICC has, then, penal and reputational costs that it can impose, which can deter abuses.[6]

Indeed, Hyeran Jo and Beth A. Simmons (2016) find that ICC action reduces the rate of intentional killing by both government forces and rebels.[7] For instance, in the aftermath of the conviction of Thomas Lubanga, they note, the M23 rebel group declared its willingness to conform to international humanitarian law and appeared to moderate its behaviour accordingly. The deterrent effect is greatest when states are concerned about their reputations in the eyes of the domestic public or the international community. Even if suspects are not apprehended, indicted individuals have fewer asylum options. This raises costs on them as well as for others considering such abuses. Of course, the ICC actions will not always deter. Some who will still 'intentionally

[5] Although there is a worry that ICC actions can undermine mediation efforts, the isolation of various groups, such as the Lord's Resistance Army (LRA) in Uganda and spoilers in Liberia, and the pursuit of accountability, can create space for more constructive and ultimately successful peace talks (Welsh 2015: 110).

[6] To be sure, what matters is not whether the ICC actions will *actually result* in these costs, but rather whether the perpetrators *perceive* that they will (Saxon 2015: 125).

[7] Jo and Simmons (2017) have since published a corrigendum to their original article, which waters down the findings in relation to rebel groups.

terrorize civilians for their personal or political purposes are difficult to deter under any circumstances' (Jo and Simmons 2016: 469).[8] Yet the ICC raises 'the risks of consequences for violations' (Jo and Simmons 2016: 469)—it makes it more costly to engage in such behaviour. Indeed, although the ICC has had little effect in states such as Sudan and Libya where it has intervened with indictments, in other cases, Jo and Simmons posit, it has mobilized domestic actors and stimulated reforms, such as in Uganda, Kenya, and Côte d'Ivoire. Another example is Guinea. The announcement of preliminary investigations into serious human rights abuses worried members of the junta, who then backed an inquiry into abuses, which was supported by statements from the Office of the Prosecutor and which helped to avoid further significant violence and a grave deterioration of the situation (Kikoler 2015; also see Saxon 2015: 151–3).

In addition to intended positive complementarity, ICC investigations can also lead to what Geoff Dancy and Florencia Montal (2017) call '*unintended positive complementarity*', that is, an improvement in *general* domestic accountability for human rights abuses, where the intention of the ICC is on high-profile crimes. States under investigation by the ICC try three times as many state officials for human rights abuses because of the 'willingness game'; when under threat from the ICC of prosecution, governments attempt to show willingness to comply with international norms in order to maintain their legitimacy (Dancy and Montal 2017). Whilst the spotlight is on and it is sensitive to international attention, reformist groups attempt to improve accountability for other crimes.

In addition to (albeit perhaps limited) deterrence, there are two further notable reasons to launch international criminal prosecutions. The first is expressivist. The launching of such prosecutions can help in the establishment of international norms against the crimes in question more generally. Regardless of the effect on the culture of impunity, the clear expression of disapproval of the crimes helps to establish further that such crimes are wrong. To that extent, David Luban argues that '[s]peaking law to power is . . . the major point of' international criminal justice, through its expressivist mode, with the aim of norm-projection, and dissemination through 'trials, punishments, and jurisprudence' (2013: 509). The argument here, then, is similar to one of the reasons to engage in naming and shaming presented in chapter 5: the expression of disapproval can help to challenge the behaviour in question, establish and propagate facts about the atrocities, and reinforce international norms around mass atrocity crimes. ICC action can reinforce the sense that mass atrocities generally are highly objectionable and not to be tolerated, and that

[8] For instance, the trial of Jean-Pierre Bemba Gombo did not stop violence in the Central African Republic (Jo and Simmons 2016: 470). Menon (2016: 160–9) also repeatedly emphasizes that the ICC will not deter determined individuals.

the international community is expected to address such abuses, in this case particularly through criminal tribunals. In other words, it can help to develop a global norm of accountability for mass atrocities.

The second reason is retributivist. Put simply, those who commit abuses deserve to be punished. Regardless of the broader effects of punishment in terms of deterring future crimes and expressing wrongdoing, those who commit the crimes governed by the Rome Statute should be punished. It is important, for instance, to attempt to bring Assad to trial. This is because the abhorrent behaviour of his regime means that he deserves to endure punishment, such as a restriction of his freedom of movement by imprisonment. To be sure, the importance of retribution is not that weighty since it concerns the underlying value of desert (for instance, Assad and his regime *deserve* punishment). Desert is only one value on the Pragmatic Approach. Even then, the importance of punishing wrongdoing to secure what *wrongdoers* deserve is secondary in importance to what the *potential future victims* deserve. The latter do not deserve to be subject to harm for which they are not liable. Qualitatively, it is more important that innocents do not receive harms that they do not deserve than that the guilty receive harms that they do deserve.[9] Quantitatively, the number of potential victims is typically likely to be much higher than the number that can be successfully prosecuted. Accordingly, considerations around deterrence are likely to be much weightier, even on desert-based grounds.

The upshot of these reasons in favour of ICC action—(limited) deterrence, expressivist, and retributive—is that there should be a presumption in favour of launching and supporting international prosecutions. The ICC Prosecutor obviously has a role-based responsibility to prosecute and carry out this responsibility in the most appropriate manner, which is determined by the various considerations discussed below. As argued in more detail in chapter 7, the use of amnesties is *de facto* absolutely impermissible: the offer of immunity for leaders from prosecution is impermissible in feasible circumstances.

However, the ICC has been subject to several objections that challenge its potential role in mass atrocities and whether it should be seen as part of the toolkit of responses. I will now consider three leading objections: (1) that ICC action exacerbates crises (the 'Moral Hazard Objection'); (2) that ICC action is politicized and so delegitimized (the 'Politicization Objection'); and (3) that linking the ICC to the R2P is counterproductive (the 'Framing Objection').

[9] This is in part because of the importance of the difference between doing and allowing, that is, it is worse to *do* harm to innocents (punish them), even if this will allow the guilty to go free. In addition, as noted in chapter 7, we need to be wary here of double-counting reasons, given that the Pragmatic Approach includes benefits to those who deserve them in effectiveness.

9.1.1 The Moral Hazard Objection

The first objection—the Moral Hazard Objection—is that the launching of a prosecution will exacerbate the ongoing situation (Goldsmith and Krasner 2003: 55; Snyder and Vinjamuri 2004: 15). Since those who have been indicted know that they will face trial if they give up arms, there is an incentive for them to continue fighting. It is therefore better to maintain only the *threat* of ICC prosecution. In addition, when a government is subject to prosecution, this provides rebels with a reason to fight; the government is delegitimized and rebels can gain international support. This means that the rebels will fight rather than negotiate. In this context, Andrew Natsios (2009), former US Special Envoy to Sudan, argues that the ICC arrest warrant against Omar al-Bashir meant that the rebels went from wanting blood money to wanting Western-style justice, which ultimately jeopardized the peace process.[10] These claims have been supported by a recent study by Alyssa Prorok (2017). This finds that ICC involvement reduces the probability of conflict termination from 21 per cent to 11 per cent. To that extent, the critics are right that there is a trade-off between peace and justice.

Although these concerns may at times undermine the case for launching a prosecution, the trade-off is conditional. There is little negative effect of ICC involvement on conflict termination when there is a good chance of domestic prosecution and when there is not a significant disparity in rates of civilians killed by rebels and government forces (either because both are using much indiscriminate force or both are not) (Prorok 2017). In addition, if there is genuine concern that ICC action will exacerbate conflict, the UN Security Council can suspend the action for twelve months under Article 16 of the Rome Statute. Moreover, even if such effects *are* likely in a particular case, this should not necessarily foreclose a prosecution. It should be reiterated here that the effect on the ongoing conflict is only one consideration. However, the importance of launching investigations and prosecuting crimes is far broader than for *the immediate conflict*. It is important (1) to deter those in *other conflicts* by establishing the rule of international law and ending the global culture of impunity, as well as (2) to contribute to related norms by expressing wrongdoing and (3) to punish those culpable. Of course, it might still be the case that, in a particular instance, a prosecution could be more harmful overall. If so, the Pragmatic Approach would not recommend this measure. However, this seems far less likely once these other considerations in favour of prosecutions have been taken into account.

[10] Also see Mills (2015*a*: 84; 2015*c*). Holmes (2014: 133–4) argues that the ICC referral made it harder for the international community to engage with Bashir, which was the only realistic way forward to resolve the crisis in Darfur.

9.1.2 The Politicization Objection

A frequently levelled objection against the ICC is that of politicization (e.g. Menon 2016: 163). This is the Politicization Objection: the ICC is supposed to be impartial, but fails in this regard, and is unduly influenced politically. This contravenes the notion, central to domestic justice systems, that criminal justice should be free from political interference. The Politicization Objection is manifest around two issues. The first is that it has largely been those from African states that have been subject to the ICC action. This has resulted in accusations of neocolonialism and has called into question the support of some African states (Mills 2015*b*: 232). In 2016, South Africa, Burundi, and Gambia indicated their resolve to leave the jurisdiction of the Court.[11] The then Information Minister of Gambia, Sheriff Bojang, claimed that '[t]here are many Western countries, at least 30, that have committed heinous war crimes against independent sovereign states and their citizens since the creation of the ICC and not a single Western war criminal has been indicted' (*The Guardian* 2016). For Bojang, the ICC is 'an International Caucasian Court for the persecution and humiliation of people of colour, especially Africans'.

The second is that rebel groups and leaders have been subject to investigations and prosecutions, but government forces and leaders have not, despite apparently similar behaviour having been committed by government forces. For example, in Uganda the ICC has not investigated atrocities committed by the government and has appeared to endorse the government's use of force against the Lord's Resistance Army and the people of Northern Uganda (Mills 2015*a*: 93). The problem is that the ICC lacks sufficient means and authority to be able to conduct sizeable investigations in states, which are often enduring conflict. It relies on the assistance of governments to help it gather materials. This means that it can be hard for the ICC to investigate governments since a government can refuse assistance (which can also limit the deterrent effects of the ICC). To the extent that the government is morally illegitimate, the ICC can be accused of assisting illegitimate governments to bulwark their positions by increasing pressure on rebel groups and delegitimizing them further.

Underlying both issues is the selectivity of the ICC. It does not launch prosecutions in all cases where it is merited and is unduly influenced by politics. The politicization of the ICC is to a large degree ingrained in the ICC in the Rome Statute. This is because, for states that have not ratified the Rome Statute, the only means of launching a prosecution is a referral by the UN Security Council. However, various permanent members of the UN Security Council are likely to veto, or threaten to veto, a prosecution that

[11] That said, South Africa's move was blocked by its High Court and Gambia, under the new leadership of Adama Barrow, reversed its decision in February 2017.

would undermine its own significant interests or that of a major ally. For instance, in 2014, Russia and China vetoed the attempt to refer the Assad regime to the ICC.

This leads some to question the links between the Council and the ICC. Louise Arbour, former Chief Prosecutor of the International Criminal Tribunals for the former Yugoslavia and Rwanda, argues that 'Security Council referrals to the ICC are . . . particularly problematic. Two referrals by the Security Council to the ICC, in the cases of Darfur and Libya, have done little to enhance the standing and credibility of the ICC, let alone contribute to peace and reconciliation in their respective regions' (2013). For Arbour, although Security Council referrals may extend accountability to states that are not signatories to the Rome Statute, they do so at the cost of shielding the permanent members and their allies from expansion of this responsibility. She asserts that 'Security Council referrals therefore expose the Court to charges of politicization, while providing the Court with no compensatory benefits such as additional financial, political or operational support'. In similar vein, Andrea Birdsall argues that the ICC was intended to be independent from the UN and the UN Security Council, but when it is used as a tool by an inherently political body such as the UN Security Council, 'this perception of independence is . . . lost which ultimately undermines the Court's credibility and legitimacy' (2015: 55).[12]

Worries about politicization also lead to calls for a less political prosecutorial strategy by the ICC. For instance, Carsten Stahn (2015: 35) argues that the prosecutorial strategy of the ICC has overemphasized its role in crisis management. He argues that in Uganda the action was guided by the desire to be the saviour of the interests of Ugandan society from the Lord's Resistance Army (Stahn 2015: 36). Similarly, ICC decision-making was influenced by political outcomes in its deferral of its decision to act in Colombia and its decision to initiate investigations in Libya, which was 'visibly geared at delegitimizing the Gaddafi regime' (Stahn 2015: 38–9). He argues that choices related to investigation and prosecution of crimes should not be driven by considerations of 'human security' (Stahn 2015: 35).

Although the critics are right to worry about politicization, these concerns should not be viewed as fatal. Although the ICC is not ideal, it works in the prevailing international context where several states refuse to be governed by a regime of international criminal justice and where great power politics are hugely important.[13] Any potential system of international criminal justice in current circumstances is likely to be heavily politicized. Even within the

[12] Similarly, Ainley (2015: 44–7) argues that there would be no practical benefits to the ICC by having more cases referred to it by the UN Security Council but there would be significant disadvantages.

[13] To be sure, some critics, such as Ainley (2015), acknowledge this.

current system, the ICC has a notable amount of independence. The Prosecutor can launch her own investigations and the UN Security Council, for all its faults, can refer circumstances to the ICC. This is a significant advance on the highly sovereigntist system that prevailed before. In other words, the ICC is somewhat remarkable because it is not *fully* politicized. In his book, *Rough Justice*, David Bosco puts the point more forcibly: '[m]ore than any other major international organization, the ICC keeps its distance from state power' (2014: 8). Bosco points to the fact that major powers can have at most only one judge and cannot threaten to withdraw support for a judge since judges are not reappointed. He also notes that the budget is approved by simple majority and that the Prosecutor and judges have almost complete discretion as to which situations to choose to investigate, even when there is a referral by the UN Security Council (Bosco 2014: 8).[14]

The worry about selectivity of the ICC has an affinity with the worries about the selectivity of humanitarian intervention, particularly prevalent in the late 1990s and early 2000s. This is the objection that humanitarian intervention is impermissible because it is carried out in places where the major powers have interests, rather than intervention in all places where required. This calls into question the moral justifiability of humanitarian intervention, the objection goes, since interests determine where it occurs. Yet, since the development of R2P, this objection to humanitarian intervention has largely been repudiated and now carries far less traction than it used to.[15] On the one hand, R2P makes it clear (particularly in the original ICISS version, which lists 'precautionary principles') that intervention cannot or should not occur in all cases because sometimes it would render the situation even worse (or would fail to meet other Just War criteria). On the other hand, what the selectivity objection shows is not that humanitarian intervention, *when it occurs*, is impermissible. Rather, it shows that there should be *more* humanitarian intervention that would meet the requisite criteria. Adopting Simon Chesterman's (2003: 54) phrasing, the central problem is 'inhumanitarian nonintervention'. The same is true of international criminal justice. The central issue is that there *should* be ICC action in situations where there is currently no action. The problem is not overzealous, partial prosecution, but rather *inhumanitarian non-prosecution*.[16] To that extent, the politicization of international criminal justice is not a reason to reject it; it is a reason to develop it further, to overcome the politicization. It should also be noted here that many of the African situations that reach the ICC are not made by

[14] Overall, Bosco (2014) argues that the ICC is independent but constrained.

[15] See Brown (2003), Pattison (2010: 169–73), and Wheeler (2000) for analyses of this objection.

[16] This is not to say, of course, that all ICC actions are humanitarian, just as it is not true that all interventions are humanitarian.

referrals of the UN Security Council or the investigator acting in *proprio motu*, but rather by *self-referrals*. This is true of the Democratic Republic of the Congo, Uganda, Central African Republic, and Mali. This casts significant doubt on the neocolonial critique of the ICC.

In fact, the partial politicization of the ICC is currently a necessary evil and cannot—and should not—be fully repudiated. In particular, some links between the ICC and the UN Security Council seem to be better than none. Although this might mean that the latter becomes politicized, the only feasible alternative seems to be for the Council not to refer situations to the ICC. This would appear to make international criminal justice *even more* selective, as only those states that have ratified the Rome Statute would be subject to its jurisdiction. The quandary, then, is whether the politicization of the ICC by connection to the UN Security Council is worse than fewer prosecutions. Sometimes, this might be the case, when the UN Security Council referral significantly weakens the ICC's legitimacy by referring to it a controversial situation that it lacks the means to investigate and prosecute fully. The UN Security Council should not refer to the ICC situations that could significantly weaken the ICC and thereby reduce its capacity to act in future cases or diminish its legitimacy. However, such potentially delegitimizing effects should not be overstated. The ICC will probably always be delegitimized in the eyes of certain actors, who might be in the future subject to ICC prosecution or are extremely sceptical about any forms of supranational, cosmopolitan justice. Their vocal complaints should not be taken to be representative. And any attempt to depoliticize the ICC—by having fewer referrals from the UN Security Council—will be unlikely to reduce these complaints. Others will differ: they will acknowledge the realities of the politicization of the ICC as the fault of the *UN Security Council*, not of the ICC, and that the ICC is necessarily political, but still desirable.

This is not to deny that the UN Security Council *should* be more impartial in its referrals. My point, rather, is that the inevitable partiality of UN Security Council referrals does not mean that the ICC and the UN Security Council should be clearly separated. Moreover, it is still important for the UN Security Council to consider, for now at least, the political nature of crises; political assessments are sometimes vital, given the highly nonideal international system. To that extent, Kurt Mills (2015*a*: 96) rightly calls for the UN Security Council to make judgements about whether a referral to the ICC would delegitimize the relevant actors and help to contribute to a resolution of the crisis or would further entrench the leadership.

The strategy of the Prosecutor should also reflect certain political considerations, such as the effects on the ongoing crisis and the future of international criminal justice. This is in part because the ICC lacks enforcement capabilities comparable to those in domestic legal systems and is heavily dependent on the cooperation of states, including for funding and support for investigations (Rodman 2012). According to James A. Goldston (2010), former Senior Trial Attorney and Coordinator of Prosecutions at the ICC, the discretion of the Prosecutor to decide which situations she pursues should reflect considerations of institutional strategy and policy, whilst remaining strictly within the limits of the Rome Statute. Claims that the Prosecutor should simply apply the law fail to grasp the complexity of the decisions to prosecute in practice (Goldston 2010: 386). The ICC is necessarily entwined in politics, which will affect its funding and future, and needs to make careful political judgements. More specifically, in order to secure its long-term future, the Prosecutor has to weigh the Court's perceived viability, efficacy (such as by prosecuting those who can be arrested), efficiency (such as by limiting the number of charges), and independence (Goldston 2010: 402). For instance, although the ICC's decision to charge Thomas Lubanga (the first person convicted by the ICC) was seen as almost too convenient, focusing too much on the use of child soldiers rather than on more heinous crimes in the Democratic Republic of the Congo, it needed to secure an arrest in order to demonstrate its practical viability (Goldston 2010: 395).[17]

The main benefit that the ICC could achieve from maintaining a purely apolitical approach might seem to be increased legitimacy amongst states and other actors. However, it is questionable how much it would be able to increase its legitimacy by operating less politically. As I have already stressed, certain states and leaders would be likely to attempt to delegitimize it even if it operates less politically, given the threat that the ICC poses to them, their general opposition to international justice, or for domestic political reasons. Several African states and leaders may continue to attack the ICC, for instance, because this is popular with certain domestic groups and elites, thereby helping them to shore up their own domestic political support. The benefits, then, in terms of increased legitimacy by operating less politically are unlikely to be significant.

By contrast, the costs of acting less politically could be much more serious. On the one hand, if it launches fewer actions because it wants to be neutral, this could reduce the deterrent effect of the ICC, as the likelihood of prosecution decreases. For instance, states may be less likely to initiate their own proper prosecutions under positive complementarity if the ICC is overly worried about keeping its hands clean. In addition, the general contribution it makes towards norms surrounding international criminal justice and mass atrocities would be smaller. If, on the other hand, the ICC launches prosecutions without consideration of the prevailing political context, it may worsen situations. Prosecuting atrocities on both sides also can be difficult in practice,

[17] Also see Bosco's (2014: 139–76) account of the careful Prosecutorial balancing act. Interestingly, Smeulers et al. (2015) find that the Prosecutor *does* generally focus on the gravest cases she can.

given the need already noted for cooperation with states. Taking action without regard to these consequences could increase the impression that the ICC is ineffective and so reduce the international support, as well as reduce the deterrent effect by decreasing the likelihood of prosecution.[18]

9.1.3 The Framing Objection

Having argued that ICC actions can play an important role in helping to address mass atrocities, let us now turn to consider the framing justice issue. On the one hand, the ICC's Chief Prosecutor, Fatou Bensouda (2012), argues that, by seeking to end impunity, the ICC has added an essential element as a tool of the R2P and that, as such, it is part of the R2P. On the other, it has been questioned (e.g. Schiff 2016) whether the ICC should be seen as part of the R2P toolkit. Central is that the R2P is viewed by some as 'toxic' and so associating the ICC with the R2P risks increasing the controversy surrounding international criminal justice. To that extent, Birdsall asserts that '[b]eing linked to R2P in Security Council deliberations can be detrimental to the ICC's perceived legitimacy as the R2P concept in itself has become controversial after Libya' (2015: 70). She notes that Russia and China object 'to any measures that include R2P language because of the negative experiences with Libya. They do not seem to explicitly object [to] ICC action, but their opposition is primarily against R2P and how the concept had been distorted during the Libya conflict' (2015: 70). The alleged toxicity stems in particular from the continuing association with R2P and military intervention. Any referral to the ICC and R2P will, the objection continues, immediately raise worries that there will be a 'slippery slope' to military intervention in the future. It may therefore seem that there should be a clearer separation of the two, at least in certain areas (Stahn 2015), such as in terms of military action under pillar three (Birdsall 2015: 72).[19]

However, such concerns should not be given too much weight. The loud claims of certain states about ICC and military intervention are often disingenuous; they are used as excuses not to support ICC action. But even without the availability of this excuse—if it were not remotely plausible—such states would use other excuses not to support an ICC referral, from the claim that peace is inimical to justice to the challenging of the ICC's jurisdiction and impartiality. The objection also probably overstates the opposition

[18] Although the ICC Prosecutorial strategy should be guided by pragmatic concerns, it seems that it should *pretend* to act purely on legal considerations in order to maintain its perceived legitimacy. See Struett (2012).

[19] Birdsall (2015) and Stahn (2015) also argue for a better connection between the R2P and ICC in certain areas, such as invoking the R2P to highlight the need for cooperation with the ICC (for example, to help ensure access for investigations).

to R2P. Contestation around R2P only really concerns its third pillar; the rest of R2P is widely accepted. And even the contestation around the third pillar of R2P does not deny that humanitarian intervention is occasionally permissible; what is at stake is *when* exactly it is.

Overall, then, ICC actions should be seen as a central part of the toolkit of the R2P. However, as we will now see, this isn't the case for refugee protection and humanitarian assistance. It does seem that these responses should not be framed under the toolkit of responses to R2P situations.

9.2 AMELIORATION 1: REFUGEE PROTECTION

It is often suggested that one way that states can fulfil the responsibility to protect to threatened populations is by accepting refugees. For instance, Brian Barbour and Brian Gorlick (2008) argue that 'there is perhaps no more direct, and in the scheme of tough choices, less controversial way to protect victims and potential victims from mass atrocity' than to 'grant asylum and ensure refugee protection' (2008: 565).[20]

Various measures could be undertaken in relation to refugees. These include ensuring that states open their borders and make it as easy as possible for threatened populations to seek asylum, as well as supporting the receiving states with the facilities needed to provide adequate housing, shelter, and protection, and facilitating the movement of refugees to third countries (Bellamy 2015*a*: 47). It helps to distinguish here between (1) the responsibility to *accept* refugees, which involves a state's responsibility to accept refugees who reach its territory, and (2) the responsibility to *assist* refugees beyond one's borders, which involves supporting refugees within the borders of another state.

It is incontrovertible that states should generally accept and assist refugees. They have weighty responsibilities to do so, which have several groundings, including a humanitarian duty of assistance (Betts 2015: 364–6). States also have a legal obligation to accept refugees who reach their borders under the Refugee Convention. Yet it is far more debatable whether accepting and assisting refugees should be *seen* as a means of addressing mass atrocities. One central issue is 'buck-passing': states may claim that by accepting and

[20] Other examples include Coen (2015: 1054; 2017) and Bellamy, who argues that asylum 'ought to be a key element of the [R2P's] repertoire of responses to atrocity crimes' (2015*a*: 47). In relation to the crisis in Syria, Welsh notes that 'neighbouring countries such as Jordan have been praised for accepting refugees as part of fulfilling the international responsibility to protect' (2014*a*: 3).

assisting refugees they have fulfilled their responsibilities and therefore are not obliged to assist in any other ways to address the situation. They can use even the partial fulfilment of this obligation to help refugees to excuse their failing to fulfil the responsibility in other ways. But perhaps far more likely is the converse form of buck-passing: they will use their more coercive responses to crises to avoid fulfilling their full responsibilities to accept and assist refugees. For instance, in the midst of the European refugee crisis, the UK government repeatedly used its aid contribution, including to refugees in Syria's neighbours, to rhetorically justify accepting only 20,000 Syrian refugees over five years, far fewer than other major European states. Thus, it might be claimed that accepting refugees should *not* be seen as part of the toolkit of responding to mass atrocities.[21]

Two clarifications are required. First, this issue also arises with other measures. As we saw in section 4.3.2, arms embargoes are alleged to be subject to the similar Fig Leaf Objection, which claims that states will use arms embargoes as a fig leaf to avoid undertaking more effective measures, such as military intervention.[22] Similarly, Mills (2015a: 85) argues that in the case of Darfur the referral to the ICC allowed the UN Security Council to give the impression that it was doing something to address the situation, even though this was not enough to protect civilians. The most serious issue, though, is the converse form of buck-passing. This is what largely prompts the need to view refugee protection (and humanitarian assistance) as separate from the toolkit of responses (that is, the risk that this will undermine refugee protection and humanitarian assistance—not simply the tackling of perpetrators). Second, this argument does not claim that states would necessarily fulfil their responsibilities towards refugees if it were not for R2P. They may well seek an alternative way of denying or reducing their responsibility. The point, rather, is that, given that R2P exists and provides one avenue for

[21] This section focuses on refugees, not internally displaced persons (IDPs). It is uncontroversial that IDPs should be a key consideration for the R2P. As Roberta Cohen (2010) argues, a comprehensive response under the R2P should take into account the needs of the internally displaced, given that IDPs are often the principal victims of crimes against humanity, ethnic cleansing, and war crimes. They are more vulnerable to attack, disease, abduction, and sexual assault, and the mortality rates are much higher amongst displaced populations than the general population (Cohen 2010: 31; Mooney 2010: 62). Indeed, the R2P doctrine developed in significant part out of the consideration of responses to IDPs. Frances Deng proposed the notion of 'sovereignty as responsibility' in the context of his efforts in regard to ensuring the better protection of IDPs, encapsulated in the Guiding Principles on Internal Displacement. The consensus forged around the responsibility to assist the protection of IDPs helped to pave the way for R2P (Mooney 2010).

[22] The Fig Leaf Objection is slightly different though: it is that states will engage in Option A in order to avoid Option B (without any reference to a sense of fair shares). The buck-passing issue concerns the worry that states will claim that they have already done their fair share in performing Option A, so are not required to perform Option B.

denying or reducing their responsibility, it makes sense to make it harder for states to wriggle out of their responsibilities. The best way of doing this is by separating out the respective responsibilities.

Notwithstanding, sometimes states might be able to *genuinely* claim that they have done their fair share and so can *legitimately* pass the buck. Consider, for instance, the fact that Lebanon hosts over one million refugees from Syria, which is more than a quarter of its population (Achiume 2015: 689). In 2013, the World Bank (2013) estimated that government expenditure in Lebanon would have to increase significantly in response to the influx of refugees and would severely strain infrastructure and affect very weak public services in already poor rural areas, where the refugees tend to be located, and that the huge increase in labour supply would increase unemployment amongst women, the young, and unskilled workers.[23] Is Lebanon excused from the other responsibilities to respond to mass atrocities in Syria, such as to name and shame, take part in economic sanctions, and monitor arms embargoes? It seems that it might be, but to assess this we need a prior conception of the fair sharing of burdens surrounding the responses to mass atrocities and serious external aggression. It is to this that we need to turn now.

9.2.1 The Fair Distribution of Burdens

In this section, I will consider the fair distribution of burdens surrounding refugees.[24] In chapter 3, I argued that, where those who are liable cannot be assigned the burdens, a fair distribution is one that (1) assigns burdens to those who agree to them, (2) assigns burdens to beneficiaries (beyond their just entitlements), and/or (3) shares the costs. In this section, I consider a related, but separate issue. This concerns how we should view the nature of burdens and, in particular, whether they should be disentangled into specific responsibilities or viewed as a whole. Thus, whereas chapter 3 focused on offering a substantive account of the fair distribution of burdens, I now consider more generally *what it is exactly that should be distributed.*

It helps to first distinguish between *isolationist* and *holistic* views on the distribution of burdens (and benefits) surrounding mass atrocities and serious

[23] To be sure, the increase in refugees might also have had some positive effects for Lebanon and, more generally, even large refugee flows can sometimes result in large improvements for the disadvantaged (Betts 2015: 366–7; Calì and Sekkarie 2015).

[24] I use the term 'burden' in relation to refugees very tentatively. This is because accepting refugees can be overall beneficial for a state (Betts 2015: 366–7), both in narrow economic terms as it is able to increase its number of skilled, young workers and in cultural terms as the richness of the welcoming society can be augmented significantly. To help to clarify the underlying ethical issues, however, I bracket these points for now.

external aggression.[25] The isolationist approach focuses on the distribution of burdens for each *particular aspect* of mass atrocities and serious external aggression. Thus, there will be accounts of the proper distribution of burdens for each of (A) accepting refugees, (B) military intervention, (C) economic sanctions, (D) naming and shaming, and so on. To give a simplified example, an assignment might be as follows: Mexico is tasked with bearing the costs of (A) accepting refugees; Argentina is tasked with bearing the costs of (B) military intervention; Brazil is tasked with bearing the costs of (C) economic sanctions; and Colombia is tasked with bearing the costs of (D) naming and shaming.

By contrast, the holistic approach considers more broadly which agents should bear the costs for *the whole range of central responsibilities*. This includes responsibilities for *all* of the potential responses to mass atrocities and serious external aggression, such as (A) accepting refugees, (B) military intervention, (C) economic sanctions, *and* (D) naming and shaming. For example, the US might be required to bear the costs of (A) accepting refugees, (B) military intervention, (C) economic sanctions, *and* (D) naming and shaming.

Before we can consider which of the isolationist or holistic accounts is preferable, two clarifications are necessary. First, more than one agent may be deemed responsible for bearing burdens. Indeed, a plausible account of the holistic approach would require all agents to bear *some* responsibility in general (e.g. in order to share the costs), but require some to bear much *greater* responsibility. For instance, the US and other major Western states might be held to have greater responsibilities, given their wealth (that is, as global beneficiaries beyond their just entitlements). Thus, although all states should bear some of the costs of measures A, B, C, and D, the US and other states might be required to bear *most* of these costs.

Second, both the isolationist and holistic approaches relate to the assignment of *burdens*. There is a further question as to who should actually *carry out* the action required by the responsibility (Hjorthen 2017). This is clear when we consider military intervention. For instance, suppose that Russia is culpable for facilitating mass atrocities in a neighbouring state. It should not be the one to carry out military intervention to redress this because doing so could be counterproductive to responding to mass atrocities, given its previous involvement. But Russia might still be required to *bear the burdens* of intervention, by, for instance, financing another state's intervention. Different agents will sometimes then be better placed to carry out the action required than those who are to bear the burdens.

How does this relate to refugees? On the holistic account, it *can* be justifiable to use the accepting and assisting of refugees as a reason to claim that one

[25] For a discussion of the merits of 'isolationist' and holistic (or, as he calls them, 'integrationist') approaches in relation to climate change, see Caney (2012). In his various works, Caney rejects isolationism.

has already fulfilled one's other obligations to respond to mass atrocities. For instance, Lebanon could perhaps plausibly claim that it does not need to bear much more of the costs of reacting to the situation in Syria, given the number of refugees that have entered its borders and the burdens that it has had to bear. Other states should bear the costs of economic sanctions, naming and shaming, and so on. By contrast, on the isolationist account, it cannot be justifiable to use accepting and assisting of refugees as a reason to claim that one has filled the general responsibilities to respond to mass atrocities. This is because each of these responsibilities is disaggregated and assessed independently. Lebanon could, then, be required to adopt other measures to help to respond to atrocities, such as naming and shaming, economic sanctions against the Assad regime, and so on (if these means are permissible).

Which of the holistic or isolationist approaches is preferable? Ideally, I think the holistic account is preferable. The (perhaps simplified) case of Lebanon illustrates why: it would seem unfair on Lebanon that its taking on a huge burden in one area does not carry over to others (as implied by the isolationist approach). It seems instead that Lebanon should not be required to bear the burdens for responding to the crisis in other ways. Other states should pick up the tab for economic sanctions, military intervention, naming and shaming, and so on. Consequently, *in principle*, there can be legitimate buck-passing when states have done their fair share in regard to one measure.

9.2.2 Illegitimate Buck-passing

Thus far, I have focused on the idealized account of burden sharing, and suggested that this favours the holistic account that permits legitimately passing the buck when agents have done their fair share. However, *in practice*, an approach akin to the isolationist approach is ultimately favourable, at least in the context of accepting refugees, whereby different responsibilities for each measure are emphasized. This is because there is not sufficient compliance with existing responsibilities in order to justify legitimate buck-passing in this context. States resoundingly fail in their responsibilities to accept and assist refugees. Even states that do take in refugees, such as Lebanon, fail to treat them sufficiently well. For instance, Lebanon has made it difficult for Syrian refugees to obtain proper legal status, which renders them vulnerable to exploitation and even slavery (Human Rights Watch 2016). States have therefore not properly fulfilled their responsibilities to accept and assist refugees and so cannot be excused. There is, then, significant non-compliance and so there cannot be legitimate buck-passing in this case.

Moreover, one of the risks of the holistic account, if put into practice, is that it could enable states to illegitimately pass the buck even more: they could use their (currently inadequate) response to accepting and assisting refugees to excuse themselves to an even greater extent from doing more in response to mass atrocities, such as humanitarian assistance, positive incentives, and diplomacy. Conversely, they may also use their other actions (such as economic sanctions or military action) to justify inaction in terms of accepting and/or assisting refugees. This may have sufficient resonance with international and domestic audiences to let them get away with this.

The emphasis, then, should be on *two sets of* responsibilities—(1) those surrounding responding to mass atrocities and (2) those surrounding refugees—in order to encourage states to live up to *all* their responsibilities. This is in order to make it more difficult to engage in illegitimate buck-passing—action in one sphere does not excuse oneself from acting in another.

9.2.3 The R2P and Refugees

Does this mean then that the issue of accepting and assisting refugees in the context of mass atrocities should be treated as separate to the R2P? There is a clear rationale for doing so: it is important to emphasize more than one set of responsibilities to avoid buck-passing and to encourage states to live up to their two sets of responsibilities.

There is, though, a countervailing and potentially compelling nonideal reason to *favour* the holistic account. This is that the current responses to accepting refugees are *so* inadequate that the R2P might provide it with some political will to encourage the international community to do more in terms of accepting refugees and internally displaced persons (Achiume 2015). The R2P can help to act as a rallying cry to encourage states to do more in this regard. It can use some of the political capital around R2P—and particularly the desire to use coercive force in response to mass atrocities—to persuade especially Western states that are more amenable to the R2P than to the refugee regime to do more in terms of assisting refugees.

The current refugee regime consists of two sets of norms: *asylum*, which concerns the obligation that states have towards refugees who reach their territory, and *burden sharing*, which concerns the obligation that states have to assist refugees in other states, such as to financially support them or to resettle some of them in their own territory (Betts 2015: 363). The existing refugee regime is much stronger on the norm of asylum than it is on burden sharing, where the norms are weak and largely discretionary (Betts 2015: 363). It might be thought that the R2P can help with the burden-sharing element. To be sure, it seems unlikely that it will help provide a compelling and comprehensive account of burden sharing, given that the R2P also suffers from an inadequate conception of the sharing of burdens (Pattison 2010: 9–10). But it could help to strengthen the sense that there is an international responsibility to accept and assist refugees.

Yet the worries about buck-passing linger. States could still respond by simply claiming that they are doing their bit in terms of R2P and so do not need to do any more in terms of accepting and assisting refugees. A more profitable strategy, then, might be to retain the isolationist account, but to make clear the *analogy* to R2P. That is, it should be emphasized that states accept that they have an international responsibility to protect militarily. If they accept that they have this responsibility, they should also accept that they have a *different*, *additional*, and *analogous* responsibility to assist and accept refugees. The responsibilities ultimately stem from the same base: the duty to protect individuals in dire need. However, it should still be emphasized that there are *two sets of responsibilities*. States generally accept those surrounding R2P, at least rhetorically. This rhetorical endorsement should be used to encourage states to live up to the second set of responsibilities surrounding accepting and assisting refugees. This would render buck-passing harder. In similar vein, William Maley, Vice-President of the Refugee Council of Australia, argues that there is a risk that states will use R2P to avoid accepting refugees and, as a result, it is best to see the norms around refugee protection (and international humanitarian law) as '*complements* to the Responsibility to Protect, members of a family of principles directed at preventing, ameliorating and confronting lethal practices that degrade our common humanity' (2015: 265).

Of course, this may be ignored, but so it seems would linking the R2P to the case for assisting refugees. As the European 'migrant crisis' demonstrated, state responses have increasingly and vehemently become militarized, focused on attempting to stop refugees from travelling, such as by targeting smugglers and closing borders. States frequently violate the law of non-refoulement, such as arguably the agreement between Turkey and European states to accept refugees (Amnesty International 2016). In addition, states such as Australia and the UK have adopted measures such as transit processing centres, where asylum seekers have their claims processed extraterritorially, in order to keep potential refugees outside their borders (Betts 2015: 371–2).

The upshot is that the sufficient acceptance of refugees, at least by Western states, is generally unlikely to be adopted, however it is framed. The perceived domestic political costs are too great for many Western leaders. Many Western states instead prefer to support internally displaced persons in their home state and refugees in other states. There is, then, a feasibility worry about advocating the acceptance of refugees as a major policy option. States in the Global South may have little choice but to accept refugees (and the issue of whether this should be seen as them fulfilling of their obligations still stands), and the treatment of refugees will often be highly inadequate in states that have failed to sign up to the Refugee Convention or simply ignore it. The duties to accept and assist refugees require that they have safe passage from their home state, such as by providing adequate search and rescue (such as in the Mediterranean) and opening borders, but many states are unlikely to do the latter. To be sure, assisting refugees is more feasible than accepting them. States such as the UK and Australia portray refugees who are distant and stay within their regions of origin as 'worthy', whereas those who move across borders are deemed less so (Betts 2015: 371). In doing so, these states claim that it is better to protect people in their region of origin, but in reality this can lead to these countries becoming increasingly unwilling to host refugees (Betts 2015: 371).

Accordingly, although accepting and assisting refugees is morally required by states, there are worries that proposing it as part of the toolkit of responding to crises will lead to unjustifiable buck-passing. It also seems unlikely to be accepted by many states, apart from, for instance, those that are misfortunate enough to be neighbouring the crisis, which may fail to look after refugees properly.

9.3 AMELIORATION 2: HUMANITARIAN ASSISTANCE

Like accepting and assisting refugees, it is relatively uncontroversial that states and other agents possess duties to give humanitarian assistance and also facilitate others, such as NGOs, in its delivery. Should humanitarian assistance then be viewed as part of the toolkit of responses to mass atrocities? In 2005, states indicated that it should. The World Summit Outcome Document on the R2P includes humanitarian means 'to help protect populations from genocide, war crimes, ethnic cleansing and crimes against humanity'.

Of course, on its own, humanitarian assistance by states and NGOs is unlikely to fully protect individuals from mass atrocities.[26] Assistance primarily aims to ensure that individuals' basic socio-economic needs are met, such as IDPs who have fled violence and those who have been cut off from the supply of basic goods and services. It can still, however, have some protective effects, such as by helping to reduce displacement, and so limit ethnic cleansing, and by reducing the desperation of vulnerable populations who may otherwise take up arms. Indeed, humanitarian organizations have, over the past two decades, orientated their efforts much more towards considerations of protection, by supporting groups that respect non-violence, by bearing witness, and by adopting other measures to reduce the vulnerability of civilians, such as by helping them flee and by providing fuel (Bellamy 2015*b*: 154–5). Moreover, it is worth highlighting that humanitarian assistance can

[26] See, for instance, Labonte (2012) on the limits of NGOs being able to offer civilian protection. Note that this section will not simply focus on states; it will also consider whether humanitarian assistance by NGOs should be viewed as part of the R2P toolkit.

help to ameliorate some of the egregious secondary effects of mass atrocities, that is, their humanitarian consequences. War crimes, ethnic cleansing, crimes against humanity, and genocide are wrong not simply in themselves, but also because they lead to grave humanitarian situations where individuals face starvation, disease, extreme poverty, and death. In other words, *intentional* mass atrocities have egregious *unintentional* negative humanitarian effects.

Should humanitarian assistance therefore be regarded as part of the toolkit of responses to mass atrocities? On the one hand, like for the distribution of refugee protection, this might seem necessary to ensure fair burden sharing. That is to say, an account of ideal burden sharing would favour the holistic approach. But, again, the isolationist approach is favourable in practice. This is because, as for the accepting and assisting of refugees, states will pass the buck. They can use their (even partial) fulfilment of the responsibilities they have in terms of humanitarian assistance to avoid fulfilling their responsibilities in terms of mass atrocities.

This is particularly worrying in the context of humanitarian assistance because governments sometimes fudge the numbers. They promise huge amounts of humanitarian assistance in response to a conflict to give the impression that they are ameliorating the situation, but then fail to deliver.[27] Alternatively, the money is drawn from the aid budget of that state, meaning that those elsewhere in the world in dire humanitarian need receive less support.[28] A better strategy, then, might be to separate the duties surrounding humanitarian assistance and those surrounding R2P. It is important that states be required to live up to both sets of responsibilities, so that they can get closer to realizing their responsibilities for both, rather than using their partial fulfilment of one to excuse their complete lack of fulfilment of the other.

Again, the worry is that there will be insufficient resources put in place to address the underlying reasons for the conflict and to find a political solution. In this context, Mills worries that aid can be a preferred course of action for rich, Western states that have enough resources to put into stopping conflict and do not want to invest troops. He argues that 'instead of bringing in surgeons (troops) to excise the tumor of war and genocide, states bring in hospice workers (humanitarians) to keep people alive until the war ultimately kills them—the so-called well-fed dead' (2015*b*: 228). The presence of humanitarians on the ground may give the impression of a satisfactory response, when the response is actually deeply inadequate (Mills 2015*b*: 233; also see more generally Mills 2015*c*).[29] Similarly, Alex Bellamy (2015*b*: 159–60)

[27] For instance, Oxfam (2015) reported that only 26.8% of the $3.5 billion towards Gaza's recovery pledged by donors at the Cairo Conference on Palestine had been released.

[28] States such as the UK use much of the humanitarian aid budget for foreign policy objectives, rather than targeting it at the most needy (Scrivener 2015).

[29] There are several other issues with the use of humanitarian aid, such as the potential for dependency on the aid organization, where local political communities are not able to provide

suggests that exaggerating the protective capabilities of humanitarian actors can encourage political leaders to mistakenly employ humanitarian action as a substitute for necessary effective political responses. An example is in Bosnia in the early 1990s, where the UN developed an obsessive focus on humanitarian assistance to the detriment of the coercive responses required. He argues that 'the chimera of humanitarian activism might help disguise or excuse political *inaction*' (Bellamy 2015*b*: 160). Moreover, as with refugees, the buck-passing may go the other way: if seen as part of the R2P, states may use their contribution to other, more coercive measures, in order to refuse to fulfil their responsibilities to give humanitarian aid.

In addition to the problem of buck-passing, the alleged toxicity of the R2P is a notable worry for humanitarian assistance, much more so than for international criminal justice. Even if only a facade, presenting the image of being neutral between the belligerents and apolitical can help humanitarian organizations to deliver humanitarian assistance. Even though the R2P is not generally toxic, the R2P is much more clearly political—or at least aspects of it are seen as such. Thus, linking humanitarian assistance to the R2P could reduce the access that certain humanitarian organizations (and potentially states) obtain. It can also lead to restrictions being placed on aid workers and even direct attacks on them. This is because government or rebel forces may perceive that the humanitarian organization, if framed as acting under R2P, will assist or lead to the international community undermining the government or rebel forces and potentially coercing them. The worry is exacerbated by the (often-false) perception that R2P can lead to regime change and the equating of R2P with military intervention. Even if this fear is not well founded, it is true that several of the measures under R2P's pillar three resist and challenge the host state, such as naming and shaming and economic sanctions. Accordingly, the alleged toxicity of R2P in this context involves the fact that it is not neutral.

To give an example, R2P was seen as unnecessarily confrontational in the efforts to negotiate access for seemingly apolitical humanitarian aid in Myanmar, in response to the crisis after Cyclone Nargis (Junk 2016: 90). For instance, the German ambassador to the UN, Thomas Matussek, was critical of the French rhetorical escalation (which invoked R2P) as deeply counterproductive and the British Minister for International Development, Douglas Alexander, rejected any public debate about R2P (Junk 2016). Matussek argues that, to avoid mass atrocities such as in Myanmar, we should, under certain circumstances, avoid the label R2P (Junk 2016: 91). This is also documented

for themselves. Aid can also fuel conflicts (Wood and Molfino 2016) and uphold rebel groups and governments, although might still be all-things-considered justified (e.g. because despite fuelling violence it addresses the needs of thousands in desperate need). For a helpful overview of the ethics of aid, see Slim (*forthcoming*).

by John Holmes (2014: 139), who was involved with the negotiations about obtaining access as the then Under-Secretary-General for Humanitarian Affairs and Emergency Relief Coordinator. Holmes argues that raising the spectre of humanitarian intervention augmented the regime's worries that the demand for entry for aid workers was really just a cover for regime change.

Given these worries about the political nature of R2P, several humanitarian organizations do not invoke R2P. Perhaps most strongly, according to Fabrice Weissman (2010: 198), a researcher for Médecins Sans Frontières (MSF), MSF opposes R2P since MSF will not make judgements on the aims of the war pursued by belligerents. This, he argues, is an 'operational principle', necessary to secure access to defend third parties.[30] Oxfam also worries about the use of R2P. According to Edmund Cairns (2014), a researcher and senior policy advisor for Oxfam, although Oxfam supports the principle of R2P to help with general advocacy, it is reluctant to cite it in relation to specific cases. The language of the protection of civilians has been used instead, he suggests, but even this is somewhat controversial, and there has been a worry about 'doubling the controversy' (Cairns 2014: 154). He argues that although citing R2P may help to build the norm in the long term, such long-term goals should not be prioritized over action to protect people from atrocities here and now. To be sure, unlike MSF, which opposes R2P in principle, invoking R2P in a particular instance is an option for Oxfam if it would help the threatened population in the short term (Cairns 2014: 158).

Although the need for humanitarian organizations to present the perception of neutrality in order to obtain access (and not be subject to poor treatment) is manifest, and prompts much of the requirement to separate humanitarianism from the R2P toolkit, it should not be overstated. It is important that the refusal to cite the R2P in order not to jeopardize access is placed in the context of numerous cases where access has been denied and restricted despite NGOs *not* citing R2P. To that extent, John Davenport (2016: 49–50) argues that the frame of neutrality has often *not* helped aid to reach victims in several notable cases. He notes that, in Syria, MSF's neutral framing and refusal to support intervention did not help it to gain access to rebel-held areas under siege. Nor, he adds, did it help to stop them from being expelled from Darfur in March 2009, nor did it prevent the intentional bombing of its hospitals in Sudan in 2015. As such, 'aid organizations may not lose much access they would otherwise have had if they publicly accept that a [coercive] response may become necessary to stop the most vicious kinds of repression

[30] Weissman also presents a more philosophical, anti-interventionist argument, which is strongly repudiated by Davenport (2016). Michiel Hofman (2014), also of MSF, argues that military intervention and coercive peacekeeping make it harder to obtain humanitarian access. But this is an objection to humanitarian intervention, not to seeing humanitarian aid as a potential option under R2P.

and brutality' (Davenport 2016: 49). Moreover, access might only be able to be enjoyed by humanitarian actors at the expense of human rights, R2P, and atrocity prevention (Bellamy 2015*a*: 43). In Sri Lanka, for instance, the UN was silent in the face of grave violations because of the fear of loss of humanitarian access, which an internal review panel later documented was a grave failing by the UN and was to the severe detriment of hundreds of thousands of civilians (Bellamy 2015*a*: 43; also see Bellamy 2015*b*: 162–4).

It is worth noting, too, that, despite the attempt at neutrality, humanitarian assistance is necessarily political. Even if humanitarian organizations strive for neutrality, or present neutrality in their rhetoric, this may simply be a facade; politics cannot be avoided.[31] Governments that are manifestly failing to protect their populations from mass atrocities and that grant access for humanitarian aid will often do so only in order to help achieve their political goals. Aid will be seized by government forces or rebel groups, or humanitarian workers will be allowed access only to certain areas, thereby strengthening rebel or governmental control. This has been patent in Syria. Aid has been used by the Assad regime to support political outcomes, despite the supposed neutral aspirations of humanitarian aid organizations (Martínez et al. 2016: 153). This is part of a more general trend, where dictators direct aid organizations away from those that they wish to displace or kill (Davenport 2016: 49).[32] If aid is not misused in favour of the government (or rebels) committing the abuses, and instead is attempted to be used neutrally, it will often be in contravention of the goals of the government or rebel group. Thus, Davenport (2016: 49) rightly argues that, in the context of a government intentionally persecuting whole segments of its population, aid organizations that are attempting to assist this population are necessarily political. As he bluntly puts it, 'in the cases to which R2P applies, humanitarian aid NGOs are *eo ipso* opposing the tyrant's war strategy; they cannot be neutral' (2016: 49).

Moreover, we need to be clear that the issue is not whether aid organizations and other actors should call for a military response, but rather whether aid should be seen as part of the toolkit of responses to mass atrocities. Although framing aid as part of the toolkit may jeopardize access *to some degree*, as aid is

[31] See, further, Rubenstein's (2015) excellent account of the ethical issues faced by humanitarian NGOs. She argues that, in contrast to the perception of them as being apolitical, they should be seen as 'somewhat governmental and highly political'. In addition to the political effects of bringing large quantities of resources into resource-poor environments, they also have 'discursive power', that is, the power to shape meanings and to frame debates (Rubenstein 2015: 70–3).

[32] Indeed, a notable worry is that state-provided aid is often handed out to the governments to distribute. For instance, Urvashi Aneja (2014) notes that India defines its humanitarian aid programmes as in line with the needs identified by the state being aided, rather than with the needs of the population. This approach, she suggests, is resonated amongst other emerging donors, such as China and Brazil, which is reflective of their pluralist conception of world order.

linked to more explicitly political measures, this is not the same as the organizations that are providing aid also calling for coercive action. Aid organizations and states could provide aid, with it seen as part of the toolkit of R2P responses, but then *not* call for more robust action. Indeed, (allegedly) neutral states and humanitarian aid organizations could play an important role in this regard, where the government in question would oppose most other measures. As such, some of the framing worries about the toxicity of R2P can be diffused.

Accordingly, the worry about framing and undermining aid neutrality should not be viewed as *very* weighty. There are important countervailing considerations, which may even mean that occasionally it might be better to link R2P and humanitarian action. But, in general, there should be notable caution and scepticism about doing so, and it would seem to be generally better not to present humanitarian aid as part of the R2P toolkit. Of course, this is not to deny that humanitarian aid is vital in the context of mass atrocities. As Bellamy (2015*a*: 40) argues, humanitarian organizations play a critical role in keeping people alive. In his words, 'these agencies have an impact' (2015*a*: 42). The point, instead, is more general: humanitarian aid should not be *framed* as one of the potential policy options in response to mass atrocities. States should still assist in the delivery of humanitarian aid, providing significant humanitarian aid themselves, and pressurize states and rebel movements to open up humanitarian corridors to allow humanitarian access.

9.4 CONCLUSION

In this chapter, I have argued that international criminal justice is a central part of the toolkit for responding to mass atrocities. This is because ICC actions can deter mass atrocities, contribute to norm development, and help to ensure that offenders are punished according to their desert. The worries about the ICC's politicization are exaggerated and the links to R2P are not likely to be toxic since states would use excuses not to support an ICC referral if they so choose. By contrast, accepting refugees and humanitarian aid, despite having clear and notable impacts on crises, should be seen as *additional* measures, to be taken alongside other options. Including them in the toolkit of responses to mass atrocities risks making it too easy for states to pass the buck and to abrogate their responsibilities. Although buck-passing might sometimes be legitimate on the holistic account of burden sharing, often it will not be, and, as such, the responsibilities should be disaggregated and emphasized separately on an isolationist approach.

This concludes the analysis of the central alternatives to war. In chapter 10, I will consider the practical and theoretical implications of the analysis.

10

The Alternatives, Just War Theory, and Pacifism

In this chapter, I will delineate the implications of the preceding analysis, both theoretically and practically. Section 10.1 will summarize the case for each of the alternatives in turn according to the Pragmatic Approach and reiterate that the alternatives should not be viewed in isolation. Section 10.2 will consider the implications for war. I will first highlight the two central themes of the book: (1) there are several normative reasons in favour of the alternatives and (2) there are further objections to war. To that extent, section 10.3 will argue that the analysis strengthens the case for pacifism. However, I will also argue that it poses a notable challenge to pacifism as well, since the alternatives face similar problems to that of war, albeit on a lesser scale. In section 10.4, I will consider the implications of the Pragmatic Approach and the assessment of the alternatives for Just War Theory, particularly for the last resort principle. In section 10.5, I will outline five implications for R2P and the responses to mass atrocities.

10.1 THE ALTERNATIVES SUMMARIZED

Let us start by summarizing how each of the measures fares according to the Pragmatic Approach, focusing on the main considerations for each measure. Despite the widespread and withering critique of economic sanctions, they are sometimes justifiable. The claims that sanctions use people as a means and intend to harm innocents are misguided. Furthermore, sanctions are sometimes effective, despite the significant costs that they can impose and unintended consequences. It is important in this regard not to focus on the senders' goals, but rather on the effects of sanctions on the enjoyment of basic human rights—this is the crux of 'morally valuable effectiveness'. Sanctions can also distribute costs more fairly amongst the agents undertaking the action and those subject to the regime by sharing the costs and, in the case of targeted sanctions, by imposing costs to a greater degree on the beneficiaries of the unjust regime.

Arms embargoes often have some (albeit limited) degree of effectiveness. Again, when assessed according to morally valuable effectiveness, this becomes clearer: they can reduce the intensity of the conflict and the amount of arms flowing around the state. The claims that arms embargoes are not complied with and so are ineffective, harm just rebels and states, and are used to avoid undertaking more robust measures are not persuasive—arms embargoes are generally justifiable on the Pragmatic Approach. This is because not only can they reduce aggregate harm, they can distribute harms more fairly (on both the moderate and strong views of the ethics of the arms trade), and often are symbolically important by helping to denounce the wrongdoing.

Naming and shaming can contribute to the tackling of the situation by imposing reputational costs on the wrongdoer, by challenging their legitimacy and persuading other states that the aggressors are acting inappropriately. Naming and shaming can also play an important role in contributing to global norms, such as R2P, that in the longer term help to advance basic human rights, and even punish the aggressor. Early on, though, dialogue may be more appropriate and mediation might be better used before criticizing. Although it can help to avoid complicity, the cutting and downgrading of diplomatic ties adds little to the expression of wrongdoing already made with naming and shaming and can, in fact, be highly counterproductive. By contrast, expulsion from international bodies can make clear the degree of disapproval and, as such, should generally be pursued.

Civilian peacekeeping can have some positive effects as it protects individuals in the face of violence, largely by placing potential reputational costs on aggressors. In addition, civilian peacekeeping tends not to *do* harm and civilian peacekeepers typically freely consent. However, at the moment, the small scale of civilian peacekeeping and the fact that civilian peacekeepers are unlikely to be deployed in areas where there is major, ongoing fighting mean that its effectiveness is circumscribed. Civilian defence could deter aggressors and, perhaps more likely, make it harder for an aggressor to achieve its ends. It can also avoid some of the problems of wars and having a regular military, such as fraught civil–military relations. But civilian defence faces a serious limitation: it is unlikely to work against external aggressors that are not interested in occupation. It can also increase harms faced by civilians and fail to uphold the norm of self-defence.

Positive economic and political inducements are more attractive. They can help to tackle and ameliorate the crisis, such as when they can persuade a recalcitrant domestic constituency. They *do* less harm and avoid the resentment of more coercive options. In addition, they can be less costly for the sending state than many of the other options, even if failed incentives can be politically costly for leaders. They may, however, reward wrongdoers, and they can, if not carefully carried out, lead to extortion and strengthen adversaries (which can undermine their effectiveness). To avoid some of these negative effects, they work best when combined with policies that are more coercive. By contrast, international amnesties should not be used because, in addition to rewarding wrongdoers, they can legitimize egregious behaviour and, in turn, undermine the prevailing and developing system of accountability for serious crimes.

Arming rebels and arming states are also typically unjustifiable, primarily because such military assistance is very likely to make the situation worse. It is difficult to ensure that those supplied the weapons will not target innocents and, moreover, military assistance often escalates conflict and increases the violations of individuals' basic human rights in the long run as weapons remain long after the conflict is ended. Military assistance also *does* harm, even if this harm is somewhat mediated by the interceding agency of rebel groups or states. Although it can also be occasionally permissible to arm even unjust rebels and legitimate states, the risks to innocent civilians of escalation and of the diffusion of arms generally render this an inappropriate measure.

By contrast, ICC actions are potentially effective measures to address the situation and improve longer-term compliance with individuals' basic human rights. This is primarily through positive complementarity, but it is also by contributing to the expressivist condemnation of mass atrocities, and, in doing so, reinforcing human protection and accountability norms. Of course, ICC actions can also punish wrongdoers. The claims that the ICC are politicized are misleading and the claims that it should be excluded from the R2P toolkit are somewhat misguided—this overstates the impact of the framing, since, even without R2P, states would surely adopt other reasons to deny the ICC's jurisdiction.

It is patent that states should generally accept and assist refugees. However, including accepting and assisting refugees as part of the toolkit of responses to crises can increase buck-passing, as states use their adoption of other measures to denounce their duties to accept refugees. Similarly, humanitarian assistance is often hugely effective by, in effect, keeping people alive, even if it does not address the situation directly. But humanitarian assistance should be viewed as separate to the toolkit of responses to mass atrocities. This is, again, because of the risk of buck-passing, as well as the risk that associating humanitarian assistance with R2P can jeopardize the potential effectiveness of assistance by undermining access.

It is important to reiterate here that the measures will often work best when combined. Although particular circumstances will determine which measures should be combined, a mix of coercive and non-coercive measures will often be most apt, since this can ameliorate some of the resentment that occurs with purely coercive measures and avoid some of the risks, such as extortion, of maintaining a purely non-coercive approach. In addition, naming and shaming should typically accompany all the other measures, in order to make clear the reason for the response, as well as in order to contribute to morally justifiable global norms and to delegitimize the offending regime.

The measures should not necessarily be deployed sequentially, from non-coercive to most coercive. On rare occasions, coercive options, such as economic sanctions (and even direct military action), may be the most justifiable option, before other measures have been tried. I will consider this issue further below, when I consider the implications for the analysis for the last resort principle in Just War Theory.

It is also worth reiterating that some measures block others, both *directly* and *indirectly*, and other measures can *enable* further ones. For instance, ICC actions can directly block humanitarian action, as humanitarians are seen as 'internationals' and be blamed for actions to prosecute human rights violations (Mills 2015*c*: 50). Virtually all measures can also indirectly block others by their consumption of political will or be used as a fig leaf to give the impression of doing something. And, as noted in section 7.4, economic sanctions can enable positive inducements and vice versa. More generally, the launching of one measure can increase the willingness of the international community to support another measure. The use of a less coercive measure first can show that it does not work, which can then enable a more coercive one. Accordingly, even if a particular measure may not seem likely to address the situation effectively, it might still be effective when broadly conceived because it will enable a more effective measure. For instance, mediation may sometimes need to be tried politically before various international actors would support measures that are more coercive, such as targeted economic sanctions.

10.2 IMPLICATIONS FOR WAR

I now want to present two implications of this analysis for war. Both implications highlight a central point that I have been reiterating throughout: the ethics of the alternatives is crucial to the ethics of war.

First, the case for war is worse than often claimed (e.g. in the ethics of war and public discourse). That is to say, once the comparison to the alternatives is made, which is vital on the comparative principles of Just War Theory (necessity or last resort), it becomes clear that war is less likely to be justifiable in response to a particular circumstance. This is because, first, there is more going for the alternatives than often presumed. More specifically, several of the alternatives are more effective than they are generally given credit for. Military intervention is not the only effective action; other measures can be effective. Comprehensive economic sanctions, targeted sanctions, naming and shaming, mediation, dialogue, civilian peacekeeping, positive inducements, ICC actions, humanitarian assistance, and accepting and assisting refugees can all have a positive impact on the immediate crisis and the protection of basic human rights.

Moreover, many of the alternatives have other considerations in their favour, in addition to their efficacy. These include the fact that some options (such as ICC prosecutions) punish wrongdoers, some options (such as positive inducements) do much less harm, some options (such as naming and shaming) contribute to morally important global norms, and some options (such as economic sanctions and arms embargoes) can distribute costs more fairly. The upshot is that this raises the bar for war to be justifiable: it needs to be more effective than the options that are often effective and, more generally, it needs to be more justifiable than the options that have much going for them in terms of the other values on the Pragmatic Approach.

Conversely, war is worse than often presumed, since it tends to do poorly on factors that are often missed on the accounts of *jus ad bellum* and, in particular, accounts of necessity, proportionality, and last resort that focus only on a narrow range of considerations (see section 2.3). As argued in section 3.4, war tends to distribute harm unfairly. War also clearly *does* harm and this harm is direct (not often mediated by the interceding agency of others)—the belligerents are fully causally responsible. It is also doubtful whether war will often punish those who deserve punishment—it is typically too blunt a tool for this and it is other measures, such as criminal prosecutions after the war, which will do this. Consequently, the bar for war to be morally permissible is likely to be higher than is often held. This is because, to overcome its various problems, it needs to be *even more* effective, so its effectiveness outweighs the other problems—and, of course, more effective than the other options. In practice, the result is that, to be justifiable, war will need to be highly likely to make a significant impact on the tackling of ongoing or impending mass atrocities or defend against serious external aggression, and other options will need to be unlikely to succeed.

The second implication is that states and other actors should not wage war without properly *considering* the case for the alternatives. Given that there is much going for the alternatives, and little going for war, we can generally presume that the alternatives are the appropriate response. It is therefore paramount to consider them in detail, when weighing up responses to mass atrocities and serious external aggression. Even if war appears in fact to be the best option, it is morally required of policymakers to scrutinize properly the case for the alternatives. Appearances might be wrong and, even if not, the use of the alternatives might diminish some of the need for such an extensive operation. Moreover, it is not enough to simply consider whether war is superior to the alternatives *at the time war is launched.* One needs to consider *throughout the war* whether the whole war or particular ongoing aspects of the war could be ceased, in favour of the alternatives. One needs to make periodic assessments, then, about the case for the alternatives.[1]

This is not to deny that occasionally there may be little time for full investigation and deliberation of all the alternatives. This is because there might be an imminent, perhaps unexpected attack, or mass atrocities might suddenly be impending, and military action might appear to be required immediately. A delay could cost thousands of lives. But such situations are rare. Unexpected, imminent attacks are the exception. The build-up in hostilities more often occurs over months and even years; likewise, there are often clear warning signs of mass atrocities.[2] Moreover, much of the worry about delay is foreclosed when it is made clear that it is not necessary to *try* the alternatives. Rather, the obligation is only to *consider* them properly. To be sure, sometimes trying them might be required, because they are relatively uncostly (in terms of basic human rights) and the situation is slow-moving. But if the situation is imminent, and war is highly likely to be the best option, all that is required is that the alternatives are sufficiently considered.

This has some notable implications for pacifism, Just War Theory, and R2P. Let us now consider these.

10.3 IMPLICATIONS FOR PACIFISM

The preceding analysis provides some grist to the mill of pacifism. In short, pacifism may appear to be more attractive, since there is more going for the alternatives than often presumed. Although, as I will discuss shortly, there are several varieties of pacifism and much contestation about its exact meaning, accounts of pacifism agree in their opposition to war and the need to seek alternatives (Cady 2010: 17).[3] In arguing that (1) war is worse than often perceived and (2) the case for the alternatives is often stronger, the preceding analysis supports these claims of pacifists. The preceding analysis also fleshes out the ethical case for the alternatives, which has not been systematized by pacifists. To put it crudely, there are numerous measures that can be taken instead of going to war and many of them have a lot going for them. This supports the pacifist's *political* project of seeking to resolve conflict without looking to direct military solutions. Indeed, the

[1] One should also reassess alternatives, to see if they need to be diminished or extended. For instance, a more extensive sanctions regime might be required (and justified), as it is clear that the current sanctions regime is not working.

[2] See the Early Warning Project (https://www.earlywarningproject.org\).

[3] On the various accounts of pacifism, see Cady (2010) and Fiala (2014*a*; 2014*b*).

account of the alternatives could serve as a blueprint for a pacifist foreign policy.[4]

In addition, the preceding analysis supports pacifism as a *theoretical* approach to the ethics of war and peace. However, this depends in part on what exactly is understood by pacifism. All pacifists agree in their general opposition to war, but differ about how strong that rejection should be. It helps here to distinguish between two approaches to the rejection of war. On what I will call the '*soft rejection of war*', with which the preceding analysis is congruent, there is general opposition to war but occasional wars may still be permissible. Such pacifists claim, for instance, that we should try to avoid war, that wars are very occasionally permissible, and that militarism is problematic. This is true of Andrew Fiala's (2006) 'practical pacifism', which holds that war may be justifiable according to the principles of Just War Theory, but the burden of proof lies with those wanting to advocate war. Likewise, Albert Einstein and Bertrand Russell both claimed to be pacifists, but supported the war against Nazi Germany, with the latter admitting that *very few* wars are worth fighting (Fiala 2014*b*). Similarly, Andrew Alexandra advocates 'political pacifism'. He asserts that 'pacifists reject the institution of war and are committed to the construction of institutional alternatives to it' (2015: 42; see also 2003), but doesn't clearly rule out all wars. The obvious objection (with which I agree) to such accounts of pacifism is that they are not clearly distinct from dovish accounts of Just War Theory, which hold that few feasible wars will meet the requirements of Just War Theory.[5]

On what I will call the '*hard rejection of war*', pacifism is understood as the claim that *war is impermissible*. The preceding analysis contributes to this hard rejection, but also poses it a challenge. Let me explain. It is important to draw a distinction between types of hard pacifism about the rejection of war. On the one hand, '*absolutist* pacifism' holds that war is *always* impermissible. On the other hand, '*contingent* pacifism' holds that war is *currently* impermissible and will be so for the foreseeable future.

[4] See Brunstetter and Brunstetter on the development of the foreign policy of the German Green Party, which involves 'engaged pacifism' and focuses on diplomatic measures and other measures short of war, rather than 'traditional pacifist responses to war such as protest, civil disobedience, and calls for disarmament' (2011: 73).

[5] Cady (2010) suggests that Just War Theory and pacifism be viewed on a continuum of opposition to war, but (as Cady seems to be aware) this does not help to avoid the overlap and, in turn, to achieve conceptual clarity. To separate the views, there would need to be a threshold of opposition to war on the continuum to make clear when pacifism starts and Just War Theory ends, but this is not offered. Nevertheless, I will still refer to this view as 'pacifism' here since several avowed pacifists adopt it, such as Fiala and Alexandra. Cheyney Ryan defines 'political pacifism' as the unconditional opposition to war as a practice, with individual wars condemned as 'instances of the practice, whatever justification they might have in isolation' (2015: 28; also see Ryan *forthcoming*).

The two most plausible objections to war by absolute and contingent pacifism are consequentialist and deontological. First, the consequentialist objection concerns the propensity for wars to cause significant harm. The suggestion, in short, is that war (either contingently or always) leads to more harm than good. This is by harming innocent combatants and innocent non-combatants, as well as by destroying infrastructure, dividing communities, undermining international order, increasing the power of the military in society, spending money on military infrastructure rather than other public services, and promoting violence as a solution to domestic and international conflict (Calhoun 2002). Any potential benefits of wars, the objection runs, are very unlikely to outweigh these costs. Second, the deontological objection largely rests around the notion that wars tend to *do* harm. That is, wars involve the *doing* of harm to innocent combatants and non-combatants, even if by not waging war more harm is *allowed*. These consequentialist and deontological objections can be conjoined. That is, war may be viewed as impermissible because it is seen as both leading to more *overall* harm and *doing* harm.[6]

To these central arguments for pacifism, the preceding analysis of the alternatives to military intervention adds further reasons for pacifism. On the one hand, as we have seen, there is more to the repudiation of war than the consequentialist concern that it increases net harm and the deontological concern that it *does* harm. These include the notion that it distributes harm unfairly, and that other options have more going in their favour, such as the fact that their harm can be mediated by interceding agency. The Pragmatic Approach therefore adds more to the pacifist critique of war, to the extent that such concerns are rarely, if ever, explicitly noted in the literature on pacifism.

In addition, the analysis of the preceding alternatives makes clear that so much can be done instead of going to war, thereby repudiating the worry that pacifism necessarily means passivism. In fact, we have seen that there is much more going for many of these alternatives than for war. They should be pursued instead of war, given that they are more likely to be justifiable on the Pragmatic Approach. On the other hand, the Pragmatic Approach poses a challenge for both absolute and contingent pacifists who endorse the hard rejection of war. Let me explain.

There are two central responses to pacifists, the first and most frequent of which is that it seems that in certain cases war is all-things-considered justifiable, such as in certain cases of humanitarian intervention (such as in

[6] Absolutist pacifism is often associated with the deontological objection. However, one may be a consequentialist absolutist pacifist—one may hold that maximizing good consequences is all that matters and that war will always do more harm than good. Conversely, one may be a contingent pacifist who advances a strong version of the deontological objection—one may hold that doing harm to innocents is always wrong and that war in current circumstances is likely to do harm to innocents, but it is conceivable in future that war may not do harm to innocents.

Kosovo in 1999) and wars of self-defence (most obviously World War II). Intuitively, then, something appears amiss with the claims of hard pacifism. This appears to be the absolute weight wrongly given by some pacifists to the difference between doing and allowing.[7] The second response is that pacifism is radically amiss with principles of common-sense morality about individual self-defence.[8] It is widely held that individuals can defend themselves against unjust attacks on a one-on-one basis. To deny this would seem hugely problematic: it would appear to suggest that it is impermissible to defend yourself if you are being attacked by a violent aggressor. But if violence—and potentially lethal force—can be used at an individual level, it is unclear why it cannot be used at the state level, if the state is under attack.[9]

The preceding analysis adds to these worries about hard pacifism, that is, when it is conceived as outright opposition to war. To start with, the option typically favoured by pacifists—non-violence—is limited.[10] Although it is important to reiterate that non-violence is highly successful in response to *internal* repression (Stephan and Chenoweth 2008), as we have seen it is far more limited when considering *international* responses. In addition, several of the alternatives, although often more justifiable than war, endure the same sorts of problems as war, albeit on a smaller scale. For instance, economic sanctions can be indiscriminate. And most of the options *do* harm, at least to some extent. The problem, then, for hard pacifism (outright opposition to war) is that it is unclear why war *in particular* is wrong. On the Pragmatic Approach, war is often wrong not because of a *qualitative* difference to the other options, but because of a *quantitative* one—for instance, its negative effects and the degree of unfairness are likely to be much greater. This leaves open the possibility that sometimes war might still be justified, if it does better on the relevant considerations.

Where does this leave pacifism? The most plausible account of pacifism is a contingent form of pacifism that accepts this point, but that maintains that war is, in currently foreseeable circumstances, likely to be far worse *quantitatively*. This would hold that war is very likely to do more harm, be ineffective overall since it will fail to tackle the situation or will lead to long-term

[7] Bazargan (2014: 4) and McMahan (2010*a*: 17–19, 24) make this point.

[8] On this point, see McMahan (2010*a*) and Narveson (1965).

[9] Pacifists respond to this claim, arguing that opposition to war at the state level does not mean opposition to defensive violence at the individual level. See, for instance, Cady (2010: 66). Perhaps the most plausible response they can make is to highlight the militarism associated with war, rather than to advocate a prohibition on individual violence.

[10] To be sure, one can reject pacifism and still accept the strong desirability of non-violence, such as in the form of civilian peacekeeping, as a response to violent situations, even if violence may sometimes be required to tackle violence (Howes 2013). This is in similar vein to the 'strategic', rather than 'principled', view of non-violence, such as taken by Gene Sharp (Coy 2013). Another way of putting this is that non-violence can be justified for consequentialist, and not simply deontological, reasons.

problems with regard to the protection of basic human rights, and unfairly distribute harm. On this view, war would need to be (and won't be) better than (1) doing nothing and (2) the alternatives. To this, the pacifist endorsing this view could add the worries about the effects of the war machine and civil–military relations, noted in section 6.4, whereby the military can pose significant risks to the society it is supposed to protect, as well as consume valuable resources that could be better spent on other public goods.

The pacifist could also add that the standard case used against pacifism—World War II—was now over seventy years ago and one might think another similar war, where there is so clearly an evil that must be defeated and the proportionality costs clearly favour fighting the war, is currently not feasible. All currently feasible wars, they could claim with a greater degree of plausibility, are unlikely to be justified, mostly because they will be disproportionate or other options could be undertaken instead. To respond to the contingent pacifist, it needs to be feasible that a war could be justified in the near future, not a war that was over seventy years ago. This is a more plausible form of pacifism that could arise from the Pragmatic Approach (and that maintains the hard opposition to war).

To be clear: I do *not* agree with this view, largely because I think that some recent wars have been justified and similar wars in the future may well be justified, such as the 1999 NATO intervention in Kosovo to protect the Kosovan Albanians, the 2011 intervention in Libya to tackle the apparent mass atrocities by Gaddafi's regime (see Pattison 2011), and the 2015 action to protect these Yazidis from the threat of genocide by ISIS. However, admittedly, the justification of these interventions is much more contested than was the case for the Allies' war in World War II. This seems to render the contingent pacifist case stronger.

In sum, the preceding analysis of the alternatives clearly strengthens the case for pacifism in its softer form, which does not reject war outright. It also strengthens the case for hard pacifism that outright opposes war, but poses a challenge to the leading versions of it, given that the alternatives face similar problems to that of war, albeit on a lesser scale. A more plausible version of pacifism can be developed from the Pragmatic Approach that avoids this challenge, although I do not subscribe to this form of pacifism for empirical reasons.

10.4 IMPLICATIONS FOR JUST WAR THEORY

Having considered the implications for pacifism, let us now consider the implications for Just War Theory. I will focus on the implications for the understanding of the Just War principle of last resort. But before doing this

I want to reiterate two general points. First, we cannot know whether a war is justified without understanding the ethics of the alternatives. This is because to know whether a war is justified, we need to look at what else could have been done instead and, in particular, the merits and demerits of the alternatives. The preceding analysis of the alternatives is therefore vital to Just War Theory if it is to guide concrete assessments about the justifiability of wars. Second, the comparative *ad bellum* requirement, fleshed out in terms of necessity or last resort, is widely held to be a necessary condition on the justifiability of war. It follows that when reacting to mass atrocities and aggression, states are morally obliged to pursue the best option/pursue war as the last resort. It also follows that, the extent to which the alternatives *are* often the best option, states are *morally obliged to pursue the alternatives.*

10.4.1 Last Resort

Last resort is a central principle of Just War Theory and is widely cited in public discussions about the use of force, but is controversial and, as we will see, its relation to the necessity principle is moot.

It helps to start by considering three accounts of last resort in the existing literature in Just War Theory, drawing on a recent, important critique of this principle by Eamon Aloyo (2015).[11] The first account is the 'Literal Account', which requires that *all* peaceful options be tried before war is permissible. One problem with the Literal Account, as famously noted by Michael Walzer, is that '[t]here is always something else to do: another diplomatic note, another United Nations resolution, another meeting' (2004: 88). War is therefore *never* an option. In addition, the Literal Account seems problematic since it holds that, even if the other options—such as mediation and the cutting of ties—are unlikely to succeed, and even if they will be counterproductive at addressing the situation, they should still be tried. It seems then that the non-literal understanding of last resort should be preferred.

The second account is the 'Reasonable Chance Account'. This is a non-literal account: it holds that only peaceful options that have a reasonable chance of success should be tried first. This improves upon the Literal Account since if, for instance, dialogue would not have a reasonable chance of success, it would not be required to be pursued before war is launched. Yet, the problem with the Reasonable Chance Account is that the options that *do* have a reasonable chance of success may still be disproportionate, indiscriminate, and unnecessary, yet require to be tried. For instance, if economic sanctions would have a reasonable chance of success at tackling mass

[11] Aloyo lists four accounts, but it is unclear that the second account that he identifies—'necessity last resort'—differs from the other three or is widely endorsed in the literature.

atrocities, but would be likely to lead to far more deaths of innocents than a targeted aerial-bombing campaign, sanctions would still have to be pursued before war would be permissible. The problem, then, with the Reasonable Chance Account is that it requires insufficient comparison of the costs and benefits of the various options. Measures that are not war are required only to be reasonably effective at addressing the situation, regardless of their various problems.

The third understanding of last resort holds that the resort to war is permissible only if it will cause the least amount of harm. Following Caney (2005*a*: 202; 249), let us call this the 'Least Awful Account'. Unlike the Reasonable Chance Account, this account of last resort is sufficiently comparative: it requires that the costs and benefits of the various options be weighed and the least awful option be chosen. War may be undertaken ahead of economic sanctions or various diplomatic measures, such as diplomatic criticism, if it is the least awful option, although this should not be understood in narrow instrumentalist terms. It could instead be applied to the Pragmatic Approach: the least awful option in terms of the likely amount of the five central values of this approach would be favoured.

However, Aloyo (2015) argues that such an account is specious. This is because, he asserts, it is not really a principle of last resort; it fails to indicate why war *in particular* should be attempted only after the other options have been tried first, given that war may be better than the other options. On this account, Aloyo argues, the last resort principle is redundant because it is already covered by other Just War principles, most notably necessity. Given the problems with these three accounts, Aloyo argues that the last resort principle should be dropped 'as a just war theory requirement' (2015: 194).

This is an important challenge, but there is a fourth, more plausible account of last resort. This is an amended version of the Reasonable Chance Account and the Least Awful Account, and has two parts. The first part is what I call '*Presumptive Last Resort*'. It holds that (1) '*war should (generally) be the last option of those that are feasible*'. The second part is what I will call 'Best Resort': it holds that (2) '*the comparatively best non-military, feasible option(s) should be tried first*'.[12]

Underlying these principles is a comparative principle that requires a weighing of the various feasible options at addressing the situation. To that extent, the underlying basis of this principle is akin to an *ad bellum* principle of necessity. As argued in chapter 2, on the Pragmatic Approach the weighing of the various goods in such a calculation should not be viewed in narrow instrumentalist terms, whereby they are each assessed simply according to their likely efficacy at addressing the situation and some of their costs. Rather,

[12] This differs slightly from my account in Pattison (2015*b*), which uses the notion of Presumptive Last Resort to cover both aspects.

it should concern the five central values on the Pragmatic Approach. Underlying Presumptive Last Resort is therefore an account of necessity that compares the various military and non-military options, weighing the various harms and benefits, considers them in relation to fairness and desert, and, in doing so, holds that *doing* harm should generally be avoided. From this basis, Presumptive Last Resort requires that war should (generally) be the last feasible option.

What grounds the presumption in Presumptive Last Resort that war is likely to be worse? First, despite some potential exceptions, war will generally be likely to be worse in narrow instrumentalist terms, given the death and destruction that it brings. This is also reflected in Walzer's claims that 'sending troops into battle commonly brings with it so many unanticipated costs that it has come to represent a moral threshold: political leaders must cross this threshold only with great reluctance and trepidation. This is the truth contained in the "last resort" maxim' (2004: 88).

Second, as already noted, beyond narrow instrumentalist calculations, the other options, such as naming and shaming, tend to be preferable. Although this might be true for many of the factors, this is clearest for doing and allowing: the other measures are generally less likely to involve as much *doing* of harm as war, even if, perhaps rarely, they *allow* for more harm overall (such as if war would sometimes be more effective at addressing the situation).

Third, epistemic uncertainty about effectiveness provides further reason for maintaining this presumption: as noted in section 2.3, it sometimes can be hard to estimate reliably the comparative efficacy of options, in which case the other values on the Pragmatic Approach can become more determinative. Indeed, we can often have a stronger sense of which ones will *do* harm. This is clear for war. We can be confident that war will typically *do* harm, even when we are unsure—which may be often—of whether it will be more effective than the other options. This gives us further reason to be highly cautious in resorting to war and so upholding the presumption. In short, we know that war will do harm, but are unsure whether it will be any more effective.

To reiterate, Presumptive Last Resort maintains, as its name suggests, a *presumption*—but not an *absolute prohibition*—against resorting to war first and in favour of pursuing other options instead. Sometimes, the presumption will *not apply* since it will be very clear that war will *do* less harm and be more effective than the other options, such as notably economic sanctions—and, more generally, be favourable in regard to the five central values on the Pragmatic Approach.[13]

Although the underlying basis of this account of last resort can be captured by other moral principles, such as necessity, this does not render the principle

[13] As such, this account of Presumptive Last Resort has some affinity with the account of last resort presented by John Lango (2014), which also is contingent and multi-factorial.

redundant. Importantly, unlike necessity, last resort contains a contingent, non-absolute presumption against war. This is practically important to include in Just War Theory in order to emphasize the wrongness of war and the case for pursuing the alternatives. It helps to separate here the (1) *underlying basis for the criteria* of Just War Theory from the (2) *practically focused criteria* of Just War Theory, which will offer presumptive guidance for thinking about war. Necessity provides the (1) underlying basis for last resort, but (2) a last resort criterion is important to include for presumptive guidance for thinking about war. Why is this? In general, it is important to have a set of presumptive criteria of Just War Theory to provide clear and practical guidance to policy-makers, as well as those advising, lobbying, and criticizing them and those involved in the public debate, all of whom may have little appetite for considering the philosophical complexities in every case. Including last resort—Presumptive Last Resort—is important in particular in order to emphasize that *sometimes* war may be permissible and other options may not, but *generally* war should be avoided and other options should be pursued.[14] The underlying aim is to encourage states and other actors to refrain from choosing a measure—war—that is generally likely to be severely suboptimal (according to the underlying principle of necessity, assessed according to the five values of the Pragmatic Approach). In addition, as work on military intervention shows (e.g. Badescu and Weiss 2010; Chesterman 2001), states (and other agents) sometimes mendaciously justify their behaviour according to the prevailing norms, despite failing to comply with them. Advocating only a more permissive principle of necessity (*ad bellum*) could result in states mendaciously, but somewhat plausibly, defending their war as the best course of action when it is not. A principle of Presumptive Last Resort, with its emphasis on not going to war, would make it harder for states to claim with a semblance of plausibility that their war is permissible, when it is not. States would have to show that they have pursued other feasible options first or clearly override the presumption.

10.4.2 Best Resort

I will now consider the second aspect—'Best Resort'—the comparatively best non-military option(s) should be tried first. This goes beyond traditional accounts of last resort to offer an account of first resort, second resort, third resort, and so on. This may go beyond Just War Theory *per se*, which is of course focused on the launching of *war*. But Best Resort is important more

[14] See, further, Brunstetter (2014), who highlights the rhetorical import of the last resort principle in US presidential debates.

generally for thinking about the ethics of foreign policy and addressing mass atrocities under R2P and serious external aggression.

What is the best resort? I have highlighted the case for mediation and negotiation as first resorts in particular. Beyond these, targeted economic sanctions, arms embargoes, naming and shaming, expulsions, civilian peacekeeping, economic and political inducements, and international criminal prosecutions are all likely to be some of the earlier options—second and third resorts (and so on)—that should be tried. Accepting and assisting refugees and humanitarian assistance are also likely to be desirable options of best resort, but should not be viewed as part of the toolkit for addressing serious external aggression and mass atrocities. The cutting and downgrading of diplomatic ties, amnesties, military assistance to rebels and states, and wars and direct military intervention are unlikely to be justifiable and so should not generally be tried unless the other options have failed or it is clear that they are highly unlikely to work.

Like Presumptive Last Resort, Best Resort may also be viewed presumptively; the particular alternatives should be the *general* response to mass atrocities and serious external aggression. This presumption should be overridden only when there is clear evidence; it should be upheld for the most part.

10.5 IMPLICATIONS FOR THE R2P DOCTRINE

Finally, let us consider five implications for the predominant framework for addressing mass atrocities: the R2P doctrine. But before doing so, I want to reiterate again a general point. The account of the alternatives helps to flesh out the international responsibility to protect. It provides a much stronger sense of what states and other actors should be doing to fulfil the second and third pillars of R2P.

The central implication for R2P is this: states should look to the leading alternatives as the primary means to fulfil the R2P. In contrast to much of the academic and public debate on R2P since its birth in 2005, the reactive and 'direct preventive' phases of R2P should not be seen as about humanitarian intervention in response to mass atrocities. R2P should instead be seen *as mostly about the alternatives*, given the strength of the normative case for them and against war. As such, the reactive (and direct preventive) part of R2P should be seen as primarily about sanctions, embargoes, naming and shaming, denying membership, civilian (and UN) peacekeeping, positive incentives, and ICC actions, rather than humanitarian intervention. Although much of the impetus around R2P arose from debates about humanitarian intervention in the 1990s and 2000s, R2P need not—and should not—put military intervention front and centre. It is often argued about the 'responsibility to prevent' by

R2P advocates that R2P is not about solely military intervention since it emphasizes the prevention of mass atrocities. In this book, we have seen that this is true of the reactive phase of R2P as well. That is, the 'responsibility to react' is far from being only about humanitarian intervention; it is primarily about non-military measures.

Second, and related, emphasizing the case for these measures when a reaction is required may help to reduce some of the toxicity surrounding pillar three of R2P. Although the degree of opposition to R2P is exaggerated by some, as discussed in section 1.2 several states are still highly sceptical of military intervention to tackle mass atrocities. Even if they accept that it is in principle justifiable, they often oppose particular instances of it. Greater emphasis on the alternatives to military intervention under pillar three (as well as pillar two) adds flesh to the bones to claims of R2P advocates that reactive measures under R2P do not equate to military intervention. In turn, this may enable more actors, such as humanitarian organizations, to be willing to frame their actions in terms of R2P, as it loses its strong association with humanitarian intervention, which may strengthen the norm of R2P further.

Third, the emphasis on the alternatives can help to reduce some of the paralysis that exists in debates about responses to mass atrocities. At the moment, with almost every crisis, significant effort is spent in terms of deliberating about the potential for military intervention. The public debate often revolves around whether there should be intervention or not. Typically, military intervention will not, however, be suitable and no agent would be willing to intervene on the scale necessary to address the situation. As Holmes (2014) argues, 'loose talk' about humanitarian intervention is extremely counterproductive. It wastes valuable time and effort debating something that will not happen and would be most likely unjustifiable. Moreover, it more broadly contributes to viewing a complex crisis in simplistic and militaristic terms, whereby full-scale military intervention will resolve all of the worries and nothing else can help tackle the atrocities. As this book has emphasized, this is a clearly mistaken view.

The fourth implication is that, since none of the measures will completely tackle the crisis, the need for the longer-term prevention of mass atrocities becomes even greater. The failings of war and humanitarian intervention are well known. But we have seen that many of the other options, although they have more going for them than direct military intervention, still suffer from several problems. It is vital, then, to tackle crises before they require any of these measures.[15]

[15] Notwithstanding, longer-term preventive measures raise their own issues (see Sharma and Welsh 2015*b*).

Fifth, there is a duty to reform. Given that none of the alternatives is perfect according to the Pragmatic Approach, yet that it is morally obligatory to pursue them (when prevention has failed and a crisis is imminent or ongoing), it is imperative for states and other organizations to improve their capabilities to use the alternatives and how they are used. This is so that they can use them more reliably and more justifiably when needed. Just as the duty to intervene necessitates a duty to reform to improve the agents and mechanisms of humanitarian intervention to help fulfil R2P (see Pattison 2010: 246–7), so the duty to adopt the alternatives implies a duty to reform to improve the agents and mechanisms around the alternatives. Such improvements might include developing stronger technological capacity for monitoring and enforcing financial sanctions, the improvement of capacity for mediation (Welsh 2014*b*: 140), and greater funding and training of civilian peacekeepers. This will help enable states and other organizations to perform the requirements of R2P.

10.6 CONCLUSION

This chapter has considered the implications of the Pragmatic Approach and the analysis of the alternatives to war. Section 10.2 highlighted the two central themes of the book: (1) there are several normative reasons in favour of the alternatives and (2) there are further objections to war. Section 10.3 argued that, although the analysis strengthens the case for pacifism, it also poses a notable challenge to it. Section 10.4 delineated the implications for Just War Theory. I argued here that last resort should be understood as Presumptive Last Resort. Section 10.5 outlined five implications for R2P.

Throughout the book, we have seen that many of the alternatives, although imperfect, are often likely to be justifiable and, in particular, are often likely to be more effective than at first sight. On the other hand, we have also seen that, although some of the alternatives face notable objections, several of these objections also apply to war and military intervention. Although there may still be the occasional need to undertake war or direct military intervention in response to aggression and mass atrocities, these cases are few and far between.

This book has attempted to rally against the favouring of militarized responses. By considering the alternatives to war, and exploring the ethical issues that they raise, we have a better appreciation that there *are* measures that can be adopted instead of war, from sanctions to non-violence. As is clear from the leading frameworks that we have on the ethics of war and peace—pacifism and Just War Theory—when reacting to mass atrocities and aggression, it is morally obligatory to pursue these alternatives, unless there are strong grounds for overriding Presumptive Last Resort.

Thus, the clear and unmistakable upshot of this book—the first detailed moral map of the ethics of the alternatives to war—is this: there are several justifiable alternatives to war. States and other actors in the international community are morally required to use them.

Bibliography

60 Minutes (1996). 'Secretary of State Madeleine Albright Interview by Lesley Stahl', 12 May.

Achiume, E. Tendayi (2015). 'Syria, Cost-sharing, and the Responsibility to Protect Refugees', *Minnesota Law Review*, 110/2: 687–761.

Adams, Simon (2016). 'The Responsibility to Protect and Alternatives to the Use of Force', Global Centre for the Responsibility to Protect, February.

Addis, Adeno (2003). 'Economic Sanctions and the Problem of Evil', *Human Rights Quarterly*, 25/3: 573–623.

Agiesta, Jennifer (2015). 'Poll: Most Americans Say Send Ground Troops to Fight ISIS', *CNN Politics*, 7 December.

Ainley, Kirsten (2015). 'The Responsibility to Protect and the International Criminal Court: Counteracting the Crisis', *International Affairs*, 91/1: 37–54.

Albright, Madeleine K. and William S. Cohen (2008). *Preventing Genocide: A Blueprint for U.S. Policymakers*, Genocide Prevention Task Force, United States Holocaust Memorial Museum, the American Academy of Diplomacy, and United States Institute of Peace.

Alexander, Larry (2000). 'Deontology at the Threshold', *San Diego Law Review*, 37/4: 893–912.

Alexandra, Andrew (2003). 'Political Pacifism', *Social Theory and Practice*, 29/4: 589–606.

Alexandra, Andrew (2015). 'Liability, War, and Peace', *Philosophical Forum*, 46/1: 41–53.

Alleblas, Tessa, Eamon Aloyo, Sarah Brockmeier, Philipp Rotmann, and Jon Western (2017). *In the Shadow of Syria: Assessing the Obama Administration's Efforts on Mass Atrocity Prevention*, Hague Institute for Global Justice Policy Report.

Allen, Susan Hannah and David J. Lektzian (2013). 'Economic Sanctions: A Blunt Instrument?', *Journal of Peace Research*, 50/1: 121–35.

Aloyo, Eamon (2013). 'Just Assassinations', *International Theory*, 5/3: 347–81.

Aloyo, Eamon (2015). 'Just War Theory and the Last of Last Resort', *Ethics & International Affairs*, 29/2: 187–201.

American Civil Liberties Union (ACLU) (2012). *Victims of Complacency: The Ongoing Trafficking and Abuse of Third Country Nationals by U.S. Government Contractors.* Available at <www.aclu.org/files/assets/hrp_traffickingreport_web_0.pdf>.

Amnesty International (2016). 'EU–Turkey Deal: Greek Decision Highlights Fundamental Flaws', 20 May. Available at <www.amnesty.org/en/latest/news/2016/05/eu-turkey-deal-greek-decision-highlights-fundamental-flaws/>.

Amnesty International (2017). *Amnesty International Report 2016/17: The State of the World's Human Rights Report.* Available at <www.amnesty.org/en/documents/pol10/4800/2017/en/>.

Aneja, Urvashi (2014). 'India, R2P, and Humanitarian Assistance', *Global Responsibility to Protect*, 6/2: 227–45.

Appel, Benjamin J. (2018). 'In the Shadow of the International Criminal Court: Does the ICC Deter Human Rights Violations?', *Journal of Conflict Resolution*, 62/1: 3–28.

Arbour, Louise (2013). 'Doctrines Derailed?: Internationalism's Uncertain Future', Global Briefing 2013, Opening Speech from the International Crisis Group's President and CEO, 28 October. Available at <www.crisisgroup.org/global/doctrines-derailed-internationalism-s-uncertain-future>.

Atack, Iain (2012). *Nonviolence in Political Theory* (Edinburgh: Edinburgh University Press).

Attfield, Robin (2009). 'Mediated Responsibilities, Global Warming and the Scope of Ethics', *Journal of Social Philosophy*, 40/2: 225–36.

Babic, Jovan and Aleksandar Jokic (2000). 'The Ethics of International Sanctions: The Case of Yugoslavia', *Fletcher Forum of World Affairs*, 24/1: 87–101.

Badescu, Cristina G. and Thomas G. Weiss (2010). 'Misrepresenting R2P and Advancing Norms: An Alternative Spiral?', *International Studies Perspectives*, 11/4: 354–74.

Baker, Deane-Peter and James Pattison (2012). 'The Principled Case for Employing Private Military and Security Companies in Interventions for Human Rights Purposes', *Journal of Applied Philosophy*, 29/1: 1–18.

Baldwin, David A. (1971). 'The Power of Positive Sanctions', *World Politics*, 24/1: 20–38.

Baldwin, David A. (1985). *Economic Statecraft* (Princeton, NJ: Princeton University Press).

Baldwin, David A. (1999). 'The Sanctions Debate and the Logic of Choice', *International Security*, 24/3: 80–107.

Baldwin, David A. (2000). 'Success and Failure in Foreign Policy', *Annual Review of Political Science*, 3: 167–82.

Ban Ki-moon (2009). *Implementing the Responsibility to Protect*, UN doc A/63/677.

Ban Ki-moon (2012). *Responsibility to Protect: Timely and Decisive Response*, UN doc A/66/874.

Ban Ki-moon (2015). *A Vital and Enduring Commitment: Implementing the Responsibility to Protect*, UN doc A/69/981.

Barbour, Brian and Brian Gorlick (2008). 'Embracing the "Responsibility to Protect": A Repertoire of Measures Including Asylum for Potential Victims', *International Journal of Refugee Law*, 20/4: 533–66.

Barnes-Dacey, Julien and Daniel Levy (2013). 'Syria: The Imperative of De-Escalation', Policy Brief: European Council on Foreign Relations, ECFR/80, May (London: European Council of Foreign Relations).

Bazargan, Saba (2014). 'Varieties of Contingent Pacifism in War', in Helen Frowe and Gerald Lang (eds), *How We Fight* (Oxford: Oxford University Press), pp. 1–17.

Bazargan-Forward, Saba (2017). 'Accountability and Intervening Agency: An Asymmetry Between Upstream and Downstream Actors', *Utilitas*, 29/1: 110–24.

BBC (2013). 'Who is Supplying Weapons to the Warring Sides in Syria?', BBC News, 14 June.

BBC (2014). 'BNP Paribas to Pay $9bn to Settle Sanctions Violations', BBC News, 1 July.

BBC (2015). 'Iran Nuclear Deal: Key Details', BBC News, 14 July.

Bellamy, Alex J. (2006). *Just Wars: From Cicero to Iraq* (Cambridge: Polity).

Bellamy, Alex J. (2011). *Mass Atrocities and Armed Conflict: Links, Distinctions, and Implications for the Responsibility to Prevent*, Policy Analysis Brief, the Stanley Foundation, February.

Bellamy, Alex J. (2015*a*). *The First Response: Peaceful Means in the Third Pillar of the Responsibility to Protect*, Policy Analysis, the Stanley Foundation, December.

Bellamy, Alex J. (2015*b*). *The Responsibility to Protect: A Defense* (Oxford: Oxford University Press).

Bellamy, Alex J. (2015*c*). 'The Responsibility to Protect Turns Ten', *Ethics & International Affairs*, 29/2: 161–85.

Bellamy, Alex J. and Paul Williams (2009). 'The West and Contemporary Peace Operations', *Journal of Peace Research*, 46/1: 39–57.

Bellamy, Alex J. and Paul Williams (2012). 'On the Limits of Moral Hazard: The "Responsibility to Protect", Armed Conflict and Mass Atrocities', *Security Dialogue*, 18/3: 539–72.

Benner, Thorsten (2013). 'Brazil as a Norm Entrepreneur: The "Responsibility while Protecting" Initiative', *Global Public Policy Institute Working Paper*, March.

Bennett, Jonathan (1995). *The Act Itself* (Oxford: Clarendon Press).

Bensouda, Fatou (2012). 'ICC Prosecutor-Elect Fatou Bensouda Talks Court's Role in R2P', The Stanley Foundation, 19 January. Available at <www.youtube.com/watch?v=suJIXSsGzL0>.

Bentall, Paul (2016). 'United Nations Targeted Sanctions and Other Policy Tools: Diplomacy, Legal, Use of Force', in Thomas J. Biersteker, Sue E. Eckert, and Marcos Tourinho (eds), *Targeted Sanctions: The Impacts and Effectiveness of United Nations Action* (Cambridge: Cambridge University Press), pp. 79–100.

Berridge, G. R. (2010). *Diplomacy: Theory and Practice*, Fourth Edition (Basingstoke: Palgrave Macmillan).

Betts, Alexander (2015). 'The Normative Terrain of the Global Refugee Regime', *Ethics & International Affairs*, 29/4: 363–75.

Beversluis, Eric H. (1989). 'On Shunning Undesirable Regimes: Ethics and Economic Sanctions', *Public Affairs Quarterly*, 3/2: 15–25.

Biersteker, Thomas J., Sue E. Eckert, and Marcos Tourinho (eds) (2016*a*). *Targeted Sanctions: The Impacts and Effectiveness of United Nations Action* (Cambridge: Cambridge University Press).

Biersteker, Thomas J., Sue E. Eckert, and Marcos Tourinho (2016*b*). 'Thinking about United Nations Targeted Sanctions', in Thomas J. Biersteker, Sue E. Eckert, and Marcos Tourinho (eds), *Targeted Sanctions: The Impacts and Effectiveness of United Nations Action* (Cambridge: Cambridge University Press), pp. 11–37.

Biersteker, Thomas J., Marcos Tourinho, and Sue E. Eckert (2016*c*). 'The Effectiveness of United Nations Targeted Sanctions', in Thomas J. Biersteker, Sue E. Eckert, and Marcos Tourinho (eds), *Targeted Sanctions: The Impacts and Effectiveness of United Nations Action* (Cambridge: Cambridge University Press), pp. 220–47.

Biersteker, Thomas J., Marcos Tourinho, and Sue E. Eckert (2016*d*). 'Conclusion', in Thomas J. Biersteker, Sue E. Eckert, and Marcos Tourinho (eds), *Targeted Sanctions: The Impacts and Effectiveness of United Nations Action* (Cambridge: Cambridge University Press), pp. 265–79.

Biggar, Nigel (2013). *In Defence of War* (Oxford: Oxford University Press, 2013).

Birdsall, Andrea (2015). 'The Responsibility to Prosecute and the ICC: A Problematic Relationship?', *Criminal Law Forum*, 26/1: 51–72.

Bjola, Corneliu (2014). 'The Ethics of Secret Diplomacy: A Contextual Approach', *Journal of Global Ethics*, 10/1: 85–100.

Bjola, Corneliu and Markus Kornprobst (2013). *Understanding International Diplomacy: Theory, Practice, and Ethics* (London: Routledge).

Blanchard, Jean-Marc F. and Norrin M. Ripsman (2013). *Economic Statecraft and Foreign Policy: Sanctions, Incentives, and Target State Calculations* (London: Routledge).

Boffey, Daniel (2014). 'Ed Miliband accuses David Cameron of "Inexplicable Silence" in Row over Gaza', *The Guardian*, 2 August.

Boothe, Ivan and Lee A. Smithey (2007). 'Privilege, Empowerment, and Nonviolent Intervention', *Peace & Change*, 32/1: 39–61.

Bosco, David (2014). *Rough Justice: The International Criminal Court in a World of Power Politics* (New York: Oxford University Press).

Brahimi, Lakhdar and Salman Ahmed (2008). *In Pursuit of Sustainable Peace: The Seven Deadly Sins of Mediation*, Center on International Cooperation.

Brazil (2011*a*). 'Responsibility while Protecting: Elements for the Development and Promotion of a Concept', UN doc A/66/551.

Brazil (2011*b*). 'Statement in Open Debate on Protection of Civilians in Armed Conflict', UN Security Council doc, S/PV.6650.

Brown, Campbell (2011). 'Consequentialize This', *Ethics*, 121/4: 749–71.

Brown, Chris (2003). 'Selective Humanitarianism: In Defence of Inconsistency', in Deen K. Chatterjee and Don E. Schied (eds), *Ethics and Foreign Intervention* (Cambridge: Cambridge University Press), pp. 31–50.

Brunstetter, Daniel (2014). 'Trends in Just War Thinking During the US Presidential Debates 2000–12: Genocide Prevention and the Renewed Salience of Last Resort', *Review of International Studies*, 40/1: 77–99.

Brunstetter, Daniel and Scott Brunstetter (2011). 'Shades of Green: Engaged Pacifism, the Just War Tradition, and the German Greens', *International Relations*, 25/1: 65–84.

Brzoska, Michael (2008). 'Measuring the Effectiveness of Arms Embargoes', *Peace Economics, Peace Science and Public Policy*, 14/2: 1–32.

Brzoska, Michael (2013). 'Research on the Effectiveness of International Sanctions', in Hendrik Hegemann, Regina Heller, and Martin Kahl (eds), *Studying 'Effectiveness' in International Relations: A Guide for Students and Scholars* (Berlin: Barbara Budrich Publishers), pp. 143–60.

Brzoska, Michael and George A. Lopez (eds) (2009). *Putting Teeth in the Tiger: Improving the Effectiveness of Arms Embargoes* (Bingley: Emerald Group Publishing).

Brzoska, Michael and George A. Lopez (2016). 'Security Council Dynamics and Sanctions Design', in Thomas J. Biersteker, Sue E. Eckert, and Marcos Tourinho (eds), *Targeted Sanctions: The Impacts and Effectiveness of United Nations Action* (Cambridge: Cambridge University Press), pp. 60–78.

Buchanan, Allen (1999). 'The Internal Legitimacy of Humanitarian Intervention', *Journal of Political Philosophy*, 7/1: 71–87.

Buchanan, Allen (2004). *Justice, Legitimacy, and Self-Determination: Moral Foundations for International Law* (Oxford: Oxford University Press).

Buchanan, Allen (2013). 'The Ethics of Revolution and Its Implications for the Ethics of Intervention', *Philosophy & Public Affairs*, 41/4: 291–323.

Buncombe, Andrew (2013). 'US Army Chief Says Iraqi Troops Took Bribes to Surrender', *The Independent*, 6 October.

Cady, Duane L. (2010). *From Warism to Pacifism: A Moral Continuum*, Second Edition (Philadelphia: Temple University Press).

Cairns, Edmund (2014). 'R2P and Humanitarian Action', *Global Responsibility to Protect*, 6/2: 146–61.

Calhoun, Laurie (2002). 'How Violence Breeds Violence: Some Utilitarian Considerations', *Politics*, 22/2: 95–108.

Calì, Massimiliano and Samia Sekkarie (2015). 'Much Ado about Nothing? The Economic Impact of Refugee "Invasions"', 16 September, Brookings.edu. Available at <www.brookings.edu/blogs/future-development/posts/2015/09/16-economic-impact-refugees-cali>.

Caney, Simon (2000). 'Human Rights, Compatibility and Diverse Cultures', *Critical Review of International Social and Political Philosophy*, 3/1: 51–76.

Caney, Simon (2005*a*). *Justice Beyond Borders: A Global Political Theory* (Oxford: Oxford University Press).

Caney, Simon (2005*b*). 'Cosmopolitan Justice, Responsibility, and Global Climate Change', *Leiden Journal of International Law*, 18/4: 747–75.

Caney, Simon (2010). 'Climate Change and the Duties of the Advantaged', *Critical Review of International Social and Political Philosophy*, 13/1: 203–28.

Caney, Simon (2012). 'Global Justice, Climate Change, and Human Rights', in Douglas A. Hicks and Thad Williamson (eds), *Leadership and Global Justice* (Basingstoke: Palgrave Macmillan), pp. 91–111.

Caney, Simon (2015). 'Responding to Global Injustice: On the Right of Resistance', *Social Philosophy and Policy*, 32/1: 51–73.

Carpenter, Ted Galen (2012). 'The U.S. Should be Wary of Arming Syrian Rebels', *US News and World Report*, 1 November.

Carriere, Rolf (2010). 'The World Needs "Another Peacekeeping"', in Christine Schweitzer (ed.), *Civilian Peacekeeping: A Barely Tapped Resource*, IFGK Working Paper No. 23 (Belm-Vehrte, Germany: Sozio Publishing), pp. 17–24.

Chang, Howard F. (1997). 'Carrots, Sticks, and International Externalities', *International Review of Law and Economics*, 17/3: 309–24.

Chenoweth, Erica (2017). 'Trends in Nonviolent Resistance and State Response: Is Violence Towards Civilian-based Movements on the Rise?', *Global Responsibility to Protect*, 9/1: 86–100.

Chenoweth, Erica and Maria J. Stephan (2011). *Why Civil Resistance Works: The Strategic Logic of Nonviolent Conflict* (New York: Columbia University Press).

Chesterman, Simon (2001). *Just War or Just Peace? Humanitarian Intervention and International Law* (Oxford: Oxford University Press).

Chesterman, Simon (2003). 'Hard Cases Make Bad Law: Law, Ethics, and Politics in Humanitarian Intervention', in Anthony F. Lang Jr (ed.), *Just Intervention* (Washington, DC: Georgetown University Press), pp. 46–61.

Christensen, James (2015). 'Weapons, Security, and Oppression: A Normative Study of International Arms Transfers', *Journal of Political Philosophy*, 23/1: 23–39.

Christiansen, Drew, S. J., and Gerhard F.Powers (1995). 'Economic Sanctions and the Just-War Doctrine', in David Cortright and George A. Lopez (eds), *Economic Sanctions: Panacea or Peacebuilding in a Post-Cold War World?* (Oxford: Westview Press), pp. 97–117.

Cicovacki, Predrag (ed.) (2013). *The Ethics of Nonviolence: Essays by Robert L. Holmes* (London: Bloomsbury).

Clayton, Govinda (2013). 'Relative Rebel Strength and the Onset and Outcome of Civil War Mediation', *Journal of Peace Research*, 50/5: 609–22.

Cochrane, Feargal (2008). *Ending Wars* (Cambridge: Polity).

Coen, Alise (2015). 'R2P, Global Governance, and the Syrian Refugee Crisis', *International Journal of Human Rights*, 19/8: 1044–58.

Coen, Alise (2017). 'Capable and Culpable? The United States, RtoP, and Refugee Responsibility-Sharing', *Ethics & International Affairs*, 31/1: 71–92.

Coghlan, Tom and James Bone (2011). 'Stop Bribing the Taleban, Bush Told Italians', *The Times*, 12 August.

Cohen, G. A. (2013). *Finding Oneself in the Other*, ed. Michael Otsuka (Princeton, NJ: Princeton University Press).

Cohen, Roberta (2010). 'Reconciling R2P with IDP Protection', *Global Responsibility to Protect*, 2/1: 15–37.

Conley-Zilkic, Bridget, Saskia Brechenmacher, and Aditya Sarkar (2016). *Assessing the Anti-Atrocity Toolbox*, World Peace Foundation.

Cook, Martin L. (2000). '"Immaculate War": Constraints on Humanitarian Intervention', *Ethics & International Affairs*, 14/1: 55–65.

Corten, Olivier and Vaios Koutroulis (2013). 'The Illegality of Military Support to Rebels in the Libyan War: Aspects of *Jus Contra Bellum* and *Jus in Bello*', *Journal of Conflict & Security Law*, 18/1: 59–93.

Cortright, David (1997*a*). 'Incentives and Cooperation in International Affairs', in David Cortright (ed.), *The Price of Peace: Incentives and International Conflict Prevention* (Oxford: Rowman & Littlefield), pp. 3–20.

Cortright, David (1997*b*). 'Incentives Strategies for Preventing Conflict', in David Cortright (ed.), *The Price of Peace: Incentives and International Conflict Prevention* (Oxford: Rowman & Littlefield), pp. 267–301.

Cortright, David and George A. Lopez (2005). 'Bombs, Carrots, and Sticks: The Use of Incentives and Sanctions', *Arms Control Today*, 35/2: 19–24.

Cowan, Geoffrey and Amelia Arsenault (2008). 'Moving from Monologue to Dialogue to Collaboration: The Three Layers of Public Diplomacy', *ANNALS of the American Academy of Political and Social Science*, 616/1: 10–29.

Coy, Patrick G. (2011). 'The Privilege Problematic in International Nonviolent Accompaniment's Early Decades: Peace Brigades International Confronts the Use of Racism', *Journal of Religion, Conflict and Peace*, 4/2. Available at <www.religionconflictpeace.org/>.

Coy, Patrick G. (2012). 'Nonpartisanship, Interventionism and Legality in Accompaniment: Comparative Analyses of Peace Brigades International, Christian Peacemaker Teams, and the International Solidarity Movement', *International Journal of Human Rights*, 16/7: 963–81.

Coy, Patrick G. (2013). 'Whither Nonviolent Studies?', *Peace Review: A Journal of Social Justice*, 25/2: 257–65.

Crawford, Neta C. (2005). 'The Justice of Preemption and Preventive War Doctrines', in Mark Evans (ed.), *Just War Theory: A Reappraisal* (Edinburgh: Edinburgh University Press), pp. 25–49.

Cull, Nicholas J. (2008). 'Public Diplomacy: Taxonomies and Histories', *ANNALS of the American Academy of Political and Social Science*, 616/1: 31–54.

Damrosch, Lori Fisler (1994). 'The Collective Enforcement of International Norms through Economic Sanctions', *Ethics & International Affairs*, 8/1: 59–75.

Dancy, Geoff and Florencia Montal (2017). 'Unintended Positive Complementarity: Why International Criminal Court Investigations Increase Domestic Human Rights Prosecutions', *American Journal of International Law*, 111/3: 689–723.

Daniels, Norman (2016). 'Reflective Equilibrium', in Edward Zalta (ed.), *Stanford Encyclopaedia of Philosophy*, Winter 2016 Version. Available at <plato.stanford.edu/entries/reflective-equilibrium/>.

Davenport, John J. (2016). 'In Defense of the Responsibility to Protect: A Response to Weissman', *Criminal Justice Ethics*, 35/1: 39–67.

Davies, Graeme A. M. and Robert Johns (2016*a*). 'R2P from Below: Does the British Public View Humanitarian Interventions as Ethical and Effective?', *International Politics*, 53/1: 118–37.

Davies, Graeme A. M. and Robert Johns (2016*b*). 'The Domestic Consequences of International Over-Cooperation: An Experimental Study of Microfoundations', *Conflict Management and Peace Science*, 33/4: 343–60.

de Soto, Alvaro (2008). 'Harnessing Incentives for Peace: An Interview with Alvaro de Soto', *Accord: An International Review of Peace Initiatives*, 19: 24–9.

DeMeritt, Jacqueline H. R. (2012). 'International Organizations and Government Killing: Does Naming and Shaming Save Lives?', *International Interactions*, 38/5: 597–621.

DeMeritt, Jacqueline H. R. (2015). 'Delegating Death Military: Intervention and Government Killing', *Journal of Conflict Resolution*, 59/3: 428–54.

Dobos, Ned (2012). 'International Rescue and Mediated Consequences', *Ethics & International Affairs*, 26/3: 335–53.

Dorussen, Han (2001). 'Mixing Carrots with Sticks: Evaluating the Effectiveness of Positive Incentives', *Journal of Peace Research*, 38/2: 251–62.

Doxey, Margaret P. (1996) *International Sanctions in Contemporary Perspective*, Second Edition (London: Macmillan).

Drezner, Daniel W. (1999). 'The Trouble with Carrots: Transaction Costs, Conflict Expectations, and Economic Inducements', *Security Studies*, 9/1–2: 188–218.

Drezner, Daniel W. (2011). 'Sanctions Sometimes Smart: Targeted Sanctions in Theory and Practice', *International Studies Review*, 13/1: 96–108.

Drezner, Daniel W. (2015). 'Targeted Sanctions in a World of Global Finance', *International Interactions*, 41/4: 755–64.

Drury, A. Cooper and Dursun Peksen (2014). 'Woman and Economic Statecraft: The Negative Impact International Economic Sanctions Visit on Women', *European Journal of International Relations*, 20/2: 463–90.

Easthom, Tiffany (2014). 'As a New Civil War Gripped the Nation, NP Scaled Up to Become the Largest Protection Agency in South Sudan', Nonviolent Peaceforce, *Progress Report*, January 2013–June 2014.

Eckert, Sue E., Thomas J. Biersteker, and Marcos Tourinho (2016). 'Introduction', in Thomas J. Biersteker, Sue E. Eckert, and Marcos Tourinho (eds), *Targeted Sanctions: The Impacts and Effectiveness of United Nations Action* (Cambridge: Cambridge University Press), pp. 1–10.

Eddy, Matthew P. (2011). 'Freedom Summer Abroad: Biographical Pathways and Cosmopolitanism among International Human Rights Workers', *Research in Social Movements, Conflicts, and Change*, 31: 209–58.

Ellis, Elizabeth (2017). 'The Ethics of Economic Sanctions', *The Internet Encyclopedia of Philosophy*. Available at <www.iep.utm.edu/eth-ec-s/>.

Erickson, Jennifer L. (2013). 'Stopping the Legal Flow of Weapons: Compliance with Arms Embargoes, 1981–2004', *Journal of Peace Research*, 52/2: 159–74.

Eriksson, Mikael (2016). 'The Unintended Consequences of United Nations Targeted Sanctions', in Thomas J. Biersteker, Sue E. Eckert, and Marcos Tourinho (eds), *Targeted Sanctions: The Impacts and Effectiveness of United Nations Action* (Cambridge: Cambridge University Press), pp. 190–219.

Eriksson, Mikael and Francesco Giumelli (2011). 'Why the EU's Sanctions against Assad's Syria Will Backfire', *Foreign Affairs*, 1 December.

Eriksson, Mikael and Peter Wallensteen (2015). 'Targeting Sanctions and Ending Armed Conflicts: First Steps Towards a New Research Agenda', *International Affairs*, 91/6: 1387–98.

Escribà-Folch, Abel (2010). 'Economic Sanctions and the Duration of Civil Conflicts', *Journal of Peace Research*, 47/2: 129–41.

Evans, Gareth (2008). *The Responsibility to Protect: Ending Mass Atrocity Crimes Once and For All* (Washington, DC: Brookings Institution Press).

Evans, Gareth (2012). 'R2P and RwP After Libya and Syria', Keynote Address to GCR2P/FGV/Stanley Foundation Workshop, Responsibility While Protecting: What's Next?, Rio de Janeiro, 23 August.

Fabre, Cécile (2012). *Cosmopolitan War* (Oxford: Oxford University Press).

Fabre, Cécile (2016). 'Secondary Economic Sanctions', *Current Legal Problems*, 69/1: 259–88.

Feaver, Peter D. (1999). 'Civil–Military Relations', *Annual Review of Political Science*, 2: 211–41.

Fiala, Andrew (2004). *Practical Pacifism* (New York: Algora).

Fiala, Andrew (2006). 'Practical Pacifism, *Jus in Bello*, and Citizen Responsibility: The Case of Iraq', *Ethical Perspectives: Journal of the European Ethics Network*, 13/4: 673–97.

Fiala, Andrew (2014*a*). 'Contingent Pacifism and Contingently Pacifist Conclusions', *Journal of Social Philosophy*, 45/4: 463–77.

Fiala, Andrew (2014*b*). 'Pacifism', in Edward N. Zalta (ed.), *The Stanford Encyclopedia of Philosophy*, Winter 2014 Edition, <plato.stanford.edu/archives/win2014/entries/pacifism/>.

Finkelstein, Claire, Jens David Ohlin, and Andrew Altman (eds) (2012). *Targeted Killings: Law and Morality in an Asymmetrical World* (Oxford: Oxford University Press).

Finlay, Christopher J. (2015). *Terrorism and the Right to Resist: A Theory of Just Revolutionary War* (Cambridge: Cambridge University Press).

Finnemore, Martha (1996). *National Interests in International Society* (Ithaca, NY: Cornell University Press).

Finnemore, Martha and Kathryn Sikkink (1998). 'International Norm Dynamics and Political Change', *International Organization*, 52/4: 887–917.

Fisher, David (2011). *Morality and War: Can War be Just in the Twenty-First Century?* (Oxford: Oxford University Press).

Fitzpatrick, Kathy R. (2007). 'Advancing the New Public Diplomacy: A Public Relations Perspective', *Hague Journal of Diplomacy*, 2/3: 187–211.

Franklin, James C. (2008). 'Shame on You: The Impact of Human Rights Criticism on Political Repression in Latin America', *International Studies Quarterly*, 52/1: 187–211.

Freeman, Mark (2009). *Necessary Evils: Amnesties and the Search for Justice* (Cambridge: Cambridge University Press).

Frey, Bruno S. and Reto Jegen (2001). 'Motivation Crowding Theory', *Journal of Economic Surveys*, 15/5: 589–611.

Friman, H. Richard (2015). *The Politics of Leverage in International Relations: Name, Shame, and Sanction* (Basingstoke: Palgrave Macmillan).

Frowe, Helen (2011). *The Ethics of War and Peace: An Introduction*, First Edition (London: Routledge).

Fruchart, Damien (2007). 'United Nations Arms Embargoes: Their Impact on Arms Flows and Target Behaviour: Case Study: Rwanda, 1994–Present', SIPRI (Stockholm International Peace Research Institute).

Fruchart, Damien, Paul Holtom, Siemon T. Wezeman, Daniel Strandow, and Peter Wallensteen (2007). *United Nations Arms Embargoes: Their Impact on Arms Flows and Target Behaviour*, Stockholm International Peace Research Institute (SIPRI) and Special Program on the Implementation of Targeted Sanctions (SPITS).

Galston, William A. (2003). 'A Sketch of Some Arguments for Conscription', *Philosophy & Public Policy Quarterly*, 23/3: 2–7.

Galtung, Johan (1967). 'On the Effects of International Economic Sanctions, with Examples from the Case of Rhodesia', *World Politics*, 19/3: 378–416.

Gardiner, John (2007). 'Complicity and Causality', *Criminal Law and Philosophy*, 1/2: 127–41.

Garwood-Gowers, Andrew (2016). 'China's "Responsible Protection" Concept: Reinterpreting the Responsibility to Protect (R2P) and Military Intervention for Humanitarian Purposes', *Asian Journal of International Law*, 6/1: 89–118.

Gilboa, Eytan (2008). 'Searching for a Theory of Public Diplomacy', *ANNALS of the American Academy of Political and Social Science*, 616/1: 55–77.

Giumelli, Francesco (2016). 'The Purposes of Targeted Sanctions', in Thomas J. Biersteker, Sue E. Eckert, and Marcos Tourinho (eds), *Targeted Sanctions: The Impacts and Effectiveness of United Nations Action* (Cambridge: Cambridge University Press), pp. 38–59.

Glaser, Daryl (2006). 'Does Hypocrisy Matter? The Case of US Foreign Policy', *Review of International Studies*, 32/2: 251–68.

Goldsmith, Jack and Stephen D. Krasner (2003). 'The Limits of Idealism', *Daedalus*, Winter 2003: 47–63.

Goldston, James A. (2010). 'More Candour about Criteria: The Exercise of Discretion by the Prosecutor of the International Criminal Court', *Journal of International Criminal Justice*, 8/2: 383–406.

Goodin, Robert E. (1988). 'What Is So Special About Our Fellow Countrymen?', *Ethics*, 98/4: 663–86.

Goodin, Robert E. (2013). 'Disgorging the Fruits of Historical Wrongdoing', *American Political Science Review*, 107/3: 478–91.

Goodin, Robert E. and Christian Barry (2014). 'Benefiting from the Wrongdoing of Others', *Journal of Applied Philosophy*, 31/4: 363–76.

Goodman, Ryan (2006). 'Humanitarian Intervention and Pretexts for War', *American Journal of International Law*, 100/1: 107–41.

Gopalan, Sandeep and Roslyn Fuller (2014). 'Enforcing International Law: States, IOs, and Courts as Shaming Reference Groups', *Brooklyn Journal of International Law*, 39/1: 73–158.

Gordon, Joy (1999*a*). 'A Peaceful, Silent, Deadly Remedy: The Ethics of Economic Sanctions', *Ethics & International Affairs*, 13/1: 123–42.

Gordon, Joy (1999*b*). 'Economic Sanctions, Just War Doctrine, and the "Fearful Spectacle of the Civilian Dead"', *Crosscurrents*, 49/3: 387–400.

Gordon, Joy (2010). *Invisible War: The United States and the Iraq Sanctions* (Cambridge, Mass.: Harvard University Press).

Gordon, Joy (2011). 'Smart Sanctions Revisited', *Ethics & International Affairs*, 25/3: 315–35.

Gordon, Joy (2015). 'Ethics and Targeted Sanctions', in Cathal J. Nolan (ed.), *Ethics and Statecraft: The Moral Dimension of International Affairs*, Third Edition (Santa Barbara, Calif.: Praeger), pp. 261–72.

Gordon, Joy (2017). 'Reconsidering Economic Sanctions', in Michael Gross and Tamar Meisels (eds), *Soft War: The Ethics of Unarmed Conflict* (Cambridge: Cambridge University Press), pp. 49–62.

Gorin, Moti and Harald Schmidt (2015). '"I Did It for the Money": Incentives, Rationalisations and Health', *Public Health Ethics*, 8/1: 34–41.

Grant, Ruth W. (2006). 'Ethics and Incentives: A Political Approach', *American Political Science Review*, 100/1: 29–39.

Grant, Ruth W. (2012). *Strings Attached: Untangling the Ethics of Incentives* (Princeton, NJ: Princeton University Press).

Griffiths, Aaron and Catherine Barnes (2008). 'Incentives and Sanctions in Peace Processes', *Accord: An International Review of Peace Initiatives*, 19: 9–13.

Gross, Michael (2013). 'Just War and Guerrilla War', in Anthony F. Lang Jr, Cian O'Driscoll, and John Williams (eds), *Just War: Authority, Tradition, and Practice* (Washington, DC: Georgetown University Press), pp. 213–30.

Gross, Michael (2014). 'The Paradox of Using Human Shields in War', *Ethics & International Affairs blog*, 6 October. Available at <www.ethicsandinternationalaffairs.org/2014/the-paradox-of-using-human-shields-in-war/>.

Gross, Michael (2015). *The Ethics of Insurgency: A Critical Guide to Just Guerrilla Warfare* (Cambridge: Cambridge University Press).

Gross, Michael and Tamar Meisels (eds) (2017). *Soft War: The Ethics of Unarmed Conflict* (Cambridge: Cambridge University Press).

The Guardian (2016). 'Gambia is Latest African Nation to Quit International Criminal Court', *The Guardian*, 26 October.

Haass, Richard N. and Meghan L. O' Sullivan (2000). 'Conclusion', in Richard N. Haass and Meghan L. O'Sullivan (eds), *Honey and Vinegar: Incentives, Sanctions, and Foreign Policy* (Washington, DC: Brookings Institution Press), pp. 159–201.

Hafner-Burton, Emilie M. (2008). 'Sticks and Stones: Naming and Shaming the Human Rights Enforcement Problem', *International Organization*, 62/4: 689–716.

Hafner-Burton, Emilie M. (2014). 'A Social Science of Human Rights', *Journal of Peace Research*, 51/2: 273–86.

Halpern, Scott D., Kristin M. Madison, and Kevin G. Volpp (2009). 'Patients as Mercenaries? The Ethics of Using Financial Incentives in the War on Unhealthy Behaviours', *Circulation: Cardiovascular Quality and Outcomes*, 2/5: 514–16.

Hanna, Jason (2015). 'Enabling Harm, Doing Harm, and Undoing One's Own Behavior', *Ethics*, 126/1: 68–90.

Hartung, William D. (2001). 'The New Business of War: Small Arms and the Proliferation of Conflict', *Ethics & International* Affairs, 15/1: 79–96.

Havemann, Chris (1998). 'Ethical Business around the World: Hawks or Doves? The Ethics of UK Arms Exports', *Business Ethics*, 7/4: 240–4.

Heinze, Eric A. (2005). 'Commonsense Morality and the Consequentialist Ethics of Humanitarian Intervention', *Journal of Military Ethics*, 4/3: 168–82.

Heinze, Eric A. (2009). *Waging Humanitarian War: The Ethics, Law, and Politics of Humanitarian Intervention* (Albany: SUNY Press).

Helm, Toby (2013). 'Poll Finds 60% of British Public Oppose UK Military Action Against Syria', *The Guardian*, 31 August.

Hillebrecht, Courtney (2016). 'The Deterrent Effects of the International Criminal Court: Evidence from Libya', *International Interactions*, 42/4: 616–43.

Hjorthen, Fredrik (2017). 'Who Should Pay for Humanitarian Intervention?', *European Journal of Political Theory*, DOI: 10.1177/1474885117697468.

Hofman, Michiel (2014). 'The Evolution from Integrated Missions to "Peace Keepers on Steroids": How Aid by Force Erodes Humanitarian Access', *Global Responsibility to Protect*, 6/2: 246–63.

Høivik, Tord and Solveig Aas (1981). 'Demilitarization in Costa Rica: A Farewell to Arms?', *Journal of Peace Research*, 18/4: 333–50.

Holmes, John (2014). 'Responsibility to Protect: A Humanitarian Overview', *Global Responsibility to Protect*, 6/2: 126–45.

Holmes, Robert L. (1989). *On War and Morality* (Princeton, NJ: Princeton University Press).

Holmes, Robert L. (ed.) (1990). *Nonviolence in Theory and Practice* (California: Wadsworth Publishing Company).

Hooker, Brad (2000). *Ideal Code, Real World: A Rule-Consequentialist Theory of Morality* (Oxford: Clarendon Press).

Hopkins, Nick (2014). 'Syria Conflict: UK Planned to Train and Equip 100,000 Rebels', *BBC Newsnight*, 3 July.

Howes, Dustin Ells (2013). 'The Failure of Pacifism and the Success of Nonviolence', *Perspectives on Politics*, 11/2: 427–46.

Hsieh, Nien-hê (2016). 'Incommensurable Values', in Edward N. Zalta (ed.), *The Stanford Encyclopedia of Philosophy*, Spring 2016 Edition. <plato.stanford.edu/archives/spr2016/entries/value-incommensurable/>.

Huemer, Michael (2010). 'Lexical Priority and the Problem of Risk', *Pacific Philosophical Quarterly*, 91/3: 335–51.

Hufbauer, Gary Clyde, Jeffrey J. Schott, Kimberly Ann Elliott, and Barbara Oegg (2009). *Economic Sanctions Reconsidered*, Third Edition (Washington, DC: Peter G. Peterson Institute for International Economics).

Hultman, Lisa, Jacob Kathman, and Megan Shannon (2014). 'Beyond Keeping Peace: United Nations Effectiveness in the Midst of Fighting', *American Political Science Review*, 108/4: 737–53.

Hultman, Lisa and Dursun Peksen (2017). 'Successful or Counterproductive Coercion? The Effect of International Sanctions on Conflict Intensity', *Journal of Conflict Resolution*, 61/6: 1315–39.

Hultquist, Philip (2013). 'Power Parity and Peace? The Role of Relative Power in Civil War Settlement', *Journal of Peace Research*, 50/5: 623–34.

Human Rights Watch (2016). '"I Just Wanted to be Treated like a Person": How Lebanon's Residency Rules Facilitate Abuse of Syrian Refugees', Human Rights Watch Report, 12 January. Available at <www.hrw.org/report/2016/01/12/i-just-wanted-be-treated-person/how-lebanons-residency-rules-facilitate-abuse>.

Hurka, Thomas (2005). 'Proportionality in the Morality of War', *Philosophy & Public Affairs*, 33/1: 34–66.

Huseby, Robert (2015). 'Should the Beneficiary Pay?', *Politics, Philosophy, & Economics*, 14/2: 209–25.

International Commission on Intervention and State Sovereignty (ICISS) (2001). *The Responsibility to Protect: Report of the International Commission on Intervention and State Sovereignty* (Ottawa: International Development Research Centre).

Jackson, Richard (2017). 'CTS, Counterterrorism, and Non-violence', *Critical Studies on Terrorism*, 10/2: 357–69.

Jackson, Thomas (2010). 'From Under Their Noses: Rebel Groups' Arms Acquisition and the Importance of Leakages from State Stockpiles', *International Studies Perspectives*, 11/2: 131–47.

Janzen, Randy (2014). 'Shifting Practices of Peace: What is the Current State of Unarmed-Civilian Peacekeeping?', *Peace Studies Journal*, 7/3. Available at <peacestudiesjournal.org/>.

Jo, Hyeran and Beth A. Simmons (2016). 'Can the International Criminal Court Deter Atrocity?', *International Organization*, 70/3: 443–75.

Jo, Hyeran and Beth A. Simmons (2017). 'Can the International Criminal Court Deter Atrocity?—CORRIGENDUM', *International Organization*, 71/2: 419–21.

Julian, Rachel and Christine Schweitzer (2015). 'The Origins and Development of Unarmed Civilian Peacekeeping', *Peace Review*, 27/1: 1–8.

Junk, Julian (2016). 'Testing Boundaries: Cyclone Nargis in Myanmar and the Scope of R2P', *Global Society*, 30/1: 78–93.

Kagan, Shelly (2012). *The Geometry of Desert* (New York: Oxford University Press).

Kaldor, Mary (2012). *New and Old Wars: Organized Violence in a Global Era*, Third Edition (Cambridge: Polity Press).

Keatinge, Tom and Florence Keen (2017). 'Humanitarian Action and Non-state Armed Groups: The Impact of Banking Restrictions on UK NGOs', Chatham House Research Paper, April.

Kerry, John (2013). 'Remarks at the United Nations Security Council', New York, 27 September. Available at <2009-2017.state.gov/secretary/remarks/2013/09/214890.htm>.

Kikoler, Naomi (2015). 'Guinea: An Overlooked Case of the Responsibility to Prevent in Practice', in Serena K. Sharma and Jennifer M. Welsh (eds), *The Responsibility to Prevent: Overcoming the Challenges of Atrocity Prevention* (Oxford: Oxford University Press), pp. 304–23.

Kinzelbach, Katrin (2014). *The EU's Human Rights Dialogue with China: Quiet Diplomacy and its Limits* (London: Routledge).

Klein, Eran P. (2014). 'Patient Health Incentives: Ethical Challenges and Frameworks', *International Journal of Behavioural Medicine*, 21/6: 995–1004.

Klosko, George (2005). *Political Obligations* (Oxford: Oxford University Press).

Koh, Harold Hongju and Todd F. Buchwald (2015). 'The Crime of Aggression: The United States Perspective', *American Journal of International Law*, 109/2: 257–95.

Krain, Matthew (2005). 'International Intervention and the Severity of Genocides and Politicides', *International Studies Quarterly*, 49/3: 363–87.

Krain, Matthew (2012). '*J'accuse*! Does Naming and Shaming Perpetrators Reduce the Severity of Genocides or Politicides?', *International Studies Quarterly*, 56/3: 574–89.

Krain, Matthew (2014). 'The Effects of Diplomatic Sanctions and Engagement on the Severity of Ongoing Genocides or Politicides', *Journal of Genocide Research*, 16/1: 25–53.

Krain, Matthew (2017). 'The Effect of Economic Sanctions on the Severity of Genocides or Politicides', *Journal of Genocide Research*, 19/1: 88–111.

Kriesberg, Louis (1981). 'Noncoercive Inducements in International Conflicts', *Peace and Change*, 7/4: 37–47.

Kutz, Christopher (2007). 'Causeless Complicity', *Criminal Law and Philosophy*, 1/3: 289–305.

Labonte, Mellissa T. (2012). 'Whose Responsibility to Protect? The Implications of Double Manifest Failure for Civilian Protection', *International Journal of Human Rights*, 16/7: 982–1002.

Lango, John (2007). 'Generalizing and Temporalizing Just War Principles: Illustrated by the Principle of Just Cause', in Michael Brough, John Lango, and Harry van der Linden (eds), *Rethinking the Just War Tradition* (Albany: SUNY Press), pp. 75–95.

Lango, John (2009*a*). 'Before Military Force, Nonviolent Action: An Application of a Generalized Just War Principle of Last Resort', *Public Affairs Quarterly*, 23/2: 115–33.

Lango, John (2009*b*). 'Military Operations by Armed UN Peacekeeping Missions: An Application of Generalised Just War Principles', in Th. A. van Baarda and D. E. M. Verweij (eds), *The Moral Dimension of Asymmetrical Warfare: Counter-terrorism, Western Values and Military Ethics* (Leiden: Martinus Nijhoff), pp. 115–33.

Lango, John (2014). *The Ethics of Armed Conflict: A Cosmopolitan Just War Theory* (Edinburgh: Edinburgh University Press).

Lazar, Seth (2010). 'The Responsibility Dilemma for Killing in War: A Review Essay', *Philosophy & Public Affairs*, 38/2: 180–213.

Lazar, Seth (2012). 'Necessity in Self-Defense and War', *Philosophy & Public Affairs*, 40/1: 3–44.

Lazar, Seth (2016). 'War', in Edward N. Zalta (ed.), *The Stanford Encyclopedia of Philosophy*, Winter 2016 Edition. Available at <plato.stanford.edu/archives/win2016/entries/ethics-deontological/>.

Lazar, Seth (2017*a*). 'Deontological Decision Theory and Agent-Centred Options', *Ethics*, 127/2: 579–609.

Lazar, Seth (2017*b*). 'In Dubious Battle: Uncertainty and the Ethics of Killing', *Philosophical Studies*, DOI: 10.1007/s11098-017-0896-3.

Lee, Steven P. (2013). *Ethics and War: An Introduction* (Cambridge: Cambridge University Press).

Lefkowitz, David (2011). 'On a Duty of Humanitarian Intervention', in Paulo Tripodi and Jessica Wolfendale (eds), *New Wars and New Soldiers: Military Ethics in the Contemporary World* (Farnham: Ashgate), pp. 87–101.

Lehmann, Julian (2012). 'All Necessary Means to Protect Civilians: What the Intervention in Libya Says about the Relationship between the *Jus in Bello* and the *Jus ad Bellum*', *Journal of Conflict & Security Law*, 17/1: 117–46.

Lektzian, David and Patrick M. Regan (2016). 'Economic Sanctions, Military Interventions, and Civil Conflict Outcomes', *Journal of Peace Research*, 53/4: 554–68.

Lepora, Chiara and Robert E. Goodin (2013). *On Complicity and Compromise* (Oxford: Oxford University Press).

Levy, Jack S. and William R. Thompson (2010). *The Causes of War* (Oxford: Wiley Blackwell).

Lopez, George A. (1999). 'More Ethical than Not: Sanctions as Surgical Tools: Response to "A Peaceful, Silent, Deadly Remedy"', *Ethics & International Affairs*, 13/1: 143–8.

Lopez, George A. (2012). 'In Defense of Smart Sanctions: A Response to Joy Gordon', *Ethics & International Affairs*, 26/1: 135–46.

Lord, Errol and Marry Maguire (eds) (2016). *Weighing Reasons* (Oxford: Oxford University Press).

Luban, David (2013). 'After the Honeymoon: Reflections on the Current State of International Criminal Justice', *Journal of International Criminal Justice*, 11/3: 505–15.

Luck, Edward (2012). 'Opening Statement of Dr Edward C Luck, Special Adviser to the United Nations Secretary-General on the Responsibility to Protect', Informal Discussion on the 'Responsibility While Protecting', United Nations, 21 February.

MacAskill, Ewen and Martin Chulov (2014). 'ISIS Apparently Takes Control of U.S. Weapons Airdrop Intended for Kurds', *The Guardian*, 22 October.

McCormack, Daniel and Henry Pascoe (2017). 'Sanctions and Preventive War', *Journal of Conflict Resolution*, 61/8: 1711–39 .

McGee, Robert W. (2003). 'The Ethics of Economic Sanctions', *Economic Affairs*, 23/4: 41–5.

McMahan, Jeff (2004). 'The Ethics of Killing in War', *Ethics*, 114/4: 693–733.

McMahan, Jeff (2005). 'Just Cause for War', *Ethics & International Affairs*, 19/3: 1–21.

McMahan, Jeff (2009). *Killing in War* (Oxford: Clarendon Press).

McMahan, Jeff (2010*a*). 'Pacifism and Moral Theory', *Diametros*, 23: 3–20.

McMahan, Jeff (2010*b*). 'The Just Distribution of Harm Between Combatants and Noncombatants', *Philosophy & Public Affairs*, 38/4: 342–79.

McMahan, Jeff (2013–14). 'Proportionate Defense', *Journal of Transnational Law and Policy*, 21: 1–36.

Mahony, Liam (1997). 'Unarmed Bodyguards', *Peace Review: A Journal of Social Justice*, 9/2: 207–13.

Maley, William (2015). 'Humanitarian Law, Refugee Protection, and the Responsibility to Protect', in Ramesh Thakur and William Maley (eds), *Theorising the Responsibility to Protect* (Cambridge: Cambridge University Press), pp. 249–65.

Maller, Tara (2009). 'The Dangers of Diplomatic Disengagement in Counterterrorism', *Studies in Conflict & Terrorism*, 32/6: 511–36.

Maller, Tara (2010). 'Diplomacy Derailed: The Consequences of Diplomatic Sanctions', *The Washington Quarterly*, 33/3: 61–79.

March, James G. and Johan P. Olsen (1998). 'The Institutional Dynamics of International Political Orders', *International Organization*, 52/4: 943–69.

Martínez, José Ciro and Brent Eng (2016). 'The Unintended Consequences of Emergency Food Aid: Neutrality, Sovereignty and Politics in the Syrian Civil War, 2012–15', *International Affairs*, 92/1: 153–73.

May, Larry (2011). 'Contingent Pacifism and the Moral Risks of Participation in War', *Public Affairs Quarterly*, 25/2: 95–112.

Mazzetti, Mark (2014). 'C.I.A. Study of Covert Aid Fueled Skepticism About Helping Syrian Rebels', *New York Times*, 14 October 2014.

Mazzetti, Mark, Adam Goldman, and Michael S. Schmidt (2017). 'Behind the Sudden Death of a $1 Billion Secret C.I.A. War in Syria', *New York Times*, 2 August.

Mearsheimer, John (2015). 'Don't Arm Ukraine', *New York Times*, The Opinion Pages, 8 February.

Meisels, Tamar (2011). 'Economic Warfare: The Case of Gaza', *Journal of Military Ethics*, 10/2: 94–109.

Mellison, Jan (2013). 'Public Diplomacy', in Andrew F. Cooper, Jorge Heine, and Ramesh Thakur (eds), *The Oxford Handbook of Modern Diplomacy* (Oxford: Oxford University Press), pp. 436–52.

Menon, Rajan (2016). *The Conceit of Humanitarian Intervention* (New York: Oxford University Press).

Milburn, Thomas W. and Daniel J. Christie (1989). 'Rewarding in International Politics', *Political Psychology*, 10/4: 625–45.

Miller, David (2001). 'Distributing Responsibilities', *Journal of Political Philosophy*, 9/4: 453–71.

Miller, David (2007). *National Responsibility and Global Justice* (Oxford: Oxford University Press).

Miller, Franklin G. and Alan Wertheimer (2010). 'Preface to a Theory of Consent Transactions: Beyond Valid Consent', in Franklin G. Miller and Alan Wertheimer (eds), *The Ethics of Consent* (New York: Oxford University Press), pp. 79–106.

Miller, Franklin G. and Alan Wertheimer (2011). 'The Fair Transaction Model of Informed Consent: An Alternative to Autonomous Authorization', *Kennedy Institute of Ethics Journal*, 21/3: 201–18.

Mills, Kurt (2015*a*). 'R2P and the ICC: At Odds or in Sync?', *Criminal Law Forum*, 26/1: 73–99.

Mills, Kurt (2015*b*). 'What Responsibilities Does the International Community Have in Complex Humanitarian Crises and Mass Atrocity Situations?', in Kurt Mills and

David Karp (eds), *Human Rights Protection in Global Politics* (Basingstoke: Palgrave Macmillan), pp. 223–44.

Mills, Kurt (2015*c*). *International Responses to Mass Atrocities in Africa: Responsibility to Protect, Prosecute, and Palliate* (Philadelphia: University of Pennsylvania Press).

Miniotaite, Grazina (1996). 'Lithuania: From Non-Violent Liberation towards Non-Violent Defence?', *Peace Research*, 28/4: 19–36.

Mitchell, David (2008). 'Room for Accommodation: Incentives, Sanctions, and Conditionality in Northern Ireland', *Accord: An International Review of Peace Initiatives*, 19: 50–3.

Moellendorf, Darrel (2008). 'Jus ex Bello', *Journal of Political Philosophy*, 16/2: 123–36.

Mooney, Erin D. (2010). 'Something Old, Something New, Something Borrowed... Something Blue? The Protection Potential of a Marriage of Concepts between R2P and IDP Protection', *Global Responsibility to Protect*, 2/1: 60–85.

Moore, Matthew (2010). 'Arming the Embargoed: A Supply-Side Understanding of Arms Embargo Violations', *Journal of Conflict Resolution*, 54/4: 593–615.

Moore, Matthew (2012). 'Selling to Both Sides: The Effects of Major Conventional Weapons Transfers on Civil War Severity and Duration', *International Interactions*, 38/3: 325–47.

Mor, Ben D. (2012). 'Credibility Talk in Public Diplomacy', *Review of International Studies*, 38/2: 393–422.

Moret, Erica S. (2015). 'Humanitarian Impacts of Economic Sanctions on Iran and Syria', *European Security*, 24/1: 120–40.

Morgan, T. Clifton (2015). 'Hearing the Noise: Economic Sanctions Theory and Anomalous Evidence', *International Interactions*, 41/4: 744–54.

Morgan, T. Clifton, Navin Bapat, and Yoshiharu Kobayashi (2014). 'Threat and Imposition of Economic Sanctions 1945–2005: Updating the TIES Dataset', *Conflict Management and Peace Science*, 31/5: 541–58.

Nagel, Thomas (2005). 'The Problem of Global Justice', *Philosophy & Public Affairs*, 33/2: 113–47.

Narveson, Jan (1965). 'Pacifism: A Philosophical Analysis?', *Ethics*, 75/4: 259–71.

Natsios, Andrew (2009). 'Waltz with Bashir: Why the Arrest Warrant Against Sudan's President Will Serve Neither Peace Nor Justice', *Foreign Affairs*, 23 March.

Newnham, Randall E. (2004). '"Nukes for Sale Cheap?" Purchasing Peace with North Korea', *International Studies Perspectives*, 5/2: 164–78.

Nincic, Miroslav (2006). 'The Logic of Positive Engagement: Dealing with Renegade Regimes', *International Studies Perspectives*, 7/4: 321–41.

Nincic, Miroslav (2011). *The Logic of Positive Engagement* (Ithaca, NY: Cornell University Press).

Nonviolent Peaceforce (2014). *Progress Report*, January 2013–June 2014.

Nye, Joseph S. (2008). 'Public Diplomacy and Soft Power', *ANNALS of the American Academy of Political and Social Science*, 616/1: 94–109.

Obama, Barack (2009). 'Remarks by the President at the Acceptance of the Nobel Peace Prize', 10 December, Oslo. Available at <obamawhitehouse.archives.gov/the-press-office/remarks-president-acceptance-nobel-peace-prize>.

Office of the Prosecutor (2007). 'The Interests of Justice', *Policy Paper on the Interests of Justice*. Available at <www.icc-cpi.int/NR/rdonlyres/772C95C9-F54D-4321-BF09-73422BB23528/143640/ICCOTPInterestsOfJustice.pdf>.

O'Grady, Siobhán (2016). 'Burundi: Sepp Blatter Tried to "Bribe" Our President to Step Down', *Foreign Policy*, 21 April.

Orend, Brian (2013). *The Morality of War*, Second Edition (Ontario: Broadview Press).

Oxfam (2015). 'World not Delivering on Gaza Reconstruction Promises', Oxfam, Press Release, 13 April. Available at <www.oxfam.org.uk/media-centre/press-releases/2015/04/world-not-delivering-on-gaza-reconstruction-promises>.

Page, Edward (2008). 'Distributing the Burdens of Climate Change', *Environmental Politics*, 17/4: 556–75.

Page, Edward (2012). 'Give it Up for Climate Change: A Defence of the Beneficiary Pays Principle', *International Theory*, 4/2: 300–30.

Pape, Robert (1997). 'Why Economic Sanctions do not Work', *International Security*, 22/2: 90–136.

Parchomovsky, Gideon and Peter Siegelman (2009). 'Bribes vs. Bombs: A Study in Coasean Warfare', *International Review of Law and Economics*, 29: 179–90.

Paris, Roland (2014). 'The "Responsibility to Protect" and the Structural Problems of Preventive Humanitarian Intervention', *International Peacekeeping*, 21/3: 569–603.

Parkin, Nicholas (2017). 'Non-violent Resistance and Last Resort', *Journal of Military Ethics*, 15/4: 259–74.

Pasternak, Avia (2009). 'Sanctioning Liberal Democracies', *Political Studies*, 57/1: 54–74.

Pattison, James (2010). *Humanitarian Intervention and the Responsibility to Protect: Who Should Intervene?* (Oxford: Oxford University Press).

Pattison, James (2011). 'The Ethics of Humanitarian Intervention in Libya', *Ethics & International Affairs*, 25/3: 271–7.

Pattison, James (2013). 'Is there a Duty to Intervene? Intervention and the Responsibility to Protect', *Philosophy Compass*, 8/6: 570–9.

Pattison, James (2014*a*). 'Bombing the Beneficiaries: The Distribution of the Costs of the Responsibility to Protect and Humanitarian Intervention', in Don Scheid (ed.), *The Ethics of Armed Humanitarian Intervention* (Cambridge: Cambridge University Press), pp. 113–30.

Pattison, James (2014*b*). *The Morality of Private War: The Challenge of Private Military and Security Companies* (Oxford: Oxford University Press).

Pattison, James (2015*a*). 'Mapping the Responsibilities to Protect: A Typology of International Duties', *Global Responsibility to Protect*, 7/2: 190–210.

Pattison, James (2015*b*). 'The Ethics of Diplomatic Criticism: The Responsibility to Protect, Just War Theory, and Presumptive Last Resort', *European Journal of International Relations*, 21/4: 935–57.

Pattison, James (2015*c*). '*Jus Post Bellum* and the Responsibility to Rebuild', *British Journal of Political Science*, 45/3: 635–61.

Pattison, James (2016). 'The Ethics of "Responsibility While Protecting": Brazil, the Responsibility to Protect, and the Restrictive Approach to Humanitarian Intervention', in Kai Michael Kenkel and Philip Cunliffe (eds), *Brazil as a Rising Power: Intervention Norms and the Contestation of Global Order* (London: Routledge), pp. 104–26.

Pattison, James (2017). 'Guns vs Troops: The Ethics of Supplying Arms', in Aidan Hehir and Robert Murray (eds), *Protecting Human Rights in the 21st Century* (London: Routledge), pp. 201–14.

Pattison, James (2018). 'The Case for Nonideal Morality of War: Beyond Revisionism versus Traditionalism in Just War Theory', *Political Theory*, 46/2: 242–68.

Peksen, Dursun (2009). 'Better or Worse? The Effect of Economic Sanctions on Human Rights', *Journal of Peace Research*, 46/1: 59–77.

Peksen, Dursun (2010). 'Coercive Diplomacy and Press Freedom: An Empirical Assessment of the Impact of Economic Sanctions on Media Openness', *International Political Science Review*, 31/4: 449–69.

Peksen, Dursun (2011). 'Economic Sanctions and Human Security: The Public Health Effect of Economic Sanctions', *Foreign Policy Analysis*, 7/3: 237–51.

Peterson, Timothy M. and A. Cooper Drury (2011). 'Sanctioning Violence: The Effect of Third-Party Economic Coercion on Militarized Conflict', *Journal of Conflict Resolution*, 55/4: 580–605.

Philips, Michael (1984). 'Bribery', *Ethics*, 94/1: 621–36.

Pierce, Albert (1996). 'Just War Principles and Economic Sanctions', *Ethics & International Affairs*, 10/1: 99–113.

Pogge, Thomas (2008). *World Poverty and Human Rights*, Second Edition (Cambridge: Polity Press).

Pollock, Lansing (1988). 'Evaluating Moral Theories', *American Philosophical Quarterly*, 25/3: 229–40.

Popovoski, Vessilin (2011). 'Fighting the Colonel: Sanctions and the Use of Force', *Jindal Journal of International Affairs*, 1/1: 148–61.

Portela, Clara (2016). 'Are European Union Sanctions "Targeted"?', *Cambridge Review of International Affairs*, 29/3: 912–29.

Portmore, Douglas (2017). 'Uncertainty, Indeterminacy, and Agent-Centred Constraints', *Australasian Journal of Philosophy*, 95/2: 284–98.

Pritchard, Michael S. (1998). 'Bribery: The Concept', *Science and Engineering Ethics*, 4/3: 281–6.

Prorok, Alyssa K. (2017). 'The (In)compatibility of Peace and Justice? The International Criminal Court and Civil Conflict Termination', *International Organization*, 71/2: 213–43.

Puri, Hardeep Singh (2016). *Perilous Interventions: The Security Council and the Politics of Chaos* (London: HarperCollins).

Quinn, Warren S. (1989). 'Actions, Intentions, and Consequences: The Doctrine of Doing and Allowing', *Philosophical Review*, 98/3: 287–312.

Quong, Jonathan (2009). 'Killing in Self-Defense', *Ethics*, 119/3: 507–37.

Ramesh, Randeep (2009). 'Sri Lanka Threatens to Expel Media as Army Closes in on Rebels', *The Guardian*, 1 February.

Rawls, John (1999*a*). *A Theory of Justice*, Revised Edition (Oxford: Oxford University Press).

Rawls, John (1999*b*). *The Law of Peoples* (Cambridge, Mass.: Harvard University Press).

Rawls, John (2005). *Political Liberalism*, Expanded Edition (New York: Columbia University Press).

Recchia, Stefano (2017). 'Authorising Humanitarian Intervention: A Five-point Defence of Existing Multilateral Procedures', *Review of International Studies*, 43/1: 50–72.

Regan, Anthony (2008). 'External versus Internal Incentives in Peace Processes: The Bougainville Experience', *Accord: An International Review of Peace Initiatives*, 19: 44–9.

Risse, Thomas (2000). 'Let's Argue! Communicative Action in World Politics', *International Organization*, 54/1: 1–39.

Roberts, Adam (2009). 'Introduction', in Adam Roberts and Timothy Garton Ash (eds), *Civil Resistance and Power Politics: The Experience of Non-violent Action from Gandhi to the Present* (Oxford: Oxford University Press), 1–24.

Rodin, David (2011). 'Justifying Harm', *Ethics*, 122/1: 74–110.

Rodman, Kenneth A. (2012). 'Why the ICC Should Operate Within Peace Processes', *Ethics & International Affairs*, 26/1: 59–71.

Rubenstein, Jennifer C. (2015). *Between Samaritans and States: The Political Ethics of Humanitarian INGOs* (Oxford: Oxford University Press).

Rudolf, Peter (1998). 'Power without Principle: Ethical Problems of International Economic Sanctions', *Law and State*, 57: 9–21.

Ryan, Cheyney (2015). 'Pacifism(s)', *The Philosophical Forum*, 46/1: 17–39.

Ryan, Cheyney (*forthcoming*). 'Pacifism', in Seth Lazar and Helen Frowe (eds), *The Oxford Handbook of Ethics of War* (Oxford: Oxford University Press).

Salehyan, Idean (2010). 'The Delegation of War to Rebel Organizations', *Journal of Conflict Resolution*, 54/3: 493–515.

Salehyan, Idean, David Siroky, and Reed M. Wood (2014). 'External Rebel Sponsorship and Civilian Abuse: A Principal–Agent Analysis of Wartime Atrocities', *International Organization*, 68/3: 633–61.

Sandel, Michael J. (2012). *What Money Can't Buy: The Moral Limits of Markets* (London: Penguin).

Sawyer, Katherine, Kathleen Gallagher Cunningham, and William Reed (2017). 'The Role of External Support in Civil War Termination', *Journal of Conflict Resolution*, 61/6: 1174–202.

Saxon, Dan (2015). 'The International Criminal Court and the Prevention of Crimes', in Serena K. Sharma and Jennifer M. Welsh (eds), *The Responsibility to Prevent: Overcoming the Challenges of Atrocity Prevention* (Oxford: Oxford University Press), pp. 119–59.

Scharf, Michael P. (2006). 'From the eXile Files: An Essay on Trading Justice for Peace', *Washington and Lee Law Review*, 63/1: 340–76.

Scheffler, Samuel (2004). 'Doing and Allowing', *Ethics*, 114/2: 215–39.

Schiff, Benjamin N. (2012). 'The ICC's Potential for Doing Bad When Pursuing Good', *Ethics & International Affairs*, 26/1: 73–81.

Schiff, Benjamin N. (2016). 'Can the International Criminal Court Contribute to the Responsibility to Protect?', *International Relations*, 30/3: 298–313.

Schirch, Lisa (2006). *Civilian Peacekeeping: Preventing Violence and Making Space for Democracy* (Uppsala: Life & Peace Institute).

Schmitt, Eric (2017). 'U.S. Begins Arming Syrian Kurds for Final Assault on Raqqa', *New York Times*, 31 May.

Schweitzer, Christine (2010). 'Introduction: Civilian Peacekeeping—A Barely Tapped Resource', in Christine Schweitzer (ed.), *Civilian Peacekeeping: A Barely Tapped Resource*, IFGK Working Paper No. 23 (Belm-Vehrte, Germany: Sozio Publishing), pp. 7–16.

Scrivener, Alex (2015). 'Do We Really Want the Military Spending our Aid Budget?', *The Guardian*, 25 November.

Security Council Report (2013). 'UN Sanctions', Special Research Report, No. 3, November.

Sen, Amartya (2009). *The Idea of Justice* (London: Penguin).

Sharma, Serena K. and Jennifer M. Welsh (2015*a*). 'Conclusion: An Integrated Framework for Atrocity Crime Prevention', in Serena K. Sharma and Jennifer M. Welsh (eds), *The Responsibility to Prevent: Overcoming the Challenges of Atrocity Prevention* (Oxford: Oxford University Press), pp. 368–93.

Sharma, Serena K. and Jennifer M. Welsh (eds) (2015*b*). *The Responsibility to Prevent: Overcoming the Challenges of Atrocity Prevention* (Oxford: Oxford University Press).

Sharp, Gene (1973). *The Politics of Nonviolent Action: Part Two: The Methods of Nonviolent Action* (Boston, MA: Porter Sargent Publishers).

Sharp, Gene (1990). *Civilian-Based Defense: A Post-Military Weapons System* (Princeton, NJ: Princeton University Press).

Sharp, Paul (2009). *Diplomatic Theory of International Relations* (Cambridge: Cambridge University Press).

Sheffield, Hazel (2016). 'Arms Trade: One Chart that Shows the Biggest Weapons Exporters of the Last Five Years: Asia was the Main Importer of Weapons in the Last Five Years', *The Independent*, 24 February.

Shin, Geuguen, Seung Whan Choi, and Shali Lou (2016). 'Do Economic Sanctions Impair Target Economies?', *International Political Science Review*, 37/4: 485–99.

Shue, Henry (1996). *Basic Rights: Subsistence, Affluence, and U.S. Foreign Policy*, Second Edition (Princeton, NJ: Princeton University Press).

Sislin, John and Frederic Pearson (2006). 'Arms and Escalation in Ethnic Conflicts: The Case of Sri Lanka', *International Studies Perspectives*, 7/2: 137–58.

Slim, Hugo (*forthcoming*). 'The Global Ethics of Humanitarian Action', in Eric Heinze and Brent Steele (eds), *The Routledge Handbook on Ethics and International Relations* (London: Routledge).

Smeulers, Allete, Maartje Weerdesteijn, and Barbora Hola (2015). 'The Selection of Situations of the ICC: An Empirically Based Evaluation of the OTP's Performance', *International Criminal Law Review*, 15/1: 1–39.

Snyder, Jack and Leslie Vinjamuri (2004). 'Trials and Errors: Principles and Pragmatism in Strategies of International Justice', *International Security*, 28/3: 5–44.

Sohn, Louis B. (1964). 'Expulsion or Forced Withdrawal from an International Organization', *Harvard Law Review*, 77/8: 1381–425.

Stahn, Carsten (2015). 'Marital Stress or Grounds for Divorce? Re-thinking the Relationship between R2P and International Criminal Justice', *Criminal Law Forum*, 26/1: 13–50.

Steiner, Hillel (1974–5). 'Individual Liberty', *Proceedings of the Aristotelian Society*, 75: 33–50.

Stephan, Maria J. and Erica Chenoweth (2008). 'Why Civil Resistance Works: The Strategic Logic of Nonviolent Conflict', *International Security*, 33/1: 7–44.

Strawser, B. J. (ed.) (2013). *Killing by Remote Control: The Ethics of an Unmanned Military* (New York: Oxford University Press).

Struett, Michael J. (2012). 'Why the International Criminal Court Must *Pretend* to Ignore Politics', *Ethics & International Affairs*, 26/1: 83–92.

Stuenkel, Oliver (2014). 'Why Brazil Has Not Criticised Russia over Crimea', NOREF: Norwegian Peacebuilding Resource Centre, Policy Brief.

Stuenkel, Oliver and Marcos Tourinho (2014). 'Regulating Intervention: Brazil and the Responsibility to Protect', *Conflict, Security, & Development*, 14/4: 379–402.

Summy, Ralph (1994). 'Nonviolence and the Case of the Extremely Ruthless Opponent', *Pacifica Review: Peace, Security & Global Change*, 6/1: 1–29.

Syrian Network for Human Rights (2017). 'Homepage'. Available at <sn4hr.org/>.

Tadros, Victor (2016). 'Permissibility in a World of Wrongdoing', *Philosophy & Public Affairs*, 44/2: 101–32.

Task Force on the EU Prevention of Mass Atrocities (2013). *The EU and the Prevention of Mass Atrocities: An Assessment of Strengths and Weaknesses*, Budapest Centre for the International Prevention of Genocide and Mass Atrocities.

Taylor, Brendan (2010). *Sanctions as Grand Strategy*, Adelphi Papers, 49/411: International Institute for Strategic Studies.

Tesón, Fernando R. (2003). 'The Liberal Case for Humanitarian Intervention', in J. L. Holzgrefe and Robert O. Keohane (eds), *Humanitarian Intervention: Ethical, Legal and Political Dilemmas* (Cambridge: Cambridge University Press), pp. 93–129.

Tesón, Fernando R. (2005). *Humanitarian Intervention: An Inquiry into Law and Morality*, Third Edition (New York: Transnational Publishers).

Tesón, Fernando R. (2006). 'Eight Principles for Humanitarian Intervention', *Journal of Military Ethics*, 5/2: 93–113.

Thale, Geoff (1997). 'Incentives and the Salvadoran Peace Process', in David Cortright (ed.), *The Price of Peace: Incentives and International Conflict Prevention* (Oxford: Rowman & Littlefield), pp. 181–204.

Thomas, Claire (2005). 'Civilian Starvation: A Just Tactic of War?', *Journal of Military Ethics*, 4/2: 108–18.

Tierney, Dominic (2005). 'Irrelevant or Malevolent? UN Arms Embargoes in Civil Wars', *Review of International Studies*, 31/4: 645–64.

Timmons, Mark (2013). *Moral Theory: An Introduction*, Second Edition (New York: Rowman & Littlefield).

Toner, Christopher (2010). 'The Logical Structure of Just War Theory', *Journal of Ethics*, 14/2: 81–102.

Toscano, Roberto (2001). 'The Ethics of Modern Diplomacy', in Jean-Marc Coicaud and David Warner (eds), *Ethics and International Affairs: Extent and Limits* (New York: United Nations University Press), pp. 42–83.

Tsai, D. F.-C. (2005). 'The Bioethical Principles and Confucius' Moral Philosophy', *Journal of Medical Ethics*, 31/3: 159–63.

Turow, Scott (1985). 'What's Wrong with Bribery', *Journal of Business Ethics*, 4/4: 249–51.

UN (2016). 'Security Council Decides against Imposing Arms Embargo on South Sudan, Designating Key Figures for Targeted Sanctions', UN Press Release, 23 December. SC/12653.

US Catholic Bishops (1992). 'The Challenge of Peace: God's Promise and Our Response: The Pastoral Letter on War and Peace', in Jean Bethke Elshtain (ed.), *Just War Theory* (New York: New York University Press), pp. 77–168.

Valentini, Laura (2015). 'Social Samaritan Justice: When and Why Needy Fellow Citizens Have a Right to Assistance', *American Political Science Review*, 109/4: 735–49.

Valentino, Benjamin A. (2000). 'Final Solutions: The Causes of Mass Killing and Genocide', *Security Studies*, 9/3: 1–59.

Valentino, Benjamin A. (2011). 'The True Costs of Humanitarian Intervention: The Hard Truth about a Noble Notion', *Foreign Affairs*, November/December: 60–73.

Vilmer, Jean-Baptiste Jeangène (2012). 'Il faut armer les rebelles syriens', *Le Monde*, 7 December.

Vines, Alex (2007). 'Can UN Arms Embargoes in Africa Be Effective?', *International Affairs*, 83/6: 1107–22.

VOA (2016). 'Cuba Says US Embargo Cost It $4.6 Billion Last Year', *Voice of America*, 9 September.

Wallace, M. S. (2017). *Security Without Weapons: Rethinking Violence, Nonviolent Action, and Civilian Protection* (London: Routledge).

Wallace, R. Jay (2010). 'Hypocrisy, Moral Address, and the Equal Standing of Persons', *Philosophy & Public Affairs*, 38/4: 307–41.

Wallensteen, Peter (2016). 'Institutional Learning in Targeting Sanctions', in Thomas J. Biersteker, Sue E. Eckert, and Marcos Tourinho (eds), *Targeted Sanctions: The Impacts and Effectiveness of United Nations Action* (Cambridge: Cambridge University Press), pp. 248–64.

Wallis, Tim (2010). 'Best Practices for Unarmed Civilian Peacekeeping', in Christine Schweitzer (ed.), *Civilian Peacekeeping: A Barely Tapped Resource*, IFGK Working Paper No. 23 (Belm-Vehrte, Germany: Sozio Publishing), pp. 25–34.

Walzer, Michael (2004). *Arguing About War* (New Haven: Yale University Press).

Walzer, Michael (2015). *Just and Unjust Wars*, Fifth Edition (USA: BasicBooks).

Weinstein, Jeremy M. (2007). *Inside Rebellion: The Politics of Insurgent Violence* (Cambridge: Cambridge University Press).

Weir, Fred (2012). 'Russian Report Criticizes US on Human Rights, US Responds "Bring It On"', *Christian Science Monitor*, 24 October.

Weissman, Fabrice (2010). '"Not in Our Name": Why Médecins Sans Frontières Does Not Support the "Responsibility to Protect"', *Criminal Justice Ethics*, 29/2: 194–207.

Wellman, Christopher Heath (2008). 'Amnesties and International Law', in Larry May (ed.), *War: Essays in Political Philosophy* (Cambridge: Cambridge University Press), pp. 249–65.

Welsh, Jennifer M. (2010). 'Implementing the "Responsibility to Protect": Where Expectations Meet Reality', *Ethics & International Affairs*, 24/4: 415–30.

Welsh, Jennifer M. (2014*a*). 'Fortress Europe and the Responsibility to Protect: Framing the Issue', EUI Forum, 17–18 November.

Welsh, Jennifer M. (2014*b*). 'Implementing the "Responsibility to Protect": Catalyzing Debate and Building Capacity', in Alexander Betts and Phil Orchard (eds), *Implementation and World Politics: How International Norms Change Practice* (Oxford: Oxford University Press), pp. 124–43.

Welsh, Jennifer M. (2015). 'Mediation and Sanctions', in Serena K. Sharma and Jennifer M. Welsh (eds), *The Responsibility to Prevent: Overcoming the Challenges of Atrocity Prevention* (Oxford: Oxford University Press), pp. 103–18.

Wenar, Leif (2008). 'Property Rights and the Resource Curse', *Philosophy & Public Affairs*, 36/1: 2–32.

Wheeler, Nicholas J. (2000). *Saving Strangers: Humanitarian Intervention in International Society* (Oxford: Oxford University Press).

Winkler, Adam (1999). 'Just Sanctions', *Human Rights Quarterly*, 21/1: 133–55.

Wolff, Jonathan (2015). 'Paying People to Act in Their Own Interests: Incentives Versus Rationalisation in Public Health', *Public Health Ethics*, 8/1: 27–30.

Wood, Reed M. (2014). 'From Loss to Looting? Battlefield Costs and Rebel Incentives for Violence', *International Organization*, 68/4: 979–99.

Wood, Reed M. and Emily Molfino (2016). 'Aiding Victims, Abetting Violence: The Influence of Humanitarian Aid on Violence Patterns During Civil Conflict', *Journal of Global Security Studies*, 1/3: 186–203.

World Bank (2013). *Lebanon: Economic and Social Impact Assessment of the Syrian Conflict* (Washington, DC: World Bank).

Wright, Oliver (2015). 'G7 Summit: President Assad Could Face Exile in Russia and the West's Plan to Tackle Isis in Syria: The Summit Suggests there is Some Common Ground with Russia on the Issue', *The Independent*, 8 June.

Zehfuss, Maja (2011). 'Targeting: Precision and the Production of Ethics', *European Journal of International Relations*, 17/3: 543–66.

Zimmerman, Michael J. (1985). 'Intervening Agents and Moral Responsibility', *Philosophical Quarterly*, 35/141: 347–58.

Zongze, Ruan (2012). 'Responsible Protection: Building a Safer World', *China International Studies*, 34, May/June.

Index